THE AVIGNON PAPACY AND
THE CRUSADES, 1305–1378

The Avignon Papacy
and
the Crusades, 1305–1378

NORMAN HOUSLEY

CLARENDON PRESS · OXFORD
1986

Oxford University Press, Walton Street, Oxford OX2 6DP

London New York Toronto
Delhi Bombay Calcutta Madras Karachi
Kuala Lumpur Singapore Hong Kong Tokyo
Nairobi Dar es Salaam Cape Town
Melbourne Auckland

and associated companies in
Beirut Berlin Ibadan Nicosia

Oxford is a trade mark of Oxford University Press

Published in the United States
by Oxford University Press, New York

British Library Cataloguing in Publication Data

Housley, Norman
The Avignon Papacy and the Crusades.
1. Crusades 2. Papacy——History——1309–1378
I. Title
909.07 D172
ISBN 0–19–821957–1

Library of Congress Cataloging in Publication Data

Housley, Norman.
The Avignon papacy and the Crusades, 1305–1378.
Bibliography: p.
Includes index.
1. Crusades—Later, 13th, 14th and 15th centuries.
2. Papacy—History—1309–1378. 3. Crusades—Finance.
I. Title.
D172.H68 1986 940.1'92 85–28967
ISBN 0–821957–1 (U.S.)

Set by Wyvern Typesetting Ltd, Bristol
Printed in Great Britain
at the University Press, Oxford
by David Stanford
Printer to the University

FOR JONATHAN

Acknowledgements

For assistance during the research and writing of this book I am indebted to the staff of the Vatican Archives, the university libraries in Cambridge, Leicester, and Liverpool, the Vatican Library, Library of Congress, and libraries of the British and French Schools at Rome. I gratefully thank the British Academy and the research boards of the Universities of Leicester and Liverpool for financial subventions. The trustees of Harvard University kindly awarded me a Summer Fellowship at Dumbarton Oaks which enabled me to work for six weeks in surroundings which Hans Mayer quite rightly described as 'a scholar's paradise'. Peter Edbury, Franz Tinnefeld, and colleagues and friends at Cambridge, Liverpool, and Leicester gave advice and encouragement, and my wife has given me alternate injections of optimism and realism. To Liverpool University I owe a very special debt of thanks: its magnificent Research Fellowship scheme helped me at a critical point in my career. Finally, the book is dedicated to a brilliant historian and inspiring teacher whose friendship I hold very dear.

NORMAN HOUSLEY

Leicester University

Contents

List of Abbreviations

(For full titles of books see Bibliography)

AA	*Acta aragonensia*, ed. H. Finke
AE	*Annales ecclesiastici*, ed. C. Baronio *et al.*
ASPN	*Archivio storico per le provincie napoletane*
ASV	Archivio segreto Vaticano
BEC	*Bibliothèque de l'École des chartes*
BEFAR	Bibliothèque des Écoles françaises d'Athènes et de Rome
BIHR	*Bulletin of the Institute of Historical Research*
CC	*Lettres secrètes et curiales du pape Jean XXII relatives à la France*, ed. A. Coulon and S. Clémencet
CDP	*Codex diplomaticus prussicus*, ed. J. Voigt
CHR	*Catholic Historical Review*
COD	*Conciliorum oecumenicorum decreta*, ed. J. Alberigo *et al.*
Daumet	*Lettres closes, patentes et curiales du pape Benoît XII se rapportant à la France*, ed. G. Daumet
Déprez and Mollat	*Lettres closes, patentes et curiales du pape Clément VI intéressant les pays autres que la France*, ed. E. Déprez and G. Mollat
Déprez *et al.*	*Lettres closes, patentes et curiales du pape Clément VI se rapportant à la France*, ed. E. Déprez *et al.*
DVL	*Diplomatarium veneto–levantinum*, ed. G. M. Thomas
EHR	*English Historical Review*
Gasnault *et al.*	*Lettres secrètes et curiales du pape Innocent VI*, ed. P. Gasnault *et al.*
Instr. misc.	Instrumenta miscellanea
JEH	*Journal of Ecclesiastical History*
JMH	*Journal of Medieval History*
Knoll, *RPM*	P. W. Knoll, *The Rise of the Polish Monarchy*
LM	*Lettres secrètes et curiales du pape Urbain V*, ed. P. Lecacheux and G. Mollat

MEFR	*Mélanges de l'École française de Rome*
Mirot *et al.*	*Lettres secrètes et curiales du pape Grégoire XI relatives à la France*, ed. L. Mirot *et al.*
Mollat, *Lettres communes*	*Lettres communes du pape Jean XXII analysées d'après les registres dits d'Avignon et du Vatican*, ed. G. Mollat
Mollat, *Lettres secrètes*	*Lettres secrètes et curiales du pape Grégoire XI intéressant les pays autres que la France*, ed. G. Mollat
OCP	*Orientalia christiana periodica*
PBSR	*Papers of the British School at Rome*
PCRCICO	Pontificia commissio ad redigendum codicem iuris canonici orientalis: Fontes, 1305–1378
Reg. Avin.	Registra Avinionensia
Reg. Vat.	Registra Vaticana
RIS	*Rerum italicarum scriptores*, ed. L. A. Muratori. 25 vols. (Milan, 1723–51)
RISNS	*Rerum italicarum scriptores*, new series, ed. G. Carducci *et al.* (Città di Castello–Bologna, 1900–)
RS	*Rolls Series*
SCH	Studies in Church History
Setton, *PL*	K. M. Setton, *The Papacy and the Levant (1204–1571): Vol. I*
SRP	*Scriptores rerum prussicarum*, ed. T. Hirsch, M. Töppen, and E. Strehlke
Vidal	*Lettres communes du pape Benoît XII*, ed. J.-M. Vidal
Vidal and Mollat	*Lettres closes et patentes du pape Benoît XII intéressant les pays autres que la France*, ed. J.-M. Vidal and G. Mollat
Vincke, *SKKA*	J. Vincke, *Staat und Kirche in Katalonien und Aragon während des Mittelalters, i*
VMH	*Vetera monumenta historica Hungariam sacram illustrantia*, ed. A. Theiner
VMP	*Vetera monumenta Poloniae et Lithuaniae gentiumque finitimarum historiam illustrantia*, ed. A. Theiner
VPA	*Vitae paparum avenionensium*, ed. E. Baluze and G. Mollat

Introduction

WRITING about events in Spain in 1339, the Florentine chronicler Giovanni Villani drew an interesting comparison between the crusading aid enjoyed by Latin Syria in the thirteenth century, and the help which the Emirate of Granada regularly received from Merinid Morocco. Just as Christians in the West had sustained the Holy Land, benefiting from papal indulgences in exchange for going to Palestine, sending troops, or donating cash, so the Moors in North Africa enabled Granada to survive both by sending a continual stream of men and money across the Straits, and by organizing occasional large-scale expeditions (*generali e grandi passaggi*).[1] Comparisons of this kind would have been impossible if informed observers like Giovanni Villani had not shared a coherent and unanimous view of what a crusade was. The pronouncements of popes, secular rulers, theorists, lawyers, and others enable us to reconstruct this view, and at the start of a study like this one it is important to give a clear definition of the crusade, and to explain its precise scope and function in the fourteenth century.

The crusade, which contemporaries usually called either a *sanctum passagium* or a *cruciata*, was a form of holy war recognizable by a number of clear characteristics. The most important of these were legal, and found expression in canon or civil law; they concerned the status and commitment of the individual *crucesignatus* rather than the organization of the expeditions.[2] At the heart of the crusade stood the plenary indulgence, or remission in full of all sins committed: the grant of the indulgence, either to all participants in a military expedition, or just to those who died in the course of the fighting, is the chief way in which a crusade can be identified between 1305 and 1378.[3] Associated with it was the mechanism by

---

[1] Giovanni Villani, *Cronica*, ed. F. Gherardi Dragomanni. 4 vols. (Milan, 1848), bk. 11, ch. 99, iii, 331–2.
[2] See M. Villey, *La Croisade: Essai sur la formation d'une théorie juridique* (Paris, 1942); J. A. Brundage, *Medieval Canon Law and the Crusader* (Madison, 1969); J. S. C. Riley-Smith, *What were the Crusades?* (London, 1977).
[3] Cf. Brundage, 145: 'the granting of [the crusade] indulgence for any expedition

which a Christian could acquire the indulgence, notably the vow which he or she made to perform specified services, and the cross displayed until the vow was accomplished. In addition, the crusader was the beneficiary of certain privileges attached to the status of *crucesignatus*. The vow, its obligations and privileges were treated fairly thoroughly by lawyers and have received detailed attention from scholars.[4]

Other important characteristics of a crusade were institutional or traditional; they were normally present in a crusade but were only loosely or indirectly based on legal principles. Some of these were inherent in crusading ideology, while others came into being as the Church grappled with the problems of assembling and financing the large-scale crusades of the twelfth and thirteenth centuries. Examples were the procurement and regulation of peace between Christians, the appointment of papal legates, and the grant of certain types of revenue. The crusade was regarded as an instrument of peace,[5] and efforts to secure peace, both at the local level and at that of international conflicts like the Anglo-French war, cannot be dissociated from the preaching and organization of the expeditions themselves. Again, the crusade was a Church enterprise, a *negotium ecclesiae*, engaged in by virtue of papal authority, and these facts were commonly expressed in the field by the presence of a papal legate who acted as the spiritual mentor of the crusaders, and in some cases as their military leader too.[6] Likewise, there were several forms of revenue traditionally associated with the crusade, notably the clerical tenth and, from Clement V's reign, other benefice taxes, but also lay donations, fines and legacies, and money raised from the redemption of vows and the distribution of partial indulgences.

The crusade can thus be visualized as a kernel of legal features enclosed within a covering of institutional practices. The latter were

may well be considered to define it as a crusade; expeditions for which it was not given can scarcely be considered crusades at all.'

[4] See in particular Brundage, *passim*; E. Bridrey, *La Condition juridique des croisés et le privilège de croix: étude d'histoire du droit français* (Paris, 1900); M. Purcell, *Papal Crusading Policy: The Chief Instruments of Papal Crusading Policy and Crusade to the Holy Land from the Final Loss of Jerusalem to the Fall of Acre, 1244–1291* (Leiden, 1975), chs. 3–6.

[5] Cf. Riley-Smith, *What were the Crusades?*, 41.

[6] This applies only to the Italian campaigns of Bertrand Du Poujet and Gil Albornoz; in other areas the role of the legate was much more restricted.

not wholly stable and were open to controversy; in particular, the definition of a crusade as a *negotium ecclesiae* offered rich material for debate in terms of war finance. In addition, the student of the crusades in the fourteenth century needs to take into account two notable strategic developments which sprang from Western thinking about the problems facing the Holy Land and crusades to the eastern Mediterranean before 1291. One was the realization that the old-style expeditions were inherently unwieldy and wasteful, and that this could be countered by breaking a crusade down into two or more stages. Essentially these would be a preliminary expedition, the *passagium particulare* or *primum passagium*, and a big follow-up crusade, the *passagium generale*. This approach originated in the late thirteenth century, probably during the reign of Gregory X, who sent four small expeditions to Syria while making preparations for a large-scale crusade.[7] After 1291 it became the obvious strategy to pursue. The *passagium particulare* would establish a bridgehead in Syria, Egypt, Armenia or elsewhere, and the 'general passage' would exploit it and complete the reconquest of the Holy Land.[8] The attractiveness of this approach led to its adoption outside the context of Palestine. Thus when the focus of crusading effort in the Levant shifted to Greece and the Aegean, the new strategy was applied there too, for example in Clement VI's hopes to capitalize on the Latin capture of Smyrna, or in John Cantacuzenus's proposals to the Pope in 1347–8.[9] But planning a crusade in two stages was complicated, calling for radical changes in traditional methods of preaching and finance; it was a challenge which the papal Curia only partially met.

The second strategic development was the greater attention which was devoted to economic warfare as a concomitant to the crusade, most importantly in relation to Mamluk Egypt and the recovery of Palestine. As early as the Third Lateran Council of 1179, Christians were forbidden to trade with Egypt in war

[7] See P. A. Throop, *Criticism of the Crusade: a Study of Public Opinion and Crusade Propaganda* (Amsterdam, 1940), 273–4.

[8] Cf. L. Thier, *Kreuzzugsbemühungen unter Papst Clemens V. (1305–1314)* (Werl, Westf., 1973), 94–6.

[9] *Lettres closes, patentes et curiales du pape Clément VI se rapportant à la France*, ed. E. Déprez *et al.* BEFAR, 3rd Series, 3 vols. (Paris, 1901–61), nn. 1397, 1462, 1569; R.-J. Loenertz, 'Ambassadeurs grecs auprès du pape Clément VI (1348)', *OCP*, xix (1953), 186–7. Cf. *Annales ecclesiastici*, ed. C. Baronio *et al.* 37 vols. (Paris–Freiburg–Bar le Duc, 1864–87), ad annum 1355, nn. 34–7, xxv, 601–2.

materials, a ban which Innocent III in 1215 extended to cover all commerce over a four year period.[10] But in the late thirteenth century fresh urgency was applied to this approach, and in the Avignonese period it became for several decades a cornerstone of papal policy. In 1369, for example, Urban V's measures in support of the Veneto-Genoese league against Egypt consisted of a trade embargo and the grant of crusading indulgences: the two went hand in hand.[11] Nor were the Mamluks the only enemies of the Church against whom this weapon was turned; the Moors of Granada, the Lithuanians, and the Italian Ghibellines were periodically subject to similar sanctions.[12]

This leads us to a very important aspect of contemporary views about the crusade and its function in Christian society. For such expeditions were by no means limited to Palestine or even the eastern Mediterranean. Since at least the first half of the twelfth century and, it can be argued, since its origins in the eleventh, the purpose of crusading endeavour was not just the recovery of Palestine for Christendom and its defence in Christian hands, but also the protection of the Catholic Church and Faith wherever these were threatened. It should be stressed that this broad definition of the crusade is the only one which contemporary sources permit, not just the records of the Church and its canon lawyers, but also the writings of chroniclers, the comments of lay authorities, and, above all, the indirect assent of the 'silent majority' who showed undeniable enthusiasm for crusades taking place outside Syria and for reasons other than the recovery of the Holy Land.[13]

By 1305 the movement had spread to many different areas of the Christian world, and crusaders had fought against many types of enemy, including Muslims, pagans such as Prussians and Tatars, Christian heretics and rebellious lay rulers, and schismatic Greeks. The motives of the papal Curia in declaring such wars to be crusades, and the political complications which arose in their course, have no bearing on the fact that the campaigns themselves

---

[10] *Conciliorum oecumenicorum decreta*, ed. J. Alberigo *et al.* 3rd edn. (Bologna, 1973), 223, 270. Cf. ibid., 300, 311–12; *Corpus iuris canonici*, ed. E. Friedberg. 2 vols. (Leipzig, 1879), ii, col. 773.

[11] *Diplomatarium veneto–levantinum, sive acta et diplomata res venetas, graecas atque Levantis illustrantia a. 1300–1454*, ed. G. M. Thomas. 2 vols. (Venice, 1880–99), ii, n. 87.

[12] See below, ch. 6, nn. 16–19.

[13] Cf. Riley-Smith, *What were the Crusades?*, 18 ff.

fitted all the contemporary criteria characterizing a crusade. The crusade had become the leading form of Christian holy war and in our period there was crusading activity, to a greater or lesser extent, on all the established fronts. In the eastern Mediterranean crusaders fought not only the Mamluks, but also the Turks of Anatolia, the Greeks of the revived Byzantine Empire, and the Tatars of the Golden Horde. In Spain they engaged the Moors of Granada and Morocco. In northern and eastern Europe there were crusades against the Lithuanians and Tatars, the pagan Finns and the schismatics of Novgorod. And in Italy crusaders fought in the armies of the popes and their allies against the Ghibellines of Lombardy, Tuscany, and the Papal State.

In order to encounter the crusading movement in its full complexity it is essential to take all these fronts into account. Daunting as the task is in some respects, there are also benefits which evade those historians who keep their attention fixed on Palestine. First, there was a considerable degree of interaction between the various areas of conflict; most importantly between the eastern Mediterranean and Italy, but also between Italy and Spain, Spain and the eastern Mediterranean, and Italy and eastern Europe. This affected not only papal policy, but also the approach of such secular rulers as the kings of France, Aragon and Hungary.[14] Secondly, by conducting a comparative survey of all the fronts we gain valuable insights into the methods, problems, and achievements of the combatants. There are points to be taken about recruitment, finance, leadership, and logistics. Thirdly, and most importantly, the crusading movement in the fourteenth century is brought into a fresh and illuminating perspective. Instead of a series of intricate and abortive projects aimed at recovering the holy places of Palestine, we have a vast range of human activity stretching from the Baltic to the Straits of Gibraltar. Here too there were many crusading projects which never materialized, and some that did led to military failure, but the standard view that the crusading movement had lost all its vigour and popularity has to be severely modified when, for instance, the successes of the Castilians and Poles are brought into the picture.

We are concerned therefore with a particular type of military expedition, examples of which occurred in many very different parts

---

[14] See N. Housley, 'Pope Clement V and the Crusades of 1309–10', *JMH*, viii (1982), 29–43; id., 'King Louis the Great of Hungary and the Crusades, 1342–1382', *Slavonic and East European Review*, lxii (1984), 192–208.

of the Christian world in the fourteenth century. Several of the questions which arise are those which apply to any military venture. We want to know how and why they came into being, the means adopted to recruit, organize, lead, and pay for the armies and fleets employed, and what they achieved. A feature peculiar to the crusades, however, is the persistent necessary for close co-operation between the papacy and the secular authorities which arose from the very nature of the movement. It gives the inquiry an added dimension. How did the papal Curia and the lay powers work together in the making of the crusades, their assembly and finance, and their control in the field? It also raises new questions. How did the Curia try to deal with the obstacles to the crusade? And how important was it in directing the activities of the Military Orders, those bodies of men whose vocation included the waging of holy war? Behind all such questions lies the problem which makes the study of the Avignon papacy of absorbing interest. One is constantly aware that the ability of the Holy See both to carry out its own policies and to influence those of other rulers is in a state of flux; but it is very difficult to set precise limits on the change which occurs between 1305 and 1378.[15] At the close of this study an attempt will be made to set such limits in the case of one field of activity which was of central importance at the Curia: the direction of the crusades.

This is an account of the papal contribution to the crusading movement rather than a survey of the movement itself. There are two good reasons for focusing on the role of the Curia. One is that writing a comprehensive survey of lasting worth is made very difficult by the unsettled state of contemporary scholarship on two subjects of great relevance to the crusades: the condition of the Western economy on the one hand,[16] and the nature and precise influence of chivalric culture on the other.[17] This more limited study, which concentrates on the papacy's actions, successes, and failures without neglecting broader issues such as the popularity of the crusade, will I hope pave the way without being too bold in its claims. Also, studying the papacy has certain tangible advantages

---

[15] See, for example, B. Smalley, 'Church and State, 1300–77: Theory and Fact', in J. Hale *et al.* (eds.), *Europe in the late Middle Ages* (London, 1965), 15–43.

[16] The most stimulating contribution of recent years to the debate about the fourteenth-century economy is B. Z. Kedar, *Merchants in Crisis: Genoese and Venetian Men of Affairs and the Fourteenth-Century Depression* (New Haven and London, 1976).

[17] See now M. Keen, *Chivalry* (New Haven and London, 1984), esp. chs. 7–12.

relating to documentation and scholarship. The riches of the Vatican Archives make it possible to elucidate and explain what the Curia was doing to a degree unparalleled for any other Christian power involved in the crusades, with the exception of Aragon and, possibly, Venice. In the case of the Avignon papacy a very large proportion of these riches have been published. It is easy to be deceived by the incompleteness of the programme devised by the French School at Rome to publish all the papal registers, and wrong to be too dismayed at that programme's recent sluggishness; for many individual scholars have helped close the gaps, at least as far as the crusading movement is concerned.

The Avignon papacy is a period of papal history which has for long been regarded as relatively self-contained, its boundaries formed by the calamitous reign of Boniface VIII and the disastrous events of 1378. This has the advantage that the period has been isolated for study by a series of outstanding French administrative historians, who have analysed its governmental and fiscal machinery with exceptional clarity.[18] This means that while the procedures of policy formation still hold many secrets, both the factors which shaped policy and the process by which it was implemented are clear enough. Despite this, it would have been much harder to write this book were it not for the many scholars who have, in comparatively recent years, thrown light on subjects and areas which constantly overlap with the crusades. One should mention in particular the work of Anthony Luttrell and Kenneth Setton on the Hospitallers and Latin Greece, Joseph Gill on papal relations with Byzantium, Paul Knoll on fourteenth-century Poland, and Philippe Contamine on military organization in France. The work of the last is especially relevant for chapters four and five. It is hard for a historian of the crusades not to feel envious that so much could be discovered about the French armies of the Hundred Years War. If we knew half as much about crusading armies in the same period, we would have cause for gratitude, for all too often, despite the comparative richness of the sources, the armies of the cross remain shadowy formations at best.

[18] See in particular Y. Renouard, *Les Relations des papes d'Avignon et des compagnies commerciales et bancaires de 1316 à 1378* (Paris, 1941); G. Mollat, *Les Papes d'Avignon.* 9th edn. (Paris, 1949), with exhaustive bibliography: for convenience I have used the English translation by J. Love (*The Popes at Avignon* (London, 1963)); B. Guillemain, *La Cour pontificale d'Avignon (1309–1376). Étude d'une société* (Paris, 1962).

I

The Campaigns:
(1) The Eastern Mediterranean

THE eastern Mediterranean world in 1305 can be considered as
three more or less separate political zones. The whole of the south-
eastern littoral, from the Syrian gates north of Antioch, through
Syria, Palestine, and Egypt westwards into the Sahara, was controlled by the Mamluk rulers of Egypt as a vast sultanate built up
between 1250 and 1291. Their lands included the holy city of
Jerusalem and the coastal cities of Syria, which in the second half of
the thirteenth century had constituted the last remnants of Christian
rule in the Holy Land. Some of these ports had been devastated by
the Muslim armies when they were conquered, as a deliberate move
intended to deny the Christians potential bridgeheads from which a
crusade of recovery might re-establish the former states. The
Mamluks were formidable opponents on land but lacked sea-
power; control of the waters between Cyprus, Alexandria, and
Syria lay in the hands of the Latin Christians, particularly the
trading cities of the West.[1]

A second zone was made up of the Christian outposts of Lusignan
Cyprus and Cilician Armenia. Cyprus had been conquered by the
Franks during the Third Crusade and had in 1191 been consigned to
Guy of Lusignan, whose descendants were to rule there until 1489.
On the whole the kings of Cyprus in the fourteenth century were
well off, reaping great financial benefits from the role of the island's
chief port, Famagusta, as an *entrepôt* for commerce between the
West and the interior of Asia.[2] But they faced serious dynastic and

[1] For the Mamluk Sultanate in this period, see M. M. Ziada, 'The Mamluk
Sultans, 1291–1517', in K. M. Setton (gen. ed.), *A History of the Crusades*. 4 vols. so
far. 2nd edn. (Madison, 1969–), iii, 486 ff.; P. M. Holt, 'The Structure of Govern-
ment in the Mamluk Sultanate', in his *The Eastern Mediterranean Lands in the
Period of the Crusades* (Warminster, 1977), 44–61; R. G. Irwin, *The Medieval Near
East: the Early Mamluk Sultanate (1250–1382)* (London, forthcoming 1985).

[2] G. F. Hill, *A History of Cyprus*. 4 vols. (Cambridge, 1940–52), ii, 195, 207, 292–
3, 369.

constitutional problems, and there was much friction with western traders; a full-scale war with the Genoese erupted in 1373. Although capable of participating to some extent in the crusading movement by supplying troops, ships, money, and advice, the Lusignan kings were generally wary of upsetting the balance of power.[3] Cilician Armenia had greater military needs and much less to contribute. The little Kingdom was under pressure, sometimes simultaneously, from the Mamluks in the south and the Turks in the north, and its appeals to the West for aid were frequent until it was finally overrun by the Mamluk forces in 1375. That the Armenians should be aided by their co-religionists in the West was a constant theme of papal policy, but it was complicated by disagreement about the form which this aid should take, and by the Curia's concern about unorthodoxy in Armenian dogma and liturgy.[4]

Several hundred miles to the West of Cyprus and Armenia lay the third zone, bordered on the south by Rhodes and Crete, and on the north by Constantinople and the Adriatic port of Durazzo; contemporaries called this area *Romania*. The political framework of *Romania* was complicated. Much of it was still in Western hands as a consequence of the dismemberment which followed the Fourth Crusade. Thus southern Greece, Morea, formed the Principality of Achaea, which had close ties with the Angevin Kingdom of Naples; a Burgundian dynasty governed the Duchy of Athens; Venice had colonies and dependencies in Crete, Euboea (Negroponte), and at Coron and Modon; and a number of minor Latin families ruled many of the islands in the Aegean and Adriatic Seas. But the Greeks had held on to northern Greece and some of the Balkan provinces of their Empire, and in 1261 they had recaptured Constantinople. In 1305 a bitter conflict was in progress between the *basileus*, Andronicus II Palaeologus, and the western usurpers. At the same time Turkish tribes, formed into emirates in the wake of the Mongol destruction of the Selchükid Sultanate, were inexorably eroding Byzantine possessions in Anatolia. As they reached the Aegean coast, the emirs, devotees of holy war, launched flotillas of raiders which brought them into hostile contact with the Latin

[3] See, for example, ibid., ii, 298 ff.
[4] See T. S. R. Boase, 'The History of the Kingdom', in his *The Cilician Kingdom of Armenia* (Edinburgh and London, 1978), 29–33; A. T. Luttrell, 'The Hospitallers' Interventions in Cilician Armenia: 1291–1375', ibid., 123–33; J. Richard, *La Papauté et les missions d'orient au moyen âge (XIIIe–XVe siècles)* (Rome, 1977), 200–17.

powers of *Romania*.[5] On the edge of this zone were the trading outposts of Genoa and Venice in the Black Sea, at Caffa and Trebizond, which at times impinged on the crusading policy of the papal Curia.[6]

In 1305 the eastern Mediterranean still formed a unity of sorts. The three zones naturally overlapped so that, for example, the Mamluks launched attacks on Armenia, Cyprus took part in naval leagues directed against the Turkish emirates, and the Latin reconquest of Constantinople could be portrayed as a first step towards the recovery of Palestine. Rhodes, held by the Order of St John of Jerusalem from 1306, was well placed for intervention in all three zones, so that Hospitaller interests in this period were multifarious. Most importantly, the whole area was bound together by the pattern of commercial routes followed by the traders of the West, especially those of Genoa, Venice, and Barcelona. But it is now clear, and was so to many contemporaries, that the three zones were all but separate from the point of view of launching a crusade from the West. An expedition could set out to recover Palestine (by an invasion of Syria or Egypt), to protect Cyprus and Armenia from Mamluk and Turkish attacks, or to defend Latin interests in *Romania*. A crusade directed at any of these objectives might help one of the others, but that help would be indirect or marginal; it was just as likely that its impact would be deleterious to Christians in a neighbouring zone, for example by altering the thrust of Muslim aggression. The Curia's appreciation of this point varied considerably between pontificates: John XXII and Gregory XI were aware of its implications, while Clement V and VI were rather less well-informed, and Urban V possessed—or at least found it convenient to display—a very hazy grasp of the geography involved. Quite apart from the problems which this led to, the existence of three zones, all with a good claim to papal attention, could only lead to the dissipation of resources which were limited to start with.

[5] See N. Cheetham, *Medieval Greece* (New Haven and London, 1981), chs. 5–8. There is no general history of the emirates, but for Aydin see the classic study of P. Lemerle, *L'Émirat d'Aydin, Byzance et l'occident: Recherches sur 'La Geste d'Umur Pacha'* (Paris, 1957).

[6] For the political and economic interests of Venice and Genoa in *Romania*, see F. Thiriet, *La Romanie vénitienne au moyen âge: Le développement et l'exploitation du domaine colonial vénitien (XIIᵉ–XVᵉ siècles)* (Paris, 1959); E. A. Zachariadou, *Trade and Crusade: Venetian Crete and the Emirates of Menteshe and Aydin (1300–1415)* (Venice, 1983); M. Balard, *La Romanie génoise (XIIᵉ–début du XVᵉ siècle)*. 2 vols. (Rome–Genoa, 1978).

The election of Bertrand de Got as Pope in June 1305 was a diplomatic triumph for the French monarchy. It is true that the former Archbishop of Bordeaux was a compromise candidate and had even attended Boniface VIII's generally anti-French Council of Rome in 1302. But this was deceptive, for Bertrand had always had good relations with Philip IV and showed that he would be amenable to the wishes of the French King, first by acceding to Philip's request that he should be crowned at Lyons, and then, in December 1305, by creating nine French cardinals in a single promotion. Soon afterwards Philip secured a number of useful concessions: the Colonna were pardoned for their part in the Anagni incident, the bulls *Clericis laicos* and *Unam sanctam* were revoked, and the King was given tenths and annates for his war in Flanders. Throughout Clement V's reign the influence exercised over papal affairs by Philip and his counsellors was profound and far-reaching.[7]

This naturally affected Clement V's crusade policy in the eastern Mediterranean. The Curia had its own objectives, essentially the same ones which it had been pursuing since 1291; in the short term it wanted to organize the defence of Frankish Greece, to send aid to Armenia, and to enforce an economic blockade of Egypt, while the long-term goal was the recovery of the Holy Land.[8] It can be seen acting independently to try to bring these aims about, by attempting to restore peace between Genoa and Cyprus, issuing letters on behalf of the Hospitallers, and working for a Genoese expedition to Armenia in 1306.[9] But in the organization of a big crusade Clement was firmly tied to the plans of Philip IV and his court. In the first years of his reign this meant, in particular, granting lavish aid to Philip's brother, Charles of Valois, the titular Emperor of Constantinople, who hoped to recover his lost Empire.[10] Thus in January

---

[7] Continuator of William of Nangis, *Chronique latine . . . de 1300 à 1368*, ed. H. Géraud. 2 vols. (Paris, 1843), i, 350–1; Mollat, *Popes at Avignon*, 3 ff.; M. Barber, *The Trial of the Templars* (Cambridge, 1978), 25–6.

[8] For Clement V's crusade policy see Thier. Although dated, F. Heidelberger, *Kreuzzugsversuche um die Wende des 13. Jahrhunderts* (Berlin, 1911), 24–80, is still of value.

[9] See *Regestum Clementis papae V, editum cura et studio monachorum Ordinis S. Benedicti.* 8 vols. (Rome, 1885–92), nn. 750–3, 1247–8, 1250, 2148, 2351–2, 2371, 2387, 2614, 4986, 7427. See also ibid., nn. 1941–4, 5103, 10477 (collection of tenths and arbitration between Armenia and Cyprus). Some financial aid was sent to Armenia in 1307: Richard, *La Papauté et les missions*, 200n.

[10] The best account of this project, although not entirely accurate, is A. E. Laiou, *Constantinople and the Latins: The Foreign Policy of Andronicus II 1282–1328* (Cambridge, Mass., 1972), ch. 7.

1306 Clement confirmed the letters of his predecessor granting Charles the proceeds of all crusade legacies, donations, and vow redemptions in France, specifying that they should be handed over to the Count when he set out.[11] Clement also levied tenths on Charles's behalf in France, Sicily, and the Neapolitan Kingdom (the *Regno*).[12] Venice was exhorted to keep its agreement with the Count on the transport of his forces and in March 1307 crusade preaching was decreed in southern Italy and Sicily, Romagna, the March of Ancona, and the Veneto.[13] Three months later Clement solemnly excommunicated Andronicus II.[14] Angevin Naples also benefited from the Pope's generosity in 1307: Prince Philip of Taranto received a two-year tenth in Achaea and some of the dioceses lying between France and Germany, to help finance his attempt to recover lands conquered by the Greeks in the Morea.[15]

Clement V thus acted in a passive role as the distributor of privileges to Capetian and Angevin princes. It is questionable whether this should be attributed to the Pope's weakness of character or the illness from which he suffered, for he was capable of initiative and energy in handling Italian affairs. Rather, he was continuing a longstanding policy of giving free rein to the crusading enthusiasm which emanated from Paris, a policy made all the more attractive by the urgent need to re-establish good relations between the French and papal courts.[16] In this respect, as in many others, it is important not to judge the strength or weakness of the Curia by the criteria applied to secular governments. The problem was that the French court paralysed the crusading movement by its failure to act. Charles of Valois was unable to get his expedition off the ground, prevaricating until, in 1310, the coalition on which he depended fell apart when Venice signed a peace treaty with Andronicus II. At the root of his failure was the fact that his elder brother withdrew his backing.[17] Philip IV dragged his feet also on the larger issue of a *passagium* to the Holy Land. In the winter of 1305–6 he had secured the valuable concession of a papal dispensation from any crusading vow taken to help the Holy Land should it threaten the safety of

[11] *Reg. Clem. V*, n. 243.
[12] Ibid., nn. 244–6.
[13] Ibid., nn. 247–8, 1768.
[14] Ibid., n. 1759.
[15] Ibid., nn. 1604–5.
[16] Cf. Housley, 'Pope Clement V', 30.
[17] *DVL*, i, nn. 32, 41–3; Laiou, *Constantinople and the Latins*, 233 ff.

France, a *carte blanche* for inaction on the slenderest of excuses.[18] Even Philip of Taranto failed to do anything substantial to help his subjects in Greece.

From 1307 Franco–papal discussions on the crusade were subsumed under the trial of the Templars, which will be considered in a later chapter. Naturally the trial complicated relations between the two courts on crusading matters. On the one hand, the inability of the Curia to resist determined French pressure was amply confirmed; for although Clement V took over the initiative in the proceedings and delayed the suppression for four years, Philip IV secured both his main aims, the destruction of the Order and the acquisition of a large proportion of its French property. On the other hand, the leading role which the French King assumed in the trial, and his claim that he was doing so partly for the good of the Holy Land, placed on his shoulders the moral duty of actually preparing his much delayed *passagium*.[19] Between the suppression of the Templars at the Council of Vienne in 1312, and his death in November 1314, Philip at least went through the motions of making initial preparations. Vienne was thus the culmination of the unsatisfactory crusade conferences which Clement had conducted with Philip IV at the start of his reign, and in the range and ambition of its decrees concerning the crusade it bears comparison—as the Pope intended it to—with the great councils of the thirteenth century.[20]

The cornerstone of the measures taken at Vienne in 1312 was the levying of a six-year tenth on the whole of the Catholic Church, a step which had complex and far-reaching consequences. The French contribution to the tenth, supplemented by a seventh year, the Pope conceded to Philip IV for his preparations.[21] In December 1312 Clement wrote to Philip permitting him to defer his assumption of the crusader's cross until Pentecost 1313, when there was to be a big gathering at Paris for the knighting of the King's sons; the

---

[18] K. Wenck, 'Aus den Tagen der Zusammenkunft Papst Klemens V. und König Philipps des Schönen zu Lyon, November 1305 bis Januar 1306', *Zeitschrift für Kirchengeschichte*, xxvii (1906), 203. Cf. Thier, 35.

[19] See Barber, *Trial of the Templars*, passim.

[20] See E. Müller, *Das Konzil von Vienne (1311–1312): Seine Quellen und seine Geschichte* (Münster-i-W., 1934). The more recent account of J. Lecler, *Vienne* (Histoire des conciles oecuméniques viii (Paris, 1964)) is unfairly dismissive of the crusade plans.

[21] *Reg. Clem. V*, nn. 8781–3, 8986–7.

expedition itself was to commence not later than March 1319.[22] A cardinal was sent to France as nuncio to give crosses to the royal family and arrange crusade preaching.[23] The assembly took place as planned and Philip, his sons, and son-in-law Edward of England all took the cross.[24] A little more than a year later Clement V died.

Clement's aspirations for a general passage were clearly doomed once the long drawn out and exhausting trial of the Templars was launched. It is likely, however, reading back from what was to occur in the two decades following his death, that the trial was not the primary reason for the frustration of his hopes. Much more important was the fact that the Pope relied almost entirely on the commitment and sincerity of Philip the Fair and his court. While a strong case can be made for the importance of crusading enthusiasm among the French nobility, Philip himself did nothing for the eastern Mediterranean and it is probable that he never came near the level of action. The crusade was an important element in his political thinking, but that thinking was orientated primarily towards local objectives, such as the internal consolidation of the monarchy and the expansion of its borders.[25] Later we shall see that to get expeditions launched a new approach was necessary in papal policy: away from the projects of the court at Paris, towards the active involvement of those powers which had tangible political or economic interests in the eastern Mediterranean. There are signs that this was already the case in the history of the one crusade to the East which was successfully mounted in Clement V's reign, the Hospitaller *passagium* of 1309–10.

The *passagium* was organized in 1308–9 as Clement's response to Armenian pleas for help and as a means of enforcing the ban on trade with Mamluk Egypt. It was to consist of a limited number of troops, 5,000 in all, who would remain in the East for five years. They would be led by the Master of the Hospitallers, Fulk of Villaret, and a papal legate. The crusade was conceived as a *passagium particulare,* which would be followed by the general passage planned by Philip IV. It was the initial intention of the

---

[22] Ibid., n. 8964.   [23] Ibid., n. 9941.

[24] Cont. William of Nangis, i, 396; *Chronographia regum Francorum*, ed. H. Moranvillé. 3 vols. (Paris, 1891–7), i, 210–12; Ptolemy of Lucca, 'Vita Clementis V', in *Vitae paparum avenionensium*, ed. E. Baluze and G. Mollat. 4 vols. (Paris, 1914–22), i, 50; John of St Victor, 'Vita Clementis V', ibid., i, 21.

[25] See S. Schein, 'Philip IV and the Crusade: a Reconsideration', in *Crusade and Settlement*, ed. P. W. Edbury (Cardiff, 1985), 121–6.

French and papal courts that Philip would be closely involved in the crusade's organization and finance. In practice the King played a minimal role, and the passage became a papal–Hospitaller project. Partly because it lacked the backing of a secular power, the crusade encountered substantial problems, including lack of funds and obstruction by French nobles, light-fingered clerics, and the Aragonese government. The expedition finally set out from Brindisi early in 1310. Its last stages are obscure, but it seems to have been used by the Hospitallers to consolidate their conquest of Rhodes. To some extent this was an unsatisfactory conclusion to Clement's efforts, illustrating the problem of control which we shall later examine in detail. But the fact remains that the expedition had been launched, thus constituting the first crusade to the eastern Mediterranean since 1291.[26]

Between the Council of Vienne and his death, other events drew Clement V's attention to the affairs of Latin Greece. Despite earlier disappointments the Pope continued to give crusading aid to Philip of Taranto, suzerain-lord of Achaea, for the defence of the Principality against the Greeks advancing from the south of the peninsula. In April 1312 Philip was granted the first three years' proceeds of the Vienne tenth collected in the *Regno*, Sardinia, Corsica, and the dioceses of Greece; Clement wrote that he made the grant at the request of the clergy.[27] A few days later the Pope followed this up by giving Philip crusade indulgences for an expeditionary force which he intended to lead to the Morea.[28] *Romania* had been thrown into turmoil in 1311 by the conquest of the Duchy of Athens by the Catalan Grand Company, an army of veterans from the Sicilian war.[29] The Curia outlawed the Company and lent its support to schemes of recovery by the exiled Brienne rulers.[30] In January 1314 Clement wrote several letters of backing for Walter of Châtillon, Constable of France and grandfather of the young titular Duke, Walter II; these included an attempt to persuade the

[26] Housley, 'Pope Clement V', *passim*; J. S. C. Riley-Smith, *The Knights of St John in Jerusalem and Cyprus, c. 1050–1310* (London, 1967), 220–6; A. T. Luttrell, 'The Hospitallers at Rhodes, 1306–1421', in Setton, (gen. ed.), *History of the Crusades*, iii, 285–6.

[27] *Reg. Clem. V*, nn. 7759–65.

[28] Ibid., n. 7893. See also nn. 7890–1, 7956–8, 8863–8, 8913–16.

[29] See K. M. Setton, 'The Catalans in Greece, 1311–1380', in his *History of the Crusades*, iii, 167 ff.; R. I. Burns, 'The Catalan Company and the European Powers, 1305–1311', *Speculum*, xxix (1954), 751–71.

[30] Setton, 'The Catalans', 181 ff.

Hospitallers to help oust the invaders.[31] The resources for an expedition to rewin the Duchy of Athens were not available, but for several decades the Curia was to number the Catalans amongst the enemies of the Church in *Romania*. Athens was placed alongside Jerusalem and Constantinople as a city to be regained by crusading endeavour.

A two year interregnum followed the death of Clement V before Jacques Duèse, Cardinal-bishop of Porto, was elected Pope in August 1316.[32] Although Philip IV and his son Louis X had died without launching a crusade, enthusiasm for a *passagium* continued in France. At the time of John XXII's election it centred on Robert of Clermont and his sons, but it never moved very far from the French court itself.[33] The crusading aspirations of the French kings and their nobility dominated the new Pope's crusade policy in the eastern Mediterranean, even more so than they had that of Clement V.[34] It is therefore necessary to examine in some detail the various phases of diplomatic negotiations between the two courts on the subject of the crusade; but before doing so it is useful to establish an overall perspective, and this can best be done by making three general points.

The first is that, while much could be achieved in the East by other Latin Christian powers, such as Venice, Genoa, Cyprus, and the Hospitallers, the only ruler capable of mounting a general passage to recover the Holy Land was the king of France. Only he had the necessary resources, in terms of men, money, and prestige. Contemporaries fully realized this; some, observing such events as the trial of the Templars, grossly exaggerated the power and influence of the French Crown and ignored its weaknesses. The missionary Jordan of Séverac even claimed that 'the king of France

---

[31] *Reg. Clem. V*, nn. 10166–8; *Acta aragonensia: Quellen zur deutschen, italienischen, französischen, spanischen, zur Kirchen- und Kulturgeschichte aus der diplomatischen Korrespondenz Jaymes II. (1291–1327)*, ed. H. Finke. 3 vols. (Leipzig–Berlin, 1908–22), ii, n. 466; A. T. Luttrell, 'The Latins of Argos and Nauplia: 1311–1394', *PBSR*, xxxiv (1966), 34–5.

[32] Mollat, *Popes at Avignon*, 9 ff.; G. Tabacco, *La casa di Francia nell'azione politica di papa Giovanni XXII* (Rome, 1953), 33 ff.

[33] Tabacco, 63 ff. Robert of Clermont was the last surviving son of Louis IX.

[34] The most detailed study of French plans from 1316 to 1335 remains C. De la Roncière, *Histoire de la marine française: les origines* (Paris, 1899), 218–43. For Philip V's plans see C. J. Tyerman, 'Philip V of France, the Assemblies of 1319–20 and the Crusade', *BIHR*, lvii (1984), 15–34.

could conquer the whole world for himself and the Christian Faith, without anybody else helping him'.[35] Moreover, since 1270 royal publicists had built on the crusading achievements and commitment of St Louis by propounding the idea that the *negotium Terrae Sanctae* was the particular responsibility and concern of France and its monarchy. Peter Dubois, for example, wrote that 'the chivalry of the Kingdom of France has hitherto been, and will very likely continue to be, the leading, firmest, and most reliable hope for the recovery and tenure of the Holy Land'.[36] The papal Curia contributed to this belief by its frequent and flattering appeals to the king and his nobility; thus Clement V wrote of Philip IV as the man most involved in the crusade after himself,[37] and John XXII wrote of 'French power, whose aid is second only to that of God in the needs and expectations of the Holy Land'.[38] It is undeniable, too, that the appeal of a crusade to recover Jerusalem was still very great at the French court,[39] and this fact needs constantly to be borne in mind lest one be led by the failure of negotiations between Paris and Avignon into concluding that they were conducted by both sides as a cynical exercise with quite other objectives.[40]

The second point is the obverse or complement of the first. By 1316 there was already a long history of deception practised by lay rulers in crusading matters in order to get their hands on the rich financial pickings; in this Philip the Fair and his advisers had set new standards of persistence, skill, and ruthlessness. Interpreting experience in such a way as to reinforce their own prejudices, contemporaries who were hostile to the court of France started to view French crusade proposals as elaborate diplomatic manœuvres aimed at securing Church revenue. Three comments on the project of Philip VI illustrate this well. Bernat Oliver, an Aragonese envoy at Avignon, reflected the scepticism current in some quarters, both within and outside the Curia, when he simply took it for granted, in a letter home written towards the end of 1333, that the recently

[35] J. Gay, *Le Pape Clément VI et les affaires d'orient (1342–1352)* (Paris, 1904), 61n.
[36] Peter Dubois, *De recuperatione terre sancte*, ed. C. V. Langlois (Paris, 1891), 128.
[37] *Reg. Clem. V*, n. 2986.
[38] *Lettres secrètes et curiales du pape Jean XXII relatives à la France*, ed. A. Coulon and S. Clémencet. BEFAR, 3rd series. 4 vols. (Paris, 1906–72), n. 53.
[39] Cf. Tabacco, 152, 323.
[40] Cf. M. Barber, 'The Pastoureaux of 1320', *JEH*, xxxii (1981), 161–2.

proclaimed general passage would never take place.[41] When the crusade did indeed founder, commentators became more caustic. Matteo Villani, noticeably anti-French on this issue, described Philip VI as 'simulating a deep desire' to go on crusade, and 'creating the impression of great preparations'.[42] Henry Knighton, writing during the Anglo-French war, put forward the standard English view:

The King of France had been given a six-year tenth by Pope John by means of the deceptive assertion that he wanted to set out for the Holy Land. The Pope believed that he genuinely wanted to carry out the project, and appointed him captain of the crusade and helped him as far as he could, but the King abandoned the whole business.[43]

Philip VI's failure to set out was of course of great value to English propagandists: Knighton asserted that the French King proposed English participation in his crusade solely as an attempt to prevent Edward III ravaging the lands of his ally, the King of Scotland.[44] Views like these are of little worth as indicators of the real reason for the failure of Philip and his predecessors, and to account for that failure we need above all to examine the planning of the crusades and the immense problems which it had to contend with. But it was a fact that both the French and papal courts benefited from the crusade in terms of extra revenue, and this led to deep suspicion at each court about the motives of the other. Two of the toughest French negotiators, Henry of Sully and Mile of Noyers, were associated with the *Chambre des comptes* faction, which in general frowned on crusade projects because of the expense which they entailed; this could only aggravate papal misgivings.[45] Such considerations did not in themselves lead to an impasse, but they were corrosive of energy and enthusiasm, making it much harder to reach an agreement which would have resulted in military action.

[41] 'Nachträge und Ergänzungen zu den Acta aragonensia', ed. H. Finke. in *Spanische Forschungen der Görresgesellschaft. I Reihe*, iv (1933), n. 58. For an earlier example of Aragonese scepticism about French crusade plans see *AA*, i, n. 145.

[42] Matteo Villani, *Cronica*, ed. F. Gherardi Dragomanni. 2 vols. (Milan, 1848), bk. 7, ch. 2, ii, 6–7.

[43] Henry Knighton, 'Chronicon', ed. J. R. Lumby. *RS*. 2 vols. (London, 1889–95), i, 476.

[44] Ibid.

[45] See J. B. Henneman, *Royal Taxation in Fourteenth Century France. The Development of War Financing 1322–1356* (Princeton, 1971), 30–2, 34, 89 ff.

The third point is that the negotiations were never carried on in a political vacuum. As Giovanni Tabacco showed, relations between the two courts throughout John XXII's reign were so close and many-sided that it proved impossible to isolate the crusade from one or more of the other areas of co-operation and conflict: Italian and imperial affairs, Anglo–French relations, Flanders, Church–State problems in France, and the government of the Kingdom itself.[46] Sometimes this worked to the advantage of the crusade, so that the Pope responded favourably to French proposals because he needed French backing on another issue; at other times it was detrimental, as when the Pope wanted to secure French intervention in Italy. So John XXII's reaction to the initiatives periodically emanating from Paris was complex: he welcomed, indeed asked for them as the only effective means of regaining Palestine for Christendom; he treated them with caution and close attention to detail because of the financial issues involved; and he judged them in the context of the contribution which the French Crown, church, and nobility were making to his many other fields of activity.

We can now turn to the negotiations themselves. There were in effect three phases, corresponding to the reigns of Philip V, Charles IV, and Philip VI.

At the time of his election John XXII voiced a conventional desire for a crusade of recovery to be launched as soon as possible; he wrote to King Robert of Naples of 'the intense longing' which he had 'to recover the precious patrimony of the Lord from the hands of the infidels'.[47] In theory Philip V, who ruled France as Regent from 1316–17 and then as King, was bound to carry out the crusade project which his father had agreed to at the Council of Vienne.[48] For this, however, more money would be needed,[49] and John both confirmed the grant of a new four-year tenth on the French church by Clement V, and made a four-year grant of annates, 'so that you can attend to the *negotium Terrae Sanctae* more quickly and with greater freedom, as you so long to do'.[50] Together with Clement's

---

[46] Tabacco, *passim*.

[47] *AE*, ad annum 1316, nn. 7–9, xxiv, 33–4.

[48] 'Chronique parisienne anonyme de 1316 à 1339', ed. M. A. Hellot in *Mémoires de la Société de l'histoire de Paris et de l'Ile-de-France*, xi (1884), 43. Laiou, *Constantinople and the Latins*, 249 ff., is useful for the negotiations with Philip V.

[49] See *AA*, i, n. 145 for one, possibly distorted, version of French demands in September 1316.

[50] *CC*, nn. 23, 27.

concessions at Vienne, this added up to eleven years of tenths and four years of annates granted to the French Crown since 1312 in connection with the crusade. Had they been collected at the normal rate of about 250,000 *livres tournois* each year, the tenths alone would have brought in 2,750,000 pounds.[51] Against this background, comments like that of Knighton are readily understandable.

It was clear from the start that Philip V's crusade proposals hinged on the settlement of the Flanders dispute.[52] The defence of the French realm, the Pope wrote to Philip in 1316, obviously took precedence.[53] The plans formulated at Vienne and embraced in full chivalric style at the 1313 assembly were being held up by the rebellion in Flanders, and throughout the following years John XXII strove to restore peace there;[54] he also intervened on the royal side in the dispute between Crown and baronage in France, worked for good relations within the royal family, and maintained an active interest in the restoration of royal finances.[55] But as the Flanders quarrel dragged on and envoys arrived from Armenia pleading for military aid, both courts began to think in terms of postponing the general passage yet further and instead sending out another *passagium particulare*. Thus the Pope wrote to the King of Armenia that Philip V would send a lieutenant with a strong army,[56] and in September 1318 the King designated Louis of Clermont, the personification of the royal conscience in crusading matters, as 'captain, leader, and governor-general' of this expedition.[57] Even a limited *passagium* would be costly, as the Hospitallers had found, and Philip continued to exert pressure for extra financial aid.[58] Early in 1318 John XXII granted a new two-year tenth for the King to pay off his debts and prepare for the crusade.[59] Philip had wanted much more: John wrote tantalizingly—for diplomatic reasons the

---

[51] In fact, as we shall see, only seven years' of tenths were collected since John XXII merged the four-year tenth into the Vienne tenth.

[52] Cf. *Chron. regum Francorum*, i, 211–12; 'Chron. parisienne anonyme', 37.

[53] CC, n. 74.   [54] See Tabacco, 108 ff.

[55] Ibid., chs. 3–7 *passim*.

[56] *AE*, ad annum 1318, n. 17, xxiv, 80. Cf. CC, n. 511.

[57] *Titres de la maison ducale de Bourbon*, ed. M. Huillard-Bréholles. 2 vols. (Paris, 1867), i, 259, n. 1509; Barber, 'The Pastoureaux', 160. For Louis and the crusade, see R. Cazelles, *La Société politique et la crise de la royauté sous Philippe de Valois* (Paris, 1958), 110–11.

[58] Tabacco, 139 ff.

[59] CC, nn. 471, 505. Cf. ibid., nn. 512–13.

Curia's written replies were often vaguely expressed—of 'certain
badly-ordered matters . . . which were not only considered useless
to the business itself, but also appeared impossible from our point of
view, and even more so from yours'.[60]

In 1319 the vanguard of the *passagium particulare* was finally
prepared. It comprised ten ships, purchased or constructed at
Narbonne and Marseilles; its aim was to be similar to that of the
Hospitaller crusade of 1309–10. Had it set out it is hard to envisage
what exactly it could have achieved, but it would at least have shown
the eastern Christians that the West was concerned for their
welfare. As it was the Italian needs of the Curia intervened
disastrously and the entire flotilla was lost in a naval battle fought
off Genoa between the Guelfs and the Ghibellines.[61] After this
setback Philip V's plans, such as they were, disintegrated. It would
obviously be very difficult to assemble another *primum passagium*,
and in 1320 both Paris and Avignon were preoccupied with the
uprising of the *pastoureaux*, a popular crusading movement, itself,
it has been suggested, a reaction to these years of abortive negotiations.[62] For the remainder of Philip V's reign talks consisted of
haggling about finance. John XXII, by now very suspicious about
Philip's motives, would grant no fresh tenths unless the strictest
provisions were made concerning their fate.[63]

The talks with Philip's brother and successor, Charles IV, followed on from this without a break.[64] Charles reacted to the news of
the latest Mamluk attacks on Armenia by formulating a detailed
crusade proposal at an assembly held at Paris in January 1323.[65] It
was almost exactly a decade since Philip the Fair's great pageant of
1313 and the negotiations which resulted from it were formally
ended: Charles informed the Pope brusquely that the Vienne tenth

[60] Ibid., n. 479; Tabacco, 143.
[61] Cont. William of Nangis, ii, 20–1; C. Bourel de la Roncière, 'Une Escadre
franco-papale (1318–1320)', *MEFR*, xiii (1893), 397–418; N. Housley, *The Italian
Crusades: The Papal–Angevin Alliance and the Crusades against Christian Lay
Powers, 1254–1343* (Oxford, 1982), 100–1.
[62] Barber, 'The Pastoureaux', *passim*. An assembly held at Paris in 1320 had
discussed the crusade but made no preparations: 'Chron. parisienne anonyme', 43;
Tverman, *passim*.
[63] N. Housley, 'The Franco-Papal Crusade Negotiations of 1322–3', *PBSR*, xlviii
(1980), 166–7.
[64] Possibly they were pursued with greater vigour because of the ascendancy at
Charles's court of the pro-crusade *parlement* faction: see Henneman, *Royal Taxation
. . . 1322–1356*, 36–7.
[65] 'Chron. parisienne anonyme', 76–7.

had all been spent.[66] Instead Charles proposed a three-fold crusade. A *primum passagium*, comparable in size to the 1319 flotilla, would sail in 1323 in aid of Armenia, a *passagium particulare* would follow in the next year or very soon thereafter, and only in the very long term would there be a general passage to liberate Palestine. The French court was acting with urgency in response to a serious situation in Armenia, where the important port of Ayas had recently been lost. Preparations for the *primum passagium* were quite advanced,[67] and the Curia issued crusade bulls to recruit fighters. But it was clear that the *passagium particulare* would necessitate very heavy taxes on the French church as well as some taxes in other countries. John XXII reacted with his customary caution, calling for and receiving detailed *consilia* from his cardinals. His reply to the King concentrated on the impossibility of taxation outside France on behalf of a French enterprise. Charles's angry reaction that the Pope had offered him 'nothing except the goods of his own Kingdom' no doubt confirmed the suspicions of some cardinals about what his motives really were, and the talks collapsed at the end of 1323.[68]

In 1328 Philip of Valois became King of France, and almost straight away he revived plans for a crusade.[69] Of course it was politically expedient for the first king of a new dynasty to exploit to the full the crusading tradition of the Capetians, just as it had been, to a lesser extent, for Philip V, but Philip VI was also the son of a dedicated, if erratic, *crucesignatus* and the heir to his policies.[70] At first Philip considered the less ambitious, and cheaper, alternative of a pilgrimage or crusade in Spain,[71] but his attention was soon pulled towards the eastern Mediterranean, perhaps as a consequence of a vigorous and moving exhortation by Peter de la Palu, the Patriarch of Jerusalem, on his return from a fruitless diplomatic

---

[66] CC, n. 1562, col. 190.

[67] See De la Roncière, *Histoire de la marine française*, 226–7. In my 'Franco-Papal Crusade Negotiations' (180) I underestimated the extent of these preparations.

[68] See ibid., 180–1, and *passim* for more detail on the events of 1322–3.

[69] See J. Viard, 'Les Projets de Croisade de Philippe VI de Valois', *BEC*, xcvii (1936), 305–16. Coverage of this phase in Tabacco, 321–34, is inadequate.

[70] See Cazelles, 96–7, for important observations on Louis IX, Philip VI, and the crusade. Henneman (*Royal Taxation . . . 1322–1356*, 89–90, 105–6) stresses the role of William of St Maure, Philip's Chancellor from 1332 to 1335, and associates the decline of the royal crusade project in 1335–6 with the dominance of the *chambre des comptes* faction after William's death.

[71] CC, nn. 4241, 4660; Tabacco, 299–310.

mission to Cairo.[72] In December 1331 John XXII gave his consent
to the preaching of a crusade, which was to commence before
March 1334.[73] This was just the preliminary move in negotiations
which were to exceed even those of 1322–3 in their complexity, and
which were conducted with great suspicion on the papal side.[74]
Philip presented his project early in 1332 and received his reply in
April. The Pope was plainly taken aback by the sheer extent of
Philip's demands: 'Your royal providence should not be surprised
that we have not replied before now. For we all know how
important this matter is, and we have no records of such great
demands being made at one time for a similar project'.[75] The talks
continued for several months before a settlement was reached in
May 1333.[76] There followed in July 1333 a long series of bulls setting
out all aspects of the expedition.[77]

The culmination of this sequence of events was an impressive
gathering in the meadows near Saint-Germain-des-Près on 1
October 1333, when Peter Roger, the Archbishop of Rouen,
preached the crusade. In this ceremonial context, reminiscent of the
1313 pageant and probably designed to convince sceptics of his
sincerity, Philip VI took the cross together with a large number of
nobles.[78] What had been arranged was a three-stage crusade similar
to that proposed ten years earlier by Charles IV. The major French
contribution would come only in the third stage, the general passage
which was planned for August 1336 and which the King himself
would lead as captain-general of the Church. Before that there were
to be two preliminary *passagia*. The first of these merits close
attention because it actually took place in 1334. The background to

---

[72] See *VPA*, ii, 288–9; G. Golubovich, *Biblioteca bio-bibliografica della Terra Santa e dell'Oriente francescano*. 5 vols. (Quaracchi, 1906–27), iii, 359–67.

[73] *AE*, ad annum 1331, n. 30, xxiv, 478–80; Cont. William of Nangis, ii, 130–1.

[74] See Giovanni Villani, bk. 10, ch. 194, iii, 173; E. Déprez, *Les Préliminaires de la guerre de Cent ans: La papauté, la France et l'Angleterre (1328–1342)* (Paris, 1902), 85–99.

[75] CC, n. 4830. See also *AE*, ad anum 1332, nn. 2–7, xxiv, 488–90; *Lettres communes du pape Jean XXII analysées d'après les registres dits d'Avignon et du Vatican*, ed. G. Mollat. BEFAR, 3rd Series, 16 vols. (Paris, 1904–47), n. 58236. For the theme of unprecedented demands, see also below, ch. 5, n. 49.

[76] CC, nn. 4978, 5092, 5096, 5151; Mollat, *Lettres communes*, n. 61299.

[77] CC, nn. 5207–27; Mollat, *Lettres communes*, nn. 60794–7; Tabacco, 321–3. Cf. 'Vita Joannis XXII auctore Heinrico Dapifero de Dissenhoven', in *VPA*, i, 174.

[78] CC, n. 5322; Cont. William of Nangis, ii, 134–5; 'Chron. parisienne anonyme', 154; *Le Trésor des chartes d'Albret I*[1], ed. J.-B. Marquette (Paris, 1973), 459–60, n. 400; Viard, 'Les Projets', 310–11; E. A. R. Brown, 'Customary Aids and Royal Fiscal Policy under Philip VI of Valois', *Traditio*, xxx (1974), 215.

this achievement, however, is not the long drawn out and ultimately sterile negotiations between Paris and Avignon, but Latin problems in the Aegean, and the reaction to these difficulties of powers such as Venice and the Knights of St John. Like the Hospitaller *passagium* of 1309–10, the naval league of 1334 is an example of the transfer of real initiative and thrust in crusading affairs to smaller Christian powers with more at stake and, perhaps, greater commitment to action.

The problem was an escalation in Turkish piracy and raiding, the chief offenders being the Emirates of Aydin and Menteshe.[79] The Venetians, who appear to have suffered most and were certainly most vociferous in their response, tried from 1325 to co-ordinate a common Western defence against the Turks.[80] When Philip VI wrote to the Doge late in 1331 asking for advice on his crusade plans, the Venetian reply included an attempt to secure French support for an expedition against the Emirates. The Doge wrote of the urgent need to enforce the embargo on trade with Egypt and to clear the seaways for the provisioning of a Western army once it had reached Palestine. Clearly the Venetians realized that the French court and nobility were not prepared to undertake a crusade solely in order to protect Venetian commerce, or even defend the lands of their Angevin cousins in Greece; it was necessary to make a strategic connection, however tenuous in reality, between the defence of *Romania* and the recovery of the Holy Land.[81] But the fact remains that the expedition of 1334 was the most important indication so far of a significant shift in crusade thinking: the orientation of endeavour away from projects of recovering the Holy Land—which experience was proving to be futile—towards the active protection of Christians and their property threatened by non-believers.

The league originated in the alliance which Venice, the Hospitallers, and Andronicus III Palaeologus concluded at Rhodes in September 1332. The allies agreed to maintain a policing force of twenty galleys over a five year period.[82] In the autumn and winter of 1333–4 Philip VI and John XXII undertook to supply four galleys

---

[79] See Lemerle, *L'Émirat d'Aydin*, 75 ff.

[80] Zachariadou, 15 ff; A. E. Laiou, 'Marino Sanudo Torsello, Byzantium and the Turks: the Background to the Anti-Turkish League of 1332–1334', *Speculum*, xlv (1970), 379–80.

[81] *DVL*, i, nn. 109–10.

[82] Ibid., i, nn. 116–17.

each, and by March 1334 the league consisted, theoretically, of
forty vessels.[83] An attempt was made to bring Angevin Naples into
the league, but King Robert was too weak, his resources over-
stretched, to do much to help. Indeed, the inability of Naples to
protect its subjects in Greece was to be one of the problems
confronting the papacy throughout our period.[84] In 1334 the ships
assembled in the Aegean and managed to inflict a heavy defeat on
the Turks in the gulf of Adramyttium, in northern Asia Minor. The
primum passagium, then, had come into being and succeeded; it
had got further than either the Franco–papal squadron of 1319 or
the flotilla planned by Charles IV in 1323, and it had done more than
the Hospitaller *passagium* of 1309–10. But the real test of Christian
unity and determination would come in 1335. In that year a force of
800 men-at-arms led by Louis of Clermont was to be landed to fight
the Turks in Anatolia. Of this little army 400 men would be sent by
the Pope and Philip VI, 200 by the Hospitallers, 100 by the King of
Cyprus, and 100 by Andronicus III. The ships needed to carry the
men and their horses would be provided by the same powers,
together with Venice and Naples: a total of seven Christian powers,
their capitals many hundreds of miles apart, would be involved.[85]
But the alliance collapsed. Concern was mounting at Paris about
Anglo–French relations, and at the end of 1334 John XXII died.

   The reign of John XXII was in some ways the high-water mark of
the crusading movement in the Avignonese period. This statement
seems hard to validate on the basis of what was achieved in the
eastern Mediterranean, and it is true that there was much more
fruitful activity on other fronts in these eighteen years. The failure
of Latin Christendom to make much impact in the East in this
period was critical, for political and economic conditions in the
West were not again to be so favourable for the organization and
financing of a general passage. John himself worked with great
energy towards this end: his correspondence about the crusade is
voluminous. It is not easy to make a cut and dried judgement on his
policy, partly because the Pope's death occurred at such a crucial
moment. Would the second and third stages of Philip VI's crusade
have come about if John had been alive to push things along? The

   [83] Ibid., i, nn. 122–4, 126–7; *AE*, ad annum 1333, n. 16, xxiv, 513–14, ad annum
1334, nn. 7–9, xxv, 3–4; CC, n. 5486.
   [84] See N. Housley, 'Angevin Naples and the Defence of the Latin East: Robert
the Wise and the Naval League of 1334', *Byzantion*, li (1981), 548–56.
   [85] CC, n. 5485.

third stage, the general passage, would almost certainly have foundered, as there were still unresolved problems of finance.[86] Also, John's approach to the crusade was so closely entwined with his policies on other issues that it is difficult to judge it in isolation. But it shared with those policies certain characteristics which now seem ominously simplistic and out of date. It involved the use of blunt coercion to try to settle complex political questions, so that in 1330 John authorized the preaching of a crusade against the Catalans to support Walter of Brienne's attempt to reconquer the Duchy of Athens.[87] It entailed very heavy Church taxation. Above all, it meant confronting the sort of problems which were inherent in trying to work in co-operation with the French court at a time when that monarchy, for all its apparent might, had very serious deficiencies.[88] Yet it is doubtful that John XXII ever saw the issues in such straightforward terms. For a man with his background and experience,[89] and working in such a Curia, 'breaking with' France was unthinkable as well as unpracticable.[90] It would take the outbreak of the Hundred Years War to bring about the radical change in papal policy which was required.

John XXII's successor, Benedict XII, was a very different sort of man whose crusade policy bears the firm imprint of his personality.[91] An ascetic Cistercian, he was far more interested in reforming the regular Church and suppressing heterodoxy than in launching crusades. If he felt any deep sentiment about Palestine it is not apparent in his bulls, as it occasionally is, beneath the conventional phrases, in the letters of Clement V and John XXII.[92]

[86] See Henneman, *Royal Taxation . . . 1322–1356*, 90 ff., on the terrible state of French royal finances in the mid-1330s. The implications of this for the crusade will be considered in ch. 5 below.

[87] See *Diplomatari de l'orient català (1301–1409)*, ed. A. Rubió i Lluch (Barcelona, 1949), nn. 150–2.

[88] See Tabacco, 334–6.

[89] Since he was born in c. 1245, his formative years were the heyday of papal–Angevin co-operation.

[90] It is noteworthy that the papal galleys of 1334 were placed under the command of the French captain, John of Cepoy: CC, n. 5486.

[91] See Mollat, *Popes at Avignon*, 26 ff. For studies of his crusading policy see G. Daumet, 'Introduction' to his edition of *Lettres closes, patentes et curiales du pape Benoît XII se rapportant à la France*. BEFAR, 3rd Series, 1 vol. (Paris, 1899–1920), xliv–lxvi; F. Giunta, 'Benedetto XII e la crociata', *Anuario de estudios medievales*, iii (1966), 215–34.

[92] See for example *Reg. Clem. V*, nn. 8986, 9941. Cf. the rather harsh judgement of Déprez, *Les Préliminaires*, 168, 401–2.

By contrast, a biographer praised him as 'a very great champion of the Faith, throughout his career the unflagging uprooter and unyielding pursuer of heretics',[93] and he earned this title by his painstaking judicial proceedings against the Cathars in the French Pyrenees, for which he had been granted the plenary indulgence in 1326.[94]

Whatever his personal feelings and objectives, Benedict inherited the crusade project which had been formulated with such difficulty by John XXII and Philip VI, and he appears to have committed himself to it without hesitation. At the end of January 1335 he confirmed all his predecessor's bulls relating to the general passage.[95] Owing to the English threat, plans for a *passagium particulare* in 1335 were shelved, but an attempt was made to revive the naval league which had done so well in 1334. Thus on 20 March Benedict wrote to Robert of Naples informing the King of a meeting which had taken place at Avignon, attended by himself, Hospitaller representatives, and envoys of Philip VI and Venice. They had agreed to send more galleys to the East, and Robert was asked to co-operate.[96] Four papal galleys were prepared at Marseilles; they were to set out in mid-May and serve for five months at a cost of 11,500 florins.[97] Andronicus III prepared twenty ships.[98] Philip VI may also have armed galleys: privileges were granted in April to his 'governor and captain-general', Hué Quiéret.[99] But other sources are silent about naval activity in the summer of 1335, and it seems likely that nothing came of these preparations.[100]

There remained Philip VI's general passage and the six-year tenth which John XXII had levied to pay for it. The escalation of conflict in the West made this project of very dubious practicality, and the energy which the French government put into its planning in 1335 fell far short of what would have been required for an expedition on this scale.[101] Benedict wrote to Philip VI on 15

[93] 'Prima vita Benedicti XII', in *VPA*, i, 206.
[94] Mollat, *Lettres communes*, n. 24466.
[95] Daumet, n. 19. Cf. *Lettres communes du pape Benoît XII*, ed. J.-M. Vidal. BEFAR, 3rd Series, 3 vols. (Paris, 1903–11), nn. 2453, 2466, 2469.
[96] Daumet, n. 28.   [97] Ibid., nn. 40, 54; Vidal, nn. 2467, 2478.
[98] Nicephorus Gregoras, *Rhomäische Geschichte: Historia rhomaike,* ed. and tr. J.-L. Van Dieten. 3 vols. (Stuttgart, 1973–9), ii², 274.
[99] Vidal, nn. 2247–50. For Hué, see Cazelles, 150n.
[100] Zachariadou, 33–4. But see also 'Les Papiers de Mile de Noyers', ed. M. Jassemin, *Bulletin philologique et historique*, (1918), 222.
[101] Froissart (*Chroniques*, ed. S. Luce *et al.* 15 vols. (Paris, 1869–1975), i², 115–18)

January 1336 asking him to help restore peace in the western Mediterranean, where wars between Aragon and Genoa, Naples and Sicily, and other belligerents, were impeding the crusade.[102] Two months later the Pope wrote with feeling of a Christendom crippled by internal conflict, and cancelled the whole crusade project.[103] On 18 December he followed this up by cancelling also the collection of the six-year tenth.[104] Philip VI's project had repercussions which lasted throughout the remainder of Benedict's reign, centring on the King's attempt to get papal permission to retain what had been collected of the tenth.[105] But to all intents and purposes the French projects which had dominated the Curia's crusade policy in the East since 1313 had finally lapsed; and since these projects rested on a view of the central place of the French within the crusading movement which had its roots in the mid-thirteenth century, these events were of yet broader significance. An era had ended.

Summarizing this development, Francesco Giunta wrote that 'we have to give [Benedict XII] the credit for having laid the basis for the release of military activity in the East from the main obstacle which had stood in the way of its implementation, the house of France'.[106] This seems overgenerous to the Pope and rather unfair to the French. For Benedict, far from taking the initiative, simply acknowledged the new political conditions which the Anglo–French conflict had created. As for the French, it will now be clear that substantial effort was put into crusade planning by Philip V, Charles

asserted that very extensive preparations were made, reflecting a tradition which was already established in his day and was unquestioningly accepted by later French historians: see, for example, Viard, 'Les Projets', 315; Déprez, *Les Préliminaires*, 123, 132; J. Delaville le Roulx, *La France en orient au XIVᵉ siècle.* 2 vols. (Paris, 1886), i, 101–2. But Froissart's account is full of inaccuracies, and the preparations as outlined by Philip VI himself are meagre: 'Les Papiers', 220–2, and cf. De la Roncière, *Histoire de la marine française*, 237–8; Henneman, *Royal Taxation . . . 1322–1356*, 104–5. According to one chronicler, Archbishop Peter Roger, who played a central role in the crusade negotiations, advised the dispatch of 6,000 men-at-arms to Scotland as early as July 1335, with the scarcely practicable proviso that this should not delay the *passagium*: 'Chron. parisienne anonyme', 164–5.

[102] Daumet, n. 139. Philip VI claimed that he had already made great exertions in the field of peace-making. See 'Les Papiers', 220–1.

[103] *Lettres closes et patentes du pape Benoît XII intéressant les pays autres que la France*, ed. J.-M. Vidal and G. Mollat. BEFAR, 3rd Series, 1 vol. (Paris, 1913–50), n. 786.

[104] Daumet, nn. 251–2; Vidal, nn. 3954–5, 3998–9.

[105] This will be examined in ch. 5 below.

[106] 'Benedetto XII e la crociata', 228.

IV, and Philip VI, and the fact that the first stage of each of their projects—the naval *passagia* of 1319, 1323, and 1334—either took final shape or came quite close to doing so, must make us review the failure of the subsequent stages with greater sympathy. Giunta's comment does, however, reflect the bitter disappointment of contemporaries at Philip VI's failure, disappointment which appears to have been deeper and more resentful than at any point since 1291. In 1340 Benedict XII wrote that the King was still subject to widespread abuse.[107] One of the most interesting products of this disillusionment is Matteo Villani's curious anecdote of an Italian religious from Antioch called Andrew, who travelled to France and cursed Philip VI for cheating the Church and bringing about a wave of Mamluk persecution of the Christians in Syria. French misfortunes up to the battle of Poitiers, Villani claimed, were a divine judgement on the King's deception of Christendom.[108]

Benedict XII had lost the mainstay of the Curia's crusade policy since 1305, but there was nothing to replace it; in particular, there was no impetus, until the last months of his reign, for a renewed naval league in the Aegean.[109] Benedict therefore adopted an *ad hoc* approach, chiefly concerned with Cilician Armenia, which continued to suffer attacks and to send frequent appeals to the West.[110] There was an Armenian ambassador at the western courts in 1335, and in October the Pope sent King Leo a grant of the plenary indulgence to cover all occasions on which he led an army against the Muslims.[111] In April 1336 Benedict wrote to Queen Constance of Armenia telling her that Latin aid would be sent as soon as possible.[112] Two weeks later bulls were sent out to the people of Sicily, Cyprus, Rhodes, Negroponte, and other Latin lands in the East informing them that they could earn the crusade indulgence by going to fight for the Armenians or sending soldiers.[113] Benedict also arranged for a shipment of grain to be sent

---

[107] Daumet, n. 713.

[108] Matteo Villani, bk. 7, chs. 3–4, ii, 7–10.

[109] Lemerle concluded that Umur of Aydin only resumed his raids on Latin Greece in 1339–40: *L'Émirat d'Aydin*, 116–28, 141.

[110] See Boase, 'History of the Kingdom', 30.

[111] Daumet, n. 55; *Acta Benedicti XII*, ed. A. L. Tautu. Pontificia commissio ad redigendum codicem iuris canonici orientalis: Fontes, 1305–1378, viii (Rome, 1958), n. 5.

[112] *AE*, ad annum 1336, n. 40, xxv, 75. Constance was the widow of Henry II of Cyprus and a leading exponent of the Latin cause at the Armenian court.

[113] Daumet, n. 175.

to Armenia to help with a famine there.[114] But he was concerned about the doctrinal errors which, he was told, flourished in Armenia. In 1341 he insisted that King Leo convene a council of his prelates to enforce Catholic teaching; he would be sent no aid until there was orthodoxy.[115]

Limited western aid in exchange for guaranteed orthodoxy: the arrangement was wholly characteristic of Benedict's approach. In other respects he was happy to follow the lead of others or to adopt policies which might yield results without major expenditure. Thus he cancelled crusade preaching in Cyprus in 1336 at the King's request, but congratulated Hugh two years later when he claimed to have won a victory over the Turks.[116] The overall theme was that of retrenchment, so that the Palestine crusade was not the only crusade of recovery to be abandoned in these years: no project for the reconquest of Constantinople had been put forward since 1320, and in 1341 the Pope responded favourably to peace overtures coming from the Catalans at Athens.[117] Warfare in the West, Benedict's desire to avoid heavy expenses, and above all the lack of initiatives coming from *Romania*, added up to inactivity. In terms of the crusade to the East, Benedict's reign was the least productive of the Avignon popes.

Benedict XII died on 25 April 1342, and within two weeks Peter Roger, previously the Archbishop of Rouen, had been elected as his successor. Once again the election had been partly a reaction against the policies of the preceding reign, for Clement VI's pontificate was characterized by generosity, display, and tolerance. From the point of view of the crusade much could be expected. Peter Roger had been a leader of the French delegation which had negotiated on behalf of Philip VI in the early 1330s, when his well-known skill as a preacher had impressed Matteo Villani.[118] He also

---

[114] See Y. Renouard, 'Une Expédition de céréales des Pouilles en Arménie par les Bardi pour le compte de Benoît XII', *MEFR*, liii (1936), 287–329.

[115] Vidal and Mollat, n. 3149 and cf. nn. 3150–5. See also W. De Vries, 'Die Päpste von Avignon und der christliche Osten', *OCP*, xxx (1964), 109 ff.

[116] Vidal and Mollat, nn. 732–3, 1673.

[117] Daumet, n. 810; Setton, 'The Catalans', 192. See also Déprez *et al.*, n. 465.

[118] Mollat, *Popes at Avignon*, 37 ff.; Matteo Villani, bk. 7, ch. 2, ii, 6–7. See also G. Mollat, 'L'Œuvre oratoire de Clément VI', *Archives d'histoire doctrinale et littéraire du moyen âge*, iii (1928), 255, 258 and *passim*; P. Schmitz, 'Les Sermons et discours de Clément VI', *Revue bénédictine*, xli (1929), 24, 30 and *passim*; Brown, 215n; Cazelles, 109n–110n; J. E. Wrigley, 'Clement VI before his Pontificate: the early Life of Pierre Roger, 1290/91–1342', *CHR*, lvi (1970), 458–61 and *passim*.

inherited sound finances as a result of the reforms and parsimony of Benedict XII.[119]

In the reign of Clement VI the slow reorientation of crusade strategy which we have seen at work in the campaigns of 1309–10 and 1334 accelerated. The central achievement of his pontificate was the organization of a Latin naval league against the Turkish emirates in Anatolia, a league totally unconnected with the recovery of the Holy Land or even the defence of the leading 'stepping-stone to Palestine',[120] Cilician Armenia. Several factors helped to bring this about. One was simply the passing of time and the expenditure of effort in vain. The veterans of thirteenth-century crusades to Syria had all died by 1342, and only very old men could now recall a time of Christian presence in Palestine. Clement, middle-aged at his election, may actually have been born in the year Acre fell. He and his contemporaries had witnessed the failure of successive attempts to launch a crusade of recovery, or even to enforce an effective blockade of Egypt. We shall see that Clement was the Pope who ended this policy of blockade. He also gave up hope of assembling a general passage. Quite apart from the problems which had wrecked the projects of the 1320s and early 1330s, the West was now afflicted by the Anglo-French war, by economic difficulties, and, from 1348, by periodic outbreaks of plague. The full impact of these events on the crusading movement we shall examine in another chapter. Here it is enough to say that they made a general passage impossible, and without the prospect of a general passage it was pointless to send out a *passagium particulare* to the south-east Mediterranean. Only in 1348, in a moment of singularly ill-timed and unjustified optimism, did Clement envisage the imminent recovery of Palestine.[121]

But urgent calls for a crusade did come from *Romania*.[122] Turkish piratical attacks reached new heights at the end of the 1330s, and Umur, the Emir of Aydin, was probably at his most powerful in

---

[119] Renouard, *Les Relations*, 36. The standard study of Clement VI and the crusade in the East remains that of Gay.

[120] For this approach to Armenia see, for example, Daumet, n. 175.

[121] *Letters closes, patentes et curiales du pape Clément VI intéressant les pays autres que la France*, ed. E. Déprez and G. Mollat. BEFAR, 3rd Series, 1 vol. (Paris, 1960–1), n. 1605.

[122] The most thorough and up to date account of the Smyrna crusade is K. M. Setton, *The Papacy and the Levant (1204–1571). Vol. I: The Thirteenth and Fourteenth Centuries* (Philadelphia, 1976), 182–223.

1341–2.[123] The Venetians were beginning to fear an assault on their finest colonial possession, Crete.[124] In 1341 Hugh IV of Cyprus and Hélion of Villeneuve, Master of the Hospitallers, sent embassies to Benedict XII pleading for aid. Bishop Lambertino of Limassol, Hugh's envoy, was to explain that unless action was taken against 'the power and malice of the Turks', they would soon occupy the whole area.[125] It was the new Pope who responded in July 1342 by sending a legate, William Court, to Venice to negotiate a league.[126] Slowly a flotilla of galleys was put together: Clement and Hugh would provide four each, the Knights of St John six, Venice and its colonies six.[127] To pay for his own galleys the Pope issued bulls levying a three-year tenth on selected provinces in the West, and decreed the preaching of a crusade to raise money through the administration of indulgences, as Clement V had done in the case of the Hospitaller *passagium*.[128]

In the spring of 1344 the galleys assembled at Negroponte. There were at least twenty-four galleys, which implies a better response than Clement had planned for: as in 1334, the exact details of participation are very hard to establish.[129] The flotilla was successful, apparently scoring a victory over the Turks on or about Ascension Day, 13 May.[130] But this success, and others which followed soon after, were overshadowed by a much more exciting event, the capture of the port of Smyrna (modern Izmir) on 28 October 1344. Smyrna was the sea outlet of the Emirate of Aydin, and it was Umur's negligence which was probably the chief cause of its loss.[131] The port was to be held by the Christians until it fell to

[123] Lemerle, 142; Zachariadou, 41–3.

[124] *Délibérations des assemblées vénitiennes concernant la Romanie*, ed. F. Thiriet. 2 vols. (Paris, 1966–71), i, 309; Setton, *PL*, 182. In April 1340 Venice saw its military power as 'the only shield' of *Romania* against the Turks: *I libri commemoriali della republica di Venezia Regesti*, ed. R. Predelli. 8 vols. (Venice, 1876–1914), ii, 85, n. 489.

[125] M. L. De Mas Latrie, *Histoire de l'île de Chypre sous le règne des princes de la maison de Lusignan*. 3 vols. (Paris, 1852–61), ii, 180–1. Cf. Gay, 28–9.

[126] *AE*, ad annum 1342, n. 17, xxv, 284–5.

[127] Déprez *et al.*, n. 341; *AE*, ad annum 1343, nn. 7–9, xxv, 294–5; *Régestes des délibérations du Sénat de Venise concernant la Romanie*, ed. F. Thiriet. 3 vols. (Paris, 1958–61), i, 53.

[128] *Vetera monumenta historica Hungariam sacram illustrantia*, ed. A. Theiner. 2 vols. (Rome, 1859–60), i, n. 985; *Acta pontificum svecica, I. Acta cameralia*, ed. L. M. Bååth. 2 vols. (Holmiae, 1936–57), i, n. 337.

[129] Lemerle, 184n, 187.

[130] Déprez *et al.*, n. 988; Setton, *PL*, 190–1.

[131] Ibid., 191–2. For Smyrna at this time, see Lemerle, 40–4.

Tamerlane in 1402. Clement VI had high hopes of using it as a bridgehead for expansion into Anatolia, and there was a remarkable, if short-lived, outburst of crusade enthusiasm in the West following the arrival of reports of Smyrna's fall.[132]

On 17 January 1345 the crusade received a severe setback when its main leaders were killed in a confused skirmish with the Turks. The Pope was arranging their replacement when, in May, the Dauphin of Viennois, Humbert II, took on the responsibility of commanding the forces at Smyrna.[133] It took Humbert some time to assemble his expedition, but he finally set sail from Venice in mid-November 1345. On the face of it Humbert should have been able to rejuvenate the league and achieve Clement's ambition of further triumphs over the Turks. He was a moderately wealthy man, dedicated to the crusade, and with the status needed to lead the volunteers assembling at Smyrna and to co-ordinate the league's activities. Clement showed that he still had hopes of the league in the summer of 1345 by stepping up the sale of indulgences and adding another two years to the tenth.[134] But the Dauphin was irresolute, pliable, and dilatory, and he had a very difficult situation to contend with. The Genoese opposed the league, seeing it as a Venetian enterprise thinly disguised as a crusade.[135] Venice itself had achieved its chief objective and may have been negotiating for peace with Umur. There was no obvious next step for the crusaders to take and they faced food shortages and disease cooped up in Smyrna.[136] The West, subject to war and economic collapse, lacked the resources and the will to respond favourably to the Pope's call for more aid. After a series of misadventures Humbert returned to the West, arriving in June 1347.[137]

What could the league now do? Soon after the Dauphin left the eastern Mediterranean its ships once again demonstrated Latin naval superiority by inflicting a defeat on the Turks at Imbros. But this victory was delusive. The league was too expensive to maintain

---

[132] See below, ch. 4, nn. 103–23.

[133] *AE*, ad annum 1345, n. 6, xxv, 358–9; Déprez *et al.*, nn. 1748–50; Setton, *PL*, 195 ff; A. S. Atiya, *The Crusade in the Later Middle Ages* (London, 1938), ch. 13 *passim*.

[134] Déprez *et al.*, nn. 1855–6; *VMH*, i, n. 1055. Cf. *Régestes*, i, 58.

[135] Gay, 71 f.

[136] 'Historiae romanae fragmenta', in *Antiquitates italicae medii aevi*, ed. L. A. Muratori. 25 vols. (Milan, 1723–1896), iii, cols. 369 ff. This is the only detailed description of the situation in Smyrna in 1346 and is unreliable: cf. Setton, *PL*, 207.

[137] Ibid., 210 ff.

over the long term, and it was not to be expected that the Turks would continue putting flotillas within range for it to destroy or capture. The papal galleys stopped operating in the summer of 1347 and Venice recalled its galleys in July 1348.[138] The best approach was to hold on to Smyrna in the hope of peaceful conditions being restored in the West, meanwhile signing a truce with Umur. Papal policy wavered; Clement had not altogether given up hope of an immediate resumption of military activity.[139] In August 1350 the league was actually renewed for a ten year period. No papal galleys were planned, but a legate, armed with a faculty to grant crusade indulgences, would preside over the small force of eight ships, which was to assemble at Negroponte before the end of the year.[140] By then, however, Venice and Genoa were at war. No amount of papal pleading could secure the promised three galleys from Venice, and in September 1351 the Hospitallers were released from their obligation to provide ships.[141] The league had come to an end.

At several points in this book we shall be returning to the Smyrna crusade, to its initiation, organization, command structure, and finance. This is partly because it is the crusade for which we possess the most detailed sources relating to the involvement of the Holy See. But it is also because of the expedition's inherent interest and significance. It will now be clear that the crusade represented the end of a long process by which western strategic thinking shifted from concentration on Palestine and the threat posed by Mamluk Egypt, to the need for a more effective defence of Latin Greece, the Aegean trade routes, and the rump of the Byzantine Empire, first against the Turkish emirates and later against the Ottoman Turks. It would be wrong to regard the shift as definitive; we shall see that it was not. But granting that a certain reorientation of strategy had occurred, how much could be achieved?

There were three outstanding problems associated with the organization of naval leagues for the defence of *Romania*.[142] One was that they upset the balance of power in the area, favouring some Latin states at the expense of others. The Genoese had been placed at a disadvantage by the 1342 league, had criticized it and helped to frustrate its aims. Secondly, the unity which the leagues brought

---

[138] *Régestes*, i, 63–4. [139] *I libri comm.*, ii, 174, n. 295; Lemerle, 226 ff.
[140] *AE*, ad annum 1350, n. 33, xxv, 492.
[141] Déprez *et al.*, n. 5052, and cf. n. 5056; Lemerle, 233–5; Zachariadou, 54–8.
[142] See Gay, 124–5.

into being between those powers which did stand to benefit was short-lived. The common threat did not create a long-term defensive alliance of the threatened. Thirdly, even had such an alliance been politically viable, it would have been difficult to sustain in military terms. As Jules Gay remarked, the league's naval capacity resembled Latin field armies: it was excellent for a hard-hitting offensive campaign, but was unsuited to long-term action.[143]

In addition, the papal Curia was not committed to a view of the crusade in the eastern Mediterranean which interpreted it exclusively as the defence of *Romania*. In terms of justification, the main reason for directing crusade resources to Latin Greece was that Christians were under attack there, and they were being attacked too in other parts of the eastern Mediterranean. Thus in September 1344 Clement responded to appeals from the Armenians by instructing his legate on the Smyrna expedition to send help there.[144] Armenia's problem at this point was the Mamluks, not the Turks, and Clement was in danger of scattering his limited resources. In the following year the Pope granted the Genoese indulgences for the defence of Caffa against Tatar attack.[145] This constituted less of a diversion than Armenia, since the Genoese were in general hostile to the Smyrna expedition; indeed, it may have been an attempt at conciliation on the Pope's part. But the fact remains that *Romania* was a vast region in which western interests were complicated and mutually antagonistic. Unlike expeditions to Palestine, crusades to *Romania* at least got off the ground; but once launched they were peculiarly susceptible to frustration, diversion, and failure.

At the end of 1352 Clement VI was succeeded by Étienne Aubert, a Limousin lawyer and career prelate, who took the name Innocent VI.[146] Innocent's ten year reign witnessed some of the most severe fighting of the Hundred Years War, including the battle of Poitiers in 1356. It was the period too of Cardinal Albornoz's campaigns in

---

[143] Ibid., 124. Umur of Aydin frustrated the 1334 league by staying in harbour while it was active: Lemerle, 100. Possibly this suggested the need for an assault on Smyrna in 1344.

[144] Déprez *et al.*, nn. 1086-7.

[145] Déprez and Mollat, n. 847; Giorgio Stella, 'Annales genuenses', ed. G. P. Balbi, *RISNS* 17², 139 and n.

[146] See Mollat, *Popes at Avignon*, 44 ff.; F. Giunta, 'Sulla politica orientale di Innocenzo VI', in *Miscellanea in onore di Roberto Cessi, i* (Rome, 1958), 305-20.

Italy, of bitter conflict between Genoa and Aragon, Genoa and Venice, and Venice and Hungary. Many parts of the West, especially France, suffered from social unrest and revolt. In the late 1350s the mercenary companies began to exploit and aggravate civil disorder in France and Italy, and in 1361 Avignon itself was struck by plague, in which nine cardinals died. In such circumstances it is not surprising that the affairs of the eastern Mediterranean had low priority at the Curia, as they did at Venice, Naples, and Paris.

Smyrna, at least, was still in Latin hands, a symbol of past successes and future hopes, albeit held by an underpaid and badly-supplied garrison and a series of incompetent or corrupt captains. Innocent VI did what he could to help the government of the port and maintain the subventions due from the other participants in Clement's league. It is from his reign that there dates the steady output of papal letters about Smyrniot affairs which lasted until 1378.[147] The existence of Latin Smyrna led Innocent to try to revive the league which had won it; indeed, as the defence of Smyrna was the joint responsibility of the four members of the Clementine league, it could be argued that in technical terms the league had never been dissolved—the captain of Smyrna, for example, was described as commanding the garrison 'in the name of the league'.[148] It was in any case a natural policy to follow, since organized Turkish raiding remained a serious problem.[149] The direction of papal interest towards *Romania* was further encouraged by hopes for the Union of the Latin and Greek Churches, hopes which were given fresh impetus at this point after a long period of silence. At the end of 1355 the *basileus* John V Palaeologus sent a detailed project for a crusade in aid of Constantinople.[150] For most of his reign Innocent VI thus pinned his hopes on the renewal of the Clementine league.

The first attempt at renewal, at least on the part of the Curia,[151] came in 1356, in political circumstances which appeared propitious because of the truce arranged between Venice and Genoa a year earlier. Writing to King Hugh of Cyprus on 1 April, Innocent

---

[147] See Appendix II.

[148] *Lettres secrètes et curiales du pape Innocent VI*, ed. P. Gasnault *et al*. BEFAR, 3rd Series, 4 vols. so far. (Paris, 1959–), n. 619.

[149] Ibid., nn. 646, 2006; Zachariadou, 60 ff.

[150] *AE*, ad annum 1355, nn. 34–7, xxv, 601–2.

[151] In July 1352 Venice approved the idea of a local league consisting of the colonies of Modon and Coron, *cum Francigenis circavicinis*: *Régestes*, i, 73.

recalled the damage done to the Turks by the original league. Since
the start of the great war between the Italian cities the Turks had
resumed their attacks, and the operations of the league were to be
revived. Hugh was asked to provide two galleys, which were to join
those sent by the Venetians and Hospitallers at Smyrna on 1 July.
He was also to send envoys to the Curia by 1 November to renew or
modify the terms of the 1350 league; Venice, Genoa, and the
Hospitallers received similar invitations.[152] Despite the outbreak of
war between Venice and Hungary, a meeting in March 1357
arranged provisional terms. As in 1350, no papal galleys were
offered, but a legate would be sent to help the captain-general and
galley commanders in directing the flotilla of six or eight ships. The
galleys were to assemble in the autumn of 1357 and operate for five
years.[153]

Although Venice issued orders for the arming of galleys,[154] it
seems unlikely that anything came of this planning; as Kenneth
Setton remarked, the Veneto-Hungarian conflict, the battle of
Poitiers, and the costly campaigns of Albornoz prevented Innocent
and the Venetians from taking the initiative or following it
through.[155] Hugh of Cyprus and the Knights of St John, meanwhile,
needed goading into action. Then in 1359 came a flurry of activity.
In May Peter Thomas was appointed legate in the East and Nicholas
Benedetti captain at Smyrna. Crusade preaching was ordered in
Italy and the Levant, and a tenth was levied to help with the legate's
expenses.[156] Venice sent two galleys and the Hospitallers provided
ships; with these forces the new legate won a victory at Lampsacus
in the Dardanelles in the autumn of 1359.[157] A league was now in
operation, for in 1360 Venice described Peter Thomas as 'the lord
legate of the league against the Turks'.[158] Philip of Mézières, Peter
Thomas's biographer, wrote enthusiastically of the legate's activity
both in preaching Catholicism and in organizing the defence of

---

[152] Gasnault *et al.*, nn. 2006, 2086, 2233; *DVL*, ii, n. 16; *Régestes*, i, 82–3. See also
Setton, *PL*, 230.   [153] *DVL*, ii, n. 19; *Régestes*, i, 85; Setton, *PL*, 230–1.
[154] *Régestes*, i, 88.   [155] Setton, *PL*, 231. See also Zachariadou, 61.
[156] *AE*, ad annum 1359, n. 16, xxvi, 43–4; *Acta Innocentii VI*, ed. A. L. Tautu.
PCRCICO, x (Rome, 1961), n. 125; L. Wadding, *Vita et res gestae B. Petri Thomae*
(Lyons, 1637), 150–61; Philip of Mézières, *The Life of St Peter Thomas*, ed. J. Smet
(Rome, 1954), 84–5, 206 ff.; O. Halecki, *Un Empereur de Byzance à Rome. Vingt ans
de travail pour l'union des églises et pour la défense de l'empire d'orient 1355–1375*
(Warsaw, 1930), 73.
[157] Philip of Mézières, 85–6; *Régestes*, i, 92.
[158] Halecki, *Un Empereur*, 73n.

Smyrna,[159] but the league was less effective than Clement VI's had been. A policy of wholehearted co-operation with the Greeks had not yet won favour, and Venice was suspicious of the intentions of Cyprus's new King, Peter I.

When Innocent became Pope, the Latin powers with interests in Greece, notably Venice, Rhodes, and Naples, had been preoccupied for more than a generation with the activities of the southern Turkish emirates; we have seen that they launched expeditions against them and achieved several victories, though without putting an end to piracy and raiding. On the other hand, they had paid little attention to the Osmanli Turks, who lived in northern Anatolia and fought mainly the Byzantine Greeks. Only the Genoese had consistent relations with the Osmanlis (or Ottoman Turks), whom they encountered in their trade and dealings with Constantinople. The Ottomans made great headway in the Byzantine civil war of 1341–7, when they fought for both sides, and in 1354 they took advantage of the destruction of Gallipoli by earthquake to occupy, rebuild, and repopulate the city.[160] They now had a foothold in Europe which controlled the crossing to their power base in Anatolia. In 1359, according to the Florentine, Matteo Villani, the Turks reached the walls of Constantinople itself, and in 1363 they captured the important city of Philippopolis.[161]

Even if Innocent VI realized the gravity of these events there was little he could do. His ability to make the Genoese or Venetians take action against the Turks was extremely limited, and his relations with both the Greeks and the schismatic Christian rulers in the Balkans were complicated. The powerful King of Serbia, Stephen Dushan, approached the Pope at the end of 1354 with the request that he be appointed a captain of the Roman church with the duty of defending the Christians in the East. But his offer was inspired chiefly by his fear of Louis of Hungary and by his own ambition to conquer Constantinople. Innocent's reaction was in turn influenced by the Pope's need for Hungarian support in Italy, which entailed sanctioning a crusade against the Serbs. This web of political contingencies was not untypical.[162]

---

[159] Philip of Mézières, 86–9.
[160] D. M. Nicol, *The Last Centuries of Byzantium 1261–1453* (London, 1972), chs. 12–14 *passim*.
[161] Matteo Villani, bk. 9, ch. 40, ii, 227–8; Nicol, *Last Centuries*, 273.
[162] Housley, 'King Louis the Great', 195.

The relative clarity and forcefulness of Clement VI's policy thus became muddied in the 1350s by the impact of events in Thrace and the Dardanelles. Ottoman victories were compelling the Curia to broaden its view of which parts of *Romania* needed to be defended. Towards the end of Innocent's reign another power, Lusignan Cyprus, made the confusion greater. In 1358 Peter I was crowned King of Cyprus, and this extraordinary man was during the next eleven years to make an important, if short-lived, impact on the crusading movement. Inevitably he thought in terms of Cypriot interests, and these were only marginally affected by events in *Romania*; of greater importance for Cyprus were Cilician Armenia and Egypt. Thus in 1359 Peter used the Cypriot galleys in the naval league to occupy Corycus in Armenia, which had been attacked by the Turks. Peter Thomas was convinced of the value of this step and supported the King, but Venice saw all too well that this was a diversion of the league's resources. The Republic's suspicions were confirmed when Peter captured Adalia in August 1361.[163] But Peter's ambitions were greater: on 15 June 1362 he sent a curious letter to the governments of the West announcing his intention, cherished *a pueritia*, of leading a crusade to reconquer Jerusalem and the Holy Land.[164] And in October he departed for the West to raise men for the task. Thus the idea of a crusade of recovery was revived almost a generation after the collapse of Philip VI's project, and at the same time that the Ottoman threat to Greece and the Balkans was growing.[165]

Innocent VI died in September 1362 after a troubled and unsuccessful reign, and it was his successor, Urban V, who received Peter at Avignon at the end of March 1363. William of Grimoard, elected after a very short conclave, was perhaps the most interesting of the Avignon popes. He was not a cardinal, yet had ably carried out a series of legations in Italy for Innocent VI; by career a lawyer and university lecturer, he was also a saintly Benedictine monk who attracted great respect and admiration.[166] Similar contradictions mark his contribution to the crusading movement, which enjoyed

[163] Philip of Mézières, 96–7; Hill, ii, 320–1.

[164] Mas Latrie, ii, 236–7. See P. W. Edbury, 'The Crusading Policy of King Peter I of Cyprus, 1359–1369', in Holt (ed.), *Eastern Mediterranean Lands*, 95, for a suggestion that the letter was written by Philip of Mézières, Chancellor of the Kingdom of Cyprus.

[165] Setton, *PL*, 237 ff.

[166] See Mollat, *Popes at Avignon*, 52 ff.

great victories in the eastern Mediterranean during Urban's reign. But these victories owed little to the Pope's initiative—rather to that of two middle-ranking lay rulers, King Peter of Cyprus and Count Amedeo VI of Savoy. Urban backed both their expeditions but took remarkably little interest in them, except as means of solving problems in the West. Papal policy in the 1360s was in fact confused and unsure of itself, totally lacking in the burning concern shown by such popes as John XXII, Clement VI, and Gregory XI.

Peter of Cyprus had announced his intention of reconquering the Holy Land, and it was his good fortune that the French throne was occupied by a King, John II, who was foolish enough to give this project his support. Urban V too was prepared to do what he could for the crusade,[167] and on 31 March 1363 he gave the cross to John, Peter, Cardinal Talleyrand of Périgord, and a following of high-ranking nobles.[168] King John was appointed leader and captain of the general passage, and was granted a six-year tenth, together with an assortment of miscellaneous revenues, annates, legacies, donations, fines, and the proceeds of usury. Measures were decreed against pirates and people who disturbed the peace in France, and prayers specified on behalf of the expedition.[169] Urban V sent letters to Charles of Navarre, Edward III, Charles IV, and other rulers asking them to keep peace with France and help the crusade.[170] The general passage was to begin in March 1365.

On 8 April 1364, however, John II died a prisoner in England, not long after his proctors had sworn on his behalf to carry out the project in accordance with the conditions attached, and before preparations had been set in motion.[171] 'Oh what grief for the Christian army which is shortly to set out for the recovery of the Holy Land', Urban V wrote to John's successor, 'to see itself bereft of the leadership of such a prudent and vigorous general.'[172] These

---

[167] The problem of what Urban expected from this project will be considered below, ch. 7, nn. 29–40.

[168] See N. Jorga, *Philippe de Mézières 1327–1405, et la Croisade au XIVᵉ siècle* (Paris, 1896), 165–6.

[169] *AE*, ad annum 1363, nn. 15–18, xxvi, 82–4; *Lettres d'Urbain V*, ed. A. Fierens and C. Tihon. Analecta Vaticano–belgica. 2 vols. (Rome, 1928–32), nn. 717, 719–22; M. Prou, *Étude sur les relations politiques du pape Urbain V avec les rois de France Jean II et Charles V (1362–1370)* (Paris, 1888), 91–102; Philip of Mézières, 105–6.

[170] *AE*, ad annum 1363, nn. 20–2, xxvi, 84–6; *Lettres secrètes et curiales du pape Urbain V*, ed. P. Lecacheux and G. Mollat. BEFAR, 3rd Series, 1 vol. (Paris, 1902–55), nn. 354, 477–86.

[171] LM, n. 745; Prou, 28.   [172] LM, n. 924.

were ritual condolences, for in reality there was no army to grieve. The project was fantastic, and few apart from John himself could have taken it seriously.[173] Quite apart from the unsettled relations with England and domestic issues in France, there was the serious plight of the French church, which would have had to bear the brunt of financing the expedition. Just a month before the decrees of 31 March 1363 which proclaimed the crusade, Urban issued a bull halving the assessment of the tenth in the northern provinces because clerical revenues had been so hard hit by war and plague.[174] The Pope also attached several provisions to his grant of a six-year tenth to try to make its collection less painful.[175] The only aspect of the project which made some sense was the idea of persuading the mercenary companies to accompany the crusade, thus ridding France of their violent behaviour.[176] Even before John's death his crusade was foundering,[177] and it is almost certain that the expedition would have been cancelled once the difficulties of organization and payment made themselves felt.

Peter of Cyprus's crusade was another matter.[178] On 25 May 1363 the Pope allowed him to precede John II to the East, making the traditional distinction between the *passagium particulare* and the general passage, which in this instance meant the realistic and the chimerical.[179] Peter could recruit men-at-arms and *routiers* in the West with the aid of crusading indulgences and privileges, which Urban specified as being exactly the same as those which fighters in the general passage would enjoy.[180] In December 1363 the King was

[173] The project has received very little attention from historians; see J. B. Henneman, *Royal Taxation in Fourteenth Century France. The Captivity and Ransom of John II, 1356–1370* (Philadelphia, 1976), 182, for the opposing views of Perroy and Cazelles. It may be significant that Urban V threatened with anathema anybody who dissuaded the King from undertaking the crusade: *AE*, ad annum 1363, nn. 16–18, xxvi, 83–4.

[174] LM, n. 221.

[175] Prou, 95–102.

[176] Ibid., 25; Delaville le Roulx, *La France en orient*, i, 120–1; N. Housley, 'The Mercenary Companies, the Papacy and the Crusades, 1356–1378', *Traditio*, xxxviii (1982), 271 ff.

[177] See LM, n. 857.

[178] The best recent account is Setton, *PL*, 245–84. Older accounts include Atiya, ch. 15; Jorga, chs. 8–9; Hill, ii, 324–34.

[179] Philip of Mézières, 105–6. Cf. *DVL*, ii, n. 54: 'viam tutam et dispositionem accommodam populo Dei cum ipsius assistentia paraturus'.

[180] 'Volentes ac concedentes quod omnes transfretantes huiusmodi plenam suorum peccaminum de quibus ut prefertur fuerint veraciter corde contriti et ore confessi veniam consequantur, ac si post dictum terminum cum eodem Rege francie

granted the proceeds of alms collected in crusade chests in Sicily, Hungary, and the dioceses of Greece, Crete, Rhodes, and Cyprus.[181] In June 1364 Peter Thomas was appointed legate for Peter's crusade in place of Cardinal Talleyrand, who had died.[182] The King toured the West recruiting and in November 1364 arrived at Venice, his chosen embarkation point and supplier of much of his transport. As usual there were problems. Western rulers made promises of help and failed to keep them. Peter was late in arriving at Venice, and many of the crusaders who assembled despaired of him and abandoned the undertaking.[183] A rebellion on Crete in 1363 threatened to divert Venetian resources and thus imperil the crusade, but it was suppressed in May 1364.[184] Similarly, a dispute between Cyprus and Genoa flared up in the summer of 1364 but was settled in the early months of 1365.[185]

On 26 April 1365 Urban V wrote to King Peter that his hopes for the crusade were reviving, as Peter Thomas had informed him that many recruits had appeared at Venice from Germany and elsewhere.[186] The King set sail on 27 June, and Urban wrote in July exhorting him to fight the Lord's war 'with open-hearted devotion'.[187] At this point Peter was at Rhodes, where he awaited the arrival of the ships and men coming direct from Cyprus. After their appearance at the end of August, and with the addition of troops supplied by the Master of the Hospitallers, Peter had an army estimated by Philip of Mézières at about 10,000 men and 1,400 horses.[188] The destination of the crusade was as yet unknown, and the King now announced his intention of attacking Alexandria, in accordance with thirteenth-century strategic ideas of liberating Palestine by negotiating from a position of strength in Egypt.[189]

transfretarent, et quod gaudere valeant omnibus gratiis et privilegiis per nos generaliter concessis omnibus qui post dictum terminum transfretabunt': Archivio segreto Vaticano, Registra Vaticana 245, f. 173^v; *AE*, ad annum 1363, n. 19, xxvi, 84.

[181] ASV, Registra Avinionensia 157, f. 108^r-v.

[182] LM, nn. 1051–3, 1080–4; Philip of Mézières, 117–19. For the preparation of the crusade, see ibid., 102–24 *passim*.

[183] Ibid., 120–1.

[184] LM, nn. 663–4, 979; *DVL*, ii, nn. 57–8, 61; Mas Latrie, iii, 742–7; Hill, ii, 327n–8n; Zachariadou, 68.

[185] LM, nn. 1602, 1609, 1619, 1649–50; Philip of Mézières, 122–3; Mas Latrie, ii, 254–66; F. J. Boehlke, *Pierre de Thomas: Scholar, Diplomat and Crusader* (Philadelphia, 1966), 258–66.

[186] LM, n. 1724.   [187] Ibid., n. 1887.

[188] Philip of Mézières, 127–8.

[189] Ibid., and cf. 134; Edbury, 'Crusading Policy', 94.

What followed was both a glorious victory and a chance tragically lost. On 10 October 1365 a surprise assault on the harbour of Alexandria succeeded and the city fell. But it could not be held; there were not enough troops and most of the crusaders wanted to return home now that they had booty in abundance. Peter I, Philip of Mézières, and Peter Thomas were not able to persuade them to stay and the expedition sailed to Cyprus on 16 October.[190]

Whatever our interpretation of Peter I's motives in attacking Alexandria,[191] and of the viability of using the city as a weapon in negotiations with the Mamluks, it is hard not to view this crusade as a serious diversion of manpower from the more menacing threat to Christendom, the Ottoman Turks.[192] Mamluk wrath had been aroused without any beneficial results: in October 1366 Urban V had to issue indulgences for the defence of Cyprus and Rhodes, both in danger as a consequence of the sack of Egypt's most prosperous city.[193] It was not until 1370 that peace was restored between Venice, Genoa, and Cyprus on the one hand, and the Sultan on the other. The capture of Alexandria had been a remarkable coup and its plundering brought rich booty to the West, but the cost for Cyprus was to be heavy.

By contrast, the less well-known crusade of Amedeo of Savoy in 1366 did more long-term good.[194] Amedeo's expedition was originally planned as part of the Franco-Cypriot project to regain Palestine; the six-year tenth which Urban granted the Count in April 1364, as one of a number of financial concessions, was justified in terms of the extra expenses which would be incurred because of the loss of the Syrian ports.[195] The collapse of the French crusade, and Peter I's failure to hold Alexandria, naturally changed this. Another crusade against Mamluk Egypt, now on its guard

[190] For capture, sack, debate, and departure, see Philip of Mézières, 131–4; Guillaume de Machaut, *La Prise d'Alexandrie*, ed. M. L. De Mas Latrie (Geneva, 1877), 68–109; Atiya, 345–69; Setton, *PL*, 267–72.

[191] See especially the new interpretation put forward by Edbury, 'Crusading Policy', 95–100 and *passim*.

[192] Cf. A. T. Luttrell, 'Popes and Crusades: 1362–1394', in *Genèse et débuts du Grand Schisme d'occident: 1362–1394* (Paris, 1980), 577; id., 'Venice and the Knights Hospitallers of Rhodes in the Fourteenth Century', *PBSR*, xxvi (1958), 206.

[193] LM, nn. 2416–18.

[194] For Amedeo's expedition see Setton, *PL*, 285–307; E. L. Cox, *The Green Count of Savoy: Amadeus VI and Transalpine Savoy in the Fourteenth Century* (Princeton, 1967), 204–39.

[195] *Illustrazioni della spedizione in oriente di Amedeo VI*, ed. F. Bollati di Saint-Pierre (Turin, 1900), 365–7, and see also 344–68 *passim*.

against Western aggression, would be senseless.[196] In January 1366 Urban V was hoping that a major crusade could be organized to help the Greeks; Amedeo would be one of its leaders, together with Louis of Hungary and Peter of Cyprus.[197] When Amedeo set out from Venice in June 1366 he was banking on a joint Hungarian–Savoyard campaign in the Balkans, but on arrival at Negroponte there was no news of Hungarian preparations.[198]

Amedeo realized that with an army of 3,000–4,000 men, no great victory over the Turks could be achieved. But two lesser tasks were at hand. One was the capture of Gallipoli from the Turks, which was successfully carried out in August 1366. The second was a campaign against the Bulgarians adjacent to the Black Sea, to help secure the return of the Emperor John V, whom the Bulgarians were preventing from travelling back to Constantinople after his visit to Buda. This too was achieved, in addition to the recapture of the Byzantine towns of Mesembria and Sozopolis. All this was useful in immediate terms, and it also showed John V that Latin aid for his Empire could be effective, encouraging him to go to the West and make his personal profession of faith to the Pope in 1369.[199] Despite the changes of course dictated by the falling away of his allies, Amedeo's crusade was thus the most successful of the expeditions to the eastern Mediterranean in our period, and this has to be ascribed primarily to the Count's own qualities of leadership and perseverance.

John V Palaeologus made his profession of 1369 in St Peter's Basilica at Rome: the Curia had carried out its first, unsuccessful return to the holy city. It was the detailed preparations for this, together with his attempts to deal with the *routiers* and prevent the resurgence of the Anglo-French war, which had occupied the second half of Urban V's reign. Letters about the military needs of the eastern Mediterranean continued to flow from the papal chancery. Thus Urban urged Naples and Rhodes to help threatened Cyprus, and encouraged the formation of a Veneto-Genoese league against the Mamluks in 1369.[200] He tried to organize aid for Armenia, asked Venice to send help to Constantinople, and

---

[196] Though in April 1366 the Venetians still feared that Amedeo might raid shipping off the coast of Syria: *I libri comm.*, iii, 46, n. 258.

[197] *AE*, ad annum 1366, nn. 1–2, xxvi, 122.

[198] Setton, *PL*, 298; Housley, 'King Louis the Great', 201–2.

[199] See Halecki, *Un Empereur*, ch. 8.

[200] LM, nn. 3026, 3032; *DVL*, ii, nn. 86–7.

facilitated John V's recruitment of western mercenaries.[201] But to the end Urban's options were circumscribed by the problem of Egypt's re-emergence as a threat, by the disappointments caused by the King of Hungary, and by his own inability to rouse armed resistance to the Turks. Above all, papal policy had become so diffuse as to lose all sense of direction; it is tempting to see in this part of the explanation for Urban's order of April 1369 that a register should be compiled of papal letters relating to eastern affairs dating back to Clement V's reign.[202]

None of the difficulties faced by Urban V diminished in the reign of his successor, Gregory XI, who was elected at the end of 1370. Gregory had been Peter Roger, a nobleman and a cardinal of twenty-two years' standing. The Roger family had already developed contacts with most aspects of the crusading movement in the East: Peter's namesake and uncle, Clement VI, had negotiated for Philip VI's planned crusade to Palestine before launching the Smyrna expedition, and his cousin, William Roger, the Viscount of Turenne, had fought at Alexandria in 1365. To this tradition Gregory XI was to give a further dimension by centring his crusade policy on the threat posed by the Ottoman Turks. For it is much easier to see the outlines of Gregory's approach than in the case of his predecessor. Indeed, in its clarity and forcefulness it much resembles that of Clement VI.[203]

Gregory's policy was shaped by three factors. One was the end of the war with Egypt in 1370, which closed hostilities in the southern Mediterranean. The second was the terrifying onrush of Turkish power in the Balkans and Greece. The danger which this presented was made clear near the start of the Pope's reign by the Turkish victory over the Serbs at the battle of the Maritza river (Černomen)

[201] *Acta Urbani V*, ed. A. L. Tautu. PCRCICO, xi (Rome, 1964), n. 166; *AE*, ad annum 1369, nn. 5–6, xxvi, 164–5; LM, nn. 3040–1; Halecki, *Un Empereur*, 382–3.
[202] LM, n. 2935. This was almost certainly the initiative which brought about the compilation of Reg. Vat. 62. See J. Muldoon, 'The Avignon Papacy and the Frontiers of Christendom: the Evidence of Vatican Register 62', *Archivum historiae pontificiae*, xvii (1979), 125–95; id., *Popes, Lawyers, and Infidels: the Church and the Non-Christian World 1250–1550* (Liverpool, 1979), 74–7, 182 n. 17.
[203] See Mollat, *Popes at Avignon*, 59 ff. Anthony Luttrell has made Gregory's crusading policy in the East the subject of a thorough and perceptive study, 'Gregory XI and the Turks: 1370–1378', *OCP*, xlvi (1980), 391–417. L. Mirot, *La Politique pontificale et le retour du saint-siège à Rome en 1376* (Paris, 1899), 11–17 is an older account which retains some value.

on 26 September 1371. Serbia, Achaea, Albania, even southern Italy, were now threatened by the Turks. Clearly the best way to counter Turkish aggression would be to launch a general passage by the great powers of the West to rescue their co-religionists in the Balkans, who now included the Greeks of Constantinople. But this was rendered impossible by the third factor, the persistence throughout Gregory XI's reign of the Anglo-French conflict. Although the Pope strove for peace between the two powers, and came quite close to success during the peace talks at Bruges, a general passage was never within his grasp. Even less was it feasible for the recovery of Palestine, and although that idea had been revived in the 1360s and continued to live a flitting, ghostly existence in Gregory's reign, it received little support at the Curia, where realism was the order of the day.[204]

Gregory XI's policy centred therefore on his attempts to stir those powers which were actually threatened by the Turks into more effective action, if possible co-ordinated. Like his uncle, Gregory thought in terms of leagues. He responded to the disaster on the Maritza river by issuing bulls to almost all the eastern Christian powers, including the Emperor John V, the Hospitallers, Louis of Hungary, Venice, and the Latin rulers of the Morea, summoning them to a congress which would assemble at Thebes in October 1373.[205] This was the sort of initiative which had been lacking under Urban V, but it did not succeed; political and religious differences were too great and the congress never met. The Pope continued to issue a trickle of letters which dealt with the formation of leagues. Thus in June 1373 he was hoping to organize a joint naval effort by the threatened powers in *Romania*, and in 1374 he attempted to interest Venice, Naples, and John V in a league.[206] But disunity and suspicion amongst the Christians in the East were greater than they had ever been. It was symptomatic that in 1374 their common administration of Smyrna, which had long been

---

[204] See especially 'Gregorio XI e Giovanna I di Napoli. Documenti inediti dell'Archivio segreto Vaticano', ed. F. Cerasoli, *ASPN*, xxiii–xxv (1898–1900), xxv, 6–8, n. 167.

[205] *AE*, ad annum 1372, n. 29, xxvi, 212; *VMH*, ii, n. 262; *Lettres secrètes et curiales du pape Grégoire XI intéressant les pays autres que la France*, ed. G. Mollat. BEFAR, 3rd Series, 1 vol. (Paris, 1962–5), nn. 1166–7, 1173–4; Halecki, *Un Empereur*, 250–62; Luttrell, 'Gregory XI', 394–5.

[206] Mollat, *Lettres secrètes*, nn. 1933–4; *Lettres secrètes et curiales du pape Grégoire XI relatives à la France*, ed. L. Mirot *et al.* BEFAR, 3rd Series, 1 vol. (Paris, 1935–57), n. 3525; Halecki, *Un Empereur*, 390–1.

crumbling, finally collapsed, so that Gregory had to place the city in the hands of the Hospitallers. Smyrna's status as a symbol of united Christian achievement and endeavour ended and it became simply an outpost of Rhodes.[207]

Frustrated in his hopes of making Christians act together, Gregory also tried to persuade them to take action separately, committing greater resources to the struggle against the Turks. Nothing could reasonably be expected of Naples under Queen Joanna. Venice was concentrating on its war with Trieste and Padua, then on securing Tenedos, and then on renewed war with Genoa and its allies.[208] But there were three Latin powers which could be expected to take firmer action. The first, and as always the most disappointing, was the Kingdom of Hungary. Louis the Great was granted another batch of crusade indulgences and privileges in 1373, accompanied by severe conditions born of bitter experience. With these, however, he did nothing.[209] There seemed more hope of Genoese naval action. The Genoese were historic allies of the Greek Empire and stood to lose heavily if Constantinople fell to the Turks and the latter controlled the Black Sea trade routes. There were plans afoot for a Genoese *passagium* in July–August 1371.[210] But in 1372 Genoa became involved in a dispute with Cyprus, in which papal interventions were numerous and fruitless.[211] In March 1376 Gregory was again counting on a Genoese *passagium*, but the city was soon at war with Venice.[212]

That left the third Latin power, the Order of St John of Jerusalem. From June 1372 Gregory was trying to effect a *reformacio* of the Order to gear it up for greater military activity in the East.[213] In February 1373 he decreed an inquest into the Knights' possessions throughout the West,[214] and at his command an assembly of brethren met in the autumn of 1373 and levied huge taxes on

[207] *AE*, ad annum 1374, n. 7, xxvi, 236; Luttrell, 'Gregory XI', 396–7.

[208] See Thiriet, *La Romanie vénitienne*, 176–8.

[209] *VMH*, ii, nn. 270–3; Housley, 'King Louis the Great', 205.

[210] Mollat, *Lettres secrètes*, nn. 228, 266; *AE*, ad annum 1371, n. 8, xxvi, 190–1; Luttrell, 'Gregory XI', 394.

[211] For example, Mollat, *Lettres secrètes*, nn. 1327, 1408, 1491, 1838, 1888–9, 1960, 2266, 2800, 2915, 3012, 3056, 3060, 3064, 3090, 3094, 3109, 3275. For the dispute, see Hill, ii, 382 ff.

[212] *AE*, ad annum 1376, n. 23, xxvi, 274–5.

[213] Luttrell, 'Gregory XI', 398–9.

[214] J. Glénisson, 'L'Enquête pontificale de 1373 sur les possessions des Hospitaliers de Saint-Jean-de-Jérusalem', *BEC*, cxxix (1971), 83–111.

the priories to pay for a passage.[215] In 1375 the numbers of troops which each priory was to supply for the crusade were specified, and in 1376 fresh measures were taken to finance the expedition.[216] But it has been pointed out that the Order possessed neither the manpower nor the money needed for the campaign;[217] its planning proceeded partly because of the iron determination of Gregory XI, and partly because the crusade suited the ambitions of Juan Fernández de Heredia, the Master's lieutenant in the West, and *eminence grise* in the Order at this point. Certainly the expedition, which finally set sail in 1378, was a disaster: there were no clear objectives at hand and the brethren landed in an obscure Albanian port near which they were ambushed by fellow Christians.[218]

Gregory's policies had been almost totally unsuccessful.[219] He had proved unable to organize any form of effective resistance to the Ottoman Turks. He had sent Constantinople so little aid that John V was compelled to become a tributary of the Turks. And he had failed to rescue the Armenians, who were finally overrun by the Mamluks in 1375. The Pope's letters of 1372 on the provision of aid to the Armenians are amongst the most vivid testimony to his helplessness.[220] It is unfair to criticize the Pope's meanness for the failure of his policies by comparing his expenditure in the East with that in Italy;[221] for the advantage of military activity in Italy was that it could be organized much more easily. Rather, what stood in the way was the fact that Venice, Genoa, Hungary, and Cyprus fought amongst themselves instead of forming a common front against the Turks. Discord and conflict within Christendom had reached terrible proportions. Just six months after Gregory XI's death in March 1378 they were made yet worse by the outbreak of a prolonged and catastrophic schism in the Church.

[215] Luttrell, 'Gregory XI', 404–5.
[216] *VMH*, ii, n. 309; Mollat, *Lettres secrètes*, nn. 3634–5; Luttrell, 'Gregory XI', 410–11.
[217] Ibid., 404, 409, 412–13.
[218] Luttrell, 'Hospitallers at Rhodes', 302–3.
[219] Cf. Luttrell's conclusion, 'Gregory XI', 414.
[220] *AE*, ad annum 1372, n. 30, xxvi, 213; Mollat, *Lettres secrètes*, nn. 517, 519.
[221] As does Luttrell, 'Gregory XI', 414.

2

The Campaigns:
(2) Spain, Eastern Europe, and Italy

(a) SPAIN

THE crusades in Spain formed one aspect of the broader movement
of conquest and settlement known as the *Reconquista,* in which
between the eighth and fifteenth centuries the Christians rewon the
whole of the peninsula from the Moors.[1] The waging of crusades in
Spain depended largely on the ability and readiness of its Christian
rulers to undertake further steps in the process of recovery; or
alternatively on their need to defend their lands against Muslim
counter-attacks.[2] With the exception of a few years in the 1340s, the
period 1305–78 was not a distinguished one in the *Reconquista.* This
is readily explained by the political and military situation in the
peninsula at the start of the fourteenth century.

The preceding century was one of great Christian successes.
Following the battle of Las Navas de Tolosa in 1212, and the
resultant collapse of the Almohad Empire, gains amounting to over
a third of Iberia were made by Aragon, Portugal, and especially
Castile under Ferdinand III. The Moors were left with Granada, a
relatively small Kingdom and a vassal state of Castile, its enormous
and powerful neighbour. But here they held out for nearly 250
years. The prolonged survival of Granada has been accounted for in
terms of the Kingdom's own strength and the weaknesses of its
Christian opponents.[3] Granada's mountainous terrain was cut
through by passes dominated by extremely strong fortresses. It had
a large and prosperous population capable of fielding good armies,

---

[1] A good introduction in English is D. W. Lomax, *The Reconquest of Spain*
(London, 1978). See also C. J. Bishko, 'The Spanish and Portuguese Reconquest,
1095–1492', in Setton (gen. ed.), *History of the Crusades,* iii, 396–456.

[2] See J. Goñi Gaztambide, *Historia de la Bula de la Cruzada en España* (Vitoria,
1958).

[3] See J. N. Hillgarth, *The Spanish Kingdoms 1250–1516. Volume I: 1250–1410.
Precarious Balance* (Oxford, 1976), 319 ff.; Lomax, 162; Bishko, 439–40.

and ready to fight to the end rather than submit to Christian rule or retreat to Africa. Just how difficult a problem Granada posed is shown by the fact that it took Ferdinand and Isabel eleven years to conquer it at the end of the fifteenth century, working with all the resources of the Early Modern State, including artillery, against a debilitated and internally divided enemy.

The odds were far less favourable to the Christians in the fourteenth century. Neither Portugal nor Aragon possessed a frontier with Granada. Besides, the main direction of Aragonese ambition was eastward, to Majorca and Sardinia; only intermittently, and with much hesitation, did Aragon's rulers think of fighting Granada. The kings of Castile faced the task of integrating their huge thirteenth-century acquisitions. Castile's efforts were hindered also by a series of royal minorities and civil wars. Its Military Orders were taken over by the nobility and lost their effectiveness. In addition, from the 1340s all three kingdoms encountered the same economic difficulties as the rest of Christian Europe.

For a long time, however, it proved impossible simply to tolerate Granada's existence. First, the Kingdom itself was a threat to Christian Spain, launching both frontier raids and more ambitious *razzias* which made *convivencia* at local or national level hard to achieve and sustain.[4] Secondly, there was always the danger that the Moors of Granada might call for help to their co-religionists in Morocco, the Merinids, just as the Spanish Moors had done in previous centuries. While it was true that they were more likely to do this if placed under heavy Christian pressure, the only long-term solution was Christian control of the Straits, especially the cities of Tarifa, Gibraltar, and Algeciras. Thirdly, by fighting the Moors the Spanish kings could lay claim to important Church revenues associated with the crusade: the tenth and the *tercias reales,* the third of the ecclesiastical tithe which was intended for the upkeep of church buildings, but which in Castile had helped to pay for the great conquests of Ferdinand III.[5] So as long as Merinid Morocco showed interest in the affairs of Andalusia, and the Christian kingdoms could overcome their internal problems long enough to field armies against Granada, envoys would appear at Avignon petitioning for crusade preaching and money. This was the case until the decisive

---

[4] Cf. Goñi Gaztambide, 263.
[5] Lomax, 157–8.

defeat of the Moroccan army at the battle of Salado in 1340, and the
sieges of Algeciras and Gibraltar, and to some extent until the
outbreak of war between Castile and Aragon in 1356.

War against Granada was difficult to wage, relatively unprofit-
able, and very expensive. All these disadvantages were made clear
in an important campaign near the beginning of our period. In
December 1308 James II of Aragon and Ferdinand IV of Castile
concluded an alliance for a joint attack on Granada in the following
summer. James would lay siege to Almería, Ferdinand to Algeciras,
and their aim would be to partition the Kingdom between them;
Morocco was a party to the alliance so there should be no North
African aid for Granada. Although the war would divert Spanish
resources from the Hospitaller *passagium* which was in gestation at
this point, Pope Clement V agreed to grant the two monarchs
crusade preaching and a three-year tenth. At first things went well:
James besieged Almería and the Catalan fleet captured Gibraltar
for Castile. But then Morocco changed sides, and early in 1310 the
sieges of Algeciras and Almería were both abandoned. The Aragonese seaborne withdrawal was chaotic, and James II had very
heavy debts and no gains. From this time onwards, Aragonese
policy towards the crusade against Granada was ultra-cautious.[6]

The crusade of 1309–10 seems to have been of considerable
importance too in shaping papal policy towards Castilian and
Aragonese petitions for crusade concessions. In support of these
demands were the considerations that the *Reconquista* was an
ancient crusade tradition,[7] and that those engaged in it had a
respectable claim to papal backing. It was an expensive undertaking
against a formidable foe. On the debit side was papal suspicion
about the motives of the Spanish kings, reinforced by a lack of
reliable information about what was really happening in Spain. The
crusade of 1309–10, which was promoted at the Curia as a well-
planned and potentially decisive blow against Granada, was called
off in a muddled fashion with slender results, and the Pope was
reluctant to allow the three-year tenth to be collected in its
entirety.[8] In the following decades even less was to be achieved,
especially by Aragon, whose rulers refused to act until they had

---

[6] See Housley, 'Pope Clement V', *passim*; Hillgarth, *Spanish Kingdoms*, 328–9;
Goñi Gaztambide, 265–77.

[7] See Riley-Smith, *What were the Crusades?*, 24.

[8] Mollat, *Lettres communes*, n. 5331. See too J. Vincke, *Staat und Kirche in
Katalonien und Aragon während des Mittelalters*, i (Münster-i.-W., 1931), 192.

substantial financial backing from the Church. Naturally this only worsened suspicions at Avignon. There was the further complicating factor that a clash of interests could occur between Spain and the Latin East. In 1309, for example, Clement V gave James II the same backing which he had accorded the Hospitaller *passagium* only when placed under great pressure.[9] Finally, there was concern at Avignon about the consequences for the Spanish church of excessive lay taxation, manifested especially by Benedict XII. At a time of crisis in 1340, Benedict expressed deep regret at having to tax the Castilian church on behalf of its King, adding that no other royal subsidy should be demanded, except the customary regalian service.[10]

Clearly there was a similarity between papal relations with the Spanish kings and those with Paris. In both instances the lay power bargained with skill and perseverance for primarily financial concessions; we shall see that in both cases this was dictated partly by a growing disparity between the costs of war and the value of the tenth. But the Spaniards had an important advantage over the French in having Moors on their doorstep. The use which they made of this is clearly shown in the instructions which James II gave to his envoys at the Council of Vienne in September 1311.[11] The Aragonese King wanted to introduce a campaign against Granada into the crusading plans which were being formulated at the Council. He told his envoys to argue their case in two stages. First, 'that it is better to work towards the destruction of the infidels in several areas than in just one'. Experience had shown that it was impossible to keep a single big army supplied in the East, besides being hard to maintain discipline between the various national contingents present. Similarly, more Spaniards would take the Cross if they could fight nearer to their homes, and the Muslims would be prevented from sending each other help, 'as they have been accustomed to do', if they were attacked on two fronts simultaneously. There would be healthy competition in winning victories between the two Christian armies.

In the second stage of his argument James concentrated on the importance of attacking Granada. It was *facilis*, since Granada

[9] Housley, 'Pope Clement V', 33–5.
[10] ASV, Reg. Vat. 128, ff. 52^v–55^v, n. 15.
[11] *Papsttum und Untergang des Templerordens*, ed. H. Finke. 2 vols. (Münster-i.-W., 1907), ii, n. 125. Goñi Gaztambide (277–81) pointed out the similarity between this proposal and the *Liber de fine* of Ramon Lull.

could be conquered in three years if the Pope gave the undertaking his full support, and a flotilla of twenty armed galleys patrolled the Straits to prevent reinforcements crossing. It was *necessarius*, because of the threat to Spain from a powerful Morocco, the poisonous influence of Granada on its Christian neighbours, and Spain's inability to supply men and horses for the crusade in the East while it had its own Muslims to contend with. And it was *utilis*, because of the ease with which an army advancing through Morocco and Tunisia, with aid from Christian islands in the western and central Mediterranean, would, *auxiliante Domino*, reach and conquer Palestine.

It is obvious that the main intention of James II in presenting these proposals was to prevent a tenth being levied in his lands for a predominantly French expedition to the East, or rather to divert the tax to a Spanish enterprise which could be viewed as part of that expedition: hence the connection which the King made between the two fronts. In 1335, when James's son presented his case against a universal crusade tax, he shifted his emphasis to the affront which it would represent to Aragonese sovereignty.[12] This was simpler, enabling him to avoid the mishmash of arguments to which his father resorted. But, strained and implausible as they appear to us, it is notable that James II considered them worth presenting to the Pope, that they were not without precedents in Spanish thinking about the crusades,[13] and that they had the backing of Arnold of Pellegrue, 'who is the most influential person in the Curia'.[14] Clement V claimed that he would not be able to persuade the Council to adopt the two-fold crusade because of the opposition of the French and English clergy; Spain carried little weight because of the comparatively small value of its tenth.[15] In the event the Italian clergy backed the project as did, of course, the Spanish, but James's plan must have foundered since there was no separate allocation of the Spanish contribution to the six-year tenth which the Council levied.[16]

In his last years Clement V wavered in his approach towards the Spanish theatre of operations. He granted crusade preaching and

[12] See below, ch. 5, n. 88.

[13] See Lomax, 82, 102.

[14] *Papsttum und Untergang*, ii, n. 130.

[15] Ibid., ii, nn. 126, 128.

[16] Ibid., ii, n. 135 and cf. n. 131; *Reg. Clem. V*, n. 9983. For this paragraph, see also Thier, 99–101.

other concessions to Ferdinand of Castile in August 1312, and in January 1313 gave way on the Aragonese share of the Vienne tenth,[17] but in the following month he withdrew this grant because the death of Ferdinand made Castilian-Aragonese co-operation unlikely.[18] This was a severe blow to James II, but until his death in 1327 he continued to try to get papal backing for a crusade against Granada so that he could procure the Aragonese share of the Vienne tenth. Thanks to the richness of the Aragonese archives and the King's passion for detailed instructions and reports, these diplomatic efforts can be traced in full.[19] But they were unsuccessful, and James II did not again fight against Granada. The débâcle at Almería went unavenged.

By this point Castile had resumed its natural role as the Spanish power which bore the brunt of the struggle with Granada. Ferdinand's death at the age of twenty-six left his one year old heir, Alfonso XI, in the hands of the *Infantes* Peter and John, and of Ferdinand's widow, Mary. Peter endeavoured to carry on the war against the Moors, and in February 1317 John XXII granted him the crusade indulgence, papal protection for his person, and a large sum from the Vienne tenth and *tercias*.[20] In 1318 the *Infante* John undertook to support the crusade, and he too was granted the crusade indulgence. This revival of the holy war in Spain attracted some attention from across the Pyrenees,[21] but it was short-lived, for on 25 June 1319 both *Infantes* were killed in an ambush while raiding.[22] The Moors were slow to take advantage of their success, and crusading activity ended for several years, although indulgences were issued in 1321 for the defence of the important Castilian fortress of Lorcia in Murcia.[23]

That Granada represented an active threat to Castile was shown not only by the disaster of 1319, but also by the victories of Ismail I,

---

[17] *Reg. Clem. V*, nn. 8459–64; *Papsttum und Untergang*, ii, n. 114; Vincke, *SKKA*, 184.

[18] *AA*, ii, n. 489 and cf. n. 488.

[19] See Vincke, *SKKA*, 183 ff.

[20] Mollat, *Lettres communes*, nn. 2921, 2924–6 and cf. nn. 4558–9; *AA*, ii, n. 492; *AE*, ad annum 1317, n. 39, xxiv, 61; Goñi Gaztambide, 284–6.

[21] Mollat, *Lettres communes*, nn. 8026–7, 8589–90 and cf. nn. 7328–33, 8020–2, 8339; 'Crónica de Alfonso XI', ed. C. Rosell, *Crónicas de los reyes de Castilla*, i, in Biblioteca de autores Españoles lxvi (Madrid, 1875), 181–2.

[22] *Documenta selecta mutuas civitatis Arago–Cathalaunicae et ecclesiae relationes illustrantia*, ed. J. Vincke (Barcelona, 1936), n. 340; Goñi Gaztambide, 288–9.

[23] Mollat, *Lettres communes*, nn. 14284–7.

who captured Huéscar and Baeza in 1324, and took and sacked Martos in 1325.[24] Luckily for the Castilians, this vigorous ruler was assassinated in 1325. In the same year Alfonso XI came of age. He was to prove a very able King, restoring order in Castile and leading his own people, and at times Portuguese and Aragonese forces also, to some of the greatest victories of the *Reconquista*.[25] In accordance with tradition he expected papal support, but he pitched his demands too high at first and received a notable rebuff.[26] It was only in 1328 that Alfonso was granted a series of concessions, comprising crusade preaching throughout Spain, a four-year tenth and two-thirds of the hotly disputed *tercias* (the remaining third being assigned to the University of Salamanca).[27] From 1328 until his death in 1334 John XXII found himself under repeated pressure from all the Iberian kings for crusade concessions as the struggle for the Straits intensified. It cannot be denied that he responded generously, albeit trying to grant nothing without exacting guarantees of action. Castile did best, so that in April 1331 Alfonso XI was granted a new four-year tenth, with the accompanying *tercias*, to start in 1332.[28] But other peninsular kings gained concessions. Alfonso IV of Aragon was given a two-year tenth and crusade preaching in 1330,[29] Philip of Navarre indulgences and a two-year tenth in the same year,[30] and James of Majorca a three-year tenth in 1331.[31]

In February 1331 Alfonso XI concluded a truce of four years with Granada and the grant of the tenth was automatically annulled.[32] But the truce failed to hold. At the end of 1332 the King was allowed to collect two years of *tercias* to make preparations to resist a Moroccan army of more than 10,000 men said to be on the verge of

---

[24] See Hillgarth, *Spanish Kingdoms*, 339; Lomax, 166.

[25] Hillgarth, *Spanish Kingdoms*, 337 ff.

[26] 'Nachträge', n. 32. See also Goñi Gaztambide, 297–8.

[27] *AE*, ad annum 1328, nn. 77–80, xxiv, 378–80, and see also Mollat, *Lettres communes*, nn. 41541, 41566–8, 46284. It was traditional in Castile to favour the universities in this manner: see Goñi Gaztambide, 334.

[28] Mollat, *Lettres communes*, nn. 53293–4; Goñi Gaztambide, 314.

[29] Mollat, *Lettres communes*, nn. 47985, 49498–9, 49741, 50771; *AE*, ad annum 1330, n. 46, xxiv, 453–4; Vincke, *SKKA*, 244. See also Mollat, *Lettres communes*, n. 50311.

[30] Ibid., nn. 48588, 48660 (cited wrongly by Mollat: see Goñi Gaztambide, 302), and cf. n. 48478; *AE*, ad annum 1330, n. 47, xxiv, 454–5.

[31] Ibid., ad annum 1331, n. 29, xxiv, 477–8.

[32] Goñi Gaztambide, 309.

crossing,[33] and in February 1333 he was granted crusade preaching in Castile for three years.[34] He could not, however, prevent Muhammad IV of Granada recapturing Gibraltar with Merinid troops in 1333. This was the most serious blow to Christian Spain for many years. As the Pope remarked to Alfonso, no doubt echoing the King's own interpretation, 'with great slaughter of the faithful, they have violently seized and, alas, taken possession of [the port], which functioned as a vital key to Christendom and your Kingdom, formerly denying and now permitting ease of entry and departure to the enemy'.[35] Under the impact of this event, the Pope agreed to the confirmation of his earlier grant of preaching, and to the levying of fresh tenths in February 1334.[36] As in 1325, the Castilians benefited from internal strife in Granada which led to the assassination of Muhammad IV in 1333. But discord within his own Kingdom stopped Alfonso launching an attempt to recapture Gibraltar, and he sealed another truce with Granada in 1334.[37]

Between 1328 and 1331 the conflict in southern Spain attracted the keen attention of several rulers in western Europe who saw in it a chance to take part in a holy war without having to initiate a *passagium* to the eastern Mediterranean.[38] As early as 1326 Count Philip of Valois was planning to undertake a pilgrimage to Santiago and to fight the Moors before returning to France; the Pope wrote to him in 1326 and again in 1327 that he and his companions would be granted the crusade indulgence if they died in action or fought for a full year.[39] In 1328 Alfonso IV communicated with King John of Bohemia in an attempt to persuade him to come to the peninsula for an expedition against Granada,[40] and in 1329 he sent an envoy, Raymond of Melany, on a tour of several courts to arrange a crusade—an interesting antecedent to Peter of Cyprus's famous

---

[33] ASV, Reg. Vat. 105, f. 387[r-v], n. 1292. These were the last year of the 1328 grant and the first of the 1331 grant.

[34] ASV, Reg. Vat. 105, ff. 388[v]–389[r], n. 1297. Provision was made for trunks to be placed in churches, with the singing of a weekly mass for those who gave alms.

[35] '[the port] quod erat fidelium et clavis potissima Regni tui, olim prohibens, nunc autem dans, liberum ingressum et exitum inimicis, non sine magna strage fidelium, expugnarunt per violentia et prohdolor occuparunt': ASV, Reg. Vat. 107, ff. 270[r]–271[r], n. 900.

[36] Mollat, *Lettres communes*, nn. 62721, 62723; Goñi Gaztambide, 314.

[37] Ibid., 314–15.

[38] Ibid., 301 ff.; Tabacco, 299 ff.

[39] CC, n. 2739; Mollat, *Lettres communes*, n. 29408.

[40] *AA*, iii, 544–5, n. 256.

tour a generation later.[41] John of Bohemia and Philip of Navarre expressed strong interest,[42] and in October 1330 Count William of Jülich was planning to lead forty knights and eighty other men-at-arms, 'with some hope that many others from the region will accompany him'.[43]

It was more than a century since rulers and nobles north of the Pyrenees had displayed this much interest in the *Reconquista*,[44] and this fact reinforces an earlier comment that the 1320s and early 1330s can be considered as the high-water mark of the crusading movement in our period.[45] But plans for a general European crusade in Spain naturally hinged on events in the peninsula, and the project collapsed in the spring of 1331 when news reached France of the Castilian truce with Granada.[46] Possibly part of the responsibility for the failure of these plans must be borne by John XXII, who did not exert himself to help organize an expedition to Spain; he refused even to receive William of Hainault when the Count journeyed to the papal court early in 1330 to discuss the Spanish crusade, evidently fearing that William, who was accompanied by a large number of troops, might put pressure on him for a reconciliation with Louis of Bavaria.[47] In August 1331 the Pope wrote an extraordinary letter to the Queen of France, agreeing to do what he could to dissuade Philip VI from going to Spain to fight the Moors, although 'it does not befit us to dissuade Catholic princes from attacking the infidels, but rather to encourage them to do so'.[48] There is truth in Tabacco's comment that John showed little enthusiasm for the Granada crusade, compared with his energetic policies in Germany and Italy, though it should be added

[41] See his report in 'Nachträge', n. 41. See also J. Miret y Sans, 'Ramón de Melany, embajador de Alfonso IV en la corte de Francia', *Boletín de la real Academia de buenas letras de Barcelona*, ii (1903–4), 192–202; id., 'Negociacions diplomátiques d'Alfons III de Catalunya-Aragó ab el rey de França per la croada contra Granada (1328–1332)', *Anuari del Institut d'estudis catalans*, ii (1908–9), 265–336.

[42] 'Nachträge', n. 41; Goñi Gaztambide, 301–2; M. Mahn-Lot, 'Philippe d'Evreux, roi de Navarre et un projet de croisade contre le royaume de Granade (1329–1331)', *Bulletin hispanique*, xlvi (1944), 227–33.

[43] *AA*, iii, 548, n. 256.

[44] See J. Fernández Conde and A. Oliver, 'La corte pontificia de Aviñon y la iglesia española', in J. Fernández Conde (ed.), *Historia de la Iglesia en España, II²: La Iglesia en la España de los siglos VIII al XIV* (Madrid, 1982), 364, for a comparison between this period and the lead-up to Las Navas de Tolosa.

[45] Ch. 1, n. 86.   [46] CC, n. 4514; Goñi Gaztambide, 646–7.

[47] Tabacco, 301–2.   [48] CC, n. 4660.

that the idea of organizing a Spanish crusade on this scale was somewhat fanciful anyway, besides being fraught with political implications.[49]

The years following 1334 were of critical importance, one of the most dramatic periods in the *Reconquista*. The Sultan at Fez, Abū al-Ḥasan, was a devotee of the jihad, and between 1331 and 1338 he built up substantial land and sea forces for intervention in Spain.[50] Faced with this threat, the Christian kingdoms displayed an uncharacteristic ability to co-operate; particularly useful to Alfonso XI was the Catalan naval help sent by Peter III of Aragon.[51] In 1339 the Castilians won a victory in which Abū al-Ḥasan's son was killed, but in April 1340 they sustained a serious naval defeat off Gibraltar. The Merinids now had command of the Straits, and concentrated an army of perhaps 67,000 men at Tarifa, which the Castilian garrison defended vigorously. Alfonso XI marched to the relief of Tarifa with an army of about 21,000 men composed mainly of Castilians and Portuguese, with naval aid from Portugal and Aragon. On 30 October 1340 the two armies joined in battle on the banks of the Salado river near Tarifa. The result was a major Christian victory.[52] Alfonso XI moved on to invest Algeciras, and the great port fell, after a hard, two year siege, in March 1344. The struggle for the Straits had been won; the Muslims in North Africa did not again intervene in strength in southern Spain.

What part did the papal Curia play in these momentous events? The urgency of the Merinid threat to Christian Spain naturally made negotiations between Avignon and the Spanish kings somewhat easier. Alfonso XI could prove that he was making crucial defensive preparations and his appeals for help had more credibility than formerly. This is not to say that relations were entirely smooth. The Kings of Portugal and Aragon were impeding the collection of John XXII's six-year tenth;[53] Alfonso IV and Peter III of Aragon continued to submit unacceptably high demands for papal grants;[54] Alfonso XI himself was criticized for confiscating

---

[49] Tabacco, 303.

[50] Hillgarth, *Spanish Kingdoms*, 339 ff.

[51] See the excellent analysis by J. A. Robson, 'The Catalan Fleet and Moorish Sea-Power (1337–1344)', *EHR*, lxxxiv (1959), 386–408.

[52] Full account of the battle in A. Huici Miranda, *Las Grandes batallas de la Reconquista durante las invasiones africanas* (Madrid, 1956), 331–79.

[53] Vidal and Mollat, nn. 1620, 1842; Vincke, *SKKA*, 250.

[54] Ibid., 252; 'Aragón y la empresa del Estrecho en el siglo XIV: Nuevos

the revenues of benefices held by foreigners and non-residents.[55] Alfonso XI fell far short of being an ideal Christian king: Benedict XII blamed the naval defeat of 1340 on the King's adultery and his murder of the Master of the Military Order of Alcantara.[56]

But the Curia responded well to the danger facing Christian Spain. In 1335 Benedict XII confirmed his predecessor's grant of February 1334, in view of 'the intolerable expenses' which Alfonso XI had to incur in his attempt to recapture Gibraltar.[57] Then, in March 1340, as the military situation reached the point of crisis, he gave Alfonso XI a new three-year tenth with *tercias,* under much the same conditions as John XXII had imposed;[58] he also decreed crusade preaching throughout Spain, and sent Alfonso a papal standard, which was carried at Salado by a French knight.[59] In April 1341 Alfonso of Portugal was granted a two-year tenth and crusade preaching.[60] Clement VI also gave Alfonso XI aid, comprising a loan of 20,000 florins in June 1343,[61] tenths, two-thirds of the *tercias,* and indulgences in October. [62]

It is impossible to gauge the precise significance of this stream of aid in terms of the Christian war effort, but it impressed contemporaries. Giovanni Villani wrote that the siege of Algeciras would have failed had it not been for the aid which Alfonso XI received from the Pope and the Church.[63] The Curia helped in other ways than the provision of money. It worked for peace between the Christian states in the peninsula.[64] It asked Genoa to permit Alfonso XI to hire ships and enlist sailors for the war, and to stop its citizens taking service with the Moors.[65] It consoled Alfonso

documentos del Archivio municipal de Zaragoza', ed. A. Canellas, *Estudios de Edad media de la Corona de Aragón: Seccion de Zaragoza,* ii (1946), 57–9.

[55] Goñi Gaztambide, 316. Cf. Vidal, n. 8043.
[56] Vidal and Mollat, n. 2803.
[57] ASV, Reg. Vat. 119, ff. 110ᵛ–111ᵛ, n. 291. Cf. Vidal, n. 2110.
[58] ASV, Reg. Vat. 128, ff. 52ᵛ–55ᵛ, n. 15.
[59] ASV, Reg. Vat. 128, ff. 56ᵛ–57ᵛ, n. 17; 'Crónica de Alfonso XI', 318, 324. Cf. Vidal, n. 8355.   [60] Ibid., nn. 9139–42.
[61] Goñi Gaztambide, 333; 'Crónica de Alfonso XI', 367–8; J. Gautier Dalché, 'A propos d'une mission en France de Gil de Albornoz: opérations navales et difficultés financières lors du siège d'Algéciras (1341–1344)', in *El Cardenal Albornoz y el Colegio de España,* i (Zaragoza, 1971), 260.
[62] ASV, Reg. Vat. 137, f. 127ʳ, n. 435.
[63] *Cronica,* bk. 12, ch. 31, iv, 57–8.
[64] Vidal and Mollat, nn. 752, 1620–1, 2286–7, 2300–1, 2469; Fernández Conde and Oliver, 'La corte pontificia', 365–6.
[65] Vidal and Mollat, nn. 2573–4, 2801.

in defeat and praised him lavishly in victory.[66] And it decreed a 'spiritual strategy' of processions, public sermons, and prayers for peace between Christians, on the eve of the battle of Salado.[67]

All this meant that the battle of Salado and the capture of Algeciras were great crusading victories.[68] Although the army which fought in 1340 was made up mainly of Castilians and Portuguese, there were some non-Iberians present; the crusade was publicized in advance and the indulgence offered to men-at-arms from beyond the Pyrenees.[69] The crusading bull included the unusual clause that the cross should be given both to Castilians and 'to other people who come [to Castile] from any outside region'.[70] The battle was preceded by mass, celebrated by the Archbishop of Toledo, Gil Albornoz. It was entirely in character with this fervent atmosphere that Alfonso XI is described in the *Crónica de Alfonso XI* as swearing publicly before the engagement that he would put aside his mistress and amend his life, and that the Portuguese were said to be encouraged at a critical point in the battle by the arrival of a relic of the True Cross.[71] The siege of Algeciras too was promoted outside Spain, in accordance with the papal concession of indulgences 'to all from the Spanish kingdoms and other parts who serve you [Alfonso XI] or give you aid in the said war and siege'.[72] The long siege attracted a number of foreign crusaders, notably King Philip of Navarre (who died at the siege in 1343), Gastón of Bearn, Roger Bernal of Castielbon, and the Earls of Derby and Salisbury.[73] Giovanni Villani described a stream of nobles from France, Germany, England, and Languedoc, staying for four or six months, and enabling the Castilians to mount an effective blockade of the port.[74]

---

[66] Ibid., nn. 2803, 2976–7; *AE*, ad annum 1341, n. 7, xxv, 228–9; Déprez *et al.*, n. 981.

[67] Vidal and Mollat, nn. 2862–7; Goñi Gaztambide, 326.

[68] Cf. ibid., 325 ff.

[69] See ibid., 324–5, for a balanced view on this matter. Cf. Fernández Conde and Oliver, 'La corte pontificia', 367.

[70] '. . . ceterorum undecunque illuc confluentium': ASV, Reg. Vat. 128, f. 57ʳ, n. 17.

[71] Goñi Gaztambide, 327; Hillgarth, *Spanish Kingdoms*, 342.

[72] '. . . omnibus et singulis de regnis Ispaniarum et aliorum quorumcumque locorum qui tibi servierint vel subsidium prestiterint in guerris et obsidione predictis': ASV, Reg. Vat. 137, f. 127ʳ, n. 435.

[73] Déprez *et al.*, n. 3256; 'Crónica de Alfonso XI', 360, 363, 377; Goñi Gaztambide, 333; Hillgarth, *Spanish Kingdoms*, 343.

[74] *Cronica*, bk. 12, ch. 31, iv, 57–8.

The successes of the early 1340s made it hard for Clement VI to refuse to grant additional financial aid to the Spanish kings even though there was little fighting for some years after 1344. Thus at the beginning of 1345 Alfonso of Portugal was given a two-year tenth on the grounds that he was continuing the struggle against Granada,[75] and in March 1346 Alfonso XI was granted a two-year tenth to help him defend Algeciras.[76] In 1347 Clement conceded a conditional two-year tenth to the Kings of Aragon and Portugal, to be collected only if their lands were attacked by the Moors.[77] Two years later Alfonso XI resumed hostilities, laying siege to Gibraltar in an attempt to complete his policy of closing the Straits to the enemy. Clement VI pressed for Genoese naval help.[78] But the besieging army was severely hit by the Black Death, of which Alfonso XI himself died on 27 March 1350. The siege was abandoned.[79]

Goñi Gaztambide characterized the period following the accession of Peter I of Castile in 1350 as marking 'a very deep trough in the history of the [Spanish] crusade'. He went on to note that

The religious ideal of holy war seems to have slumbered. All that occurred were projects, sporadic attempts, ephemeral campaigns, make-believe crusades; there was no methodical, persistent activity in pursuit of the national goal of the *Reconquista*.[80]

A recent writer has qualified this prevailing view, pointing out that there was a vigorous tradition of frontier warfare which subsisted even when the peninsula's kings showed no interest in Granada.[81] The fact remains, however, that between 1350 and 1378 there was little crusading activity: few envoys came to Avignon with projects for fighting the Moors, and there were very few bulls decreeing crusade preaching. One of the main reasons was the extremely unfavourable political situation in the two leading kingdoms. Castile from 1350 was ruled by Peter I, who became an enemy of France and the papacy and showed no interest in a renewed assault on Granada, his policy being directed rather against the other Christian kings of Iberia.[82] His successor, Henry of Trastámara,

---

[75] *AE*, ad annum 1344, n. 53, xxv, 347–8.
[76] Ibid., ad annum 1346, nn. 61–2, xxv, 400–1.
[77] Déprez and Mollat, n. 1410.   [78] Ibid., nn. 1997, 2020.
[79] Hillgarth, *Spanish Kingdoms*, 344.   [80] Goñi Gaztambide, 336.
[81] See Bishko, 439 ff.
[82] Hillgarth, *Spanish Kingdoms*, 372 ff., esp. 374.

had too many problems within Castile to think of the *Reconquista*.[83] Nor did Granada feature, except marginally, in the ambitious plans of Peter III of Aragon.[84] Most importantly, Castile and Aragon were at war from 1356 to 1366, a bitter struggle which exhausted both countries.

The papacy's reaction to these developments was complicated by its own policies outside Spain. It was the aim of Innocent VI and Urban V to counteract the growth of English influence in Castile, and this made the Curia sympathetic towards Peter of Aragon, despite his systematic erosion of ecclesiastical rights in his Kingdom. Thus, although Innocent VI told his legate in Spain to work for peace in 1356,[85] and complained two years later that the war between the two Kingdoms was permitting the Moors to grow stronger,[86] the Curia began to give unofficial support to Aragon. In 1362 England and Castile entered into a formal alliance, and in 1366 Bertrand Du Guesclin led an invasion of Castile by the mercenary companies. His expedition was sponsored and partly financed by Urban V, who represented it as a crusade against the Moors; it is just possible that this was how the Pope really saw the campaign, though his primary aim was simply to get the companies out of southern France, and his secondary one to overthrow Peter I.[87]

With the assassination of Peter and the accession of the pro-French Henry of Trastámara, Urban was able to resume traditional policies of peacemaking and incitement to the crusade. In February 1370 he told his nuncios to try to make peace between the Christian kingdoms and then to preach the crusade which Henry II wanted to lead in order to protect his southern provinces.[88] The crusade in Spain was now attractive to the Curia for financial reasons, for it had begun the practice of granting crusade tenths and reserving a part of the proceeds for itself. Thus in 1376 Ferdinand of Portugal was given a two-year tenth, of which half was to go to the Holy See.[89] In such circumstances it is doubtful whether the Curia expected a crusade to materialize: it was a fiscal manœuvre similar to the granting of licences for trade with Mamluk Egypt.

---

[83] Ibid., 385 ff. [84] Ibid., 353.

[85] *Bulas y cartas secretas de Inocencio VI (1352–1362)* ed. J. Z. Aramburu. Monumenta Hispaniae Vaticana: Seccion Registros iii (Rome, 1970), n. 257.

[86] Ibid., n. 337.

[87] See Housley, 'Mercenary Companies', 275–6.

[88] *AE*, ad annum 1370, n. 18, xxvi, 179. Cf. LM, n. 3107.

[89] *AE*, ad annum 1376, nn. 19–22, xxvi, 272–4.

If Granada's strength constituted an insuperable obstacle to the completion of the *Reconquista*, some contemporaries were already thinking of carrying the crusade outside Spain. During the reign of Alfonso XI the Moorish King of Montesclaros in Africa, Abdallah, intimated his secret desire to be baptized, and in 1354 Peter I asked Innocent VI for papal support so that he could help Abdallah carry through the plan. The King wanted crusade preaching throughout Spain, and the despatch of a papal banner, 'bearing the sign of the same life-giving cross and a picture of the keys, by which the door of salvation is opened to the faithful'.[90] But relations between Peter and Innocent were already tense and the Pope was sceptical about the scheme. Although he congratulated Abdallah on his conversion, he insisted on much more detailed Castilian proposals before giving anything.[91] The project came to nothing.

A second area of crusading endeavour associated with the *Reconquista* was the Canary Islands. Several Christian maritime powers showed interest in these in the early decades of the century.[92] Then on 15 November 1344 Clement VI granted the Islands as a papal fief to Louis de la Cerda, a princely descendant of Alfonso X with estates in both Spain and France. Louis was to pay an annual rent of 400 florins to the *camera*.[93] At this point he was trying to assemble an expedition to conquer the Islands, and in January 1345 this was given crusade status at Louis's request.[94] Clement VI took other steps to sponsor his new vassal's expedition. In December 1344 he wrote to the Kings of Portugal, Castile, and Aragon asking them to allow Louis to hire ships and recruit men, and purchase arms and supplies for his forthcoming crusade. He also wrote to other western rulers asking for their support.[95]

The replies from the Spanish monarchs, two of which were by a fortunate chance recorded in the papal registers, reveal a keen

---

[90] *Bulas*, n. 61.

[91] Ibid., nn. 61, 63. Peter had severe political problems at this point: Hillgarth, *Spanish Kingdoms*, 376–7.

[92] See J. Vincke, 'Der verhinderte Kreuzzug Ludwigs von Spanien zu den Kanarischen Inseln', in *Gesammelte Aufsätze zur Kulturgeschichte Spaniens*, xvii = *Spanische Forschungen der Görresgesellschaft, I Reihe*, xvii (1961), 57.

[93] *AE*, ad annum 1344, nn. 39–47, xxv, 341–4; Mollat, 'L'Œuvre oratoire', 253, 259; Schmitz, 'Les Sermons', 21, 32. For Louis, see G. Daumet, 'Louis de la Cerda ou d'Espagne', *Bulletin hispanique*, xv (1913), 38–67.

[94] ASV, Reg. Vat. 166, f. 200ʳ, n. 296 (cited incorrectly by Goñi Gaztambide, 335).

[95] Déprez *et al.*, nn. 1314–15, 1348–9.

awareness of what the newly-discovered Islands might have to offer. Alfonso XI of Castile replied that 'the acquisition of the Kingdom of Africa [sic] is known to be our royal right and that of nobody else', but that he would display his reverence towards the Holy See by allowing Louis to conquer the Canaries.[96] Alfonso of Portugal wrote that the Islands belonged to him since his subjects had discovered them;[97] although he would not oppose the crusade, it would receive no Portuguese support, especially as the country's resources were all needed 'for the defence and extension of the Faith' in Iberia.[98] Peter III of Aragon at first gave the expedition his active backing, probably because he saw the Canaries as a possible zone of Catalan expansion. But when Genoa invoked the clauses of a treaty with Aragon against the crusade, Peter withdrew his support, and the expedition never set sail.[99] The extension of the *Reconquista* southwards had to wait until the fifteenth century.[100]

(b) EASTERN EUROPE

Throughout most of the thirteenth century crusading activity in eastern Europe had been directed at the consolidation and extension of Christian rule in lands adjacent to the Baltic Sea, Livonia and Prussia.[101] While these campaigns were in progress a substantially new and powerful state had been created to the south by a people related by language to the Prussians. This people, the Lithuanians, suffered greatly from Mongol attacks in the 1240s and 1250s, and under their pressure one ruler called Mindaugas succeeded in welding the various principalities into a single political unit. Lithuanian society was less advanced than either its Latin Christian or Russian Orthodox neighbours, but it was militarized and aggressive, in some ways similar to the Frankish West of the eighth century. To a considerable extent its economy depended on the profits of raids and on tribute payments from the Russians.

---

[96] Ibid., n. 1316.
[97] There had been a Portuguese expedition to the archipelago in 1341.
[98] Déprez *et al.*, n. 1317.
[99] See Vincke, 'Der verhinderte Kreuzzug', *passim*; Fernández Conde and Oliver, 'La corte pontificia', 368–9. Goñi Gaztambide's account (334–5) is inaccurate.
[100] See Bishko, 448. For missionary activity see Fernández Conde and Oliver, 'La corte pontificia', 408 ff.
[101] See E. N. Johnson, 'The German Crusade on the Baltic', in Setton (gen. ed.), *History of the Crusades*, iii, 556–75; E. Christiansen, *The Northern Crusades: The Baltic and the Catholic Frontier 1100–1525* (London, 1980), chs. 4–5.

Belligerent and tough, the Lithuanians were also pagans, given to the worship of a curious catalogue of nature gods. Mindaugas accepted baptism at one stage and was even sent a crown by Pope Innocent IV, but this was a political gambit, and until 1386 Lithuania remained a vigorously pagan state.[102] Lithuanian paganism, the violent nature of relations between the Grand Principality and its Catholic neighbours, and the well-established tradition of crusading in this part of Europe, together explain the series of crusades directed against the Lithuanians in the fourteenth century.

The main recipients of crusading favour were the Poles.[103] After nearly two centuries of disunity, the Kingdom of Poland was reunited in January 1320 when Vladislav Lokietek was crowned King in Cracow. Papal backing had been instrumental in his climb to the throne. In a petition of 1318 in which the people of Poland asked John XXII to grant Lokietek the crown, two points were of particular significance. One was that Poland's immediate dependence upon the Holy See and its payment of the ancient tax of Peter's Pence provided justification for papal support. The other was that if Poland were a kingdom again it would be able to display greater vigour in its struggle against the pagan Lithuanians and the Orthodox, and therefore schismatic, Ruthenians of Halicz-Vladimir, the 'regnum Galiciae et Lodomiriae' which straddled the frontiers of Little Poland in the east. Despite the opposition of King John of Bohemia and the Teutonic Order, John XXII responded to these arguments by giving his blessing to the proposed coronation.[104]

On the solid foundations of Poland's crusading role and its valuable contribution to papal finances, a relationship of friendly co-operation and mutual aid was established which lasted throughout our period. One of its features was papal support for the new Kingdom in its long drawn out conflict with the Teutonic Knights.[105] Another was an impressive series of crusade bulls and

[102] Ibid., 133 ff.; Muldoon, *Popes, Lawyers and Infidels*, 57–8, 90.

[103] See P. W. Knoll, *The Rise of the Polish Monarchy: Piast Poland in East Central Europe, 1320–1370* (Chicago–London, 1972); K. Tymieniecki, 'The Reunion of the Kingdom, 1295–1333', in *The Cambridge History of Poland (to 1696)*, ed. W. F. Reddaway *et al.* (Cambridge, 1950), 115–24; O. Halecki, 'Casimir the Great, 1333–70', ibid., 167–87.

[104] *Vetera monumenta Poloniae et Lithuaniae gentiumque finitimarum historiam illustrantia*, ed. A. Theiner. 4 vols. (Rome, 1860–4), i, n. 236; Knoll, *RPM*, ch. 1, esp. 37–9.

[105] See below, ch. 8, nn. 61–71.

other forms of aid, which were despatched from Avignon to the Polish court. These began in September 1319 with a bull to Vladislav acceding to his request for the grant of an indulgence of a year's enjoined penance to him and his followers 'on all occasions when you have to lead an expedition against the pagans, schismatics or other infidels, or the enemies of the Catholic faith'.[106]

The main danger from Ruthenia was that this vulnerable *regnum* might be absorbed either by Lithuania or by the Tatars of the Golden Horde. King Vladislav tried to persuade the Pope to grant him crusading aid on the basis of this contingency in 1321, and three years later he wrote again after the deaths of the last two princes of the house of Roman made the threat of a Tatar occupation of Ruthenia greater.[107] John XXII responded to such appeals in the summer of 1325 by granting the crusade indulgence to all Poles who died fighting pagans and schismatics over the course of a five year period, together with lesser indulgences for those who fought and survived.[108] It is unlikely that the indulgences were published, however, since Poland entered into an alliance with the Lithuanians in the autumn of 1325; the Polish heir to the throne, Casimir, was wed to the Lithuanian princess Aldona after her conversion to Christianity.[109] Until 1340 the thrust of Polish diplomacy was northwards, directed at the recovery of the Baltic provinces, illegally seized, so the Poles claimed, by the Teutonic Knights. Polish and Lithuanian armies operated together against the Knights and King Vladislav did what he could to hinder the 'crusade' which John of Bohemia led against the Lithuanians in 1328.[110]

By the late 1330s King Casimir, who succeeded Vladislav in 1333, was beginning the re-orientation of policy towards the east which marked Polish diplomacy in the following decades.[111] The immediate occasion for this renewed interest in Halicz-Vladimir was the revival of Tatar power. The danger was aggravated when the pro-Catholic ruler Boleslaw-George was assassinated by his boyars in April 1340. Casimir invaded Ruthenia in 1340, and in the autumn prepared for the inevitable Tatar counter-attack. Pope Benedict

---

[106] *VMP*, i, n. 242.

[107] *AE*, ad annum 1324, n. 53, xxiv, 273–4; Knoll, *RPM*, 45.

[108] *VMP*, i, nn. 316, 334, 338.

[109] Knoll, *RPM*, 45–7.

[110] Ibid., 51–4. I have not been able to find a crusade bull relating to this expedition.

[111] Knoll, *RPM*, 121 ff.

XII was persuaded of the gravity of the threat, and in August 1340 sent bulls decreeing the preaching of a crusade in Poland, Hungary, and Bohemia.[112] Casimir inflicted a crushing defeat on the Tatars in January 1341, but was unable to consolidate his hold on Ruthenia because of his preoccupations in the west.[113] With the Treaty of Kalisz of July 1343, his relations with the Teutonic Order were at last stabilized, and he wrote to Clement VI asking for financial aid to build up his defences in the east. The Pope responded by granting a two-year tenth on 1 December 1343; this meant losing the Polish church's contribution to the three-year tenth for the crusade against the Turks, which was levied on the same day.[114]

In 1349 Casimir led another army into Ruthenia and took several important fortresses; by the end of the year he had formally incorporated the 'regnum Galiciae et Lodomiriae' into his dominions.[115] The Tatars had suffered terribly from the Black Death and the Golden Horde was unable to prevent Casimir's territorial advances, but the Lithuanians put up a determined struggle. In 1350 they recaptured several castles from the Poles. Casimir despatched an eloquently phrased petition to Avignon pleading for help, and in March 1351 Clement VI granted him a four-year tenth, of which he reserved a half for his own needs.[116] A Lithuanian attack in 1351 was repulsed with valuable Hungarian aid, but the situation was still serious in 1352, as the Lithuanians hired Tatar troops.[117]

An appeal to Avignon resulted in a crusade bull against the Tatars, a virtual reissue of Benedict XII's bull of 1340.[118] This preaching was renewed in November 1354.[119] It was money that the King needed most, however: he was forced to borrow very substantial sums at this time.[120] It must have been galling that two years' proceeds of the 1351 tenth were reserved for the papal *camera*. The papal collector in Poland, Arnold de Caucina, was persuaded to lend Casimir over 13,000 florins, but in February 1354 Innocent VI

[112] *VMH*, i, nn. 958–9.
[113] Knoll, *RPM*, 132–3.
[114] *VMP*, i, nn. 604–5.
[115] *The Chronicle of Novgorod 1016–1471*, tr. R. Michell and N. Forbes. Camden 3rd Series, xxv (London, 1914), 143; Knoll, *RPM*, 140–2.
[116] *VMP*, i, nn. 702–3.
[117] Knoll, *RPM*, 148–51.
[118] *VMP*, i, n. 713.
[119] *VMH*, ii, n. 18.
[120] Knoll, *RPM*, 152.

refused to sanction the use of cameral funds for the war in Ruthenia, and demanded that they be repaid.[121] In November he yielded to the extent of granting the King a three year moratorium on his debts to the *camera*.[122] The papacy's 'special relationship' with Poland was running through a stormy patch, mainly because both powers were heavily reliant on taxes from the Polish church.

Fresh Church aid was forthcoming in 1355, for the 1351 tenth had expired and the Pope levied another four-year tenth of which, as before, Casimir was allotted half.[123] The conflict over Ruthenia continued in the following years, with raiding by Poles, Tatars, and Lithuanians.[124] The diplomatic background was intricate: Poland's greatest enemy, the Teutonic Order, brought papal censure on itself by helping the Lithuanians against Casimir while continuing to organize its own curious form of war against the pagans; conversely, it was in Casimir's interests to settle the problem of Ruthenia so as to free his own hands to deal with the Knights. In 1363 the King started to prepare for a major campaign in the east, and as usual petitioned for papal aid. He was granted a bull conferring the crusade indulgence on all who died fighting, covering a twelve year period.[125] The royal army carried out a successful expedition in 1366, but a Lithuanian raid into Mazovia in 1368 led to another petition to Avignon. In his reply to this on 15 May 1369 Urban V granted a two-year tenth for the rebuilding of castles razed by the pagans and the strengthening of Poland's defences.[126]

The crusade against the Lithuanians was thus primarily a Polish concern, with occasional participation by the Hungarians. It was conducted in a series of campaigns and raids over a thirty year period in an area comprising Ruthenia, Mazovia, and Little Poland, the overall context being Casimir's bold attempt to bring Halicz-Vladimir under his personal rule in order to safeguard his Kingdom's eastern frontier. Since the conflict could be represented as a religious one, the King was able to secure a series of bulls of great use in military and financial terms: he made between 10,000 and 15,000 Polish marks from the tenths which he was granted by the Curia.[127] Just as in the cases of the French and Spanish kings, the

---

[121] Ibid.; Gasnault *et al.*, nn. 762–3. [122] Ibid., n. 1210.
[123] *VMP*, i, n. 742. [124] Knoll, *RPM*, 157 ff.
[125] *VMP*, i, n. 833.
[126] Ibid., i, n. 882. Cf. Knoll, *RPM*, 2
[127] Knoll (*RPM*, 176) reached a total of 11 or 12 years of tenths, or 13,500–15,000 Polish marks. I estimate a total of only 8 years, or 10,000 marks.

crusade brought Casimir great profits, and it would be wrong to ignore them when assessing his motivation as a crusader. But a recent historian of the King's reign has warned against a cynical interpretation of his actions in this respect, both because of Casimir's own piety and because of the development, at the papal and Polish courts, of the idea that Poland formed an *antemurale Christianitatis,* a strategically important yet exposed and vulnerable bulwark of the West, similar to fifteenth-century Hungary.[128] So while political and commercial contacts between Poland and Lithuania were as significant as those between the Spanish kingdoms and Granada, in both cases the difference of religion made anything more than a *modus vivendi* impossible.

Further north, in the lands west of Lake Ladoga, there was another religious confrontation, here between the Swedes and Norwegians on the one hand, and the pagan Karelians and schismatic subjects of Novgorod on the other.[129] A list of *supplicationes* submitted by a papal collector in about 1322 included the plea that the Pope should grant crusade indulgences to the Swedes who were being attacked by pagans and schismatics,[130] and in February 1323 John XXII granted the plenary indulgence to Norwegians who died while fighting the *Fumar* (Finns).[131] King Magnus was able to derive considerable revenue from crusade taxes levied for his wars in this area. In 1326 he was assigned a share of the Vienne tenth, and in 1351 he was granted half of a four-year tenth.[132] The latter tax was levied on the same day as its equivalent in Poland, and the two clearly represent an attempt by Clement VI, faced by mounting financial difficulties at the end of an expensive reign, to improve his position by tax compromises with these far-off kings. But Magnus was not a man to keep a bargain: if Casimir was eastern Europe's equivalent of the victorious Alfonso XI, Magnus was its James II.

Both Poland and Sweden had embattled eastern frontiers. Hungary's situation was more complicated. The Hungarians certainly faced the threat of occasional Lithuanian raids and, more import-

---

[128] Ibid., 174–7. See also id., 'Poland as *Antemurale Christianitatis* in the Late Middle Ages', *CHR*, lx (1974), 381–401; G. Rhode, *Die Ostgrenze Polens. Politische Entwicklung, kulturelle Bedeutung, und geistige Auswirkung. I Band. Im Mittelalter bis zum Jahre 1401* (Cologne–Graz, 1955), 242–60.

[129] See Christiansen, *Northern Crusades*, 171 ff., esp. 182–90.

[130] *Acta pont. svecica*, i, n. 191.   [131] *AE*, ad annum 1323, n. 21, xxiv, 213.

[132] *Acta pont. svecica*, i, nn. 207, 214, 398–9. Cf. *VMP*, i, nn. 702–3, and *Acta pont. svecica*, i. nn. 429, 477.

antly, attacks by the Tatars. In addition, Hungary had a claim of its own to Ruthenia and King Louis the Great (1342–82) was heir to the Polish throne until 1370, and thereafter King of both countries. Papal aid to the Hungarians for war in the north was therefore frequent, though less so than in the case of Poland. In February 1314 Clement V gave King Charles-Robert a three year grant of the crusade indulgence for soldiers who died fighting, a bull probably intended for warfare with the Tatars and Lithuanians;[133] this grant was repeated in February 1325 by John XXII, a few months before his identical concession to the Poles.[134] In 1325 the Pope refused Charles-Robert financial aid from neighbouring kingdoms—it is hard to envisage which *regna* were meant[135]—but in June 1332, soon after an important victory over the Tatars, he granted the King a third of a recent three year levy of annates, together with a third of Hungary's contribution to the Vienne tenth, for the defence of the Kingdom against the *Rutheni*. The larger share of the taxes was taken by the Pope for his wars in Italy.[136] This was followed two years later by a renewal of the now standard three year grant of the crusade indulgence 'in articulo mortis'.[137]

True to form, Benedict XII was less generous with money, asking for a clarification of royal requests in 1335, but he sent the King a six year grant of the indulgence 'in articulo mortis' in 1339.[138] This was the period of Casimir's penetration of Ruthenia, in which Hungary too became involved. The crisis which broke out in Halicz-Vladimir in 1340 thus affected Hungary, and crusade preaching was decreed there.[139] In the early years of his reign King Louis made several interventions in Halicz-Vladimir and Poland. The most important of these occurred in 1351–2; Hungary was once more included in the crusade preaching ordered by Clement VI in May 1352, and on 15 July Louis was granted a generous four-year tenth.[140] The papal letters make it clear that one reason for this large concession was the King's agreement to release several members of the Neapolitan royal family, captured in his Italian expedition of 1350. Again in

---

[133] *AE*, ad annum 1314, n. 13, xxiv, 21–2.
[134] Mollat, *Lettres communes*, n. 21500.
[135] *VMH*, i, n. 771.   [136] Ibid., i, nn. 845, 865–8.
[137] Ibid., i, n. 894. Cf. *AE*, ad annum 1334, n. 26, xxv, 11–12.
[138] Vidal and Mollat, n. 478; *VMH*, i, n. 945.
[139] Ibid., i, n. 959. For fuller details of the events recounted in the next five paragraphs, see Housley, 'King Louis the Great', *passim*.
[140] *VMP*, i, n. 713; *VMH*, i, nn. 1249–51, 1253.

1354 Hungary was included in the renewal of crusade preaching,[141] but soon afterwards the conflict in Ruthenia became less vehement and Louis was able to turn his attention away from his northern frontier.

The advantage of Hungary's geographical position was that there were several other fronts where its king could represent his war with his neighbours as a crusade. One of these was the south, where Louis hoped to conquer and dismember the schismatic Kingdom of Serbia ruled by Stephen Dushan. There were precedents for crusading in this area, and Charles-Robert had made advances which had earned him papal praise and support.[142] Moreover, the Curia was committed to encouraging Louis's war against pagans and schismatics in order to divert him from the Neapolitan Kingdom.[143] But Stephen Dushan was a clever opponent with a sound grasp of the interplay of politics and religion in the Balkans. He opened negotiations with Avignon on Church Union and even, at the end of 1354, offered his services as captain of the Roman church with the duty of defending the Christians in the east.[144]

Innocent VI was attracted by the idea of a negotiated Union and alarmed by the recent successes of the Turks. In addition, he knew that if he granted Louis a crusade, Hungarian troops would be directed as much against Catholic Dalmatia and Venice as against the schismatic Serbs. The Pope was anxious to prevent a full-scale war between Hungary and Venice because he was hoping to secure Venetian participation in a renewed naval league in the eastern Mediterranean. All these factors induced Innocent to send nuncios to Serbia to discuss Union in 1355.

In 1355–6, however, a new consideration helped to erode the Pope's doubts about the proposed Hungarian crusade. Military and financial aid from Hungary was urgently needed in Romagna to tip the balance in favour of the papal troops fighting there under Cardinal Albornoz. It was probably this factor, together with the failure of the mission sent to Serbia, which led the Pope to grant Louis crusade preaching against the Serbs in 1356, as well as a three-year tenth. In exchange for this Louis was appointed standard-bearer of the Church and given the task of furnishing substantial aid

---

[141] Ibid., ii, n. 18. See Matteo Villani, bk. 4, ch. 5, i, 306–7 for a Hungarian campaign against the Tatars in 1354.

[142] *AE*, ad annum 1320, nn. 1–2, xxiv, 118.

[143] Ibid., ad annum 1352, n. 6, xxv, 528–9.   [144] Gasnault *et al.*, n. 1249.

to Albornoz in Romagna.[145] He was also to combat heresy in his own lands,[146] to refrain from attacking the Catholic Kingdom of Albania and Duchy of Durazzo,[147] and to co-operate with the efforts of a papal nuncio to restore peace between himself and Venice.[148] As it turned out, Louis's contribution to the Romagna war was not as effective as the Pope hoped that it would be, and the King's chief success was against Venice, which was forced to accept humiliating peace terms in 1358.

The agreement which Louis reached with Innocent VI in 1356 had echoes throughout the following two decades, as the last three Avignon popes all tried to persuade the King to intervene more forcefully in Italy, or at least to permit them to tax the Hungarian church for that purpose.[149] But Louis would neither send large armies to Lombardy, nor use his considerable military strength to hold up the Turkish advance in the Balkans. His chief interest was in winning lands from the Bulgarians, a notable example being the capture of Vidin in 1365. Louis secured some papal backing for this; in April 1368 Urban V wrote praising the King's intention 'to approach in person the lands of the unbelievers, the schismatics and Patarenes, the enemies of the Catholic Faith, with your army, in order to wage war on them'.[150] Hungary's interests called for a determined crusade against the Turks, but Louis preferred the easier target of the schismatic Balkan states. His people would, of course, pay dearly for this in the fifteenth century.

Apart from a short and savage crusade against the followers of Fra Dolcino in Piedmont in 1306–7,[151] it was also in East Central Europe that this period's main crusading activity against heretics took place. There were important settlements of Cathars in Bosnia, Transylvania, and Dalmatia.[152] In February 1327 John XXII ordered the Dominican Prior of Hungary to organize crusade

---

[145] Ibid., nn. 2267, 2316–17.

[146] Ibid., n. 2328.

[147] Ibid., n. 2267.

[148] Ibid., n. 2230.

[149] As reported by Matteo Villani, Louis's demands for aid in exchange for personal combat in Italy were exceptionally high: bk. 10, ch. 5, ii, 310, and bk. 10, ch. 45, ii, 344–5.   [150] *Acta Urbani V*, n. 141.

[151] See Bernard Gui, 'De secta illorum qui se dicunt esse de ordine apostolorum', ed. A. Segarizzi, *RISNS* 9⁵, 26–8; 'Historia fratris Dulcini heresiarche', ibid., 6–13.

[152] See M. D. Lambert, *Medieval Heresy: Popular Movements from Bogomil to Hus* (London, 1977), 142 ff.; B. Hamilton, *The Medieval Inquisition* (London, 1981), 80.

preaching against such groups, only to cancel it a few months later when he realized that he had encroached on the authority of the well-established Franciscan Inquisition in Hungary.[153] Such full crusade preaching was rare: usually the Curia adopted the more limited procedure laid down in the early thirteenth century, of granting indulgences to laymen as a reward for giving armed support to the machinery of the Inquisition.[154] The first instance of this which I have discovered occurred in July 1318, when John XXII ordered the Dominican Prior of Greece to deputize some brothers with theological training to investigate heresy 'in the regions of Greece'. Anybody who took up arms against the heretics would enjoy the remission of three years of enjoined penance, while the plenary indulgence would be granted to those who died.[155] Exactly the same guidelines were given in 1327 in a letter to the Dominican Prior of Hungary, dealing with heretical ideas being propagated in Hungary by 'enemies of the cross from remote parts of Germany and Poland, and the surrounding regions'.[156] And in 1340 Benedict XII wrote of heretics in Bohemia who were attacking and robbing Catholics. He granted the crusade indulgence 'in articulo mortis' to Ulrich, lord of Novadomo in the diocese of Prague, and his followers, who intended to fight these brigands.[157]

(c) ITALY

The popes of the thirteenth century, especially from Innocent IV onwards, made extensive use of the crusade in implementing their temporal policy in Italy. In particular, the crusade became associated with the alliance between the papacy and the Angevin dynasty of Naples, which acted as the sheet-anchor of the Guelf cause from Charles of Anjou's acceptance of the Sicilian crown in 1264. But the last decades of the century brought disaster for Angevin Naples, and a severe setback for its papal suzerain. The Sicilians rose in rebellion against Charles I, threw out his troops and officials, and, with Aragonese help, invaded southern Italy with such success that the complete rout of the Neapolitan monarchy seemed imminent.

---

[153] *VMH*, i, nn. 791, 794–6.

[154] See N. Housley, 'Politics and Heresy in Italy: Anti-Heretical Crusades, Orders and Confraternities, 1200–1500', *JEH*, xxxiii (1982), 195 ff.

[155] *Acta Joannis XXII*, ed. A. L. Tautu. PCRCICO, vii² (Rome, 1952), n. 18. See also Mollat, *Lettres communes*, nn. 7861–3.

[156] *VMH*, i, nn. 787–90.

[157] *AE*, ad annum 1340, n. 72, xxv, 220–1.

By a great military effort, facilitated by the issuing of crusade indulgences and very heavy clerical taxation, the Angevin forces regained the lost south Italian provinces. But they could not reconquer Sicily, and the independence of the island was accepted when the Treaty of Caltabellotta was sealed in 1302. This in itself was a great blow to Pope Boniface VIII, but it was also part of a broader and complex crisis in papal affairs whose chief constituents were political chaos in the Papal State, the fracture of the Guelf system of alliances, and a bitter and resounding conflict between Boniface and Philip IV.[158] The temporal policy of the thirteenth-century papacy thus ended in failure, though not in the total ruin which some historians have described, and which had seemed close at hand in 1240, 1264, and 1282.

Too much was at stake for the Avignon papacy to give up its claim to rule in central Italy, or the frequent interventions in the political affairs of the Tuscan and Lombard cities which that rule implied. But under Clement V the allies and the money were lacking for a determined attempt at reconstruction. Clement did, however, launch one crusade in Italy which achieved startling success, proved that the use of force could be effective, and may have had an important morale-boosting impact on the shapers of papal policy. For when Venice gave active backing to a revolt against papal suzerainty at Ferrara in 1308, Clement reacted with uncharacteristic resolution. Early in 1309 he sent a cardinal-legate with a small army to rally resistance to the Venetians, and declared a crusade against them. The legate, Arnold of Pellegrue, faced severe problems and the campaign hung in the balance in the summer of 1309, but the Venetians had yet worse difficulties and had to submit in 1310. This success was important: not only did it restore Ferrara briefly to papal rule and, according to the Rector of Romagna, raise the papacy's prestige in the region to new heights; it also showed that the Curia's Italian policy—including the use of the crusade—was not doomed to failure, as some contemporaries, such as the anti-clerical publicist Peter Dubois, were starting to assert.[159]

The repercussions of the Italian expedition of Henry VII included the revival of the Guelf structure of alliances and the emergence of a

---

[158] See Housley, *Italian Crusades*, 15–23; J. R. Strayer, 'The Political Crusades of the Thirteenth Century', in Setton (gen. ed.), *History of the Crusades*, ii, 343–75.

[159] See Housley, *Italian Crusades*, 24–5; id., 'Pope Clement V', *passim*; 'Cronica di Bologna', *RIS* xviii, col. 319.

network of powerful and aggressive Ghibelline lords in Lombardy and Tuscany. This was the political context of the legation of Bertrand Du Poujet from 1319 to 1334. He was to co-operate with the troops of Robert of Naples and Florence against the Ghibelline forces, and himself commanded sizeable and costly armies of mercenaries.[160] There were also crusaders, recruited from 1321 onwards by the release of a series of bulls against the Visconti and Estensi families, Raynaldo Bonacolsi of Mantua, and Cangrande della Scala of Verona. Du Poujet operated mainly in Lombardy, but crusaders fought too in Tuscany on behalf of Florence, and in the eastern provinces of the Papal State, where the Church's officials had to contend with their own Ghibelline *signori* and communes. From 1327 to 1330 these various theatres of conflict were to some extent co-ordinated by the Italian expedition of Louis IV of Bavaria, whose election as German King John XXII had bitterly opposed. Early in 1328 the Pope issued crusade indulgences for fighting Louis, and the Guelfs succeeded in driving him out of the peninsula. But it was an ephemeral triumph: by the end of John XXII's reign his policies had clearly failed and the Curia was no nearer to dominating political affairs in central and northern Italy than it had been twenty years earlier.[161]

The legation of Bertrand Du Poujet represented the first major exertion of the papacy's military and financial power in the Avignon period. A pattern had been established, and when, in 1353, Pope Innocent VI sent Cardinal Gil Albornoz to Italy to regain control over the Papal State, it was predictable that fresh crusades would be declared against the governments which resisted him.[162] Albornoz was able to subdue the western provinces of the State in 1354, and reached a settlement with the Malatesta of Rimini in 1355, but he was then faced with the strong opposition of Francesco Ordelaffi, lord of Cesena and Forlì, and the Manfredi of Faenza. In October 1354 Ordelaffi and the Manfredi had been pronounced heretics on the grounds of contumacy, and in the winter of 1355–6 Innocent VI sanctioned the preaching of a crusade against them.[163] The crusade

---

[160] P. Partner, *The Lands of St Peter: The Papal State in the Middle Ages and the Early Renaissance* (London, 1972), 312 ff.

[161] Housley, *Italian Crusades*, 25–9; 'Cronica di Bologna', col. 338; 'Chronicon astense', *RIS* xi, cols. 260–1.

[162] Gasnault *et al.*, nn. 352–432; Partner, 339 ff.

[163] Gasnault *et al.*, nn. 1143–4, 1865, 1867, 1871, 1876; 'Cronica d'Orvieto', *RIS* xv, cols. 684–5; *La vita di Cola di Rienzo*, ed. A. M. Ghisalberti (Florence–Rome–

progressed well in 1356,[164] but Bernabò Visconti secretly hired Conrad of Landau's army of mercenaries and sent it to relieve Ordelaffi. Albornoz extended the crusade to include the mercenaries on the grounds that they were helping a heretic, and preaching was successful, but it was bribery rather than force which robbed Ordelaffi of his German troops in 1357, enabling Albornoz to complete his conquest of Romagna, with some Hungarian help.[165]

Thus far Albornoz's successes had been extremely expensive, costing over half a million florins and necessitating Church taxation at least as heavy as that imposed by John XXII, and in much less favourable economic circumstances.[166] Without the aid of crusade preaching, which was promoted with energy, the financial burden of the campaigns would have been even greater; it is questionable whether the Church could have sustained it.[167] From 1357 Innocent VI insisted on a reduction of these costs, and for some years the conflict died down, but in 1360 the Curia again entered into a war with the Visconti of Milan, the most powerful of the Lombard tyrants and consistent opponents of papal policy in northern Italy. Innocent's successor, Urban V, pursued the war with determination, bringing new measures of clerical taxation to bear and, in March 1363, declaring Bernabò Visconti to be a heretic.[168] As a consequence of this step the Pope decided to renew the crusade: 'Since we have no hope of his conversion . . ., after the publication of this sentence, which we intend to promote in various parts of the world, we propose preaching the word of the life-giving cross against the sentenced man.'[169] In a dramatic gesture worthy of Gregory VII, the Pope knelt in front of the altar and called on Saints

Geneva, 1928), 111; F. Filippini, *Il cardinale Egidio Albornoz* (Bologna, 1933), 110–11; Housley, 'Mercenary Companies', 259.

[164] Gasnault *et al.*, nn. 2020, 2237; 'Cronica d'Orvieto', col. 685; 'Cronaca malatestiana', ed. A. F. Massèra, *RISNS* 15², 21; *I libri comm.*, ii, 240, n. 129, 246, n. 156; Filippini, 114–15.

[165] Housley, 'Mercenary Companies', 259; Filippini, 132–3, 149–50, 151–2; 'Cronica di Bologna', col. 447.

[166] Partner, 345; G. Gualdo, 'I libri delle spese di guerra del cardinal Albornoz in Italia conservati nell' Archivio Vaticano', in *El Cardenal Albornoz*, 579–607. For Church taxation see Gasnault *et al.*, *passim*.

[167] *Vita di Cola di Rienzo*, 119, 120; Filippini, 180, 194–5.

[168] *Acta pont. svecica*, i, n. 640; *Codex diplomaticus dominii temporalis Sanctae Sedis*, ed. A. Theiner. 2 vols. (Rome, 1861–2), ii, n. 375.

[169] Ibid. See also Filippini, 307–8, 318.

Peter and Paul to execute his sentence against Bernabò.[170] The crusade was stepped up after the papal victory at the battle of Solara in April 1363, and Albornoz was instructed to preach the crusade both within and outside his legatine area.[171]

During the reign of John XXII, the French court had exerted pressure on the Curia to end its crusades in Italy so that it could concentrate on the launching of an expedition to the eastern Mediterranean.[172] In 1363-4 these events were echoed in the diplomatic efforts of the Kings of France and Cyprus, whose chief agents were Philip of Mézières and Peter Thomas.[173] In May 1363 Urban V relied on Albornoz's judgement as to the feasibility of peace with Bernabò Visconti,[174] and in July he assured the legate that there would be no crusade to the Holy Land until the tyrant was either defeated or reached a peaceful settlement with the Church.[175] In August the Pope seemed determined to carry on with the war,[176] but in September a truce was arranged, and at the end of November Urban turned down an offer of help from Thomas Beauchamp, the Earl of Warwick.[177] Androin de la Roche, a leading representative of the 'doves' at the Curia, was sent to Lombardy as legate in December, and in the summer of 1364 peace was concluded.[178]

It could not last: the territorial dispute between Bernabò and the Church was too complex, mutual suspicion too deep, and the presence of the mercenary companies made war too tempting. When Urban sent his brother, Anglic Grimoard, to Italy as legate at the end of 1367, the new appointment signified a return to the military solution; in May 1368 the crusade against Bernabò was revived, with preaching in Italy, Germany, and Bohemia to enlist soldiers for the expedition of Charles IV.[179] The new war was complicated by the activities of the companies and, in 1369, by the

---

[170] Matteo Villani, bk. 11, ch. 41, ii, 433-4.

[171] LM, n. 383 and cf. nn. 384, 386; *Storia di Milano V: la signoria dei Visconti (1310-1392)*, ed. Fondazione Treccani degli Alfieri (Milan, 1955), 422-3.

[172] See Housley, *Italian Crusades*, 84-7.

[173] Matteo Villani, bk. 11, ch. 32, ii, 428; Jorga, 206-20.

[174] LM, n. 387.

[175] Ibid., n. 535, and see too nn. 470, 510-12, 527-9 for recruitment on behalf of the crusade against Bernabò Visconti.

[176] Ibid., n. 557.   [177] Ibid., n. 682.

[178] Partner, 351-2. Androin was, however, given a faculty to grant the crusade indulgence to people who died fighting for the Church: ASV, Reg. Avin. 156, f. 41ᵛ, n. 37.

[179] *AE*, ad annum 1368, nn. 1-3, xxvi, 150-1; LM, n. 2757.

revolt of Perugia against papal rule. The rebel city hired the soldiers of Sir John Hawkwood, and in February 1370 Anglic Grimoard was given a faculty to preach a crusade against the mercenaries and their employers. This proved successful in bringing about Perugia's submission.[180]

For almost the whole of Gregory XI's reign the Church was at war in Lombardy or Tuscany. It was in these years that the Guelf diplomatic system, strong until 1332 and periodically revivified since, finally collapsed when the Florentines grew so anxious about papal intentions in Tuscany that they turned against the Curia and actively encouraged rebellions in the Papal State (1364–5).[181] Gregory concentrated his efforts on the financing of the war, maintaining taxation of the Church at a very heavy rate.[182] He does not appear to have launched full-scale crusades. Instead he adopted the practice of granting the plenary indulgence *in articulo mortis* to the soldiers of his legates and allies. The first of these grants was issued in August 1372 to the 'retainers, servants, and hired soldiers' of Amedeo of Savoy, who had entered into an agreement with the Pope a month earlier for the supply of 1,000 'lances' against Bernabò and Giangaleazzo Visconti.[183] It was followed by a stream of similar grants up to 1376.[184] These were supplemented by traditional crusade measures such as the commutation of vows and the collection of legacies and ill-gotten gains.[185] The Pope also employed crusading terminology, so that after the defection of Sir John Hawkwood to the papal cause the mercenary captain was somewhat incongruously described as 'a champion of Christ, an athlete of the Lord, and a soldier of the Christian Faith'.[186]

[180] *Codex dipl.*, ed. Theiner, ii, n. 467; 'Cronaca malatestiana', 34; 'Vita Urbani V auctore Wernero canonico ecclesiae Bunnensis', in *VPA*, i, 391; Partner, 355–6.

[181] *Storia di Milano*, 467 ff.; Partner, 358–65; Mirot, 19 ff.

[182] See, for example, *Acta pont. svecica*, ii, nn. 768, 782 ff., 815; Mirot *et al.*, nn. 879, 2395, 2462 and *passim*; Mollat, *Lettres secrètes*, nn. 430–2; J. Glénisson, 'Les Origines de la révolte de l'état pontifical en 1375: les subsides extraordinaires dans les provinces italiennes de l'église au temps de Grégoire XI', *Rivista di storia della Chiesa in Italia*, v (1951), 156–7 and *passim*.

[183] ASV, Reg. Vat. 264, f. 203^{r-v}; *Storia di Milano*, 471; Cox, *Green Count of Savoy*, 267–8.

[184] Mollat, *Lettres secrètes*, nn. 946, 987, 1108, 1615–16, 2191, 2820, 3736, 3816; Mirot *et al.*, nn. 2757, 2923, 3256, 3296, 3837.

[185] Mollat, *Lettres secrètes*, nn. 3745, 3752, 3825, 3840; Mirot *et al.*, nn. 2255, 2275, 2283, 2629, 3172, 3417, 3422, 3790.

[186] *Calendar of Entries in the Papal Registers relating to Great Britain and Ireland: Papal Letters*, comp. W. H. Bliss and J. A. Twemlow. 14 vols. (London, 1893–1960), iv, 118 and cf. 114. See also *Codex dipl.*, ed. Theiner, ii, n. 534.

Crusades against Christian lay rulers were thus an important feature of the crusading movement in the Avignonese period, scarcely less so than in the thirteenth century. There can be no doubt that much of the military and financial muscle of the Church in its Italian wars derived from the use of the crusade as a means of supplementing manpower and revenue. But, as in the case of the other crusades considered in this chapter, it is very hard to gauge the extent to which such extra resources tipped the balance in favour of the papal or Guelf cause. Time and again the historian can trace the issue of the bulls and the levy of the taxes, follow the course of the preaching and the collection of the money, and is then stopped on the threshold of military action by the inadequacy of the sources. Usually the dividing line is the transition from documentary to narrative sources. Detailed as the chroniclers are in their descriptions of the raids, skirmishes, prolonged sieges, and rare pitched battles which constituted warfare in fourteenth-century Italy, they seldom tell us much of the contribution made by crusaders, an approach reflected in modern histories of the period.[187]

Two examples illustrate the problem well. Matteo Villani related that preaching against Francesco Ordelaffi brought Cardinal Albornoz the assistance of many crusaders to supplement the 2,000 hired men-at-arms in the papal army; but how many crusaders there were, and whether they were cavalry or infantry, trained soldiers or armed civilians, is not specified.[188] Writing of the same events, the biographer of Cola di Rienzo mentioned that there were 12,000 crusaders and 30,000 mercenaries.[189] Figures as high as these are very suspect, and although they may reflect the relative importance of the two forces, it is impossible to be sure without corroborating evidence. All we can say with certainty is that the crusaders made enough of a contribution to be noticed by chroniclers, and to cause their Ghibelline enemies to react to their presence with savage hostility.[190]

Even if the response to crusade preaching in Italy had been overwhelming, it would not have brought ultimate victory to the

---

[187] See, for example, the very detailed narrative in the *Storia di Milano*, with its comparatively few references to the crusade on 155–6, 170, 172, 386, 393, 422, 443, 473.

[188] Matteo Villani, bk. 6, ch. 20, i, 483, bk. 6, ch. 45, i, 502. Cf. Filippini, 125n.

[189] *La vita di Cola di Rienzo*, 112.

[190] See, for example, J. Larner, *The Lords of Romagna: Romagnol Society and the Origins of the Signorie* (London, 1965), 92.

Church, because the problems facing the Curia were not just military ones. They included the difficulty of establishing an effective government in the Papal State, the emergence and expansion of a strong Visconti state in Lombardy, and the general instability of Italian politics, which was aggravated by the activities of the mercenary companies. So although he was able to defeat Florence in the War of the Eight Saints and to return to Rome in 1376, Gregory XI was no more successful in his long-term aims than his predecessors had been. Despite their substantial financial resources, and their employment of some of the best captains and most capable administrators of the age, the Avignon popes failed in their Italian policy, which meant that their Italian crusades failed also. There is a striking comparison to be drawn with the failure of their policy in the eastern Mediterranean. There too a number of important victories were achieved, at great cost, which could not be followed through, partly because the crusaders lacked a firm power-base, partly because their enemies were too strong, the problems they faced too complex, and partly because of deep flaws in papal policy itself. It is a similarity which we shall observe at several points in this book, and it is the more interesting because of the way in which the two fronts had been linked in papal thinking about the crusade since the reign of Innocent III. Neither in Italy nor in the East could a crusade be fought to a genuinely successful conclusion; in both cases money spent was, all too often, money wasted.

3

The Making of a Crusade:
Propaganda, Pressure, and Policy

THE crusade was a *negotium Christi*, a war which was fought on
Christ's behalf, and all orthodox Catholics in the fourteenth century
accepted that its promulgation lay in the hands of the *vicarius
Christi*, the pope.[1] By 1300 the juristic underpinning of this authority had been fully elaborated by canon lawyers, who had discussed it in terms of the just war tradition, and the exclusive power
of the pope to grant the crusade indulgence and exercise control
over the crusader's vow.[2] The fourteenth-century legal commen-
tator, Honoré Bonet, reflected a general viewpoint when he wrote
that 'all the great expeditions which were made in times past beyond
the sea, against the Saracens, were made with the consent of the
holy father of Rome; and those who have read the histories of times
past well know this'.[3] This consent, he added, the pope was by no
means bound to give. The pope alone, acting with—but not necessarily in accordance with—the advice of his cardinals, had the
authority to declare a crusade, to have it preached by churchmen,
and to sanction the financing of the war by the collection of Church
taxes and lay oblations.

By a logical extension of this authority, the pope could also cancel
the crusade, call off the preaching, absolve crusaders of their vows
or commute them to the performance of other acts of piety or the
payment of a sum of money. He could halt the collection of crusade
taxes and other sources of revenue, decree the return of what had

---

[1] As Peter Roger put it in a sermon delivered at the Curia in 1333, 'nullus alius
potest passagium generalis [sic] indicere': D. Wood, '*Omnino partialitate cessante*:
Clement VI and the Hundred Years War', in *The Church and War*, ed. W. J. Sheils.
SCH 20 (Oxford, 1983), 188n. Even critics of individual crusades did not deny the
general authority of the pope: see below, ch. 6, nn. 176–7.
[2] See F. H. Russell, *The Just War in the Middle Ages* (Cambridge, 1975), 195 ff.;
Villey, 97–104; Brundage, 90–1, 105–6, 133, and ch. 3 *passim*.
[3] Honoré Bonet, *The Tree of Battles*, tr. G. W. Coopland (Liverpool, 1949), 127.

been collected, or transfer these proceeds to another cause deemed equally important to the Church. This power of cancellation was exercised, sometimes quite dramatically. In March 1336 Benedict XII postponed Philip VI's crusade project and absolved the King of his vow. He wrote that he was taking this step after discussions with cardinals and royal advisers, on the grounds that other nations were incapable of supporting the French effort, while France itself would be put at risk if the King left it for a long period of time. The clerical tenth levied by John XXII on Philip's behalf was cancelled, and the Pope decreed the return of what had been collected.[4] Ten years later Clement VI effectively ended the Smyrna crusade by encouraging Humbert of Vienne to negotiate a truce with the Turks. Again it was discord in the West which prompted Clement's decision: the efforts of the past two years could not be prolonged because the essential flow of men and money had been cut off by such conflicts as the Hundred Years War.[5] For this reason both popes regarded their moves as temporary. Benedict told Philip VI that he was to carry on with his preparations so that he could set out at a later date, and Clement instructed Humbert to restrict his truce with Umur to a maximum length of ten years, hoping that by then peace would be restored in the West.

Papal authority over the crusade was not restricted to the promotion, cancellation, and postponement of expeditions. Two centuries of crusading in a wide variety of settings had infused a certain degree of flexibility into the institution and how it could be handled. This applied above all to the indulgence. The Curia could change the terms of the indulgence to make it more, or less, attractive, thus acting as a spur or a curb on recruitment. In Spain in November 1309 the terms of the indulgence offered to those who fought against the Moors were significantly extended at the urgent request of James II.[6] In 1356 Cardinal Albornoz was permitted to reduce the period of time for which a crusader was supposed to fight in Romagna because, 'as you have informed us, there are many who devoutly want to take part in this salutary endeavour, but who cannot afford to spend a whole year doing so because of their

---

[4] Vidal and Mollat, n. 786. Cf. Daumet, nn. 210, 260; Vidal, nn. 3954–5, 5139–40.

[5] Déprez *et al.*, nn. 2956–7.

[6] *Reg. Clem. V*, nn. 5092–3. For the nature of the extension see below, ch. 4, nn. 60–2.

poverty or for other genuine reasons'.[7] And in 1363 Albornoz was again allowed to shorten the specified period of service, besides subdividing the twelve months in such a way that they could be served over several years.[8] The pope could also extend the preaching of the crusade to fresh Church provinces to bolster recruitment. He could introduce extra provisions which, especially in the sphere of finance, could make a big difference to a crusade already under way. Lastly, he could divert resources from one project to another, by authorizing the commutation and redemption of crusade vows.[9]

Many of these refinements dated back to the reign of Innocent III and on paper they look impressive. But in practice they were subject to two major limitations. One relates to the nature of the crusade as a voluntary enterprise largely dependent on the enthusiasm of the laity and the readiness to co-operate of the clergy. A crusader could not, for instance, be ordered to fight for a cause different from that for which he had taken the cross, and modifications introduced when an expedition was in progress often led to confusion and irritation amongst Church and laity.[10] Men-at-arms whose vows were cancelled, deferred, or made subject to redemption became disillusioned, cynical, and apathetic, and churchmen too regularly taxed or burdened with crusade preaching became recalcitrant and lax. After the problems which had arisen in this regard in the thirteenth century, the Avignonese Curia was driven to use its powers with discretion.

The second major limitation on the exercise of papal authority was the attitude of the secular powers. Both the crusader and the taxpaying ecclesiastic were the subjects of lay rulers, and in the fourteenth century such rulers had the steadily increasing ability to control their subjects' movements and actions. If it was inconvenient for a king that his fighting men and administrators go

---

[7] Gasnault *et al.*, n. 2020. For the use which Albornoz made of this faculty, see Matteo Villani, bk. 7, ch. 80, ii, 69–70, bk. 7, ch. 84, ii, 72–3.

[8] 'Et quia idem terminus dicti anni continui aliquibus forsan nimis longus et incommodus redderetur, aut forsitan ipsum annum interpolatum infra duos annos complere non possent, Nos de tue eximie circumspectionis industria et fide preclara in hiis et aliis plenarie confidentes, fraternitati tue abreviandi dictum annum et eum interpolatum extendendi ultra dictum biennium, aliquibus tamen specialibus personis cum eadem venia si et prout tibi videbitur expedire plenam concedimus tenore presentium facultatem': ASV, Reg. Vat. 245, f. 146^{r-v}.

[9] For examples of commutation and redemption see below, ch. 4, nn. 147–62.

[10] See, for example, Housley, *Italian Crusades*, 129n. In 1323 Charles IV asked that the terms of the indulgence issued on behalf of his planned *passagium* be made quite clear: CC, n. 1685.

on crusade, then his officials and his civil lawyers gave him the power and the legal arguments to stop them going. Almost all the wide-ranging aspects of papal authority mentioned earlier were heavily qualified by this consideration, starting with their keystone, the pope's right to launch crusades. The pope might have the power to proclaim a crusade, but it meant little if publicity, preaching, and the ability to tax were denied him. And theory was catching up with practice, in that secular rulers were beginning to assert that their consent was an essential prerequisite to the declaration of any crusade which would affect them. Thus in 1335 Alfonso IV of Aragon argued that, while the pope enjoyed *plenitudo potestatis* in crusading matters, in practice he did not launch a general passage without convening a meeting of secular rulers to gain their approval.[11]

The fourteenth century was rich in vetoes on crusading activity imposed by lay powers, most notably the French Crown.[12] In 1307 Charles of Valois explained to the Venetians that he could not recruit soldiers, collect his crusade tenth, or even leave France himself to fight the Greeks, because of the impending conflict with Flanders.[13] Two years later French knights on their way to Granada to fight the Moors were prevented from crossing the frontier on the grounds of Philip IV's decree against the export of horses, arms, and money.[14] In 1331 Philip VI put pressure on the Pope not to grant the crusade indulgence to French nobles who wanted to fight in Spain, and in 1345 the King refused to allow either Bertrand des Baux or Bishop Raymond of Thérouanne to take up their appointments as captain of the papal galleys and legate in the Smyrna crusade.[15] And in 1376 Charles V prohibited all French men-at-arms from going to Prussia, the eastern Mediterranean, or anywhere else outside France without first obtaining royal permission.[16]

The French Crown was not the only offender. In May 1309

---

[11] *Documenta selecta*, n. 509.

[12] Cf. P. Contamine, *Guerre, état et société à la fin du Moyen Âge: Études sur les armées des rois de France 1337–1494* (Paris–La Haye, 1972), 4–5.

[13] *DVL*, i, n. 32.

[14] *AA*, iii, n. 93.

[15] *CC*, n. 4514; Déprez *et al.*, n. 1704.

[16] *Mandements et actes divers de Charles V (1364–1380)*, ed. L. Delisle (Paris, 1874), n. 1263. In peacetime rulers actively encouraged their nobles to travel abroad to gain experience and establish a reputation which would redound to their lords' advantage: Keen, *Chivalry*, 224–7.

Clement V complained that James II of Aragon had forbidden Hospitaller Knights and other fighting men in his territories to desert the forthcoming campaign against Granada in favour of the Order's *passagium* to the East, and that the King had banned the export of arms and horses.[17] In 1345 Alfonso of Portugal informed Clement VI that he would not permit any of his men-at-arms to accompany Louis de la Cerda on his expedition to the Canaries because they were all needed in the struggle against Granada.[18] At times crusade preaching was stopped at the urgent request, or demand, of the local lay power, as in 1336, when Benedict XII postponed preaching in Cyprus until an expedition actually set out from the West: King Hugh had written that preaching was of little use at the moment and only provoked the Muslims.[19] A halt was also called to preaching in Cyprus in 1346 and 1351,[20] and in 1345 Clement VI acceded to Philip VI's request that the indulgences for Smyrna should not be preached in France because of the Anglo-French war.[21] These instances exclude the occasions on which preaching was not set in motion at all because it was clear that it would meet with oppposition from the officials of the lay power.

As with men, so too with specie. Philip IV's measures against Boniface VIII had shown that it was possible even in a large kingdom with a long land frontier to place and enforce severe restrictions on the export of coinage and precious metals; and he was by no means the first to take such steps.[22] Faced with wars of their own, many fourteenth-century rulers impeded the transference of crusade funds. In 1317 English officials were stopping papal agents from collecting legacies and donations for the crusade, and in 1363 collectors met with similar obstacles in Hungary; the ramshackle nature of contemporary administration enabled both Edward II and Louis to feign ignorance of what was going on, but it was clearly royal policy in both cases.[23] Such rulers were not antipathetic to the crusade: Edward often talked of going on

---

[17] *Cartulaire général de l'Ordre des Hospitaliers de S. Jean de Jérusalem (1100–1310)*, ed. J. Delaville le Roulx. 4 vols. (Paris, 1894–1906), iv, n. 4860. Fulk of Villaret had predicted that this would happen: ibid., iv, n. 4681.

[18] Déprez *et al.*, n. 1317.

[19] Vidal and Mollat, nn. 732–3.

[20] Déprez and Mollat, nn. 1081, 2496.

[21] Déprez *et al.*, n. 1704. See also Wood, 189.

[22] See Purcell, 156–7, for examples from England, Scotland, Norway, Sweden, and Aragon.

[23] *Cal. of Entries*, ii, 132; *VMH*, ii, nn. 98–9.

crusade with the French king, and we have seen how deeply involved Louis became with the movement.[24] But they could not afford the draining off of men and money which a crusade entailed. Philip VI's indecisiveness when Peter de la Palu, his Seneschal of Beaucaire, took the cross in 1344, is a good example of the conflict between a genuine desire to support the crusade, and the need to provide for a major office of state.[25] Much the same can be said of his refusal to allow the Count of Eu, his Constable, to absent himself from France in order to carry out a vow of fighting in Granada.[26] What often tipped the balance against the crusade was the escalation of conflict within Christendom, as shown by the papal letters of 1336 and 1346 cited earlier.

The attitude of the Venetians calls for special treatment. With Genoa incapacitated by civil discord for much of our period, and Pisa in decline as a naval power, the importance of Venice as the provider of shipping for a crusade to the East increased; the city was also well placed to help or hinder the papal forces operating in Lombardy and Romagna. On three notable occasions Venice actively obstructed crusading enterprises. In 1346 its authorities were preventing people taking ship for Smyrna—ironically, a crusade which the Republic had itself initially promoted.[27] Ten years later Innocent VI complained that the Doge had forbidden preaching at Venice against Francesco Ordelaffi, and was hindering the transport of supplies by sea, 'even from the Church's own lands', for the use of the papal army outside Forlì.[28] And in 1366 the Republic prohibited the use of Venetian ships to carry men-at-arms, horses, armour, timber, and supplies to Cyprus, ordering too that if Peter of Cyprus made another attack on Mamluk lands, the Venetian *bailli* in Cyprus was to forbid any Venetian subject to accompany it.[29]

Venetian action in all three cases was dictated not by a general dislike of crusading enterprises, but by the fact that the city's own interests were imperilled. In 1346 the government was reacting to the threat of a shortage of manpower, while in 1366 it was desperately trying to repair the damage caused to its commercial

[24] *AE*, ad annum 1317, nn. 45–6, xxiv, 63–4; *Cal. of Entries*, ii, 423, 439; above, ch. 2, nn. 140–50.

[25] Déprez *et al.*, nn. 674–5, 708, 1524–30, 1639. For Peter, see Cazelles, 274.

[26] Mollat, *Lettres communes*, n. 54386.

[27] Déprez and Mollat, n. 1273; Déprez *et al.*, n. 2956.

[28] Gasnault *et al.*, n. 2216, and cf. n. 2227. [29] Mas Latrie, ii, 285–9.

relations with Egypt by the sack of Alexandria. Most interesting is
the tangled web of considerations which shaped Venice's opposition to the Romagna crusade. This is revealed by the correspondence between Venice and Innocent VI in 1356–7. The
background was formed by Louis of Hungary's proposal for a
crusade against Serbia—which would also be directed against
Venice—and by papal hopes of renewing the Clementine league
and bolstering the defence of Smyrna.[30] Thus, while Innocent
wanted to remain on good terms with Venice, he also wanted
maximum coverage for his crusade preaching, an end to Venetian
trade with Ghibelline cities in Romagna, and the unopposed provisioning of his army. Venice, on the other hand, needed to placate
the Pope in order to prevent the grant of crusade privileges to
Louis,[31] but it feared that a Church victory in Romagna would
benefit Hungary; in addition, as the Doge pointed out, the
Republic's economic ties with Romagna were vitally important.[32]
To complicate the situation still further, both powers were profiting
from a triangular arrangement for the transfer of funds between
Venice, Avignon, and Barcelona.[33] The net result was a highly
apologetic Venice, and the avoidance of a head-on clash like those
which had occurred in similar circumstances in the past.[34]

But lay powers did not simply impose limitations on papal
authority in the negative sense of presenting obstacles to its exercise. They also began to encroach on that authority itself, and in this
respect the fourteenth century marked a significant advance. For if
secular rulers objected to crusades at certain times, they approved
of and eagerly sought them at others. Waging holy war was an
attractive prospect because of the extra resources which it placed at
the disposal of a king or prince. Apart from the material resources,
which form a major theme of this book, there were less tangible, but
nonetheless important assets such as prestige, the various benefits
of papal backing, and the spiritual value of prayers and processions.[35] That these too were considered worth having is shown by

[30] See Gasnault *et al.*, nn. 2006, 2015, 2088, 2233.

[31] Ibid., nn. 2230, 2267, 2272–3.

[32] *I libri comm.*, ii, 257–9, nn. 207, 211, 214, 216.

[33] Ibid., ii, 221, n. 35, 244–5, n. 148, 248, n. 164, 257–8, n. 208.

[34] Gasnault *et al.*, n. 2216; Housley, *Italian Crusades*, 111.

[35] In 1360 Albornoz ordered that prayers be said after the 'Pater noster' during
Mass throughout Italy on behalf of the Church's struggle against Bernabò Visconti:
Matteo Villani, bk. 10, ch. 2, ii, 308. Cf. Brundage, 157–8.

the efforts made by rulers to give their enterprises a 'sacred' quality without trying to get them officially declared crusades. Important individuals and institutions such as universities were approached to assert publicly that a war was just, Church prayers for victory were demanded, and successes were celebrated by thanksgiving services and ex-voto offerings.[36]

In this propaganda conflict the crusade remained a potent reference point and was often deployed. In 1302 an unknown French cleric preached a sermon in support of Philip IV's war in Flanders which illustrates the two chief ways in which this could be done. First, by placing the Flemish conflict in the context of the great achievements of the French monarchy on behalf of the Church, a case could be made for viewing it as a type of holy war. Secondly, the settlement of the dispute in Flanders was essential if Philip the Fair was to lead a crusade to recover the Holy Land, so the French were conducting a form of preliminary crusade in the West. The conclusion was that 'he who wages war against the King [of France] works against the whole Church, against Catholic doctrine, against holiness and justice, and against the Holy Land'.[37] This was only the tip of an iceberg of official and semi-official propaganda emanating from France in the decades after 1270, which made full use of the tradition of St Louis and Charles of Anjou.[38]

The ground was thus well prepared for French propaganda in the early phase of the Hundred Years War. Apart from the defence of the realm from unprovoked attack, its major themes were the delay which this had caused to Philip VI's crusade plans, and the fact that Edward III was allied with the heretical Louis IV. Such were the aspects which Philip told his bishops to stress in their sermons in 1337.[39] Three years later, in his reply to Edward III's challenge to a

---

[36] See H. J. Hewitt, *The Organization of War under Edward III 1338–62* (Manchester, 1966), 160–5; W. R. Jones, 'The English Church and Royal Propaganda during the Hundred Years War', *Journal of British Studies*, xix (1979), 18–30.

[37] J. Leclerq, 'Un Sermon prononcé pendant la guerre de Flandre sous Philippe le Bel', *Revue du moyen âge latin*, i (1945), 165–72, with quotation at 170. See also E. H. Kantorowicz, *The King's Two Bodies: A Study in Medieval Political Theology* (Princeton, 1957), 249–55.

[38] See J. R. Strayer, 'France: the Holy Land, the Chosen People, and the Most Christian King', in T. K. Rabb and J. E. Seigel (eds.), *Action and Conviction in Early Modern Europe* (Princeton, 1969), 3–16; J. N. Hillgarth, *Ramon Lull and Lullism in Fourteenth-Century France* (London, 1971), 106–13.

[39] Henneman, *Royal Taxation . . . 1322–1356*, 129.

duel, Philip asserted that the English King's wilful and unjust war had held up the crusade, and constituted an affront to the Church.[40] But these themes were not pursued with as much vigour as one might expect, either because they were rather hackneyed or because Philip was wary of making too much use of a project whose postponement had given rise to a wave of popular indignation against himself. After sixty years of frequent use, French crusade-related propaganda was wearing thin.

In fact it was Edward III who made most imaginative propaganda use of the crusade. He centred his arguments on two claims: that Philip VI had used his crusade plans as cover for warlike preparations against England, and that he himself had genuine crusade aspirations which Philip was impeding. Edward thus countered the tradition of St Louis with a rival English tradition based on the reputation of his grandfather, Edward I. The first claim can be seen in Edward's comment of 1340 that Philip was attacking England 'with the ships, which he had pretended to be preparing for a holy passage overseas'.[41] Its impact is visible in the passage from Henry Knighton already quoted.[42] As for Edward's own aspirations for a crusade, these were cited in 1335, 1339, and 1340.[43] The cleverest use of this theme was in 1339, when Edward expressed sympathy for the Christians overseas who were being ill-treated by the Sultan because of the crusade supposedly planned by Philip VI.[44] Edward's advantage was that since his government had put forward no actual plans for a crusade, as the French court had repeatedly done over the previous decades, it was not tainted by failure and could arouse real expectations as a centre of activity, especially once English military prowess had been demonstrated in the early victories of the war. Of course nothing could be done while England was at war, but there are signs that Edward was placed in an

---

[40] Thomas Walsingham, 'Historia anglicana', ed. H. T. Riley. *RS*. 2 vols. (London, 1863–4), i, 229–30.

[41] Ibid., i, 219. Cf. the King's comment in 1337: 'galiotas et alias naves guerrinas quas fecit sub colore ficto praefati passagii fabricare, versus Angliam destinavit, et captas plurimas naves Anglicanas submerserunt, necnon partes Australes insulae eiusdem hostiliter invaserunt, rapinas, homicidia et incendia perpetrantes': Canon of Bridlington, 'Gesta Edwardi III', ed. W. Stubbs. *RS* (London, 1883), 132.

[42] Ch. 1, n. 43.

[43] Henry Knighton, i, 476; Thomas Walsingham, i, 201; Vidal and Mollat, n. 2981. See also *Les Grandes Chroniques de France*, ed. J. Viard. 9 vols. (Paris, 1920–37), ix, 134.

[44] Thomas Walsingham, i, 201.

awkward situation by the Treaty of Brétigny: Walsingham related that knights from Spain, Cyprus, and Armenia came to the Smithfield tournament of 1362 to ask the King to aid their countries against the Muslims.[45]

In such circumstances could the crusade itself be safe from the manipulation of lay rulers such as the kings of England and France? In 1360, following the French attack on Winchelsea in the previous year, all English males between the ages of sixteen and sixty were arrayed for the defence of the country against a possible French attack. Henry Knighton added that 'the archbishops and bishops granted great indulgences throughout their sees to all who journeyed to the coast to defend the Kingdom against its enemies, and allowed each of them to choose his own confessor at will'.[46] We can conclude that partial indulgences were granted for the defence of the realm, and it is quite possible that other instances of this could be found for both England and France, particularly the latter, where the English threat could be assimilated to that posed by the *routiers*. In such passages as the above we have clear signs of the onset of the 'national crusades' which occurred during the Great Schism.[47] It was of course the Schism which made such a development possible, but its role was that of a catalyst: the essential preconditions, in terms of governmental aims, the readiness of the clergy to assist the lay powers, and popular acceptance of crusading against a national enemy, were all fully developed by 1378. Partial indulgences like those issued in 1360, together with the aggressive use of the crusade for propaganda purposes, and the diversion into the Anglo-French war of revenue, arms, and shipping intended for the crusade to the East, added up to a substantial threat to papal authority.

It is important not to exaggerate this development, because under the Avignon papacy the central core of that authority remained intact. The full crusade indulgence, the administration of vows, the official preaching of the cross, were all to be obtained only by persuading the Curia to issue the relevant bulls. This meant that although the popes themselves initiated crusade projects comparatively rarely, and were often subject to extraordinary diplo-

---

[45] Ibid., i, 296–7.   [46] Henry Knighton, ii, 110.
[47] See E. Perroy, *L'Angleterre et le Grand Schisme d'occident* (Paris, 1933), 166–209; A. K. McHardy, 'The English Clergy and the Hundred Years War', in *The Church and War*, 171–8.

matic pressure, their Curia retained its traditional role in the launching of a crusade, functioning as a clearing-house of crusade plans and ideas. A crusade was 'made'—in the sense that the all-important bulls were issued—as the result of the interaction of papal policy with the co-operation or active push of a wide range of lay rulers. The working of this complicated mechanism of commitment varied from front to front, and they need to be examined separately. At the end it will be possible to reach a conclusion about the overall part played by the Curia.

From the point of view of the initiation of a crusade, Spain and eastern Europe had several similarities. Helmut Roscher, in his analysis of the crusading policy of Innocent III, concluded that these were the theatres over which that Pope and his successors had least control.[48] A similar conclusion was reached in a recent book on the crusades promoted by the Teutonic Order in Prussia: the popes of the thirteenth century would have liked to exert greater influence on these campaigns, but a stream of legates proved unable to implement the theocratic aims of their masters.[49] The same was true of the Avignon popes, who rarely if ever took the first steps in initiating a crusade against either the Moors of Granada and their Merinid allies, or the Lithuanians, Tatars, and other pagans between the Baltic and the Black Sea. The Curia relied on the secular powers *in situ* to take the lead in crusading matters; above all, it was kings, of Castile, Aragon, Portugal, Majorca, Poland, and Hungary, whose initiative lay behind the campaigns.

There were two connected reasons for this. First, it was the acknowledged responsibility of the Christian king to defend his Church and people against attack, and the bulls to Casimir of Poland show that the Curia fully acceded in the protective role of the monarch.[50] It followed from this that a king who took his coronation and anointing seriously would object to papal intervention on a regular basis. There was a potential clash here between the rights of a king, and the authority of the pope in the *negotium Christi*, but it was one which in Spain had already been resolved in the king's favour, and papal relations with Hungary and Poland

---

[48] H. Roscher, *Papst Innocenz III. und die Kreuzzüge* (Göttingen, 1969), 181–91, 198–213.

[49] Christiansen, ch. 5 *passim*. Cf. Purcell, 88–91.

[50] *VMP*, i, nn. 604–5, 702–3, 713, 742, 833, 882.

followed much the same course. Secondly, the Curia was conscious of its own ignorance of the detailed local situation. It could remedy this only by sending agents to the spot to submit lengthy reports, or by ordering the local clergy to keep it informed. Neither method proved satisfactory. The nuncio Galhard de Carceribus sent detailed accounts of the situation in Poland, but they were biased in favour of the Poles and their demands.[51] According to allies of the Teutonic Knights, Galhard and his fellow nuncio Peter Gervasii were 'the special friends, virtually the retainers, of the Kings of Hungary and Poland'.[52] Similarly, John Guilbert, Clement VI's nuncio in Sweden, may have become committed to King Magnus's policies from 1350.[53]

If nuncios could be won over in this way, there was little hope of receiving objective reports from the local clergy. In July 1310 Clement V responded to Ferdinand of Castile's request for fresh Church aid by ordering the Archbishops of Compostella, Toledo, and Seville to convene provincial councils to advise the Pope about the course he should follow. The reply of the clergy of Seville clearly demonstrated that the King had no cause to worry about his Church's disloyalty. Their report praised Ferdinand's achievements in glowing colours:

Once he had manfully expelled the enemies of the Faith, he acquired the fortress called in the vernacular Gibraltar. The fruits of this conquest have provided much exultation and profit to all Christians, as well as bringing terror and lamentation to the filthy nations of the Saracens.

It was now necessary to close the Straits, and for that purpose, 'although the churches and churchmen of this Kingdom are oppressed by great poverty for the reasons given above', they advised Clement to levy a tenth and *tercias* on the Castilian church 'for such a period of time as your sanctity should see fit'. The tax should also be imposed in Portugal.

Because of these considerations, and with the help of these subsidies, we firmly believe and hope that, with the Lord's help, the filthy nation of

[51] Ibid., i, n. 519; Knoll, *RPM*, 93–5.
[52] *Codex diplomaticus prussicus*, ed. J. Voigt. 6 vols. (Königsberg, 1836–61), iii, n. 21.
[53] P. Riant, *Expéditions et pèlerinages des Scandinaves en Terre Sainte au temps des Croisades* (Paris, 1865), 404–6.

Saracens living in the said Kingdom will shortly be wiped out, and the Kingdom brought into the orthodox Faith.[54]

Even reports like this must have been of value, however, since Clement V complained in 1310 that the Archbishop of Braga was not continuing his predecessors' policy of keeping the Curia informed of Muslim threats to Castile and how they could be countered.[55] And in 1326 John XXII, suspicious that there might be ulterior motives behind the young Alfonso XI's recent foundation of a crusading confraternity at Seville, told the city's archbishop and others to send him details of its membership, aims, and characteristics.[56]

It was another matter when the civil power was weak. On such occasions the Curia took a greater part in organizing the defence of a region on the periphery of Christendom, measures which often involved the deployment of the crusade. This was the case, for example, in Castile during the minority of Alfonso XI. John XXII gave his full support to the promotion of a crusade by the Infantes Peter and John in 1317–19, authorizing preaching, levying a subsidy on the Castilian church, issuing a special prohibition of trade with Granada, and endeavouring to prevent discord between the regency government and the nobility.[57] After the defeat and death of the two regents in 1319 the Pope continued to give valuable support, acting through his legate, William of Sabina. Crusade funds were released for the defence of the realm, indulgences preached on behalf of Lorca, and the garrison duties of the Military Orders stepped up. Active papal involvement in Castilian affairs continued until Alfonso reached his majority in 1325.[58]

The kings of Spain and eastern Europe secured crusading aid for

[54] ASV, Instrumenta miscellanea, n. 490, *a.* 1311 (misdated in *Reg. Clem. V*, n. 10455). Quotations in text are as follows: 'Castrum illud quod Gibraltar vulgariter appellatur, expulsis inde fidei inimicis, viriliter acquisivit. Cuius acquisitionis beneficium non solum universis et singulis qui Christi nomine vocantur exultationis et utilitatis non modice dedit initium, sed sarracenorum fetidis nationibus terrorem intulit et lamentum . . . Hiis ergo considerationibus et subsidiis oportunis firma credulitate speramus, favente domino, quod agarenorum fetida natio que dictum Regnum inhabitat in brevi poterit extirpari et Regnum predictum perduci ad cultum fidei orthodoxe.'

[55] *Reg. Clem. V*, n. 6379.

[56] Goñi Gaztambide, 644–5.

[57] *AE*, ad annum 1318, n. 36, xxiv, 90; Mollat, *Lettres communes*, nn. 2924–5, 7328–33, 8021, 8026–7, 8339.

[58] Ibid., nn. 12620, 14213–15, 14284–6. See also Fernández Conde and Oliver, 'La corte pontificia', 364.

their projects by presenting petitions (*supplicationes*), setting out in detail the requests of the rulers, and argued at Avignon by well briefed and often resourceful envoys.[59] What they wanted was all or part of the wide range of privileges, spiritual, legal, and financial, which had become attached to the status of crusader, and particularly that of crusading king. In July 1309, for example, the *supplicationes* of James II of Aragon were as follows: an improvement in the terms of the indulgence granted to those who fought in, or contributed money to, the royal army; faculties for the Bishop of Valencia to commute vows and provide absolution to the financial benefit of the crusade; the quicker transfer of crusade funds to the royal treasury; and permission for the Bishop of Valencia to give the cross to knights from southern France and Navarre who wanted to fight in Granada.[60] The importance of financial measures is clear from the petition presented to John XXII by the Kings of Castile and Portugal in 1330. The Pope was to grant them a double clerical tenth lasting five years, to levy a tax of annates, also for five years, to cede a percentage of intercalary fruits for four years, and to transfer alien priests holding Castilian and Portuguese benefices, who were objecting to such swingeing taxation.[61]

Petitions from Poland and Hungary followed a similar pattern. Typical was the *rotulus regis Polonie* of June 1363, which requested crusading indulgences and privileges for those who helped Casimir to defend the Kingdom against the assaults of Lithuanians, Tatars, and other infidels and schismatics.[62] At other times Casimir asked for the grant of partial indulgences to Christians who prayed for him and for his crusading endeavours, for papal pressure on neighbouring kings to help Poland defend its neophytes from attack by pagan Lithuanians, and, at the end of 1350, for a personal grant of the Jubilee Indulgence on the grounds that the King had been actively engaged in war against the pagans since June, and had been unable to go to Rome.[63] Louis of Hungary's earliest *supplicatio*, in 1342, was for the renewal of a grant of the plenary indulgence *in articulo mortis* to his subjects who fell while fighting Hungary's non-

---

[59] Not all have survived, despite a ruling that incoming correspondence be preserved 'in archivio curiae romanae': *Acta Inn. VI*, n. 93.

[60] *Documenta selecta*, n. 148.

[61] *AE*, ad annum 1330, n. 44, xxiv, 452.

[62] *Acta Urbani V*, n. 29, and cf. n. 29a.

[63] *Analecta Vaticana 1202–1366*, ed. J. Ptasnik. Monumenta Poloniae Vaticana iii (Cracow, 1914), nn. 336, 347, 375.

Catholic neighbours, as well as for permission for his soldiers to eat meat during Lent if necessary, on nutritional grounds.[64]

In the presentation of such petitions tactics played a large part. There were powerful arguments to be put across, such as the declaration of crusading zeal, the invocation of tradition, and the assertion of financial need. All three are apparent in the preamble to the requests submitted by Alfonso XI of Castile in March 1328:

Most holy father, you well know in your wisdom and prudence to what extent we desire, above all, to serve God and bring honour to the Catholic Faith with all our might, as a true son of the Church and a Catholic Christian, and to suppress and smash the faithless and loathsome race of the Saracens, the enemies of the true Faith, just as did the kings from whom we are known to descend. Since the revenues of our kingdoms will not be enough to carry out such a difficult and holy enterprise in a fitting manner, and hoping to secure timely aid through the grace and generosity of the Apostolic See, we have had our envoys petition you, that your holiness should mercifully agree to grant certain concessions which are expedient to ourselves, our kingdoms, and our subjects.[65]

The appeal to precedent was particularly important, not just in Spain but also in eastern Europe: when a papal collector in Scandinavia submitted a request to John XXII for crusade indulgences on behalf of the Swedes, he cited Alexander III's crusading bull against the pagans of the Baltic littoral.[66]

There were other tactics of value. Promises could function as subtle bribes, such as Louis of Hungary's assurance in 1355–6 that his conquest of schismatic Serbia would lead to its reunion with Rome, or the suggestion of Polish envoys in 1351 that the successful defence of the newly conquered provinces in Ruthenia would result in the foundation of eight new sees, one of them metropolitan.[67] There were also warnings, such as Vladislav Lokietek's reminder to John XXII in 1324 that a Tatar conquest of Poland would rob the Curia of its annual receipts of Peter's Pence, and crude threats, like James of Aragon's assertion in 1309 that public opinion would blame the Pope if the King had to end his crusade in Granada through lack of papal support.[68] Similarly, Alfonso IV's contacts

---

[64] *Acta Clementis VI*, ed. A. L. Tautu. PCRCICO, ix (Rome, 1960), nn. 1, 1a. Cf. *VMH*, i, n, 871.

[65] *AE*, ad annum 1328, n. 76, xxiv, 377.

[66] *Acta pont. svecica*, i, n. 191.

[67] *AE*, ad annum 1356, nn. 24–6, xxvi, 11–13; *VMP*, i, n. 702.

[68] *AE*, ad annum 1324, n. 53, xxiv, 273–4; *AA*, ii, n. 482.

with extra-peninsular rulers in 1328–31 may well have been intended to exert pressure on the Pope to grant Aragonese demands.[69] More welcome at the Curia were detailed reports of success, which could be sent to Avignon to encourage the grant of further privileges. Thus Charles-Robert of Hungary sent news of his victory over the Tatars to John XXII in 1331,[70] and in 1341 Alfonso XI sent Benedict XII full details of his victory at the Salado river, together with captured Muslims and enemy standards, the Castilian royal standard, and the King's horse.[71] An Italian chronicler even claimed that Alfonso sent the Pope a full tenth of his booty, 160,000 florins; but Alfonso's money problems, and the absence of a papal letter of thanks make this very unlikely.[72] In August 1366 Urban V was presented with a captured Mamluk standard, and other booty from Alexandria, by an envoy of Peter of Cyprus.[73] The demonstration of gratitude for past favours thus paved the way for future requests.

The Avignonese Curia favoured petitions which put their case in terms of military need, of Christians and their property threatened by infidel aggression: the just war tradition continued to exercise a strong grip on papal thinking about the crusade.[74] Thus in 1324 King Vladislav of Poland related how, since the deaths of the last two princes of Ruthenia, the Tatars had pressed hard on Poland's frontiers, and it was necessary to stop them occupying the Principality to the detriment of his Kingdom's security. He asked for help 'in crusade preaching and other forms of aid'.[75] In 1326 Magnus of Sweden asked for the grant of crusading taxes to help him resist the mounting attacks of pagan tribes adjoining his lands.[76] A request from Poland in 1351 described an alliance between the Lithuanians and Tatars which threatened to devastate all Poland, and in 1369 Casimir of Poland was granted a crusade tenth to rebuild four castles destroyed in a pagan raid on the diocese of Cracow.[77] The picture presented by this characteristic sample of

[69] See Fernández Conde and Oliver, 'La corte pontificia', 364.

[70] *VMH*, i, n. 845.

[71] *AE*, ad annum 1341, n. 2, xxv, 225–6; 'Prima vita Benedicti XII', 202; 'Crónica de Alfonso XI', 330–1.

[72] See Goñi Gaztambide, 331.

[73] 'Vita Urbani V auctore Wernero', 387; *Délibérations*, ii, 38.

[74] See Riley-Smith, *What were the Crusades?*, ch. 2 *passim*.

[75] *AE*, ad annum 1324, n. 53, xxiv, 273–4.

[76] *Acta pont. svecica*, i, n. 207.

[77] *VMP*, i, nn. 702, 882.

supplicationes is that of an embattled Christian frontier struggling against pagan aggression.

The same picture emerges from most of the Spanish petitions. In 1316 the Catholics of the Balearic Islands were granted indulgences, at the request of their King, to defend themselves against North African pirates.[78] The Muslim recapture of Gibraltar in 1333 led to petitions from Alfonso XI stressing the strategic importance of the lost port.[79] Seven years later the crusade preaching and tenths granted to Alfonso XI followed the exposition by the King of the build-up of Merinid forces to avenge a recent defeat.[80] Like the kings of eastern Europe, the Spanish monarchs sometimes resorted to somewhat flimsy arguments in their search for a defensive cause to back up their petitions. Early in 1345 Alfonso of Portugal asked for crusade taxes for the defence of the realm, basing his request on the claim that since Castile's truce with the Moors, the full weight of Merinid power would be directed westwards.[81] In 1309 James II's envoy argued before the Curia that the Moors of Granada and their co-religionists in Morocco were growing restless because of plans for a general passage to the Holy Land, even though this would have little or no effect on them.[82]

But the grand theme of *defensio Christiane fidei* was accompanied by a less regular, but still impressive, counterpoint of *dilatatio Christiane fidei*, a war of expansion aimed at extending the Faith. This played an important role in the Spanish crusade petitions, so that in 1343 and 1346 Alfonso XI could be granted indulgences and taxes to help with the expenses first of besieging and then of defending Algeciras, whose capture and defence for Christianity were viewed in terms of expansion.[83] Portugal's reply to Clement VI's request for aid for Louis de la Cerda in 1345 referred to the country's efforts in 'the defence and extension of the Faith' in Iberia.[84] Spain, of course, was somewhat special since all the crusades there, whatever their immediate goal, fitted into the long-term context of the recovery of a once Christian land, but *dilatatio*

---

[78] *AE*, ad annum 1316, n. 26, xxiv, 41.

[79] John XXII was probably adopting a Castilian phrase when he described Gibraltar as 'clavis potissima regni tui': Goñi Gaztambide, 314n.

[80] *AE*, ad annum 1340, nn. 40–3, xxv, 205–6.

[81] Ibid., ad annum 1344, n. 53, xxv, 347–8.

[82] *AA*, ii, n. 477.

[83] ASV, Reg. Vat. 137, f. 127ʳ, n. 435; *AE*, ad annum 1346, nn. 61–2, xxv, 400–1.

[84] Déprez *et al.*, n. 1317.

also made occasional appearances in petitions and bulls relating to eastern and northern Europe.

One crusade which poses undeniable problems of legal interpretation is Louis de la Cerda's projected conquest of the Canary Islands. Clement VI's enfeoffment of the Prince in November 1344 implied that the Pope adhered to the view of papal authority over pagans which had been expounded by Hostiensis: that with the coming of Christ all lawful lordship was transferred to the faithful, and that the pope had the right to deprive non-believers of their lands and vest them in a Christian prince. While this right was not to be abused, one acceptable reason for exercising it was the promotion of missionary activity, and Louis's crusade was justified in terms of his solemn undertaking to construct and endow churches for the conversion of his subjects:

Divine mercy has appointed us as gardener and guardian of the vineyard of the Lord of Sabaoth, and we seek not only to protect it, lest it should be harmed by the incursions of evil beasts, but also to extend its cultivation. Willingly therefore, and as far as we can with God's aid, we grant appropriate favours and honours to those who show themselves assiduous and devout labourers for the spread of the vine's cultivation—that is, of God's holy Church.[85]

This does not, however, explain the Pope's reference to the inhabitants of the Islands as 'enemies of the Christian Faith',[86] unless they had already proved hostile to missionaries sent there, which we would expect to be mentioned. Clement VI's treatment of the Canary Islands project remains a rare and puzzling example of the survival of the tradition of Hostiensis at a Curia whose policies were largely in accordance with the more moderate views of Innocent IV about the property rights of pagans.[87] It is possible that Clement was more sympathetic towards this tradition than other Avignonese popes: in 1343 he even included *dilatatio fidei* amongst the goals of the Order of St John, and it is notable how rapidly the idea of *dilatatio* entered his approach towards the Smyrna crusade.[88]

Apart from the merits of the project itself, three main considera-

---

[85] Ibid., n. 1314. Cf. Muldoon, *Popes, Lawyers and Infidels*, 15–18.

[86] *VPA*, ii, 428. Cf. Thomas Walsingham's comment that 'incolae non sunt Christiani nec de secta Machometi': i, 265.

[87] Muldoon, *Popes, Lawyers and Infidels*, 88–91 and cf. 104, 134–5.

[88] Déprez *et al.*, nn. 341, 1844, 1855.

tions shaped the way the Curia responded to the petitions presented
to it. The first consideration was whether the proposal conflicted
with some aspect of the Curia's crusading policy. Such conflicts
were infrequent since Spain and eastern Europe were relatively
self-contained fronts: events there rarely impinged on the central
preoccupations of the papacy, Italy and the Turks. But there were
some rulers who had interests in two or more fronts, especially
Louis of Hungary. Initially the Curia tried to bind together the
King's various projects, so that in 1356 Innocent VI appointed him
captain of the Roman church, with the mandate first to defeat the
Ghibellines and then to conquer the Serbs.[89] Subsequently the
Curia attempted to guide Louis in a certain direction—usually
northern Italy—by holding out financial and other enticements.[90]
Both approaches were based on earlier policy towards such rulers as
Charles of Anjou, and neither succeeded, because Louis remained
his own master.

It was not only kings whose crusading efforts the papacy tried to
direct in this manner. For much of this period the appeal of
crusading to the western nobility was a general one, unrelated to
specific fronts. Between 1363 and 1365, for example, the young
Thomas Beauchamp thought of fighting in Italy, the Latin East, and
Prussia,[91] and according to John Capgrave, Henry of Lancaster
went on crusade in Granada, Prussia, Rhodes, and Cyprus.[92]
Humbert of Vienne only turned to the Smyrna crusade after
showing interest in Louis de la Cerda's proposed crusade to the
Canaries.[93] This encouraged the Curia to believe that it could direct
the activities of such princes and nobles by graduating the terms of
the indulgence offered, to make the spiritual reward of combat on
one front appreciably greater than that of another. Thus Clement V
was reluctant to grant James II's request for full crusade privileges
for his crusade in 1309 because he hoped to retain some Spanish

[89] Gasnault *et al.*, n. 2267.
[90] See below, ch. 5, nn. 128–32.
[91] LM, nn. 682, 940; *Cal. of Entries,* iv, 19. He appears to have gone to Prussia
eventually. See M. Keen, 'Chaucer's Knight, the English Aristocracy and the
Crusade', in V. J. Scattergood and J. W. Sherborne (eds.), *English Court Culture in
the Later Middle Ages* (London, 1982), 54–5.
[92] John Capgrave, 'Liber de illustribus Henricis', ed. F. C. Hingeston. RS
(London, 1858), 161 (quoted below, ch. 6, n. 213); K. Fowler, *The King's
Lieutenant: Henry of Grosmont, First Duke of Lancaster 1310–61* (London, 1969),
20–1, 26, 45, 103–10.
[93] Gay, 62.

resources for the Hospitaller *passagium*;[94] similar thinking may account for the fact that so many of the bulls addressed to the Poles, Hungarians, and Scandinavians offered the plenary indulgence only *in articulo mortis*.

Such a policy had no real chance of influencing events. Kings like James II resented their enterprises being treated as second-class crusades and pressed, successfully in his case, for an extension of the indulgence.[95] And it is questionable whether the indulgence was uppermost in the thoughts of men like Thomas Beauchamp and Henry of Lancaster when they looked for a crusade to fight in; there were too many easier ways of gaining it. This type of 'roving crusader' seems to have been attracted by quite other factors. The Lithuanian *Reysen* conducted by the Teutonic Knights, which probably constituted their most favoured battleground, had no discernible spiritual rewards attached.[96]

The second consideration influencing papal treatment of the petitions was a financial one. For much of the Avignonese period the current fiscal requirements of the Holy See could only be met by regular taxation of the churches of Spain and the eastern European kingdoms, and this taxation was threatened by the rival claims put forward in the *supplicationes*.[97] In such circumstances there were only two courses of action open to the Curia. It could exclude taxes altogether from the privileges granted, restricting its financial concessions to the collection of donations, legacies, and other lesser sources of money. Pope Gregory XI, for instance, declined to tax the Hungarian church in 1373 for Louis's crusade against the Turks, although he granted the King full concessions in other respects. The omission was caused by the Pope's own need to tax the Hungarian clergy for his struggle against the Visconti, a conflict which Gregory ranked alongside the defence of the Balkan states against the Turks.[98] The Pope took a firm stand on this, telling high-ranking Hungarian churchmen that they were to stop preaching the crusade if royal officials impeded the collection of the papal tenth.[99]

---

[94] *AA*, iii, n. 97. In March 1309 James II complained that 'aliqui tam milites et etiam clerici quam alii homines de terra nostra ad illud passagium se iuramento obligaverunt': ibid., iii, n. 91.   [95] *Reg. Clem. V*, nn. 5092–3.

[96] See below, ch. 6, nn. 208–15, ch. 8, nn. 35–7, for fuller discussion of these issues.

[97] For Spain see Fernández Conde and Oliver, 'La corte pontificia', 380, 400 ff.

[98] *VMH*, ii, nn. 270–3.

[99] Mollat, *Lettres secrètes*, n. 1769, and see also n. 1744.

But this was rare. For reasons which we shall examine, the popes accepted the legal right of Catholic rulers to Church aid when they were engaged in a crusade; a straightforward refusal to grant any form of tax was something the Curia was driven to issue only when it was suffering the severest of financial constraints—as it was in 1373.[100] More often it adopted a second course of action, one which was characteristic of Church–State relations in the fourteenth century: a tax would be granted, but the Curia would reserve a proportion of the proceeds for its own uses. Compared with similar arrangements with the kings of France and England, the pope was able to claim a large share, such as two-thirds in Hungary in 1332;[101] a half in Sweden in 1326,[102] in Poland, Sweden, and Norway in 1351,[103] in Poland in 1355,[104] and in Portugal in 1376;[105] and a third in Castile in 1352.[106]

These two considerations related to the needs of the Catholic world and the papal *camera*. By contrast, the third centred on the reputation enjoyed by the petitioner and the Curia's assessment of his motivation and reliability. The Curia had to evolve a policy for dealing with the petitions of such crusaders *manqués* as James II of Aragon, Magnus of Sweden, and Louis of Hungary. Some petitions were rejected outright; such was the fate of a list of substantial financial demands submitted by Alfonso XI in 1330, which John XXII described as without precedent.[107] Others were returned with a request for more details. Charles-Robert of Hungary was asked for clarification of some of his demands in 1335,[108] and in 1354 Peter of Castile was asked to send details of 'the nature of this enterprise, its circumstances, conditions, and all its advantages', in connection with his North African project.[109] At other times the Curia passed a project but displayed its uncertainty by giving it only qualified approval. Thus in July 1310 Clement V sanctioned crusade preaching for the defence of newly acquired Gibraltar, but only if it was essential for the port's protection, if there was no other way of defending it, and if delay would be hazardous.[110]

---

[100] See Glénisson, 'Les Origines', 156 ff. and *passim*.
[101] *VMH*, i, n. 865.   [102] *Acta pont. svecica*, i, n. 207.
[103] Ibid., i, n. 398; *VMP*, i, n. 702.
[104] Ibid., i, n. 742.
[105] *AE*, ad annum 1376, nn. 19–22, xxvi, 272–4.
[106] Déprez and Mollat, n. 2611, and cf. nn. 2650, 2660.
[107] *AE*, ad annum 1330, n. 45, xxiv, 452–3.
[108] *VMH*, i, n. 900.
[109] *Bulas*, n. 61.   [110] *Reg. Clem. V*, n. 6380.

But the most common way of dealing with the problem of sincerity was to issue a conditional grant, in which the concessions were hedged about with guarantees. The envoys of the negotiating ruler would specifically accept these and he himself, or his fully accredited proctors, would swear an oath to abide by them. In this way a form of insurance policy for action was established. While this sort of grant was not new—a good early example is Honorius III's agreement with Frederick II at San Germano in 1225[111]—it was issued more frequently and became more complex after about 1300. The conditional grant was in fact a corner-stone of Avignonese policy on the crusade, and all possible care was taken to eliminate loopholes which the committed ruler could exploit to evade his obligations. The many conditions which the Curia attached to the grant generally fell into three groups.

The first group dealt with military matters: the size of the army, leadership, the duration of the conflict, its strategic goals. For example, in 1328 Alfonso of Castile was granted crusade preaching, tenths, and *tercias* on condition that his proctors undertook various obligations in his name. The King's ritual protest that the idea of guarantees was a new one should be treated with some scepticism although, as we shall see, it is possible that the system was tightened up by John XXII at this time. Alfonso agreed to fight 'in a forceful and efficacious manner, both by sea and by land, for the exaltation and expansion of the Catholic Faith', for a period of four years. If the King could not go in person, he was to delegate a captain, a man of proven orthodoxy, rectitude, and reliability, who would have at his disposal at least 1,000 men-at-arms. This force was to defend Alfonso's subjects, and if possible attack Granada to reduce the lands held by the Moors.[112] In March 1340 Benedict XII stipulated that Alfonso XI was to fight in person for three months of each year covered by his privileges.[113] Similarly, in 1376 Ferdinand of Portugal was to fight with vigour, 'both defending the lands of Christians from the impious nations of the said kings and enemies [of Granada], and also attacking these kings and enemies'.[114] And in 1373 Louis of Hungary was to agree to take command of an army by

---

[111] See T. C. Van Cleve, 'The Crusade of Frederick II', in Setton (gen. ed.), *History of the Crusades*, ii, 440–1.

[112] *AE*, ad annum 1328, n. 77, xxiv, 378–9. Cf. conditions imposed in 1331: ASV, Reg. Vat. 99, ff. 19ʳ–21ʳ, n. 1004.

[113] ASV, Reg. Vat. 128, ff. 52ᵛ–55ᵛ, n. 15.

[114] *AE*, ad annum 1376, n. 21, xxvi, 273.

May 1374 with the strategic goal of expelling the Turks from the Balkans.[115]

A second group of conditions concerned the handling and fate of the revenue raised for the crusade. The need in this instance was to prevent the sort of situation described by the papal collector in Portugal in 1328, who complained about the crusade 'which the King is pretending [to wage], so that he can hold onto the Holy Land tenth'.[116] To try to deal with this contingency, the Curia began to impose conditions which were often extraordinarily detailed and specific. Typical, and therefore worth quoting at length, were those which John XXII attached to his grant of tenths and *tercias* to Alfonso XI in April 1331.

On all occasions, and during all periods when, through a truce or other arrangements, you have reason to stop waging the said war during the time specified above, you are also to stop receiving all the above-mentioned subsidies. And when you resume the conflict, as long as this occurs within the said four-year period, you will receive the said subsidies in proportion to the time which remains of the said four-year period, and during which you carry on with the resumed war. For the intervening period, when you stop waging the war, you must receive absolutely nothing in your own person, or in that of another or others, of the said subsidies. In addition, if the said truce should be extended beyond a year, not only must you stop receiving the said subsidies for the entire span of the said truce, but also the aforesaid executors and their sub-collectors will cease exacting and collecting the tenth and *tercias* and call off the whole procedure.[117]

The conditions which Gregory XI attached to his grant of a tenth to

---

[115] *VMH*, ii, n. 271.

[117] Mollat, *Lettres communes*, n. 42497.

[117] 'Quotiens vero et quamdiu infra dictum tempus ab eiusdem negotii prosecutione negotii [sic] sive per treugas sive aliis contigit te cessare, totiens et tamdiu cessabis a receptione subsidiorum quorumlibet predictorum et cum huius negotii prosecutionem infra dictum tamen quadriennium resumes, pro rata sequentis restantis temporis de dicto quadriennio quo dumtaxat dictum sic resumptum negotium prosequaris recipies subsidia supradicta, ita quod pro medio tempore quo ad huius negotii prosecutione cessabis nichil omnino per te vel alium seu alios recipies de subsidiis memoratis, hoc pretere nichilominus observando, ut si predicte treuge ultra annum forsitan protendatur, nonsolum per te per totum tempus dictarum treugarum ut premittitur ab eorumdem subsidiorum receptione cessetur, sed etiam executores predicti et subcollectores eorum ab exactione et collectione decime et duarum partium tercie predictarum et qualibet executione premissorum omnium abstinebunt': ASV, Reg. Vat. 99, f. 20ʳ, n. 1004. Cf. the conditions imposed on Peter of Cyprus and Amedeo of Savoy in 1363 on the collection of alms, which included the submission of annual accounts to the papal legate: ASV, Reg. Avin. 157, f. 108ᵛ; *Illustrazioni*, 357–8.

Ferdinand of Portugal in 1376 added the details that the King was to act with the advice of his prelates in spending the proceeds on the war with the Moors, and that during truces and other lulls in the fighting the money was to be sent to Avignon, 'so that during the period in which you refrain from pursuing the matter, you receive absolutely nothing from the said subsidies'.[118] Ultimately the main sanction behind such conditions was spiritual: the concern of kings about their own chances of salvation if they broke their solemn oaths, and the fear of their officials about the excommunication which hung over the heads of those who misspent crusade funds.[119] How effective this sanction was remains to be seen.[120]

The third group of conditions related to the period after the crusade. Whatever the legal justification of crusades in Spain and eastern Europe, the Curia was aware that they often entailed the conquest of non-Christian lands and peoples. It was anxious that the conquered should be converted to Catholicism, given pastoral care, and ruled with justice and moderation. In Spain it was laid down that churches were to be built, a system of tithes established, and severe restrictions placed on the practice of the Muslim Faith.[121] In the Balkans, Louis of Hungary was prepared to swear that he would rule benignly over the conquered schismatics of Serbia, and that he would protect the privileges and immunities of churches in the lands which he incorporated into his Kingdom.[122]

It will be clear that although the Curia did not take as active a role in the initiation of crusades in Spain and eastern Europe as it did in Italy and the eastern Mediterranean, its grant of crusade status was by no means a foregone conclusion. At various times petitions were turned down or sent back for more details. The privileges granted were often less than those asked for, and usually accompanied by conditions which dealt with every important aspect of the proposed campaign. Often money was denied or had to be shared with the papal *camera*. The Curia acted with caution, guided in part by what it understood to be the merits of each project, but more importantly by the dictates of its overall crusade policy, its growing financial needs, and the ever-present fear of deception.

[118] *AE*, ad annum 1376, n. 20, xxvi, 273.
[119] See, for example, *VMH*, ii, n. 272.
[120] Below, ch. 5, nn. 90–113, 123–7.
[121] See, for example, *AE*, ad annum 1328, nn. 78–9, xxiv, 379. Cf. *COD*, 380 (decree of the Council of Vienne).
[122] *AE*, ad annum 1356, nn. 24–6, xxvi, 11–13.

It remains true, however, that it was other fronts which held the attention of the papacy. We will look first at the 'interior' front, the use of the crusade as a weapon against baptized Christians. This means primarily the series of crusades waged against Ghibelline powers in Italy; but it is also necessary to include the issuing of crusade indulgences for resisting the *routiers* in France and Italy, and the hopes entertained, in the early decades of the century, for a Latin reconquest of Constantinople through the launching of a crusade.

As in the case of Spain and eastern Europe, it was not hard to find legal precedents and arguments for these concerns. Popes from Innocent III onwards had established the legitimacy of crusades against rebellious Christians in terms of the harm which they were doing to the Church, the succour which they rendered to heretics, and the obstacles which they posed to an expedition to the East.[123] In the case of the Greeks, the themes of recovery and obdurate schism were joined, at the turn of the century, by a growing fear of Turkish power and the need for a strong, which meant a Latin, Constantinople.[124] The granting of indulgences against the companies posed a slight problem since the thirteenth century had not given rise to such campaigns, but it was solved partly by employing the sort of charges used against the Ghibelline tyrants, and partly by reaching back into the precedents afforded by twelfth-century legislation against brigands and those who hired them.[125]

There was, then, an impressive arsenal of arguments; no new legal ground needed to be broached. It is clear that not only the Curia but also the kings of France and Naples, the Commune of Florence, and other authorities in or attached to the Guelf network of alliances knew of these arguments and gauged their importance in the making of a crusade. When Charles of Calabria, the eldest son of Robert of Naples, pleaded for a crusade against Louis the Bavarian in the early months of 1327, he knew that the German King had committed enough offences to validate the enterprise along traditional lines.[126] Similarly, when the Florentines wanted to mobilize crusading resources against Castruccio Castracane in 1328, they presented their request in terms of legal justification: the lord

---

[123] Housley, *Italian Crusades*, ch. 2 *passim*.
[124] *Reg. Clem. V*, n. 243.
[125] Housley, 'Mercenary Companies', 265–6.
[126] Id., *Italian Crusades*, 145.

of Lucca was guilty of aiding heresy—*fautoria heresiae*—by giving his support to Louis.[127] Forty years later the French King, Charles V, argued the case for a full-scale crusade against the mercenary groups in France on the grounds that the *routiers* merited condemnation as schismatics. Since schism always led to heresy, and since the *routiers* were showing themselves to hold unorthodox beliefs by opposing the Church and displaying contempt for the penalties imposed by the Pope, they should be subjected to the full rigours of the crusade.[128]

Just as in Spain and eastern Europe, the Curia responded most readily in cases of urgent military need. The crusade against Venice in 1309 was a response to the critical situation in Romagna, where it seemed to Clement V that the Venetian seizure of Ferrara might bring about the destruction of the Church's temporal power. The Florentines in 1328 pointed to the serious deterioration of the Guelf position in central Italy. The crusade was declared against the company of Conrad of Landau in July 1357 because his soldiers threatened to undo all the painstaking work of Cardinal Albornoz in the eastern provinces of the Papal State. In 1361 Innocent VI preached a crusade against the *routiers* who were menacing the papal court itself at Avignon. And the papacy responded repeatedly to the pleas of the civil authorities in France and Italy for the issue of indulgences against companies which were holding individual communities to ransom.[129] By contrast, one chronicler described Albornoz making the decision not to declare a crusade against Giovanni di Vico because the situation did not seem to call for it.[130]

Granted that the petitions emanated from papal legates and allies, and were therefore greeted with greater sympathy than those coming from the courts of Spain and eastern Europe, these aspects seem broadly comparable to the process described above. The big difference is in the role played by papal policy. For 'interior crusades' were closely linked to the current shape and thrust of the Curia's crusade policy, particularly as it related to the royal house of France and the Guelf powers in Italy. As an example of justification, pressure, and policy converging without noticeable strain to

[127] Ibid., 147.

[128] Housley, 'Mercenary Companies', 264.

[129] Id., *Italian Crusades*, 147; id., 'Pope Clement V', 37; id., 'Mercenary Companies', 259–60, 262, 264. The 'Cronica d'Orvieto', col. 684, makes the point well in connection with the crusade against Francesco Ordelaffi.

[130] ' . . . non li pareva da tanto': *La vita di Cola di Rienzo*, 105.

bring about a crusade, we can take Clement V's support for the expedition planned by Charles of Valois to retake Constantinople, as expressed in his series of bulls dated January 1306.[131] The justification for the crusade was tailor-made and Clement made no important additions. It is clear that he issued the bulls because of an agreement reached with Philip IV during their meeting at Lyons at the end of 1305: the pressure is apparent. But the bulls also fitted in with papal policy at this time, displaying the closest of co-operation with France, the concept of reconquering Constantinople as a 'stepping-stone' to Palestine, and the taxation of the French church to pay for the crusade projects of the French Crown. The Valois scheme was rooted in the Franco-papal alliance and, as Charles explained to the Venetians in July 1309, he had to catch the sustained attention of both Pope and King to make any progress with it.[132]

But papal policy changed, causing disharmony and bitterness. There are examples of powerful diplomatic pressure or urgent military need, operating within well established legal traditions, failing to bring about the desired result. The most important instances derived from a conflict of needs between Italy and the eastern Mediterranean, and will be considered below. But there were other reasons for papal policy to alter, notably the decision to abandon the coercive approach in favour of negotiation and compromise. This meant, for instance, that requests from Naples for a renewal of the crusade against the Sicilians were rejected by John XXII and probably by Benedict XII; papal policy towards Sicily had become less aggressive than in the days of Martin IV and Boniface VIII.[133]

One of the best examples of heavy pressure for an 'interior crusade' failing because of a change in papal policy is the French Crown's relations with Flanders in the early years of John XXII. It is clear that from 1316 the French court was pressing for a tougher papal approach towards the rebels in Flanders, and that the new Pope was ready to go some way in this direction because his plans, on the crusade and other matters, called for French disengagement in the County. In September 1316, for instance, John confirmed the grant of a four-year tenth for the Flanders war.[134] But Philip V wanted more: there is strong evidence that he was working for a full-

---

[131] *Reg. Clem. V*, nn. 243–8. [132] *DVL*, i, n. 41.
[133] Housley, *Italian Crusades*, 36. [134] CC, n. 23, and cf. n. 27 (annates).

scale crusade. In July 1319 he replied to a request from Louis of Clermont for royal pressure on the Curia to sanction a *passagium* to the East. The King wrote that if it proved impossible to make peace with the Flemish rebels, he intended to ask the Pope for aid against them, 'in both spiritual and temporal forms'. This aid would, he hoped, include 'the things included in the above-mentioned articles, or some of them', which were crusading indulgences, privileges, legacies, and subsidies. If the Pope refused to grant these, Philip would ask for them on Louis's behalf for the *passagium* to the East.[135]

It is not clear from what point Philip thought along these lines, but by 1317 the correspondence between Pope and King about Flanders was using arguments and language which are very familiar from the thirteenth-century crusades against the Staufen and the Sicilians. In August 1317, in a letter of admonition to the envoys of Robert of Flanders, the Pope accused the Flemings of several offences traditionally associated with the worst enemies of the Church: they were disturbing all Christendom, delaying the French crusade to the East, ignoring papal sanctions, and seizing clerical property.[136] In March 1318 Philip V's envoys called for papal support, 'both spiritual and temporal', against the rebels; the use of the phrase may indicate that this was to include the crusade. The Pope prevaricated on the grounds that the time was not right, peace was still possible. But he added that if the stubbornness of the Flemings led to further conflict and the crusade was held up, then the French cause, which was God's too, would have papal backing.[137] By March 1319 John was threatening excommunication and interdict, which were so often first steps towards a crusade,[138] but on 26 March he wrote to Philip that he had turned down the pleas of his envoys for aid against the Flemings, 'because it seemed to us and the cardinals . . . that the said petition could not have been granted by us without offending justice and the dignity of the Church'.[139] Philip's reply to Louis of Clermont post-dated this letter, but if he did make another attempt to secure the crusade it was not successful.

---

[135] *Titres de la maison ducale de Bourbon*, i, 282–3, n. 1633, and see also 263, n. 1526.

[136] CC, n. 367, and cf. n. 197.

[137] Ibid., n. 530. Cf. Cont. William of Nangis, ii, 11.   [138] CC, n. 800.

[139] Ibid., n. 830. Tabacco (121) cited this letter without trying to explain it. On the French background see Tyerman, 18–19.

Why the rebuff? Certainly not for the reasons which John XXII gave, because a crusade against the Flemings was fully in accordance with both French and papal thinking. As we have seen, the French monarchy and some French churchmen had been accustomed since the start of the century to think of the conflict in Flanders as a species of holy war.[140] And there were ample legal precedents in the crusades authorized in the thirteenth century against groups accused of hindering a crusade to the East, such as the English rebel barons in the 1260s and the Sicilians in 1282. Ten years earlier a crusade against the Flemings might have been declared, along similar lines to that declared against the Greeks. But papal policy had changed. John XXII was trying to bring about a subtle but important alteration in Franco-papal relations, to work in close harmony with Paris on a wide range of issues without subordinating papal interests to those of France. The Pope wanted peace in Flanders, not a French conquest, and he was sceptical about the sincerity and reliability of Philip V. The King was several times rebuked for misapplying Church funds and failing to make any real preparations for his *passagium* to the East.[141] So there was no crusade against the Flemings, the gradual abandonment of the proposed crusade against the Greeks, and a return in depth to the waging of crusades for specifically papal aims in Italy.

The fronts which we have examined so far had an important feature in common. For all there were resident powers which were capable of applying pressure on the Curia to declare a crusade on the basis of existing arguments for holy war, usually in response to a military crisis: kings in the case of Spain and eastern Europe, Guelf rulers, papal legates in charge of armies, and threatened local authorities in that of the 'interior' front. The Latin East departed from this pattern; there was no single authority there which could channel and interpret information, and present clear and consistent demands with the required diplomatic push. It is of course notorious that political power was fragmented in Latin Syria in the thirteenth century, but this did not matter so much because the defence of the Holy Land, however interpreted strategically,

---

[140] Above, n. 37. The author of the 'Chronique des comtes de Flandres' viewed the papal sanctions against the Flemings as an important weapon in Philip V's armoury: Hillgarth, *Ramon Lull*, 76n.

[141] See, for example, CC, nn. 364, 667.

enjoyed unquestioned priority. After 1291 the longstanding tendency of the crusading movement in the East to splinter was encouraged by the number and geographical spread of the Christian powers there.

None of the Avignon popes had the advantage of firsthand knowledge of the eastern Mediterranean possessed by Urban IV and Gregory X. They relied on detailed information and suggestions from their agents in the East, and on the whole they were fortunate in their choice of legates, especially Peter Thomas and Peter of Pleine Chassagne. Peter Thomas's espousal of the needs of the Smyrna garrison and then of the Cypriot crusade undoubtedly helped to keep some of the Curia's attention focused on the East at a time of crisis in Italy.[142] Thus after the return of King Peter's crusade to Cyprus in 1365 the legate wrote to both Urban V and Charles IV pleading for aid to continue the war against the Mamluks.[143] He was not afraid to blame the Pope for the failure of the crusaders to retain Alexandria: 'This misfortune is really your responsibility, for if enough people had come and the Church had made a big enough contribution, there would have been no difficulty in holding on to the city'.[144] His fervent commitment to the cause of the crusade led Peter to exceed his authority, so that in 1363 Urban V cancelled the preaching which he had set in motion in southern Italy, channelling the money, arms, and other goods which his preachers had collected into the crusade against the Visconti.[145] Presumably such actions lay behind the legate's rebuke two years later.

Scarcely less resourceful than Peter Thomas was Peter of Pleine Chassagne, Clement V's legate, who sustained the initiative of the Hospitaller *passagium* and the Vienne Council through the papal vacancy of 1314–16. Peter had some of his later namesake's independence: he held onto his legatine title, contrary to practice, after Clement's death, and in 1317 successfully defended his record in the East in a hearing at the Curia.[146] The careers of the two men show how thin was the dividing line between the vigorous performance of legatine duties and disobedience to papal command. The

---

[142] Boehlke, 156–294.

[143] Philip of Mézières, 135–40, esp. 139–40.

[144] 'Tibi quasi imponitur plaga praesens, quia si venisset populus in sufficientia, si providisset de aliquo ecclesia, nulla excusatio fuisset de tanti loci custodia': ibid.

[145] ASV, Reg. Vat. 245, f. 76^{r-v}. Cf. Boehlke, 178.

[146] Golubovich, iii, 147–51.

independence they were both tempted to display reinforces the
point made earlier in connection with the activities of the nuncios
Galhard de Carceribus and John Guilbert in Poland and Sweden:
prolonged work in the field inevitably led papal agents to see
problems and openings not perceived at Avignon, and to develop
initiatives of their own. It was a difficulty common to most
centralized, immobile governments and we shall see that it had
widespread implications.

The Curia had other sources of information about events in the
East. Some rulers, such as the usurper Amalric of Cyprus, sent
envoys to the pope with detailed information. But Amalric's envoys
never reached the Curia (their galley was lost at sea), and even if
they had, it is doubtful that Amalric, whose hold on power was
illegal and tenuous, would have sent the objective assessment of
conditions in Cyprus and the Holy Land which Clement V wanted.[147] To add to the ideas and news coming from its agents and
local rulers, the Curia had the crusade treatises which appeared in
abundance in the early fourteenth century; Gregory XI had at least
fifteen of these in his library.[148] But much of this recovery literature
was far too generalized to be of practical use, and many of the ideas
it expressed were uncongenial to the Curia—an example being
Marino Sanudo's suggestion that the Church should bear the
burden of financing at least the initial stage of the proposed
crusade.[149]

Petitions from resident powers remained the best way of getting
action, and there was a steady flow of letters and envoys to Avignon
pleading for papal aid. The Curia was usually prepared to concede
indulgences to those already fighting or easily recruited. In some
cases these indulgences were granted *in articulo mortis* only, for
example, to the hired soldiers of Martin Zaccaria who fell defending
Chios in 1323 and 1325,[150] to those who died defending Greece
against the Turks in 1364,[151] and to Christians who were killed while

---

[147] Mas Latrie, iii, 680–1.

[148] Luttrell, 'Gregory XI', 394.

[149] Marino Sanudo Torsello, 'Liber secretorum fidelium crucis,' in *Gesta Dei per
Francos, sive orientalium expeditionum et regni Francorum Hierosolymitani historia*,
ed. J. Bongars. 2 vols. (Hanover, 1611), ii, 35–6. Cf. the heavy Church taxes
proposed by Fulk of Villaret: *Cartulaire général*, iv, 109, n. 4681.

[150] Mollat, *Lettres communes*, nn. 16977, 22117. Chios under the Zaccarie
attracted considerable attention in the West as a 'strategic outpost' of Latin
Christendom. See Lemerle, 50 ff.; Balard, i, 467–9.

[151] ASV, Reg. Vat. 246, f. 238ʳ⁻ᵛ.

bringing supplies to combatants against the Turks in 1372.[152] But this restriction did not always apply. Plenary indulgences were granted to all who fought for a year in Armenia in 1336,[153] to Genoese who spent a year in the defence of Caffa in 1345,[154] and to Frenchmen who sailed to help defend Cyprus and Rhodes in 1366.[155]

This was the simplest form of crusading activity, involving very little organization by the Curia, bringing with it few complications and little risk of deception. There is no way of knowing for certain how many individuals in the West or the East responded to such bulls, or how many came to the Curia to seek specific grants of the indulgence. In June 1355, for example, Innocent VI issued a letter of commendation, addressed to the Master of the Hospitallers, on behalf of a French nobleman called Adhemar 'de Monteauroso', 'who is setting off to overseas parts to fight against the enemies of the faith'.[156] The letter has enjoyed fortuitous survival in a miscellaneous collection in the Vatican Archives; we do not know if Adhemar did set off or where he was planning to go (possibly Smyrna), and most importantly how many followed a similar path. But it is a reminder that the fourteenth century should not be considered just from the vantage point of the major *passagia*.

Nevertheless, it was the major expeditions which called for hard thinking on the part of the Curia, and in this respect crusades destined for Palestine and *Romania* demand separate treatment. The making of a crusade of recovery to Palestine in effect meant detailed negotiations with the French monarchy, first in the period 1305–35, and then, briefly, in 1363–4. The most striking feature of these bargaining sessions is the extent to which they resemble the Curia's negotiations with the kings of Spain and, to a lesser degree, those of eastern Europe. The French kings argued their case with the same stress on their crusading zeal, appeals to precedent, and rich array of bribes and threats; the Curia countered with the same insistence on binding obligations and cast-iron guarantees. The reason for the similarity is quite clear: there was an almost identical background of high financial odds and mutual suspicion. The difference was that in the case of the French and the crusade to the East the stakes were even higher than in that of Spain, and the main

---

[152] Mollat, *Lettres secrètes*, n. 1202.
[153] Daumet, n. 175.
[154] Déprez and Mollat, n. 847.
[155] LM, n. 2416.
[156] ASV, Instr. misc. n. 6292.

reason for this was the difficulty of the enterprise. Military failure in Spain, or eastern Europe, would be a grave setback; its equivalent in the eastern Mediterranean could hardly be less than a catastrophe.[157]

Behind the complicated and often brutal interplay of tactical advantage which characterized the Franco-papal negotiations,[158] the Curia clung to certain principles and approaches which recur with regularity. One was a deep-rooted scepticism about the value of a *passagium generale*. There was no doubt that for the long-term goal of reconquering Palestine a general passage was essential, but for the short-term aim of, for example, helping the Armenians, large-scale crusades were to be avoided. They aroused wild expectations which were always disappointed; they had a long history of misdirection; and they served the cause of the Muslims by giving them unity and vengefulness. In 1363 Urban V wanted to make financial provision for the defence of eastern Christians who would be attacked by the Muslims 'with greater ferocity and animosity' in the wake of the planned French crusade.[159] And the view was expressed by some cardinals in 1323, and by Benedict XII in 1336, that it was better to have no crusade at all than to allow this to occur.[160]

A second principle generally adhered to by the Curia when negotiating with Paris related to its Italian wars. The Avignon popes were usually not prepared to promote a full-scale crusade to the East if to do so would cause serious harm to their Italian policy, especially its financial foundations. In 1322, for example, Charles IV put forward his complicated proposal for a *passagium* in relief of Armenia and Cyprus at a time of mounting costs in Lombardy; John XXII's display of caution about the project was at least partly motivated by the exigencies of the Visconti war.[161] Forty years later a similar collision of interests led Urban V to assure Albornoz that 'we will not permit the preaching of the cross for an overseas expedition, as we have already explained to our very dear sons in Christ King John of France and King Peter of Cyprus, until the

---

[157] Worse still, the catastrophe might be blamed on the Church: CC, n. 1693.

[158] For a good example of the calculated use of brutality, see Housley, 'Franco–Papal Crusade Negotiations', 178.   [159] Prou, 101.

[160] CC, nn. 1691, 1693, 1696, 1699, 1701–2; Vidal and Mollat, n. 786. Critics of the Smyrna crusade at the French court turned this argument to their own advantage: Déprez *et al.*, n. 1704.

[161] Housley, 'Franco–Papal Crusade Negotiations', 172, 181–2.

matter of the said heretic [Bernabò Visconti] has been brought to a successful conclusion by war or his submission'.[162] The popes were capable of yielding to pressure: indeed, shortly after writing this letter Urban V permitted peace negotiations with an undefeated Bernabò, for reasons which have been disputed.[163] But they tried to maintain the policy of their predecessors—Italy came first.

This was just one aspect of the broader issue of timing. One of the richest themes in crusading thought was the concept of a *tempus acceptabile*, which had received brilliant treatment at the hands of St. Bernard in the early twelfth century and had been a constant feature of crusade literature ever since.[164] By the fourteenth century it had become a political and military matter rather than a theological one, and the Avignon popes continued to assert that God would intervene to make the situation in the West or amongst the Muslims particularly favourable for the launching of a major crusade. *Tempus acceptabile* was a theme which Clement VI, himself a remarkable orator, thought highly of. In 1345-6 he wrote that Christian success at Smyrna had introduced such a period,[165] and he was clearly thinking along the same lines in March 1348, when he wrote an enthusiastic letter of commendation for two travellers from the East bearing the news that Mamluk Egypt was in political and military chaos, backing them with a call to liberate the Holy Land.[166] Again in 1363 Urban V considered that the crusade aspirations of the French and Cypriot Kings had ushered in a *tempus acceptabile*.[167] Peter of Cyprus had told the Pope that the Muslims were hard hit by civil strife, plague, and the loss of Satalia, so that 'in these times the strength of the Saracens and Turks can easily be shattered, and the recovery of the Holy Land take place'.[168]

---

[162] '. . . nec ad predicationem crucis in negotio transmarino permittemus procedi, sicut hoc carissimis in Christo filiis nostris Johanni francie et Petro Cipri Regibus perdiximus, nisi dicti heretici negotio per bellum vel conversionem eius feliciter expedito': ASV, Reg. Vat. 245, f. 214ᵛ.

[163] There is substantial disagreement on this between Filippini (321–34) and J. Smet (in Philip of Mézières, Appendix VI, 213–17).

[164] See Villey, 118, 146–7. The phrase originated in 2 Cor. 6:2.

[165] *AE*, ad annum 1346, n. 63, xxv, 401. Cf. *VPA*, ii, 289, in relation to Philip VI's crusade project. See also Wrigley, 458n.

[166] Déprez and Mollat, n. 1605. See also M. W. Dols, *The Black Death in the Middle East* (Princeton, 1977), 57, 154, 190 ff.

[167] *AE*, ad annum 1363, nn. 20–2, xxvi, 84–6; *DVL*, ii, n. 54.

[168] *AE*, ad annum 1363, n. 15, xxvi, 82. In 1366 Urban considered that a *tempus acceptabile* had come for the Greeks to embrace Union: *AE*, ad annum 1366, nn. 1–2, xxvi, 122.

But the most interesting occurrence of the *tempus acceptabile* theme came in 1375, when a series of factors together made up a pattern of optimism very rare in the late fourteenth century.[169] First, in March 1375 papal efforts for an Anglo-French peace conference finally succeeded, and talks began at Bruges which brought about a one-year truce on 27 June.[170] Secondly, the spring also saw peace talks between the Church and Visconti Milan, which led to a one year truce in Lombardy at the beginning of June.[171] The two greatest wars in the West had been brought to a temporary halt, and this in itself led to the third factor, the need to find employment for the mercenaries who would be released from the various armies. Finally, in April, when this combination of opportunity and problem was already in the offing, a French squire called John Du Château arrived at the Curia from the East with news similar to that which so impressed Clement VI in 1348: the Muslim world was the victim of a wave of apocalyptic terror. Miraculous conversions had taken place and the time was ripe for a crusade; even a small Christian army could achieve much.[172]

In the letters which Gregory XI wrote between spring and autumn 1375 in response to this situation, a conflict can be perceived between the idea that this striking convergence of factors might represent the long awaited *tempus acceptabile*, and the realization that the economic and political condition of the West forbade action on a large scale. In letters to Charles V and the delegates at Bruges the Pope struck an optimistic tone, reiterating the traditional theme that a crusade to the East could provide suitable employment for the discharged French and English soldiers: 'It is to be hoped that many, who have committed appalling crimes, could be purged of them in the Lord's war, through the action of his mercy'.[173] On 1 July the Pope took steps to find out how many people would be prepared to enlist in a crusade,[174] but already his optimism was crumbling; there was ominous news of the talks between Florence and Milan which would lead to a formal

---

[169] See Mirot, 63.
[170] E. Perroy, *The Hundred Years War*, tr. W. B. Wells (London, 1959), 166–7.
[171] *Storia di Milano*, 484–6.
[172] Mirot *et al.*, n. 1852. Cf. ibid., nn. 1853–65.
[173] Ibid., n. 1896, and cf. nn. 1897–1907, 3713; Mirot, 68n–69n.
[174] *Lettres de Grégoire XI*, ed. C. Tihon. Analecta Vaticano–belgica. 4 vols. (Brussels–Rome, 1958–75), iii, n. 3263. Cf. ibid., iii, n. 3264; Mollat, *Lettres secrètes*, nn. 3382–3.

alliance of the two powers on 24 July, ushering in renewed war in Italy.[175] By the end of October Gregory was pouring cold water on the crusading ardour expressed by Joanna of Naples, steering her in the direction of a limited naval league against the Turks.[176] Realism had prevailed.

So persuasive was the atmosphere of optimism in 1375 that Gregory XI sanctioned the brief revival of plans for a *passagium* to Palestine, partly because this was the form of eastern crusade which would have most appeal for the *routiers*. But the Pope's letter to Joanna is more revealing of his overall policy, with its accurate and gloomy assessment of the Turkish menace to the Balkans, Achaea, and even the *Regno* itself. The recovery of the Holy Land, he wrote, was indeed a long-term goal of Christendom and would be facilitated by the defeat of the Turks, but Gregory was in no real doubt about priorities in the East:

Opposing the said Turks can not only be considered as a work of Faith, but it is a better contribution towards the defence of the said Principality [Achaea] and Kingdom [Naples]; it is easier and more important to help those in danger, lest they perish, than to attempt, at present, the recovery of the Holy Land, which has been occupied for so long.[177]

This brings us to the naval leagues formed against the Turks in *Romania*. In Chapter One I stressed that these represented a significant shift in crusade strategy, and their formation thus raises not just the question of how important the Curia was in the initiation of individual leagues, but also the fundamental issue of how the transition occurred from a crusade to recover Palestine to one intended to defend *Romania*.

In terms of crusading theory, the war against the Turks presented no problems. As Gregory XI put it in his letter to Queen Joanna, it was an *opus fidei*, a holy activity, and this approach was followed by the Curia throughout our period; there are no signs of opposition at the papal court towards this view.[178] Thus, once the problem of Turkish aggression was brought to the attention of the Curia, it was wholly natural to conceive of a military response in the form of a

---

[175] See G. A. Brucker, *Florentine Politics and Society, 1343–1378* (Princeton, 1962), 282–94.
[176] 'Gregorio XI e Giovanna I di Napoli', *ASPN*, xxv, 6–8, n. 167.
[177] Ibid.
[178] I cannot, therefore, agree with Lemerle's comment (181n) that the leagues were crusades only in a 'technical' sense.

crusade, a *sanctum passagium*.[179] The problem which arose was the
familiar one of priorities within the crusading policy of the Curia.
For the French court, reflecting the views of the French nobility,
was obsessed with the recovery of the Holy Land, and it had great
influence not only on the papacy but also on the Hospitallers and
Angevin Naples. While there were real prospects of a crusade of
recovery, crusading activity in *Romania* had either to be fairly
minor in scope, or to be related in strategic terms to the passage to
the Holy Land.

Until the early 1330s, therefore, the two chief characteristics of
crusade activity in Greece were its orientation towards French
interests, and the fact that it was so often linked to the *recuperatio
Terre Sancte*. This was the case with the bulls which Clement V
issued to Charles of Valois and Philip of Taranto for fighting the
Greeks; in 1312, for example, it was asserted that Philip was going
'in aid of the Holy Land, to the region of *Romania*'.[180] Clement V
was careful to state that Frenchmen and Italians who had taken the
cross for a crusade to the Holy Land and who went to fight with
Charles of Valois against the Greeks could not commute their vows,
although posthumous commutation would be granted to those who
died in the field.[181] Clement V and John XXII gave much backing to
Briennist and Angevin opposition to the Catalans in the Duchy of
Athens, also recognizable as a Franco-Guelf objective.[182] When the
issue of Turkish piracy arose in about 1320, the Curia simply placed
the Turks alongside the Greeks and Catalans as enemies of Latin
Christianity. Thus in 1322 indulgences were granted to the
inhabitants of Achaea, who had complained of attacks 'from the
schismatic Greeks, Bulgars, Alans, Turks, and various other infidel
peoples'.[183] John XXII was not averse to issuing indulgences for
fighting the Turks, but he did not envisage a radical shift from
Palestine to *Romania*; in the crusade discussions with Charles IV
which took place at this time the ultimate objective remained the

---

[179] *Délibérations*, i, 211–12.
[180] *Reg. Clem. V*, n. 7893. Cf. ibid., n. 243.
[181] Ibid., nn. 247, 1768.
[182] See, for example, ibid., nn. 7890–7901, 10166–8; *AA*, ii, n. 466; *I libri comm.*,
i, 191, n. 100; *Diplomatari de l'orient català*, nn. 105, 110, 120.
[183] 'Vos et ecclesie romane fideles aliarum parcium adiacencium Romanie a
scismaticis Grecis, Bulgaris, Alanis et Turchiis aliisque permixtis infidelium nationibus impugnaciones, depopulaciones, captivitates, servitutes et carceres et alias
diversorum generum penas et cruciatus multiplices patiamini': ASV, Reg. Vat. 74, f.
93ᵛ, n. 209.

recovery of the Holy Land, and the immediate aim help for Armenia against the Mamluks.[184]

But if the French court kept papal policy centred on Palestine, another great western power was laying the diplomatic foundations for the shift which would occur. Venice, with its fleets and colonial bases, held the key to effective military operations in *Romania*, and the Republic's aims in the region were very different from those of Paris and Naples. With the treaty of 1310 the Venetians entered a period of better relations with the Greeks,[185] and they also refused to join in military action against the Catalans, preferring the negotiations which produced the settlements of 1319, 1321, and 1331.[186] Negotiations did not succeed, however, with the Turks. Beginning in June 1318, Venetian documents started to record their attacks on the Republic's ships and territory, and by 1325 Venice was considering forming a league against them.[187] In 1327 the Senate decided to instruct its colonial officials to discuss this with the Hospitallers, Martin Zaccaria of Chios, and Andronicus II Palaeologus. As Angeliki Laiou has pointed out, the inclusion of the *basileus* showed how radically Venetian policy had been reformulated since the days of Charles of Valois's schemes of *revanche*.[188]

The road leading from the Senate decision of 1327 to the fully-fledged league of 1334 was a complicated one, involving a compromise between the French-inspired Palestine project and the new crusade simply *contra Turchos*. Essentially there were three developments. One was the successful formation, in September 1332, of an anti-Turkish naval league consisting of Venice, Andronicus III, and the Hospitallers.[189] Secondly, there was Philip VI's agreement to take part in the league. Possibly this showed that Venice had been successful in arguing that the league represented a *primum passagium* to the Holy Land;[190] but it is more likely that Philip hoped, by making a contribution to a Venetian project, to lay the city under an obligation towards his own general passage.[191]

[184] ASV, Reg. Vat. 74, f. 3ᵛ, n. 7, ff. 3ᵛ–5ʳ, n. 8; Housley, 'Franco–Papal Crusade Negotiations', *passim*.

[185] *DVL*, i, n. 46; Laiou, *Constantinople and the Latins*, 267 ff.

[186] *DVL*, i, nn. 70, 108; *Régestes*, i, 25, 27; K. M. Setton, *Catalan Domination of Athens 1311–1388*. Revised edn. (London, 1975), 26–7, 32–5.

[187] *DVL*, i, nn. 61–3.

[188] Laiou, 'Marino Sanudo Torsello', 381, 386, and *passim*.

[189] *DVL*, i, n. 116; *Régestes*, i, 25–7, and see also 28, 30.

[190] *DVL*, i, nn. 109–10, 122–3, 127. Cf. Cont. William of Nangis, ii, 145.

[191] This can be inferred from *DVL*, i, n. 123.

Thirdly, there was the collapse of papal policy in northern Italy in 1331–2, which made John XXII more responsive to pleas from Paris and Venice for his involvement in all this activity. This meant that while the Pope was apparently unaware of the extent of Venice's progress on the league as late as August 1333, during the following autumn and winter he took a much more prominent role, including the league in the brief of his legate in Italy.[192]

It would be wrong to lay too much emphasis on the implausible Venetian arguments about the league's services to the Palestine crusade.[193] In reality a strategic breakthrough had been made. It is significant that from 1334 crusading activity against both the Greeks and the Catalans ceased. The Turks were now seen as the chief enemies of Christendom in *Romania*, and when Benedict XII attempted to revive the league in 1335 he wrote of his desire 'to give some defensive aid to the Christians of *Romania*, who are being severely attacked and oppressed, so we are told, by the infidel Turks'.[194] No reference was made here to the Holy Land. The change had come about almost entirely through Venetian initiative and diplomatic push.[195] John XXII was interested mainly in Italy, to some extent in French plans for a crusade to Palestine, and only thereafter in the problem of the Turks. But if the Curia was not willing—or able—to take the lead, events in 1333–4, together with the indulgences issued on earlier occasions, showed that it was at least ready to sanction what was happening.[196]

One of the major differences between the league of 1334 and that of 1342 was the much more impressive role played by Clement VI; outside the Italian peninsula there was no other crusade in this period in which the initiative lay so fully in the hands of the pope.[197] Two reasons account for this. One was the willingness of the Latin powers on the spot to accept, and even to lay stress on, papal sponsorship of a joint endeavour in order to secure the help of the West generally. Thus the Bishop of Limassol, Cyprus's envoy, was

---

[192] *AE*, ad annum 1333, n. 13, xxiv, 511–12; *DVL*, i, n. 124; Housley, *Italian Crusades*, 69.

[193] The Venetians argued that the expedition would have to be supplied from the Black Sea and its supply ships would be attacked. See *DVL*, i, n. 110, and cf. CC, n. 5247; *AE*, ad annum 1333, n. 16, xxiv, 513–14.

[194] Daumet, n. 40. See also Déprez, *Les Préliminaires*, 107n–8n.

[195] Lemerle (98–9) exaggerated the role played by John XXII.

[196] See *AE*, ad annum 1333, n. 15, xxiv, 513. Cf. Laiou's comment, 'Marino Sanudo Torsello', 383n.

[197] Cf. Luttrell, 'Venice and the Knights Hospitallers', 203.

told 'to petition our said lord, the Pope, to be inspired by piety to provide a suitable solution to the above problems, especially as it is his responsibility to furnish a remedy in this matter, in his capacity as the head of all Christendom'.[198] Secondly, Clement was able to accept this role because he had advantages which John XXII had lacked, notably a well-stocked treasury, only minor expenses in Italy, and no pressure from Paris for a crusade to the Holy Land.

Initially, of course, Clement responded to pleas for help against the Turks, which, he later claimed, reached him with such urgency that they could not be ignored.[199] Granted that the league did not call for the recruitment of large numbers of men-at-arms or the assembly of quantities of supplies, the speed with which the Pope acted is impressive. He was elected in May 1342, and in June the Doge was already replying to an enquiry from Avignon about what course of action should be taken. By November Clement was arranging details of the league with the Cypriots and Hospitallers, and pressing Venice to join it.[200] The Venetian government decided in January 1343 to contribute a quarter of the galleys in the league; it also made valuable suggestions about the size and duration of the planned *passagium*.[201] The Pope maintained the pace in the spring and summer months of 1343, notably in a batch of letters written in August and September. Attempts were made to expand the league; those already in it were reminded, in forceful tones, of their obligations; and provision was made for the leadership and financing of the expedition.[202]

To a considerable extent, the successful assembly of the league's flotilla in the spring of 1344, just two years after it was first suggested, has to be credited to Clement's personal authority, energy, and commitment to the project. He had established a tradition of papal initiative in the organization of naval leagues, which would be followed both by himself in 1350 and by Innocent VI and Gregory XI at later dates. With Clement VI, moreover, the nature of the league as a form of crusade was fully established. Theoretically, the 1334 league had been a *primum passagium*, the

[198] Mas Latrie, ii, 180–1.
[199] Déprez *et al.*, n. 1704; Gay, 28–9.
[200] *Régestes*, i, 49; *AE*, ad annum 1342, n. 17, xxv, 284–5; *I libri comm.*, ii, 117–19, nn. 18, 22, 24; Setton, *PL*, 183.
[201] *DVL*, i, n. 136. The figures for galleys and *usserii* were slightly different from those suggested in 1342.
[202] Déprez *et al.*, nn. 333–41.

first stage of what was intended as a three-part crusade; essentially it was the first instance in *Romania* of a type of expedition geared to the circumstances of the south-east Mediterranean.[203] The league of 1342, on the other hand, was planned as a self-contained instrument with an intended life of at least three years, aimed at a problem which had grown considerably over the previous decade.[204] The league, and its successors, constituted a substantially new type of crusading venture and it is not surprising that, as we shall see in the next chapter, Clement himself did not grasp the full implications of this.

It would be misleading to close this chapter on the high note of Clement VI's undoubtedly important, even decisive, role in bringing the Smyrna crusade into existence. For it was clearly an exception to the rule. Clement himself, a decade earlier, had helped lead a French deputation which exerted enormous pressure on the Curia to sanction Philip VI's crusade project; and this was only a particularly well-documented and important example of the sort of pressure which was constantly placed on Avignon from Spain, eastern Europe, and even the papacy's own allies in Italy. This itself was less dangerous, in the long run, than the encroachments on papal authority over the launching of a crusade which were beginning to be made by the more advanced monarchies of the West. It could indeed be said that it was when pressure ceased to be placed on the Curia that the situation would be really perilous, in that the role of the pope as the validator of the *negotium Christi* was being denied or bypassed.

This would have been cold comfort for the popes and cardinals, forced periodically to work out means of ensuring that would-be crusading rulers lived up to their promises, of reconciling projects presented to the Curia with their own crusading and fiscal policies, of avoiding the launching of a crusade which might be diverted and produce a major scandal. A gloomy view would be that not only had the initiative passed to the secular powers, but that all endeavours

---

[203] Had it come to anything, a precedent would have been Venice's treaty of alliance with Charles of Valois in 1306, in which it was stipulated that 12 galleys would be sent on ahead on the major *passagium* against the Greeks, 'ad custodiam maris et terrarum, nec non ad nocendum inimicis comunibus in Imperio': *DVL*, i, n. 27. This was a significant advance on the Orvieto treaty of 1281, reflecting Venetian doubts about Charles's ability to get the major *passagium* off the ground.

[204] Ibid., i, n. 136.

to fit the resulting activity into a coherent pattern in line with the Curia's own goals were doomed by the lack of effective sanctions and came down, in the end, to an attempt to safeguard narrowly papal interests and claim a share of the taxes granted for the *camera*. But this is too pessimistic: to begin with, the aims of the secular powers and the papacy were not that incompatible. And in the last resort, the Avignon popes could always resist demands—there was not yet another pope to go to.

A balance has to be struck between the power and influence of the lay rulers—which even in the papal sources appear overwhelmingly impressive at times—and the less noticeable strengths of the Holy See, especially its diplomatic dexterity and resilience. Despite the undoubted failures, some of which sprang from the Curia's own inconsistent policies and conflicting interests, the balance is not as unfavourable to the popes as one might expect. In Spain and eastern Europe the Curia was able to shape projects, to accommodate them to its own needs and guard against its fears. Dealing with the 'interior' front, it retained the biggest say in the procedure. And in the eastern Mediterranean some important achievements arose from papal initiatives. To concentrate on the role of monarchy in the making of a crusade is thus to miss much of the subtlety of the exercise, to oversimplify a complex process.[205] Nor is this surprising in view of the nature of the crusade and the history of the crusading movement: it would have been a catastrophe indeed if the Avignon papacy had totally lost control of one of its most important functions.

[205] To this extent I disagree with Muldoon's conclusion in 'The Avignon Papacy', 190–3, particularly with reference to the papal practice of issuing 'standard-form' letters.

4

Crusade Recruitment:
The Role of Pope and Church

ONE striking characteristic of the crusades launched in this period is that those setting out to recruit an army knew not just how many men they wanted, but also of what calibre—men-at-arms, heavily-armed infantry, or crossbowmen—and, in many cases, how long they would be required. This formed part of a general trend in fourteenth-century warfare towards greater precision in the planning and assembling of armies. Military activity was increasingly expensive and called for attention to detail to cut out waste. In the case of the crusades, this might not have been possible had there been a general passage, a type of expedition by its very nature amorphous and only partially subject to official control. But no such crusade was successfully launched. Those that were, required comparatively small, expert forces. As we have seen, the numbers to be raised and the duration of hostilities were usually agreed in advance with the Curia as a precondition for the granting of crusade status; these agreements were not always adhered to, but they furnish useful guidelines to what contemporaries considered feasible.

Numbers are given most frequently in the case of crusades to the eastern Mediterranean, because both men and horses had to be carried by sea, and the numbers which were involved dictated the amount and type of shipping needed. Thus it was laid down in 1308 that the Knights of St John were to recruit 1,000 cavalry and 4,000 infantry for a five year period, for their *passagium*.[1] In a letter to Philip IV written in January 1309 the Master of the Hospitallers described in some detail the hiring of these men, the assembly of 500 brethren from the western priories to accompany the expedition, and the hiring and construction of the vessels required; he added, characteristically, that it was all costing 'an inestimable amount' of

[1] *Reg. Clem. V*, n. 2988.

money.[2] Three years later Philip of Taranto was granted the crusade indulgence for an army of 2,000 horsemen and 4,000 foot which was to accompany him to Achaea to fight the Greeks.[3] Similarly, in the complex negotiations between the French and papal courts in 1322–3 the numbers who were to take part in both preliminary *passagia* were debated in detail, together with the time-scale involved.[4] The same applied to the naval leagues of 1334 and 1342.[5] In May 1363 Peter of Cyprus was given details by the Pope of exactly how many men he could recruit in the West for his crusade: 200 noble men-at-arms in France, 2,000 horse and 6,000 foot elsewhere; only in the recruitment of *routiers* was the King given *carte blanche*.[6] These latter would be signed with the cross by their ordinaries provided the bishops judged them to be suitable fighters.[7] Details were commonplace too in talks between the Curia and the Spanish kings, although the Aragonese objected to specific conditions.[8] Only in the case of eastern Europe are we left with an impression of uncertainty at the Curia about how many should be expected to participate. But here too it is likely that the sovereigns knew approximately how many fighters they wanted.

How were soldiers raised? A distinction should be drawn between territorial princes and other powers recruiting for a crusade. The former used standard procedures for hiring fighters; there was no reason to lay aside established and reliable mechanisms of recruitment because the war was a crusade. When the French kings planned their *passagia* to the East they clearly envisaged using the system of letters of retainer which Philippe Contamine analysed as their chief means of putting together a volunteer force at this time.[9] Thus the costing of Charles IV's projected crusade of 1323 bears a marked resemblance to that of an actual expedition to Gascony in 1326–7,[10] and in August 1335 Philip VI drew up a list of salaries payable to the different kinds of fighters

---

[2] *Cartulaire général*, iv, n. 4841.
[3] *Reg. Clem. V*, n. 7893.
[4] Housley, 'Franco–Papal Crusade Negotiations', *passim*.
[5] See, for example, CC, n. 5485; Déprez *et al.*, n. 341.
[6] *AE*, ad annum 1363, n. 19, xxvi, 84.
[7] ASV, Reg. Vat. 245, f. 173ᵛ.
[8] See below, ch. 5, nn. 50–1, 67.
[9] Contamine, *Guerre*, 55–62, esp. 59.
[10] M. Jusselin, 'Comment la France se préparait à la guerre de Cent ans', *BEC*, lxxiii (1912), 220–1; Contamine, *Guerre*, 65–6n; Henneman, *Royal Taxation . . . 1322–1356*, 64.

who enlisted for his crusade. They were the standard rates for the period: twenty shillings *tournois* a day for bannerets, ten shillings for knights, and five shillings for squires.[11] Philip V had proposed the same rates of pay for his crusade.[12]

Other leaders also used familiar methods. It has been shown that in the army of Amedeo of Savoy in 1365–6 about a half of those recruited had close legal and social ties to the Count; they came from Amedeo's own household or were his hereditary vassals and their followers.[13] The little that we know of the Spanish, Polish, and Hungarian crusade armies of this period suggests that the same applied there.[14] These were first and foremost national armies. The only abnormal feature was the arrival of foreigners who had taken the cross. But the organization of royal armies was supple enough to absorb such men without strain;[15] there is a parallel in the way the French armies dealt with the contingents sent or led by neighbouring princes allied with France, during the early phase of the Anglo-French war.[16]

Two notable exceptions to this rule were the papacy and the Teutonic Order: they were in a more difficult position since they relied heavily on fighters who were not normally subject to their political authority. But in neither case did serious problems arise. In Italy those who took the cross against the Ghibellines were assimilated into the paid armies of the Church for the period of their service.[17] And in Prussia a refined system of communications kept the Knights informed of what volunteers they could expect; when these arrived they were treated with generosity but firmness.[18] Nobody in our period started out to create a crusading army of any size without experience of military organization and some sort of administrative base: the Hospitallers in 1308–9 and Peter of Cyprus

[11] F. Lot, 'Projets de Croisade sous Charles le Bel et sous Philippe de Valois', *BEC*, xx (1859), 509; Henneman, *Royal Taxation . . . 1322–1356*, 105. See also below, n. 129.

[12] CC, n. 1688. The same rates of pay were cited by Charles of Valois in 1323.

[13] Cox, 207–8.

[14] Bishko, 442. L. Garcia de Valdeavellano (*Curso de historia de las instituciones españolas de los orígenes al final de la Edad Media* (Madrid, 1968), 613–28) does not deal with the services of crusaders.

[15] At the battle of Salado Alfonso XI tactfully allowed a French knight to carry the papal banner which he had been sent. See 'Crónica de Alfonso XI', 324.

[16] Contamine, *Guerre*, 50–1.

[17] Exactly how this was done remains hard to say. See Gualdo, 606, and cf. above, ch. 2, nn. 187–90.

[18] Christiansen, 148 ff.

in 1363–5 had a core of their own brethren and vassals on whom they could rely.[19] But it was powers like these, operating outside their territorial bases, who faced the greatest difficulties in co-ordinating the complex procedures of recruitment, assembly, and shipping.

One perennial problem was desertion. In 1344, for example, Clement VI tried to retrieve the wages paid to sailors who had deserted the papal galleys in the Smyrna crusade.[20] Twenty years later, recruits who had assembled at Venice to sail under Peter of Cyprus despaired of setting out because the King was delayed, and left for home. Peter had to set about recruiting a paid force of men-at-arms, to whom Peter Thomas distributed crusade crosses; these men were later supplemented by Cypriots and Hospitallers.[21] It was in relation to such campaigns that the crusade vow may still have had some disciplinary effect: *crucesignati* who refused to obey orders during the Hospitaller crusade of 1309–10 were threatened with the loss of their privileges.[22]

This leads us into the part which the Church played in the process of recruitment. Traditionally it exerted influence in two ways, through its preaching and the spiritual rewards which it offered. The quality of preaching was much less important than it had been; the fourteenth century had no Peter the Hermit or Fulk of Neuilly, indeed it had little place for them.[23] Latin Christians were still, at least in the first half of our period, capable of displaying the popular enthusiasm for crusading which had once been so marked, but it did not depend on the expertise of preachers; it came from extraneous factors beyond papal control, indeed often not approved of by the Curia.[24] Innocent III and his immediate successors had geared up the secular Church and the Orders of friars to the preaching of the crusade in the pulpit and its advocacy in the confessional. Nothing more could be done without straining the Church's resources or

[19] Above, n. 2. Cf. P. W. Edbury, 'Feudal Obligations in the Latin East', *Byzantion*, xlvii (1977), 335–6. According to Philip of Mézières (125), Cyprus provided 60 ships for the crusade of 1365.

[20] Déprez *et al.*, nn. 815–17.

[21] Philip of Mézières, 120–1, 124–6, 127–8. See Guillaume de Machaut, 111, for Peter's payment of the mercenaries at their discharge.

[22] *Reg. Clem. V*, n. 2988.

[23] Fr. Venturino of Bergamo made an impression by his preaching against the Turks: Gay, 67 and n. See also Déprez *et al.*, n. 591. Philip of Mézières (119, 124, 126, and cf. 89, 97, 103–4) emphasized Peter Thomas's work as a crusade preacher, but this was conventional eulogizing.

[24] See below, nn. 98–123; ch. 6, nn. 178–216.

damaging its reputation. Thus John XXII rejected a curious suggestion by Philip VI in 1333 that prelates should pretend to take the
Cross at crusade gatherings in order to stir the laity into action. The
Pope wrote that this would do more harm than good, and he did not
miss the chance to make a broader comment on what the suggestion
revealed about the French court's attitude towards the crusade:
'We fear lest, by making such suggestions, you may offend your
Redeemer greatly, in which case you would not die unpunished: in
the same way that, as many believe, some of your predecessors who
perhaps practised deception in the matter of the Holy Land were
punished'.[25]

The geographical spread of preaching mattered more because its
extension might lead to the participation of foreign volunteers. The
importance of this consideration is clear both from the steady flow
of crusaders who crossed the Pyrenees and Alps to take part in
campaigns in Spain and Italy, and from the frequent attempts made
by rulers to get the crusade preached outside their own territories.
Thus in 1309 James II of Aragon pressed the Pope for recruitment
on his behalf in southern France and Navarre, in 1328 Robert of
Naples tried to get preaching against Louis the Bavarian extended
to France, and in 1333 Alfonso IV's envoy at the Curia fought hard
to prevent the crusading services of the Majorcans being transferred
from the Spanish to the eastern Mediterranean sector.[26]

But it was through the terms of the indulgence which it offered
that the Curia had most influence on recruitment. For unimportant
as the precise terms of the indulgence were for the individual
'roving crusader', they clearly mattered in the recruiting of large-
scale crusade forces,[27] and papal treatment of the indulgence is
therefore worth looking at in some detail.

Throughout the Avignon period the crusade indulgence was that
first couched by Innocent III a century earlier: 'a full pardon for
those sins for which they have truly performed contrition in their

---

[25] CC, n. 5270.
[26] *Documenta selecta*, n. 148; Housley, *Italian Crusades*, 113; 'Nachträge', nn.
56–7.
[27] Above, ch. 3, n. 96: the crucial difference is between an individual nobleman
looking for a front to fight on, and a lay power faced with the problem of organizing
an effective army. Cf. the great attention to detail on this matter in the negotiations
of 1332–3 between Philip VI and John XXII: Mollat, *Lettres communes*, n. 61324
passim.

hearts and confession through their mouths . . . and, as the reward of the just, an increase in their eternal salvation'.[28] This was sometimes referred to as 'that pardon for sins which has customarily been granted to those who set out in aid of the Holy Land'. It amounted to the full remission of the *poena* which arose from sin, together with a promise of greater joy in heaven, provided that the crusader was truly repentant and had submitted to canonical confession, thus being absolved of the *culpa* (guilt) of his sins. It was the process of absolution from guilt which was crucial to a Catholic, since the unabsolved sinner could expect eternal punishment rather than the temporal punishment left after absolution. This could explain why contemporaries very often described indulgences in terms of the remission of both *poena* and *culpa*, a technical inaccuracy: they simply wanted to stress that nothing would be lacking.[29] The point was that a properly administered crusade indulgence amounted to a guarantee of the immediate admission of the *crucesignatus* to heaven after death.

Before examining developments in the fourteenth century, it is necessary to look at how Innocent III had treated this indulgence in 1215, when it was promulgated in authoritative fashion at the Fourth Lateran Council.[30] In its full form it was granted only to those who went on crusade in person and at their own expense. In addition, two other categories of beneficiary existed. Those who went on crusade at the expense of others,[31] and those who sent a group of fighters in accordance with their financial resources and social status, received the 'full pardon of sins', shorn of the clause relating to an additional, heavenly reward. And below this came a

---

[28] *COD*, 270–1. Cf. A. Gottlob, *Kreuzablass und Almosenablass: Eine Studie über die Frühzeit des Ablasswesens* (Stuttgart, 1906), 137–9.

[29] See, for example, 'Cronica di Bologna', cols. 393, 447; 'Cronica d'Orvieto', col. 684; 'Chronicon mutinense', *RIS*, xv, col. 627; 'Chronicon astense', col. 261; *La vita di Cola di Rienzo*, 111; Giovanni Villani, bk. 9, ch. 242, ii, 294, bk. 12, ch. 31, iv, 57–8, bk. 12, ch. 39, iv, 68–70; 'Historiae romanae fragmenta', col. 370; Froissart, vi, 75; Guillaume de Machaut, 22; *Ecclesiae venetae antiquis monumentis*, ed. F. Cornaro. 12 vols. (Venice, 1749), vii, 280–2. It is clear from Matteo Villani, bk. 11, ch. 41, ii, 433–4, that this did not entail a fundamental misunderstanding of the sacrament of penance. See also W. E. Lunt, *Financial Relations of the Papacy with England*. 2 vols. (Cambridge, Mass., 1939–62), ii, 448.

[30] It formed the conclusion of the decree *Ad liberandam*, which was devoted to the organization of the Fifth Crusade: *COD*, 267–71.

[31] I think it highly unlikely that the Curia intended that *any* crusader who received a financial subsidy in the course of an expedition should descend from the first to the second category; rather, it applied to those in receipt of a regular wage.

third category of contributors, Christians who donated a sum of money or gave help or advice; such only 'shared in' the indulgence, their reward being the remission of penance equivalent to a speci- fied period of time which their souls would otherwise have spent in purgatory. Innocent's schema or schedule was copied with only minor changes at the two Lyons councils of 1245 and 1274 and can be regarded as the definitive approach of the thirteenth-century papacy towards the indulgence.[32]

Innocent III's intentions are quite clear. He was reserving the indulgence at its fullest for those who fought in person, and without placing a major financial burden on the Church or the lay leaders of the expedition. The second category was part of the Pope's pains- taking response to the growing financial strain on the organizers of crusades at the end of the twelfth century: *crucesignati*—for it is clear that these people still took the cross—who forfeited their share of the *augmentum salutis aeternae* which was enjoyed by those who made the greatest sacrifices in Christ's service. The third category too was in part a response to financial pressures, but it also arose from the Pope's earnest concern to broaden popular partici- pation in the crusading movement by granting partial indulgences to all who wished to help without making the full legal commitment of taking the cross.

Now let us see what became of this schema in the Avignon period. Laying aside minor variations of wording, it was treated in three main ways. The first of these was overall adherence to Innocent's threefold division of service and reward, with some small but interesting changes. One such was the addition of the clause that if a *crucesignatus* died *en route* to a campaign, or hostilities ceased while he was performing his period of service, he would still receive the indulgence promised.[33] The first part of this was only the explicit statement of what had long been a standard ruling.[34] Similar was Urban V's ruling of 1369 that those who fought in the Veneto- Genoese league against the Mamluks should receive the indulgence if they died of wounds incurred, or illness contracted, in the course of the campaign, even though they failed to serve out the stipulated year.[35] A more unusual variation was the ruling that those who

[32] See Purcell, 23–31, 195, 198–9; Brundage, 154.
[33] Examples include ASV, Reg. Vat. 74, ff. 3^v–5^r, n. 8; *Reg. Clem. V*, n. 9941; Daumet, n. 175; Gasnault *et al.*, n. 1876; *Codex dipl.*, ed. Theiner, ii, n. 467.
[34] Brundage, 151–2.   [35] *DVL*, ii, n. 87.

fought throughout a crusade would gain the full indulgence, but those who fought for a year, either in one period or in a series of shorter periods which added up to a year, would only 'share in' the indulgence. This curious clause was applied to the crusade of the Infantes of Castile in 1317–18, an expedition which was to last for three years in all.[36] Two variations can best be explained as attempts to bolster recruitment. One was the extension of 'participation' to those who sent a soldier or soldiers without stretching their financial resources as far as inclusion in Innocent III's second category would have demanded.[37] The other was the merging of Innocent's first two categories so that the full indulgence, including the *augmentum salutis aeternae*, was granted to all who took the cross, whether to fight in person or to send deputies.[38]

By 1305 the Church had long adopted the practice of granting the crusade indulgence to groups connected with the preparation of a crusade rather than its progress in the field; these included not just those who sent deputies,[39] but also preachers, collectors, diplomatic envoys, proctors, and even the wives of *crucesignati*.[40] The Curia had come to accept that those who maintained order at home during a crusade were entitled to spiritual rewards, and one of the most interesting of the fourteenth-century measures relates to this practice. In July 1333 John XXII agreed to grant the crusade indulgence to twelve regents who would be selected by Philip VI to govern France during the King's absence in the East. To a hundred others who would stay behind for the same reason the Pope granted the indulgence on condition that they made a substantial financial contribution to the expedition, and to all who defended France 'in person or in another way' he promised partial indulgences.[41] To some extent this was a logical development of the longstanding

---

[36] ASV, Reg. Vat. 63, f. 314[r–v], n. 1102; Reg. Vat. 68, f. 232[r–v], n. 1695. In these cases those who died *en route* to the front would also only 'participate in' the indulgence.

[37] See, for example, *Reg. Clem. V*, n. 9941; *DVL*, ii, n. 87; *VMH*, ii, n. 270.

[38] Examples include *Thesaurus novus anecdotorum*, ed. E. Martène and U. Durand. 5 vols. (Paris, 1717), ii, col. 720; *Codex dipl.*, ed. Theiner, i, n. 710; Gasnault *et al.*, n. 1876. See also Appendix III.

[39] In 1366 Urban V reminded Charles V, Joanna of Naples, and the Prince of Wales that they could earn a full indulgence by sending men in aid of Cyprus and Rhodes. See LM, n. 2418.

[40] Brundage, 153–5; Purcell, 57–62. Missionaries too received the crusade indulgence: *Acta Joannis XXII*, n. 48.

[41] CC, n. 5207. This was in response to substantial pressure from French negotiators. See Mollat, *Letters communes*, n. 61324, 240.

practice of granting Church protection to crusaders' lands: the clause follows the formal placing of the Kingdom under the guardianship of St Peter. But it was easy to misconstrue it as papal acceptance of the Capetian–Valois propaganda theme that to defend France was to perform a holy task. The pattern is familiar,[42] and it is somewhat ominous that Peter Dubois had earlier suggested the granting of the crusade indulgence to those who helped restrain warmakers in the West.[43]

The second way in which the Avignonese Curia treated Innocent III's schema was to abandon his tripartite arrangement altogether and grant the crusade indulgence only to those Christians who died in action or of wounds received there.[44] This form of indulgence we encountered in the last chapter as a means of 'downgrading' the crusade. It is unlikely that those who fought in such a campaign took the cross, since the legal framework of the vow would be hard to apply. Instead a priest would hear the soldier's confession and grant him the indulgence when he was close to death. The Curia attempted to guard against abuses by attaching stringent conditions to the grant of indulgences *in articulo mortis*: the recipient usually had to be 'sincere in his faith and devoted to holy mother Church'; he had to promise satisfaction to those he had wronged; and it was specified that the indulgence would not apply in the case of sins committed on the strength of the pardon itself.[45] Associated with this type of grant is that of the remission of a specified period of enjoined penance to all who fought against those designated enemies of the Faith, such as the grant to Vladislav Lokietek in 1319.[46] A grant of the crusade indulgence *in articulo mortis* was sometimes combined with that of the remission of enjoined penance, as in Poland in 1325, and in the case of military action against heretics.[47]

---

[42] See above, ch. 3, nn. 37–40. Cf. Clement VI's letters of 1346–7 granting Philip VI and John of Normandy the plenary indulgence on all occasions when they faced death *pro regni defensione*: Déprez *et al.*, nn. 2928, 3409. See also *VPA*, ii, 304–5.

[43] *De recuperatione terre sancte*, 9–10.

[44] See, for example, ASV, Reg. Vat. 74, f. 93ᵛ, n. 209 (Frankish Greece); Reg. Vat. 74, f. 3ᵛ, n. 7 (Armenia); *AE*, ad annum 1323, n. 21, xxiv, 213 (Norway); *VMP*, i, n. 316 (Poland); *VMH*, i, n. 945 (Hungary); *Codex dipl.*, ed. Theiner, ii, n. 355 (Italy). I have found no examples of this in the case of Spain.

[45] See, for example, *Acta Ben. XII*, n. 5; ASV, Reg. Vat. 264, ff. 77ᵛ–78ʳ, f. 189ʳ⁻ᵛ. Cf. ibid., f. 203ʳ⁻ᵛ.

[46] *VMP*, i, n. 242. Cf. the curious grant to Alfonso XI of Castile in 1345: *AE*, ad annum 1345, n. 53, xxv, 348.

[47] *VMP*, i, nn. 316, 334; *VMH*, i, n. 787; *Acta Joannis XXII*, n. 18.

Clearly this type of concession had become the standard papal response to a situation which called for some identification of military service with spiritual reward but did not need, or would not benefit from, full-scale crusade preaching. A good example is the organization of armed defence against the *routiers* in France and Italy, so that the grant of indulgences *in articulo mortis* was the usual papal reply to pleas for help coming from harassed local authorities.[48] It is interesting to find it becoming the usual form of indulgence too in the struggle against the Visconti: Gregory XI issued more than a dozen such grants to the followers of the Church and its allies between 1372 and 1376.[49] Perhaps military professionalism had made even the occasional use of voluntary crusaders to supplement the Church's paid armies—the practice under earlier Avignon popes—an obsolete approach. On the other hand, the Curia was presumably persuaded that the troops paid by itself and its allies would fight better if they had a guarantee of spiritual as well as material wages.

The Curia was the more willing to be liberal in its grant of indulgences *in articulo mortis* in that they were uncomplicated and called for little organization on the part of the Church. Like licences to trade with Egypt, they were often granted for several years at a time—usually three, but in one instance twelve—and could be renewed on request. The soldiers hired by Martin Zaccaria to defend Chios, for example, were granted a three-year indulgence in 1323, extended for another three years in 1325.[50] A grant to the soldiers of Otto of Brunswick in September 1373 contained the clause that 'they [the indulgences] are valid only for the duration of the said war, and while the alliance between ourselves, the Church, and your nobility, is in operation'.[51] The corresponding disadvantage of issuing these indulgences was that the lay powers concerned often expressed disappointment at the limited nature of the grant, and pressed for more; this implies that fighting men perceived the distinction involved.[52]

It is, however, the third approach which the Avignonese Curia

---

[48] See Housley, 'Mercenary Companies', 260–1, 264.

[49] See above, ch. 2, nn. 183–4.

[50] ASV, Reg. Vat. 74, f. 186^{r-v}. n. 515; Reg. Vat. 78, f. 301^r, n. 882.

[51] 'presentibus iamdictis guerra ac liga que inter nos eandemque ecclesiam ac nobilitatem tuam viget durantibus tantummodo valituris': ASV, Reg. Vat. 265, f. 198^v.

[52] Housley, 'Mercenary Companies', 260–1, 264.

took towards Innocent III's schema which is most interesting, because it was clearly a response to renewed financial pressures in the crusading movement. Every crusade army in our period, with the exception of some of the *ad hoc* groups which tried to engage the *routiers,* included large numbers of paid troops. This was bound to be the case since, as we have seen, recruitment followed established patterns such as the drawing up of indentures and letters of retainer. These men may have been crusaders too, fighting as deputies under Innocent III's second category: there is usually no way of knowing and for our present purpose it is not important. The point is that these men had to be paid. But with economic problems and the growing rivalry of national taxes, the returns from crusade taxes were shrinking. A way had to be found to top up such revenues.[53]

Innocent III had provided a partial solution by allowing people to earn some remission of sins by donating money. But Innocent's schema had two disadvantages from the point of view of fund-raising. First, it was not possible to secure the full indulgence by making a simple cash donation. Provision had to be made for the despatch of troops to fight vicariously. This aspect of Innocent's approach was probably related to his hope that each Christian community would organize a number of its members to fight in person, an aim idealistic in its day and never fully achieved.[54] It was too difficult for the potential *crucesignatus* to find the soldiers, hire them, and, most importantly, ensure that they would not desert. Thus in 1307 Bishop John of Prague wrote of the inadequacies of the practice whereby the family of a deceased man paid mercenaries to go and fight in Prussia on his behalf; either the surrogates failed to go or they returned early, giving little help to Prussia and endangering the soul of the beneficiary. The Bishop considered it better that the money be paid to the Teutonic Order.[55] This was indeed the only practicable solution to the problem of deputized service: that any man or woman with the necessary resources should be able to give the money to an authority which would then assume the burden of organizing the contingent.[56] The second disadvantage in Inno-

---

[53] For this paragraph, see Brundage, 194–5.

[54] See Purcell, 189–90. At times it was achieved by some self-governing Italian cities: below, nn. 94, 115, 131–2. Peter Dubois thought along similar lines: *De recuperatione terre sancte,* 15–16.   [55] *CDP,* ii, n. 55.

[56] Although the passage is not entirely clear, Maureen Purcell (119) appears to have thought that this had been achieved by 1215. But the text of *Ad liberandam* makes a clear distinction between the sending of troops and the donation of money.

cent's schema was that the clause on sharing in the indulgence was too vague, leaving too much for individual preachers and confessors to decide. Many Christians were unwilling to give cash unless they knew what they would gain by so doing. A scale of payment and remission was needed.

Some thirteenth-century popes and their agents, already pressed by rising costs, had made alterations to Innocent's schedule. On occasion the full indulgence was offered in exchange for a specified proportion of a donor's property or income.[57] More importantly, Innocent III's provision for the redemption of vows had been exploited so that people were encouraged to take the cross with the intention of redeeming their vows very shortly afterwards in exchange for payment.[58] But neither approach constituted a satisfactory solution in the long term. Systematic vow redemption was clearly an abuse which the Curia turned its back on before 1291, and any other form of financial administration of the indulgence which could be devised smacked of simony. There was also the practical consideration that if the indulgence was made readily available for cash, personal participation would suffer.[59] The Avignonese Curia thus inherited a policy on the distribution of indulgences which was inherently confused, shaped by financial need on the one hand, and practical and theological considerations on the other. What was its own solution?

At the very beginning of our period, in 1308–9, Clement V addressed himself to both disadvantages of Innocent III's schema. The Hospitaller *passagium*, an army of 5,000 men, was to be financed without the levy of a special tax, and the Pope launched a determined campaign to raise lay donations. Adapting ideas of his predecessors,[60] Clement decreed that a Christian who gave a sum equivalent to what he or she would have spent in accompanying the general passage which was planned to follow the Knights' preliminary *passagium*, would gain the full crusade indulgence. He also established a scale of lesser indulgences together with the sum to be paid for each.[61] In November 1309 the same measures were applied

[57] Purcell, 60; Housley, *Italian Crusades*, 130–1.
[58] Purcell, 118–32; Brundage, 68 ff.; Throop, 82–95.
[59] Purcell, 95–7; Brundage, 153; Throop, 191.
[60] Purcell, 125–6n; Brundage, 77–8 (a decretal of Innocent III included in the *Compilatio tertia*).
[61] *Reg. Clem. V*, nn. 2989–90. The first measure applied only to non-combatants: fighting men were expected to take part in the general passage.

to the Granada crusade, at the insistent request of James II. The
Aragonese could earn a plenary or lesser indulgence by paying
subsidies to the royal treasury.[62] It was a short-lived concession:
when indulgences were next granted for the Granada war, in 1312,
the Innocentian schema was restored.[63]

It is not possible to say how successful Clement's measures were.
Italian and French chroniclers were impressed by the sums and
goods deposited in the Hospitaller chests and collected by the
Order's agents: 'they collected much linen cloth, armour, many
horses, money, and jewels'.[64] We possess a number of notarial acts
testifying to the deposit of large sums of money at Linköping in
Sweden.[65] But in some areas the Knights encountered opposition to
the collection of their money. Thus in 1314 one of their officials
complained that the Venetian authorities had sequestrated the
money collected by his lieutenant in Germany; he demanded the
return of the money in the names of the Pope and the King of
France.[66] As late as 1321 the money donated to the Order in Castile
and Portugal had not been handed over.[67] It is noteworthy too that
the sums collected were not large enough to stop the Order plunging
into severe debt at this time.[68]

One problem of this approach was how to involve the donors
psychologically in the progress of the crusade to which they were
making an 'armchair contribution'. The Hospitallers appear to
have attempted to deal with this difficulty, for an interesting aspect
of their fundraising campaign is the statement in one of the Swedish
acts that those who gave money to the *passagium* were to be enlisted
as *confratres* of the Order. In January 1313 Leonard de Tibertis,
whom the Master had designated as his proctor to collect the
proceeds of the indulgences, appointed lieutenants to gather in the
money contributed in Scandinavia. They were told 'to receive
Christ's faithful, the helpers [*adiutores*] of the said passage, into the
fellowship of confraternity, so that they share in all the spiritual

[62] Ibid., nn. 5092–3.

[63] Ibid., nn. 8461–4.

[64] Mas Latrie, ii, 131n. See also Cont. William of Nangis, i, 371; Giovanni Villani,
bk. 8, ch. 104, ii, 137.

[65] *Acta pont. svecica*, i, nn. 128–30, 138–9. Money collected in Sweden can be
compared with the proceeds of the tenth there: Riant, 395–6.

[66] *I libri comm.*, i, 143–4, n. 630. See also Luttrell, 'Venice and the Knights
Hospitallers', 202.

[67] Mollat, *Lettres communes*, nn. 13043–4.

[68] See below, ch. 8, nn. 95–101.

benefits already earned, or to be earned, by the brethren of the said Hospital both overseas and in the West'.[69]

The neatness of Clement V's schema was that it killed two birds with one stone. It kept the expedition to the desired size—though not without problems, as we shall see—while providing some of the extra funds which a sea-borne *passagium* required, and which could not be supplied by Church taxes because these would be needed for the subsequent general passage. The point was not lost on contemporaries. Writing in 1312, the Venetian crusade theorist Marino Sanudo argued along much the same lines with his usual combination of enthusiasm and painstaking detail. Sanudo was determined to make his crusade of recovery as practical a proposition as possible. As its first stage he wanted a force of just 300 horse and 15,000 foot to establish a bridgehead in Egypt. It would be made up mainly of professional sailors, oarsmen, crossbowmen, lancers, and engineers, 'who cannot be enlisted except for wages because they are poor people, and none of them could afford to take the Cross even if they wanted to, because of their poverty'.[70]

To pay for this professional *passagium*, and also to exclude undisciplined volunteers, Sanudo suggested the distribution of indulgences in exchange for cash:

I reverently ask and suggest . . . that if somebody wants to take the cross to go in person at his own expense, it seems more useful to me that the sum of money which he would spend in going across in person with the Church's army, be handed over to the Church, or to somebody deputized for this by the Church, to be spent on the wages of hired troops. In exchange for this, the donor should receive the indulgence which your holiness thinks fitting. For mercenaries pay more attention to the orders of their captain than crusaders do, and obey them better.[71]

Although the Venetian hesitated to suggest that the full indulgence be offered in exchange for cash, he was in effect proposing Clement V's measure, and for much the same reason. Nor was Marino Sanudo the only one to perceive the advantages of Clement's schema. In 1319 Louis of Clermont wanted John XXII to grant his

---

[69] *Acta pont. svecica*, i, n. 132. See also Riley-Smith, *Knights of St John*, 242 ff.
[70] 'Liber secretorum fidelium crucis', 74. For the dating of book two, see Delaville le Roulx, *La France en orient*, 33n. In 1308 Clement V expected the sailors and rowers who accompanied the Hospitaller *passagium* to take the Cross: *Reg. Clem. V*, n. 2988.
[71] 'Liber secretorum fidelium crucis', 74, and cf. 81, 90.

proposed *passagium* 'the same indulgences, graces, and privileges which Pope Clement gave to the Hospitallers for the Holy Land'. This was one of three proposals for raising the cash needed.[72]

It was, however, some time before the Curia made another outright attempt to use the appeal of the crusade indulgence to raise money along the lines of Clement V's bulls. In general it reverted to older formulae, although there was a notable exception in 1340, when Benedict XII conceded the full indulgence to all who gave Alfonso XI of Castile a sum equivalent to the cost of a year's service in the field.[73] Then, in September 1343, Clement VI issued the bull *Insurgentibus contra fidem*, to help defray the costs of the naval league against the Turks. The purpose of the preaching decreed in the bull was clearly financial. The Pope described how he had responded to news of Turkish attacks by organizing the league, and how he intended to pay for the papal galleys in the first year by direct subventions from the *camera*, and in subsequent years through the levy of the tenth.

The matter in hand necessitates a very great outlay of money and calls for larger revenues [than the tenth alone]. The charitable aid of the faithful is of the greatest importance to help it along, and so we are making provision to invite the contributions of the said faithful with certain spiritual rewards—that is to say, indulgences and remissions.[74]

It was for this reason that the crusade was to be preached and that a plenary indulgence was offered to all who gave what they would have spent had they fought for a year. Chests were to be placed in churches and the proceeds would be collected by papal agents. The preaching was stepped up in July 1345 when the friars were drafted in as special preachers.[75]

Clearly circumstances were very similar to those in 1308–9. A small-scale expedition was being sent to the eastern Mediterranean. There was no opportunity for most Christians to take part in the crusade in person, or even to send deputies, yet it was undoubtedly a holy work, a *negotium fidei*, for which spiritual benefits could be made available; and the heavy costs of the league had to be met,

---

[72] *Titres de la maison ducale de Bourbon*, i, n. 1633.

[73] Goñi Gaztambide, 323. John XXII appears to have resisted the pressure applied by Philip VI's envoys in 1332–3 for a liberal interpretation of the indulgence (Mollat, *Lettres communes*, n. 61324, pp. 237, 241; CC, nn. 5207, 5210), although there were abuses in the way it was subsequently administered ('Les Papiers', 214).

[74] *Acta pont. svecica*, i, n. 337.   [75] Déprez *et al.*, nn. 1855–6.

although, unlike 1308–9, a clerical tenth was being levied. But it is noticeable that only one of Clement V's measures was revived by his successor: there was no scale of indulgences, just the usual Innocentian third category relating to partial indulgences. Indeed, Clement V's scale was not revived by the Curia before 1378. This could explain why the preaching of indulgences for the Smyrna crusade was less successful than in the case of the Hospitaller *passagium*, for it did not catch the attention of the chroniclers and Clement VI was later to complain that he was prevented from continuing the league's activities by lack of funds.[76] On the other hand, economic conditions had deteriorated and were no longer propitious for the raising of cash.

The financial administration of the indulgence was now firmly associated with naval activity against the Turks, and it is not surprising that Clement VI's measure was repeated by Innocent VI in May 1359 when he sent Peter Thomas to the East as his legate in charge of the renewed naval league. Again the crusade indulgence was made available to all who contributed what they would have spent in the course of a year's service.[77] The faculty was used by Peter Thomas, for on 28 September 1361 he commissioned Franciscan and Dominican friars to preach the crusade at Venice, handing out crosses to all who wanted to go to Smyrna, send deputies 'or offer help from their resources'. The money which the friars collected was to be placed in the hands of two reliable persons chosen by the Doge, who would send it on to Crete, 'because we plan, with God's aid, to assemble a fleet in the near future against the enemies of the Faith'.[78] There can be little doubt that Gregory XI too would have revived his uncle's measure if his plans for a naval league had reached fruition.

In April 1363 Urban V introduced a clause into his crusade bulls against Bernabò Visconti which went a stage further than this measure of Clement V, Clement VI, and Innocent VI. The crusade indulgence, he instructed Albornoz, was to be offered not only to those who fought in person or sent troops, but also to people who 'give you another form of subvention, which you or your agents judge to be acceptable'.[79] Urban was coming very close to the

---

[76] Ibid., n. 2957; Déprez and Mollat, n. 2060; *DVL*, i, n. 172.

[77] Wadding, 150–7.

[78] *Ecclesiae venetae antiquis monumentis*, vii, 280–2.

[79] '. . . subventionem aliam exhiberent tuo, vel eorum quibus hoc committeres iudicio, acceptandam': ASV, Reg. Vat. 245, f. 144ᵛ, and cf. f. 146ʳ.

forthright 'sale' of the indulgence which was soon to be sanctioned by the popes during the Great Schism.[80] But it was an approach which the Curia failed, at this stage, to pursue: in his bull of 1368 against Bernabò Visconti, Urban withdrew the additional clause.[81]

The papacy, then, was hesitant. Without wishing to play down the importance of the measures which we have just examined, the fact remains that the majority of bulls issued in our period adhered to the framework of Innocent III's schema; they were directed primarily at the recruitment of crusaders, and only in a subsidiary sense at fundraising. Why was the Curia so conservative? We cannot be sure, but the evidence points to a continuing concern about the religious and practical consequences of raising money by selling remission of sins—or at least, what would appear as such. As in the thirteenth century, these factors were in conflict with urgent financial need. Clement V was driven to introduce his measures of 1308–9 by the fact that he could not raise Church taxes for the *passagium*. The better off Clement VI may well have baulked at the simoniacal implications of Clement V's scale of payment and reward, even though he was himself very liberal in his interpretation of the concept of a Treasury of Merits.[82] These suppositions are supported by the fact that Benedict XII's concession to Alfonso XI in 1340 came at a time of crisis for the King, whose military expenses were crippling him,[83] while in 1362 Urban V complained of the 'most heavy and burdensome expenses' which the war against the Visconti imposed on the Church.[84] When, after 1378, these difficulties grew yet worse, a series of precedents thus existed for the more radical developments of the Schism.

It is not enough, however, just to examine the crusade bulls. For there was often a big difference between the approach laid down by the Curia, and the abuses which crept in during the preaching. For

---

[80] As early as March 1381 Urban VI offered the crusade indulgence 'eis insuper qui suis dumtaxat expensis iuxta quantitates et facultates suas destinabunt, vel tibi seu alteri per te deputando ministrabunt sufficiencia stipendia, ut destinare valeas, idoneos bellatores per dictum tempus moraturos et bellaturos ibidem': *Wykeham's Register*, ed. T. F. Kirby. 2 vols. (London–Winchester, 1896–9), ii, 205–6. See also Lunt, ii, 535 ff. This and similar developments during the Great Schism call for detailed investigation.   [81] ASV, Reg. Vat. 249, f. 108[r–v]. See Appendix III.

[82] For example, in his treatment of the Jubilee Indulgence of 1350: see below, n. 162.

[83] He had to pawn his crown jewels to raise money. See Hillgarth, *Spanish Kingdoms*, 341.

[84] 'gravissimarum expensarum onera': ASV, Reg. Vat. 245, f. 32[r].

example, Italian chroniclers report abuses in the preaching of the crusade against the Ghibellines and the Great Company in 1355–7 which are strikingly reminiscent of those reported a century earlier in connection with the redemption of vows.[85] Matteo Villani recounted what happened when the Bishop of Narni preached at Florence in 1355–6. His agents exceeded their brief, 'forgiving sins and absolving from vows of all descriptions in exchange for sums of money which varied according to what they could get'. In the city, and the towns and villages of its *contado*, women and the poor were allowed to hand over woollen and linen cloth, and grain, to pay for the indulgence.[86] The chronicler of Modena, too, complained that the preachers in his city did things for which they appeared to have no papal authority, 'remitting *poena* and *culpa* for all sins, with the exception of the four [reserved] cases, to anybody who handed over money in accordance with his resources'.[87] 'A very great deal of money' was collected at Bologna too, probably by offering the full indulgence in exchange for cash.[88] According to one historian, this sequence of events caused 'a grave scandal and discontent amongst the population', though this is probably to exaggerate.[89]

The chroniclers saw all this as the clear abuse of delegated authority, but it was not that simple. The decision to adopt this liberal approach seems to have originated with Cardinal Albornoz, as the chance survival of one of the legate's letters informs us. For in February 1356 Albornoz appointed the Patriarch of Grado as preacher in the provinces of Aquileia, Grado, and Ravenna. In the letter of commission Innocent VI's bull is quoted, but with significant additions introduced by the legate (in italics):

We also declare that a full pardon for their sins can be enjoyed by those who, at their own expense, and in accordance with their resources and ability, send suitable fighters to remain and work in the field for the said period of time. *If they prefer, they can send the customary wages of the said fighters each month for the specified period of time* [a year]: *that is to say, the seven florins for a man-at-arms, and three florins for a footman, which the Church has become accustomed to pay its troops.*[90]

---

[85] See Throop, 87 ff.; Purcell, 124–9.
[86] Bk. 6, ch. 14, i, 478–9.   [87] 'Chronicon mutinense', col. 627.
[88] 'Cronica di Bologna', col. 447. In this instance it is specified that people took the cross and redeemed their vows for cash.
[89] Filippini, 308, and see too 194–5. Cf. Goñi Gaztambide, 291–2, 334, for abuses in Spain.
[90] *Appendice ai Monumenti ravennati . . . del conte M. Fantuzzi*, ed. A. Tarlazzi.

This document raises a number of questions which we are not able to answer. Was Albornoz acting within his brief according to papal instructions which we do not possess? He was allowed a certain amount of independent action by Innocent VI, and this move may fall within that category.[91] Were there other instances of papal legates and nuncios, and even secular rulers, making important changes and additions to the crusade bulls sent them, with or without papal permission to take such steps? And, perhaps the most tantalizing question, was Albornoz employing a procedure on the indulgence which he had learnt in Alfonso XI's campaigns in Spain, and which was quite common there? The letter is a salutary warning against relying exclusively on papal sources when examining developments in the Avignonese period: for it is another variation on the theme of papal control over events and its steady erosion. In a sense the infringement was more serious than that examined in the previous chapter, since it related to the Curia's own machinery of preaching and recruitment.

Albornoz's instructions were roughly in accordance with Innocent III's proposals for vicarious service, and came about quite naturally once the idea of the crusade as a work of condign satisfaction had been thrust into the background. The trouble was that rates of payment could be lowered in times of crisis, and this led to anomalies and discontent.[92] Matteo Villani furnished details of just such a development occurring in 1357, when the Bishop of Narni returned to Florence to preach against the Great Company. In the previous year Innocent VI had allowed Albornoz to reduce the period of time for which a *crucesignatus* had to fight in Romagna, and the Bishop eagerly capitalized on this concession.[93] He announced that twelve people could club together to pay the salary of one man-at-arms to serve for six months. The payment of fifteen days' wages, or three and a half florins according to the rates quoted by Albornoz in 1356, thus earned the crusade indulgence, and it appears from the chronicle that the Bishop did not even insist

---

3 vols. (Ravenna, 1869–86), ii, n. 155, 278 and cf. 276. See also *I libri comm.*, ii, 240, n. 129. Albornoz introduced a number of other measures relating to the privileges of *crucesignati*.

[91] See above, ch. 3, nn. 7–8.

[92] Cf. Purcell, 65: 'The distributor with a genuinely urgent cause on hand was dangerously open to the temptation of offering indulgences at bargain prices for the sake of a maximum immediate gain.'

[93] Gasnault *et al.*, n. 2020.

on the soldier being found, hired, and sent off by each group, but simply took the money himself to be forwarded to Albornoz. Not surprisingly he collected large sums, between 1,000 and 1,500 florins each day, 'mainly from women and the poor'. Then the communal authorities intervened. As they had already debated sending armed help to the legate, they negotiated with the Bishop and 'it was agreed that the army would serve on behalf of the whole commune, so that everyone could enjoy the pardon'. So the Bishop announced in July 1357 that all Florentines, together with their subject *contadini* and communes, who confessed within three months would receive the full indulgence.[94] Such was the result when the concept of vicarious service was carried to its logical extreme.

Any consideration of the way the crusade indulgence was handled in the fourteenth century thus has to take into account several levels of activity. The Curia sent out bulls which themselves illustrated a wide range of approaches, from straightforward adherence to the formulae of Innocent III and the Fourth Lateran Council, to a phraseology which in practice—though never in theory—entailed the distribution of the crusade indulgence in exchange for cash payments. We have at least one instance of a hard pressed legate treating a crusade bull as a fiscal device, while at the same time using it to recruit soldiers. And distortion inevitably crept in at the level of preaching, through preachers who, even if not guilty of corruption or an excess of zeal, cannot always have understood, or adhered to, the fine distinctions within the bulls which they worked with. Finally, there were the many false pardoners against whom the Church waged a constant struggle, but who naturally battened on a system which was at once ramshackle and profitable. Despite the restraint displayed by some of the Avignon popes, the overall trend was all too clear.

Within the crusading armies themselves the Church wanted trained and trustworthy fighters, *Christi milites*. In its praise of its champions it dwelt equally on their religious zeal, military prowess, and courage. Charles of Valois, for example, who led or proposed leading expeditions on a variety of fronts, was described by Clement V as

[94] Matteo Villani, bk. 7, chs. 80, 84, ii, 69–70, 72–3.

assisting the said Church and its faithful at opportune moments, thinking only of God's business, with a fervent spirit, a strong arm, and readiness for action; sparing no labours, he has endangered himself and his people for the defence of the Faith and the liberty of the Church.[95]

By contrast, the Curia had long before made the decision that the old, infirm, and untrained in war should not be encouraged to take part in crusading expeditions. Thus John XXII in 1333, and Urban V in 1363, wrote that only those who would be useful in the planned general passage should be allowed to take the cross.[96] Secular authorities agreed; the rulers of Venice voiced a common sentiment in 1332 when they wrote in derogatory terms of the 'vile and unwarlike people' who would want to accompany the crusade which Philip VI was planning.[97] The rationale of the measures taken by Clement V in 1308–9, and by Clement VI in 1343, was that civilians could earn even as much as a plenary indulgence without clogging the wheels of the military machine. But logical and practical as this approach was, it proved no easier to implement in the fourteenth century than it had in the twelfth and thirteenth. Concepts of planning and strategy dating back to Innocent III had not yet submerged the pilgrimage element in the crusading movement. As late as 1332 the Venetians clearly doubted whether it would be possible to exclude non-combatants from a general passage. For the true experience of crusading remained a personal, not a vicarious one, and the early part of the Avignon period gave rise to two outbursts of popular enthusiasm for the crusade which ignored papal policy on participation in spontaneous attempts to revive the idea of a People's Crusade.

The first outburst occurred in 1309 as a result of the preaching for the Hospitaller *passagium*. Large numbers of peasants and the urban poor in England, Picardy, Brabant, Flanders, and Germany defied the Pope's clearly expressed aim of restricting the size of the expedition by indiscriminately, and illicitly, signing themselves with the cross.[98] The movement grew rapidly in the spring and summer months of 1309. It was incapable of making any real contribution to the crusade because, although probably not as disorganized and

[95] *Reg. Clem. V*, n. 1768.

[96] CC, n. 5210; *AE*, ad annum 1363, nn. 17–18, xxvi, 83–4.

[97] *DVL*, i, n. 110. Cf. G. Servois, 'Emprunts de Saint Louis en Palestine et en Afrique', *BEC*, xix (1858), 293; Brundage, 69.

[98] Clement V expressly forbade preaching for personal participation: *Reg. Clem. V*, n. 2988.

rapacious as the chroniclers claimed, it lacked the basic preparatory measures needed. Some of the participants hoped to arrange transport down the Danube, but most headed for the Mediterranean, in the hope that Clement V and Fulk of Villaret would make use of their zeal and enthusiasm. In July 30,000 or 40,000 people were said to have arrived at Avignon clamouring for a general passage. The Hospitallers neither wanted their services nor had the ships to transport them. Clement V was sympathetic towards their plight, but in the circumstances there was nothing he could do. In a letter written on behalf of the German *crucesignati* he granted partial indulgences to both them and their sponsors, told them to reassemble when the general passage was announced, and dispersed them to their homes. In the course of the summer and autumn months the movement fizzled out.[99]

The 'People's Crusade' of 1309 had some of the aspects of a social revolt: it may have coincided with high food prices, and its participants acted to form by killing such Jews as they could lay their hands on. The one which followed in 1320 was more clearly related to the deteriorating economic conditions of the previous years, especially the terrible famine of 1315–17. The *Pastoureaux*, or 'Shepherds' Crusade' of 1320 was on a larger and more violent scale than its predecessor. Several Jewish communities were subjected to attack.[100] John XXII reacted more harshly than Clement V had done. In June, writing to the Archbishop of Narbonne and his suffragans, he cast doubt on the motives of the *Pastoureaux*, 'who are pretending that they want to cross over in aid of the Holy Land'. This was hard to believe since they lacked arms, leaders, and transport. On the other hand, they had committed acts of robbery and violence against clerics, Jews, and the laity, and they constituted an obstacle to the crusade plans of Philip V. The Pope ordered their dispersal through the use of Church censures and, when necessary and feasible, the action of the civil authorities.[101]

Malcolm Barber has shown that the movement of 1320 sprang at least in part from the cruel psychology of royal policy in France over the previous decades, and from the continual stimulation of crusading fervour amongst the population at large without the provision of

[99] Ibid., n. 4400; Housley, 'Pope Clement V', 36. The references in Clement's letter to *crucesignati* who had been sponsored shows that the movement had its respectable participants.

[100] See Barber, 'The Pastoureaux', *passim*.

[101] CC, n. 1104, and see also nn. 1105–7, 1111, 1113–15, 1131.

an outlet for the energy thus aroused.[102] In this light, it is interesting to compare both it and its predecessor with a third outbreak of popular enthusiasm which was inspired by a real crusading success, and was greeted and encouraged with excited approval by the Curia rather than with ambivalence or hostility. That the news of the capture of part of Smyrna by the naval league in October 1344 was received in the West with exhilaration is not surprising, given the hopes invested in the league, the sale of indulgences on its behalf, and the lack of any comparable success in the eastern Mediterranean within the lifetime of contemporaries. But the scale of the enthusiasm which resulted in 1344–5 has not been given its full due by historians.[103] It was deep-rooted enough to be stimulated rather than discouraged by the news of the massacre of the league's leaders on St Anthony's Day, and lasted until the departure of Humbert of Vienne in the autumn of 1345. One factor in maintaining enthusiasm was the circulation of a curious letter describing a fabricated Christian victory near Smyrna in June 1345, in which 70,000 Turks died for minimal losses amongst the crusaders.[104] Another was the occurrence of miraculous signs testifying to God's favour. In July 1345 Clement VI wrote of the widespread appearance of 'shining crosses' which cured the illnesses of those who observed them, and there was a notable vision of the Virgin carrying the infant Christ, in a church at Aquila, in southern Italy.[105]

In some Italian cities comparatively large groups of individuals responded to these events by taking the cross and setting out in 1345–6 to fight at Smyrna. After the Aquila miracle 'many *Aquilani* and some others from the countryside took the cross and went to fight against the infidels'.[106] It was in Tuscany and Lombardy that the preaching had its greatest response: this second phase of the Smyrna crusade was in fact a peculiarly north Italian venture. Giovanni Villani, who is usually reliable on local events and numbers, wrote of 400 men setting out from Florence, 350 from Siena, and contingents too from other cities in Tuscany and the Po valley.[107] The necrology of the convent of S. Maria Novella at

---

[102] 'The Pastoureaux', 159–62.

[103] Only Gay (65 ff.) has given it much attention.

[104] Cf. Thomas Walsingham, i, 301, on another massive Christian victory reported in 1364.

[105] Déprez *et al.*, n. 1844; 'Storie pistoresi', ed. S. A. Barbi, *RISNS* 11[5], 214.

[106] Ibid., 214 and cf. 215–16. [107] Bk. 12, ch. 39, iv, 68–70.

Florence records the names of six Dominicans who took the cross 'for the *passagium* against the Turks'.[108] The chronicler of Bologna described three groups setting out from the city between October 1345 and April 1346, the first two consisting of forty men and the third of more than a hundred.[109] The assertion by the author of the 'Historiae romanae fragmenta' that 'in the entire Christian world there was not a city, a village or a country from which numerous people did not flock to take the cross' can be dismissed as fanciful rhetoric,[110] but it is likely that several thousand did depart, mainly from Italy. In July 1345 the Pope wrote that 'an innumerable multitude' of the noble and powerful were preparing to go on crusade 'to exact revenge for the injuries of the crucified redeemer'; some of these were guilty of the most heinous crimes and had been forgiven by their enemies.[111] This associates the preaching with the periodic outbursts of peacemaking which occurred in the Italian cities in the later Middle Ages, though rarely in the context of the crusade.[112]

It is clear from Clement's letter that the Pope approved of these signs of popular enthusiasm and gave his sanction to the miracles which had been reported; these showed 'that God approves of the matter of the defence and extension of the orthodox Faith' at Smyrna.[113] The Curia did its best to encourage enthusiasm by stepping up crusade preaching in July 1345.[114] People taking the cross from the hands of clerics and setting out to fight in a crusade which had already achieved a remarkable success, and for which extra manpower was urgently needed, was obviously a very different matter from groups of peasants or the urban poor living off the land and killing innocent Jews. Those going to Smyrna from the Italian cities were organized with the care and attention to detail customarily displayed by the communal regimes. The contingents from Florence and Bologna, for example, were well equipped and

---

[108] *Necrologio di S. Maria Novella, 1235–1504*, ed. S. Orlandi. 2 vols. (Florence, 1955), i, 70, 71–2, 77, 78–9, 81, 100. Cf. M. D. Papi, 'Santa Maria Novella di Firenze e l'*Outremer* domenicano', in F. Cardini (ed.), *Toscana e Terrasanta nel Medioevo* (Florence, 1982), 99–100.

[109] 'Cronica di Bologna', cols. 393–4, 399.

[110] 'Historiae romanae fragmenta', col. 370.

[111] Déprez *et al.*, n. 1844.

[112] See J. Heers, *Parties and Political Life in the Medieval West*, tr. D. Nicholas (Amsterdam, 1977), 197–205.

[113] Déprez *et al.*, n. 1844. Cf. ibid., n. 1855.

[114] Ibid.

had high ranking leaders.[115] And when a group of poor Pistoians approached their city's General Council in October 1345 with a request for financial support for their proposal 'to go overseas against the infidel Turks and Saracens', it was agreed to give a subsidy of ten pounds to all who followed the communal standard. The money would be forwarded to a citizen residing at Venice, who would hand it over to the crusaders once they had boarded ship, 'and not before'.[116]

On the other hand, the excitement of 1344–5 created problems not dissimilar to those of 1309 and 1320 because it took the Curia by surprise and proved hard to co-ordinate.[117] In 1345 Humbert of Vienne was organizing his expedition in aid of Smyrna as the official leader of the crusade.[118] But many of the new *crucesignati* would not wait for the Dauphin's orders and trickled eastwards independently.[119] Waiting for a passage at Venice, they quarrelled so much that the Pope had to intervene in May 1345 to restore order.[120] They were overcharged by the Venetians and others for the voyage to Smyrna, and when they arrived there they found nothing much to do. The part of the town held by the league became overcrowded, and many fell ill and died.[121] Such problems arose from enthusiasm which, welcome though it was in some ways, could not be effectively channelled by the Church. It was altogether safer to rely on ordinary procedures for military recruitment.[122]

But the problem went rather deeper than this. The popular

---

[115] Giovanni Villani, bk. 12, ch. 39, iv, 68–70; 'Cronica di Bologna', cols. 394, 399.

[116] A. Chiappelli, 'Contributo di Pistoia ad una crociata contro i Turchi', *Bullettino storico pistoiese*, i (1899), 113–15.

[117] The author of the 'Historiae romanae fragmenta' complained that the crusade was not preached properly: 'Haec ad crucem suscipiendam adhortatio per omnes Christiani imperii provincias minime predicata fuit, neque servatus ordo, quem custodiri necesse erat. Eiusce rei fama una populos adeo commovit, ut vehemens animorum et hominum ardor ac desiderium undique emerserit': col. 370.

[118] The 'Historiae romanae fragmenta' views his appointment as Clement VI's reaction to the uncontrollable success of the preaching (ibid.). This is unlikely.

[119] Cf. Gay, 67: 'Il n'est pas certain que les croisés . . . aient reconnu Humbert pour leur chef.'

[120] Ibid., 175–6.

[121] 'Historiae romanae fragmenta', cols. 370 ff. The crusaders arrived at a time of famine conditions in *Romania*. See Zachariadou, 45–9, 52.

[122] In 1383 Henry Despenser's successes in Flanders brought a flow of unwanted crusaders across the Channel, despite the Bishop's stringent measures intended to keep tight control over numbers. See Thomas Walsingham, ii, 78–80, 95.

movements of 1309 and 1320 sprang partly from a widespread failure to grasp, or accept, the new strategy of co-ordinated *passagia*. By contrast, the disorganized preaching of 1344–5 and its unfortunate consequences were the result of confusion at the Curia itself about the nature and goals of the crusade against the Turks. As we have seen, Clement VI launched the league of 1342 as a self-contained naval enterprise without territorial objectives. But euphoria induced by the dramatic and unexpected success at Smyrna caused the Pope, whose outlook had been shaped in large measure by the negotiations of the 1320s and 1330s, to transform the league into a form of *primum passagium* which should now be followed by a larger expedition, somewhere between a *passagium particulare* and a general passage. The foothold at Smyrna he seems to have viewed as the equivalent in *Romania* of the bridgehead which the Latins never managed to secure in Syria or Egypt (except briefly in 1365): by July 1345 he was writing of 'the defence and extension of the Faith' in Anatolia.[123] But the Pope's own experience should have taught him that a 'follow-up' crusade had to be prepared well in advance, rather than preached and assembled only when news arrived of the success of its spearhead. This lack of co-ordination, together with the absence of assertive lay leadership, explains the débâcle of 1345: a belief in *tempus acceptabile* was no substitute for proper strategy.

The richness of fourteenth-century sources, at least those relating to crusades in the eastern Mediterranean and Italy, enables us to form a very clear impression of the technical aspect of taking the cross, whether to fight in person or to send deputies. A letter from Albornoz to preachers of the crusade against Francesco Ordelaffi, written in June 1357, reveals the procedure followed in the administration of the indulgence. The preachers, the Bishop of Rimini and the General of the Servite Friars, were given the responsibility

of hearing either in person, or through others whom you choose for the task, the confessions of all who have taken the sign of the life-giving cross and wish to confess, of imposing on them the salutary penance prescribed in the letters which we have sent you separately, and of absolving them in accordance with the usual Church formula; you may also shorten the period

---

[123] Déprez *et al.*, n. 1844. Cf. ibid., n. 1855.

laid down in the papal letters for those who labour in person or send soldiers in proportion to their resources . . .[124]

Those who took the cross, then, received absolution after confession, the penance imposed taking the form of military service by themselves or others.[125] Further light is thrown on how the indulgence operated in the latter case by a letter which Clement V wrote in 1309 to the Bishop of Lérida, in which the Bishop was granted permission to gain the indulgence by sending a group of horse and foot to the Granada crusade:

We grant that as soon as the said cavalry and infantry begin to contribute to the war, the indulgences which we issued to all who set out for the said Kingdom [Granada], to participate in this matter, should start to take effect on your behalf, provided that you carry out the things laid down in the said indulgences.[126]

The Bishop thus started to benefit from the indulgence, like a *crucesignatus* who fought in person, as soon as his troops took the field, but only derived the full benefit if they fought for the prescribed period of time.

Conditional vows, widespread in the thirteenth century,[127] retained their popularity, particularly in connection with the rather problematic projects of the French court; too many French nobles had earlier been trapped into undertaking obligations which they could not discharge.[128] Amaury, the Viscount of Lautrec, was one of the French noblemen who took the cross at Saint-Germain-des-Près on 1 October 1333 in response to the preaching of Archbishop Peter Roger. Since this was the high-water mark of Philip VI's crusade project, when a settlement had been reached with the Curia and the biggest obstacles to the crusade had been overcome, it is instructive to observe how many loopholes Amaury wrote into his vow. His fulfilment of it was made contingent upon a list of conditions: that Philip actually set out within the period agreed on; that the King guaranteed wages for Amaury and his companions (three knights and six squires); that the Viscount be free to return

---

[124] C. Piana, 'Il Cardinal Albornoz e gli ordini religiosi', in *El Cardenal Albornoz*, 491. Cf. Philip of Mézières, 126.

[125] See Housley, *Italian Crusades*, 133, for a thirteenth-century example.

[126] *Reg. Clem. V*, n. 4031.

[127] Throop, 94–5; Purcell, 129.

[128] See Cont. William of Nangis, ii, 65–6, 81, for popular resentment directed against Louis of Clermont.

from the East whenever he wanted to, 'if and when it pleases me'; and that he was in sound health at the time of the expedition's departure. If the King declined to accept these conditions, then the vow would be considered null and void: 'in that case, it will be as if I had not received the said cross when it was handed to me, and I will remain as I was previously, so that I am not placed under any obligation by the aforesaid matters'. Amaury also specified that his heirs were not to be obligated by his vow, a major preoccupation of fourteenth-century *crucesignati*.[129] This detailed document is in effect a letter of retainer between Amaury and the King, and forms a good illustration of the pattern of recruitment outlined at the start of the chapter.[130]

Italian chronicles describing the Smyrna crusade and the expeditions against the Ghibellines portray the organization of small units of crusaders in some detail. The force which set out from Florence in 1345 had its own constables and banners, and wore white tunics with red crosses and the lily of Florence.[131] In the case of the small army which Florence sent to help Albornoz in Romagna in 1357 we have figures for both *crucesignati* and deputies. The latter comprised 700 men-at-arms and 800 crossbowmen; they were accompanied by 200 cavalry and 2,000 infantry, made up of 'individual groups (*masnade*) of crusading citizens and *contadini*'. It is interesting to observe that some 2,200 individuals preferred personal service to securing the plenary indulgence through the fighting of deputies.[132] The 'Cronaca malatestiana' gives a detailed account of the preaching in 1356 at Rimini, from the taking of the cross by leading members of the Malatesta clan and 600 of their supporters, to a solemn ceremony involving the Church's standard, and concluding with the summer and autumn campaigns against Cesena and Faenza.[133]

It will be clear that although most crusading armies in our period were composed of professional fighters who were usually getting

---

[129] *Le Trésor des chartes d'Albret*, 459–60, n. 400.

[130] For another good example see *Titres de la maison ducale de Bourbon*, i, n. 2083.

[131] Giovanni Villani, bk. 12, ch. 39, iv, 68–70. He drew a distinction between those who went 'di loro voluntà', and those sent 'alle spese di chi volle il perdono'.

[132] Matteo Villani, bk. 7, ch. 85, ii, 73–4. Again, the distinction is made between those 'crociati che v'erano di volontà', and the troops sent on behalf of the commune.

[133] 'Cronaca malatestiana', 21. See also P. J. Jones, *The Malatesta of Rimini and the Papal State* (Cambridge, 1974), 79–81.

paid for their services,[134] the difference between an ordinary army and a crusading army was not just one of nomenclature. The Church still wanted people to assume the cross and many did so. On occasion, such as the Salado campaign of 1340 and the Cypriot crusade of 1365, this brought with it an atmosphere of penitential zeal characterized by masses, processions, and crusade sermons while in the field.[135] It also constituted a legal commitment which had to be regulated by the Church. Most importantly, the pope had to fix a time limit for service. This was normally a year,[136] though it could be more (three years for Castilians who undertook to campaign in Granada in 1317–18)[137] or less (six months in 1373 for Hungarians who were to fight the Turks).[138] Bulls for Spain often specified service 'by sea or by land', a recognition of the importance of combined land and sea operations against Granada.[139] On occasion leadership was dealt with, so that Castilians who took the cross in 1328 were to follow their king 'or his lieutenant, lieutenants or people'.[140] But such instructions were not usually necessary as the command of the crusade was either implicit, as in the national armies which fought in Spain and eastern Europe, or firmly stated elsewhere, as with the papal captaincies held by the French kings or their representatives.

Whether he was paid or unpaid, the subject of the crusade's leader or a foreign volunteer, the *crucesignatus* had a special legal status which entitled him to claim a wide range of privileges. By 1305 these had evolved into a fixed corpus of rights, and they changed little in the Avignon period. The most important, and most frequently reiterated in the crusade bulls, were Church protection for the lands and dependents of the crusader, a duty normally exercised by the crusader's ordinary;[141] freedom from paying

---

[134] Some still preferred to fight 'in expensis propriis' and gain the fullest form of indulgence: e.g. the estimated 5,000 French nobles who took the cross in 1316. See *AA*, i, n. 145.

[135] 'Crónica de Alfonso XI', 323 ff.; Philip of Mézières, 126.

[136] In 1323 Cardinal Pierre Tessier considered a year standard on the grounds that a shorter period would constitute an insufficient penance. See *CC*, n. 1696.

[137] ASV, Reg. Vat. 63, f. 314^r–v, n. 1002; Reg. Vat. 68, f. 232^r–v, n. 1695.

[138] *VMH*, ii, n. 271. Cf. Déprez and Mollat, n. 726 (Smyrna crusade, 1345).

[139] See, for example, ASV, Reg. Vat. 63, f. 314^r–v, n. 1002; Reg. Vat. 128, f. 57^r, n. 17.

[140] 'cum eodem Rege Castelle vel eius vicario seu vicariis et gentibus': ASV, Reg. Vat. 87, f. 168^r–v, n. 2476. Cf. Reg. Vat. 128, f. 57^r, n. 17: 'cum eodem Rege Castelle vel eius exercitu' (1340).

[141] Bishop William Durand laid special emphasis on this. See Atiya, 67–70.

interest on debts; and exemption from the payment of extraordinary taxes and tolls.[142] In the case of clerics who took the cross, the Curia often issued letters, either as general rulings or addressed to individual *crucesignati*, permitting them to receive the fruits of their benefices *in absentia*, and to mortgage these for a limited period of time to help pay their expenses on crusade. There are instances of this for the eastern Mediterranean, Spain, and Italy.[143] The crusader also had obligations arising from his vow, not least that of refraining from criminal acts while performing it. As Urban V wrote to the English Company in Italy in 1364 in connection with their hoped for participation in the Franco-Cypriot crusade, 'we urge you with fatherly affection to take care to refrain from injuring or doing harm to any of the faithful from this point onwards, since those who aim to serve God must abstain from offending him'.[144] As events in eastern and southern France were to reveal, the Pope's exhortation had little effect.[145]

There was a range of other issues relating to the crusade vow and the ramifications of the crusade as a penitential act which called for the attention of the Curia; they resulted in letters which, again, broke no fresh ground but serve to underline the continuing importance of the crusade as a European institution, deeply embedded in the juridical practices of the period.[146] Many letters dealt with problems about the vow. Perhaps because of earlier abuses,[147] commutation of crusade vows became much rarer, although examples still existed: Eblonus de Venthadoro, a nobleman from the diocese of Limoges, had his vow of crusading in the East commuted to one of fighting in Italy for a year with ten companions in 1324.[148] In 1309 James II of Aragon wanted the Pope to commute the vows made by some of his subjects to fight with the Hospitallers in the East, so that they would accompany him to Granada instead.[149]

---

[142] These were not usually stated except in special circumstances. But see LM, n. 891; *VMH*, ii, n. 271; Brundage, 160–9, 179–84.

[143] *Reg. Clem. V*, nn. 2987, 3988; CC, n. 5208; Mollat, *Lettres communes*, nn. 22479, 45734, 60796; *Documenta selecta*, n. 153.

[144] LM, n. 891.

[145] Housley, 'Mercenary Companies', 275–7.

[146] Brundage (111–13) commented on the thinness of canonistic commentary on the crusade in our period.

[147] See Purcell, 106–114; Brundage, 133 ff. The sources which I have examined do not support Brundage's view that the Avignon popes continued a policy of widespread commutation and redemption.

[148] Mollat, *Lettres communes*, n. 19866. Cf. Housley, *Italian Crusades*, 99–100.

[149] *AA*, iii, n. 91.

Some non-crusade vows were commuted into participation in a crusade. Thus in 1346 the new Archbishop of Smyrna was given a faculty to commute vows, except those of religion and chastity, to participation in the crusade against the Turks.[150]

More common, though again less so than in the thirteenth century, was the grant of absolutions from crusading vows in exchange for a sum of money. The amount to be paid usually depended on the rank and resources of the *crucesignatus*. In 1306 Count Robert of Clermont was absolved of his vow to fight in the East on condition that he subsidized others with 10,000 *livres* of undebased money.[151] In the following year, by contrast, a canon of Bordeaux called Raymond of Pins was absolved for only fifteen *livres*, possibly a mark of favour from his former archbishop.[152] Odo of Grandison, the formidable Swiss veteran of the Syrian crusades, was absolved from his crusade vow in 1319, at his own request, because of his age and the fact that he saw little chance of discharging it.[153] Aged *crucesignati*, who had taken the cross when a crusade of recovery seemed imminent, were not uncommon in the early fourteenth century. In 1311, for instance, the seventy year old chaplain of Bishop Antony Bek was absolved of his crusade vow.[154] Antony Bek, himself *crucesignatus*, was a veteran of the Lord Edward's expedition of 1270.[155] Similarly, in 1335 Count William of Hainault was absolved of his crusade vow because he claimed that his arthritis was so bad that he could no longer ride a horse.[156]

The Curia also issued absolutions from non-crusade vows in exchange for donations to a crusade. Widespread dispensation from vows of abstinence and pilgrimage was one of the ways in which Clement V planned to finance the Hospitaller *passagium* in 1308;

[150] Déprez and Mollat, n. 980.
[151] *Reg. Clem. V*, n. 610. Robert again took the cross in 1316 and made similar arrangements for redemption in 1317, this time at a cost of 3,000 *livres parisis*: *Titres de la maison ducale de Bourbon*, i, n. 1471, and cf. ibid., n. 2025.
[152] *Reg. Clem. V*, n. 2227.
[153] Mollat, *Lettres communes*, n. 9566. The very large sum paid for redemption, 10,000 florins, reflects Odo's continuing dedication to the crusade.
[154] *Reg. Clem. V*, n. 6907.
[155] C. M. Fraser, *A History of Antony Bek, Bishop of Durham 1283–1311* (London, 1957), 11, 164–5.
[156] *Lettres de Benoît XII*, ed. A. Fierens. Analecta Vaticano–belgica (Rome, 1910), n. 167. For other examples of absolution, see *Reg. Clem. V*, nn. 1867, 4224; Mollat, *Lettres communes*, n. 19540; Déprez et al., n. 2740.

money was to be collected throughout the five year duration of the expedition. In the case of pilgrimages, the donor was to contribute what he or she would have spent on the journey, and trips to Jerusalem were excluded. Both of these rulings were now standard practice.[157] A faculty to dispense from some vows was given to the Bishop of Valencia in 1309 on behalf of James II and the Granada crusade.[158] Other fronts benefited from the practice: the Holy Land in the case of a knight and his family in Ireland in 1320 who had sworn to go to Santiago,[159] *Romania* in that of Scandinavians in 1350 who were unable to carry out their pilgrimage vows because of illness or old age,[160] and the Italian front in that of a cleric at Salzburg in 1326 who had vowed to go to Rome.[161] The most spectacular single grant was made by Clement VI in 1352. He conceded the Jubilee Indulgence of 1350 to all the inhabitants of Majorca who carried out a programme of visiting local churches, in exchange for a single payment of 30,000 florins 'to be spent in aid of the Christian Faith, and against the enemies and rebels of the said Faith and Church, or for other pious uses in accordance with our ruling'.[162]

By 1305 the practice was well established of setting a personal or financial contribution to a crusade as the penance imposed by the Church or as the legal sentence of a civil authority.[163] It was continued throughout our period.[164] In 1309, for example, Arnold of Pellegrue was given a faculty to absolve those guilty of murdering clerics on condition that they help the papal army fighting Venice.[165] In the same year the Bishop of Valencia was permitted to absolve Aragonese excommunicated for trading with Alexandria, provided that they paid the proceeds to James II for the Granada crusade.[166] Most examples in the early decades of the century specify service in a *passagium* to the eastern Mediterranean. Thus in

---

[157] *Reg. Clem. V*, n. 2996.

[158] Ibid., n. 4524.   [159] *Cal. of Entries*, ii, 196.

[160] *Acta pont. svecica*, i, n. 385.

[161] Mollat, *Lettres communes*, n. 26151. See also ibid., n. 60843.

[162] J. Vincke, 'Der Jubiläumsablass von 1350 auf Mallorca', *Römische Quartal-schrift*, xli (1933), 301–6.

[163] Throop, 95–100; Brundage, 126n; Purcell, 114–18.

[164] Peter Dubois had ambitious plans for sending trouble-makers to the Holy Land. See *De recuperatione terre sancte*, 7–8, 10, 17.

[165] *Reg. Clem. V*, n. 5087.

[166] Ibid., n. 5090. The context of this characteristic grant will be examined in ch. 6 below.

1310 Philip IV remitted the punishment to be incurred by Bertrand de Lamothe, his wife, and their accomplices in the murder of Arnaud Carbonnel, provided that Bertrand and his male accomplices took the cross to participate in the next general passage to the Holy Land.[167] An Italian nobleman was sentenced to go on crusade in 1319 as part of his penance for the murder of a bishop; he was to accompany the next *passagium* East.[168] Several years later a French nobleman and papal *familiaris*, Amanieu of Astarac, was sentenced by Charles IV to fight for two years in Cyprus or Armenia with a following of six men.[169] Taking part in Philip VI's planned crusade was imposed on Frenchmen guilty of offences against the Church in 1333,[170] and one of the provisions for the absolution of the Della Scala in 1339 was that they send twenty men-at-arms to the East in the next general passage.[171] By 1339 the insertion of a clause relating to a general passage was a meaningless exercise, and in many such instances the penalty was presumably remitted or changed into a straightforward money transaction.

Until the end of the Avignon period, however, other fronts where personal service was more feasible continued to receive treatment in this respect. A personal or financial contribution to the Smyrna crusade was considered by Clement VI in 1345 as a possible penance for a nobleman who had illicitly seized Church revenues in the diocese of Troyes, and for a cleric in Provence who was guilty of murder.[172] A year later Clement offered absolution to the excommunicated members of the Catalan Grand Company if they furnished 100 horse and 100 foot for the crusade.[173] Innocent VI reached an agreement with Louis of Bavaria, the son of the excommunicated Emperor, that he would send 100 men-at-arms to serve in Italy for a year in exchange for absolution; Albornoz was later given a faculty to compound on this with Louis's own son Meinhardus.[174] Allies of Bernabò Visconti were to be absolved in 1363 on condition that, 'as a special form of penance', they serve against the despot 'in accordance with the nature of their guilt and

---

[167] *Registres du Trésor des chartes. Vol. I: Règne de Philippe le Bel*, comp. R. Fawtier (Paris, 1958), n. 1123, and cf. nn. 1124, 1913, 1944.

[168] *AE*, ad annum 1319, n. 13, xxiv, 109.

[169] CC, n. 1951, and see also nn. 1952–4, 2000–3; Hill, ii, 198.

[170] CC, n. 5221.   [171] *AE*, ad annum 1339, n. 68, xxv, 181.

[172] Déprez *et al.*, nn. 1806, 1921.

[173] *Diplomatari de l'orient català*, n. 189.

[174] *Codex dipl.*, ed. Theiner, ii, nn. 368, 372.

their resources'.[175] At times a number of offences were covered, as in Clement V's bull of February 1313 on behalf of Philip IV's crusade project. Absolution was offered to laymen who had been excommunicated for visiting the Holy Sepulchre against papal or legatine prohibition, or for using violence against clerics, and to clerics who had celebrated the divine offices while under interdict.[176] The corollary was that the crusade formed just one among a group of penalties imposed. For instance, Clement V included participation in an expedition to the eastern Mediterranean amongst the *condempnationes* which he imposed on the leaders of a number of rebel towns in the March of Ancona, alongside heavy fines and punitive pilgrimages.[177]

Common to all such measures was the idea that holy work could be advanced and sin punished at the same time: 'with the aim of promoting both the salvation of souls and the goals of the holy Roman church' was how Urban V put it in 1363.[178] A similar concept, that of the consequences of sinful activity being so handled that they yielded beneficial fruit, underpinned the standard procedure whereby the whole or part of the proceeds of theft and usury were channelled into a crusade, always provided that the victims of the crime could not be located.[179] Again, examples of this procedure can be found for all the crusading fronts. Clement V introduced it in 1309 and 1312 in the case of the Granada crusade, adding that there was to be no composition with notorious usurers for less than a half of their profits.[180] Clement VI made such a provision on behalf of Humbert of Vienne in 1346,[181] and the profits of usury from the southern French dioceses were allocated to the French crusade project in 1363, as they had been to earlier French proposals.[182] Amedeo of Savoy was granted the profits of usury and penitential fines in his lands in 1364 for a period of six years,[183] and

---

[175] ASV, Reg. Vat. 245, f. 197ᵛ. Earlier examples of this abound: e.g. *Lettres de Jean XXII*, ed. A. Fayen. Analecta Vaticano-belgica. 2 vols. (Rome, 1908–12), i, n. 1529.

[176] *Reg. Clem. V*, n. 9941.

[177] Ibid., n. 5537.

[178] 'Animarum saluti ac utilitati sancte Romane ecclesie quantum cum deo possumus prospicere intendentes': ASV, Reg. Vat. 245, f. 197ᵛ.

[179] Brundage, 175, 186. Peter Dubois suggested that a similar procedure be applied to bad debts. See *De recuperatione terre sancte*, 126–7.

[180] *Reg. Clem. V*, nn. 4048, 8459–60.

[181] Déprez *et al.*, nn. 2333–4.

[182] LM, nn. 344–7.   [183] *Illustrazioni*, 344 ff.

the collection of such fines for the war in Lombardy was decreed on several occasions by Gregory XI.[184] A comparable measure was the issuing of dispensations from canonical irregularity to clerics in exchange for the donation of money to the crusades, an approach particularly favoured by John XXII.[185]

These examples, which could easily be multiplied,[186] constitute a powerful argument against dismissing the legal institutions of the crusade in the fourteenth century as unimportant. The amount of papal correspondence dealing with the indulgence, vow, and related issues does not match that of the decades between the Fourth Lateran and Second Lyons Councils (1216–74): that is hardly to be expected. But the volume of work remains significant, and it is not necessary to assert that papal rulings were always executed,[187] or that they reflect in a direct manner the popularity of the crusade, to find this noteworthy. Even if no new problems were encountered, and no new juridical ground covered, the clerks in the penitentiary and *camera* had good cause to be familiar with established procedures.

[184] Mollat, *Lettres secrètes*, n. 3752; Mirot *et al.*, nn. 2255, 2275, 2283, 3172, 3417, 3790.

[185] See, for example, *Reg. Clem. V*, n. 5095; Mollat, *Lettres communes*, nn. 9918, 10658–9, 10879, 11708, 11863, 12411, 12514, 13297, 18838, 19963, 20006, 25452, 26055, 26813, 27020, 27128, 27951, 28170; *Lettres d'Urbain V*, n. 1766.

[186] For example by a systematic analysis of episcopal registers from this period, which contain much material about individual crusading vows.

[187] See, for example, *Codex dipl.*, ed. Theiner, ii, nn. 368, 372.

5

War Finance and Crusade Taxation

THROUGHOUT the previous two chapters the question of finance has loomed large. The financing of a proposed crusade was a key issue both in the way projects were presented at Avignon, and in the shaping of the papal response to them. Similarly, the main reason for the trend towards a predominantly financial administration of the indulgence was the problem of costs. The gravity of this problem can be gauged from the aftermath of the three crusades of 1309–10, a particularly good example because it illustrates the situation virtually at the start of our period, and in relation to the three principal crusade fronts. The Aragonese Crown, the Hospitallers, and the Holy See all found themselves burdened with heavy debts, to such an extent in the case of the first two powers that their military activity was curtailed for some years.[1] The economics of crusading in the Avignonese period was so complex and critical an issue that it calls for chapter-length treatment.

(a) THE COST OF WAR

Just how serious was the rise in war expenditure, and what were its causes? Such questions are less easy to answer than one might imagine. A large percentage of costs was made up of wage bills, and documentation exists for the wages paid to its soldiers by the French Crown from the reign of Philip II onwards. But a simple comparison between two dates is impossible.[2] To begin with, knights and squires were paid at different rates; and whereas a royal army in the thirteenth century contained a high proportion of knights, the mounted troops in its fourteenth-century equivalent were chiefly squires—knighthood had become a much rarer status. So for most men-at-arms the rise in pay between 1270 and 1370 would have been

---

[1] Housley, 'Pope Clement V', 39–40.
[2] The following two paragraphs are based chiefly on the painstaking analysis by Contamine, *Guerre*, 94–106.

from 7*s*. 6*d*. of Tours a day to 10*s*. a day, rather than from 7*s*. 6*d*. to 20*s*. (the pay of a knight-bachelor). This rise of 33 per cent, however, is unreliable as an indication of the costs facing the French Crown because of the coinage mutations of the period. The relatively stable currency of the mid-thirteenth century was plunged into chaos by the actions of the last Capetian and early Valois kings. Expressed in real terms (grams of gold), the wages paid to knights, squires, and foot sergeants between 1335 and 1351 did not rise at all, although in terms of the *livre tournois* their pay had doubled. This debasement of the silver coinage brought both benefits and problems for the Crown: the latter was able to increase the profits which it derived from minting, but faced inflationary prices because it regained its own debased coins in taxes. There is a further complicating factor in the many additional payments made to hired troops, such as travelling costs, compensation for horses lost in action, the household expenses received by all leaders of contingents of twenty-five or more men-at-arms, and above all the system of paying *grands gages* to accelerate recruitment.[3]

All this means that it is rarely that one can pinpoint a definite rise in the pay of all grades of fighter in real terms, though it seems that the late 1360s did see one such rise.[4] Two things we can say with certainty. One is that the French monarchy, having accepted the obligation to pay all professional fighters in its service, whether they were fighting as volunteers or had been summoned to discharge a legal duty, was faced by consistently high and possibly rising expenses in its wage bills.[5] The other is that its revenues, both its so-called 'ordinary' income and the funds which it got from hard-won war subsidies, were throughout most of our period inadequate for the costs which it faced.[6] Much the same can be said of any western state which wanted efficient armies at its disposal.

The last point is the heart of the issue. The most striking aspect of

[3] Henneman, *Royal Taxation . . . 1322–1356*, 21–2, 126n.

[4] Cf. Contamine, *Guerre*, 98: '. . . le temps de Charles v marque d'ailleurs une manière d'apogée pour les gages des gens de guerre au service de la monarchie'.

[5] On the obligation to pay see ibid., 50. In terms of the crusade, the situation was complicated by the fact that magnate *crucesignati* had surrendered to the Crown their right to collect crusade taxes levied on their local clergy; while the Crown benefited from the taxes, it now had to subsidize contingents which in the thirteenth century would have been self-supporting. See, for example, 'Les Papiers', 223.

[6] For excellent illustrations of this problem, see Henneman, *Royal Taxation . . . 1322–1356*, 21n–2n, 126n, 291.

warfare in this period is the growing intensity of the conflicts.[7] Armies were, if not bigger, at least more professional than their feudal antecedents, capable of remaining in the field for the whole year. They were better organized and contained growing numbers of specialists, sappers, engineers, artillery experts. Larger garrisons were needed for fortresses of strategic importance.[8] At the same time naval warfare was becoming more important, concepts of strategy evolving which embraced fighting on land and sea; this was particularly the case in Spain during the struggle for control of the Straits.[9] Waging this advanced, sophisticated form of war called for quite an efficient bureaucracy and for sustained, heavy national taxation. The ruler would win who was prepared to commit his subjects' resources to their limits, deploying to the utmost both their loyalty and his coercive power.

This affected crusade finance in two important ways. First, crusades everywhere were subject to the same problem of rising costs as any other war. In a crusade memorandum prepared for the Council of Vienne in 1311–12, William of Nogaret warned that wage bills had doubled: 'today you can hardly get a hundred knights for the wages or expenses for which you could formerly get two hundred'.[10] The same was true of Spain; as the envoys of the kings of Castile and Aragon repeatedly put it, war against Granada entailed 'endless expenses', which royal revenues alone could not sustain.[11] The crusade to recover Palestine presented the most daunting problems in this respect. In its reply to Philip VI's request for advice on his project in 1332, Venice estimated that 20,000 horse and 50,000 foot would be needed to take and hold the Holy Land.[12] By comparison, the fielding of armies totalling 28,000 horse and 16,700 foot in 1340 represented a massive and short-lived effort on

[7] See C. T. Allmand, *Society at War: The Experience of England and France during the Hundred Years War* (Edinburgh, 1973), *passim*.

[8] The cost of guarding France's long frontier rose from an estimated 29,000 *livres* per month in 1327 to 57,000 *livres* in 1339. See Henneman, *Royal Taxation . . . 1322–1356*, 126.

[9] Robson, *passim*, and esp. 391–8 for the heavy costs involved. See also *AE*, ad annum 1346, nn. 61–2, xxv, 400–1; 'Crónica de Alfonso XI', 367–8; Gautier Dalché, *passim*.

[10] Mas Latrie, ii, 129.

[11] '. . . immensa profluvia expensarum': ASV, Reg. Vat. 114, f. 26ᵛ, n. 747. Cf. *AE*, ad annum 1328, n. 76, xxiv, 377–8, ad annum 1330, n. 44, xxiv, 452, ad annum 1346, nn. 61–2, xxv, 400–1.

[12] *DVL*, i, n. 110. Marino Sanudo Torsello considered 2,000 horse and 50,000 foot necessary for the general passage: 'Liber secretorum fidelium crucis', 90–1.

the part of the French Crown.[13] Nor was it only a question of paying the troops needed. As the Venetians remarked, Philip would have to carry with him siege and construction machinery and materials.[14] And, as Clement V noted in 1312, John XXII in 1333, and Urban V in 1364, the loss of a Christian foothold in Syria presented further financial problems, 'so that this crusade calls for greater expenses than were formerly required'.[15] Given these considerations, of which few underestimated the gravity, it is astonishing that *passagia* of recovery were seriously planned.

Rising costs also affected the crusade in an indirect way. They made contemporary rulers even less tolerant of the collection and export of money for non-national, crusading purposes than their thirteenth-century predecessors had been. The expensiveness of war in the fourteenth century probably lay at the root of the tensions which the crusade created in relations between the Curia and secular rulers throughout the West. It is with these tensions that much of this chapter will deal; but we need first to examine the context within which they developed, that of Church taxation for the crusades.

(b) CRUSADE TAXATION: THE BACKGROUND

The thirteenth century was one of rapid changes in the arrangements for financing crusading ventures. The changes sprang from Innocent III's introduction of a benefice tax directly related to the crusade: the fortieth of 1199 and the twentieth of 1215. These were the precursors of the tenth, the standard levy on clerical revenues— though not on all revenues or all clerics—which in the following decades became established as the corner-stone of crusade finance. The tenth revolutionized the procedure of paying for crusading expeditions. In place of the mixture of feudal levies and tentative national taxes which characterized the twelfth century, a straight- forward tax now existed which could be collected with relative ease; the clergy complained loud and long, but caught between the pressure of pope and king they had no effective means of resistance.[16]

---

[13] Contamine, *Guerre*, 70; Henneman, *Royal Taxation . . . 1322–1356*, 141–53.
[14] *DVL*, i, n. 110.
[15] *Reg. Clem. V*, n. 8986; CC, n. 5211; *Illustrazioni*, 365–7. The expense involved in mounting a crusade to the East was a point continually made in negotiations: e.g. 'Les Papiers', 216. For the heavy cost of Peter of Cyprus's crusade see Edbury, 'Crusading Policy', 99; Hill, ii, 317–18.   [16] See, for example, Lunt, i, 240–7.

The effect of this innovation on the expeditions themselves was profound. The most expensive of the crusades to the East in the thirteenth century was almost certainly that of Louis IX, 1248–54. It has been estimated that of the total royal outlay for the crusade, which was later calculated at 1,500,000 *livres* of Tours, about two-thirds, 950,000 *livres*, was paid from the proceeds of the five-year tenth imposed on the French church. The economies and abuses to which the royal administrators had to resort to collect the remaining third (about two years' worth of normal Crown revenue), show clearly that but for the contribution of the Church the French monarchy would have been left with intolerable debts. The relative solvency of Louis's crusade thus rested on the broad shoulders of the French church, which also paid heavily in the form of temporal regalia. The King's second expedition, in 1270, was also financed largely by the clergy; on this occasion it only paid a three-year tenth, but the army was smaller than that of 1248.[17]

Much the same can be said of another major crusading venture of the mid-thirteenth century, the invasion and conquest of the Kingdom of Sicily by Charles of Anjou in 1265–8. The campaign was financed chiefly by the levy of a three-year tenth on the Church in France and the dioceses bordering it in the east: this tenth, which probably brought in about 700,000 *livres* of Tours, proved enough to pay the French army which defeated both Manfred and Conradin. Without the tax, the invasion would have been impossible to finance; Charles did not possess the resources needed, and ordinary papal revenues, even supplemented by charitable subsidies, were inadequate. Hence the overriding importance of securing Louis IX's consent to the taxation of his church.[18]

The French church complained bitterly about this series of taxes in the 1250s and 1260s, and it may have been this which induced Gregory X, at the Second Lyons Council, to try to shift some of the financial burden back onto the laity. Quite apart from traditional measures for collecting the charitable and penitential donations of laymen, Gregory also proposed the levy throughout Christendom of a poll tax of one penny, of Tours or Sterling, each year, for the benefit of his crusade to the Holy Land.[19] This was a clear attempt

---

[17] See J. R. Strayer, 'The Crusades of Louis IX', in Setton (gen. ed.), *History of the Crusades*, ii, 490–4, 510–11; W. C. Jordan, *Louis IX and the Challenge of the Crusade: A Study in Rulership* (Princeton, 1979), 79–104, 215.

[18] Housley, *Italian Crusades*, 222–31.   [19] Purcell, 27–8, 197–8.

to return to the national taxes of the twelfth century, but there is no sign of it succeeding. Gregory himself acknowledged the need for increased Church taxation by quadrupling the tax levied at the First Lyons Council and instituting a much more systematic procedure for collection. The most substantial contribution made by the laity at this point probably derived from the redemption of crusade vows, but the profits from this certainly could not compare with the tenth.[20]

The most intensive exploitation of the tenth came at the end of the century, in the struggle for Sicily (1282–1302). To pay the armies and fleets of the kings of Naples, France, and Aragon, all of whom were at various times fighting the Sicilian rebels on the papacy's behalf, the Curia levied a series of tenths of unprecedented severity on the western Church. Hardest hit were the clergy of France, Provence, the Arelate, and Aragon. Even with the flow of cash which this brought about, the military and diplomatic costs of the prolonged conflict created a crisis of credit which had widespread repercussions. By the turn of the century it was clear that the ability of the Curia to levy the tenth in favour of itself or its allies was essential to the status of the Holy See as a power to be reckoned with.[21]

The clerical tenth, which in Castile tended to mean the *tercias* as well,[22] was thus, in 1305, the corner-stone of the whole structure of crusade finance. It had become a crucial element in all negotiations between the Curia and secular princes about the granting of Church aid. Whenever proctors or envoys came to the Curia they had instructions to secure tenths, and we possess a mass of detail about the talks which they entered into, particularly in the cases of Aragon and France.[23] There is much detail too on how the collection of the tax was organized: on the procedure for paying, the exempt groups, the penalties for refusal to pay, and the storing and transmission of the cash. What we lack is the theoretical underpinning of this great fabric of diplomacy and organization; for the tenth was not dealt with in canon law and there is no set of principles and definitions to

---

[20] Ibid., 122n, 142, 197.

[21] Housley, *Italian Crusades*, 231–45.

[22] A. Oliver and J. Fernández Conde, 'La epoca de las grandes conquistas', in Fernández Conde (ed.), *Historia de la iglesia en España*, II², 32–40, esp. 36.

[23] The very density of this diplomatic material is daunting. Vincke remarked of Peter III of Aragon that 'allein die Geschichte seiner Zehntpolitik könnte Bände füllen': *SKKA*, 253.

which we can turn to elucidate the diplomatic manœuvrings which dominate the period. Three questions are especially hard to answer.

First, was the clerical tenth in the fourteenth century still recognizably a crusade tax? Clearly not, if this means that all tenths levied were related to crusading ventures. By 1300 many western rulers had developed a practice of national taxation which owed much, in terms of precedent, to the national crusade taxes of the twelfth century.[24] They argued that the clerical order, previously exempt from lay taxation, must contribute to taxes raised for the defence or other urgent needs of the realm. The share paid by the Church was usually expressed as a tenth of its revenues, and *decimae* paid for purposes unconnected with the crusade thus became common. The attempt which the Curia made under Boniface VIII to fight off this secular encroachment on Church liberties failed.

By 1305, therefore, two types of tenth existed, the crusade tenth and the tenth paid as the Church's share of a national tax. The two were differentiated by their justification: the defence of the Faith and the Catholic Church, inherently international in tone, and that of a particular political unit in which the clerics to be taxed had possessions and therefore responsibilities. This is not to deny that there were significant overlaps between the two types. In Spain the *Reconquista* had both a national and a crusading complexion which made the claims of the kings on the revenues of their churches doubly strong.[25] Similarly, in Hungary and Poland the crusade taxes levied in the fourteenth century were at the same time national taxes *pro defensione regni* against the pagans on their borders. The fact remains, however, that taxation of the Church for crusading purposes continued during the Avignonese period as a separate category of tenth. Envoys at the Curia petitioning for tenths for crusading causes presented their masters' cases in traditional crusading terms, and the bulls levying the tenths were descendants, in both style and wording, of the early thirteenth-century letters which justified the tax in the language of holy war.

The problem was that there were now frequently two claims and two ideologies in competition for the tenth. The pope needed the

---

[24] Kantorowicz, 232 ff.; R. C. Smail, 'The International Status of the Latin Kingdom of Jerusalem, 1150–1192', in Holt (ed.), *Eastern Mediterranean Lands*, 24–5.

[25] See, for example, *AA*, iii, p. xlix.

tenth for his wars in Italy or the East; the local ruler needed it for national purposes.[26] The Curia had no chance of winning the tug of war. Driven away from the tenth, increasingly it exploited other forms of benefice tax: subsidies, annates, intercalary fruits. The rigorous collection of these taxes by John XXII was associated with his crusading struggle against the heretical Ghibelline *signori*; partial indulgences were offered for the provision of subsidies.[27] But such was the appeal of justifying taxes in terms of national need that by 1378 the Curia was attempting to transfer the basis of its taxation measures to the legal conception of a corporate Church, which could be taxed by analogy with national kingdoms. Thus Gregory XI wrote to Louis of Hungary in 1372 that he was taxing churchmen, 'who, amongst Christ's faithful, are particularly subject [to our authority], following the example of secular princes, who seek and obtain the help of their subjects when pressed by their needs'.[28] In the twelfth century national taxation had borrowed ideas from the crusades; in the fourteenth century the trend was reversed.[29]

The second question concerning the tenth is: what rights, if any, did the clergy possess in the granting of tenths for the crusade? In the Romano-Christian tradition which dominated western European thinking about taxation the consent of the taxed held an important place.[30] But the crusade tenth evaded this tradition; it was peculiar in that its purpose was the waging of a holy war, a war whose direction lay uniquely in the hands of one man, and that man the holder of a plenitude of power in spiritual matters. When Innocent III levied his fortieth of 1199 he did not seek the consent of the clergy; on the other hand, he did not punish for refusing to pay and he offered spiritual rewards for payment.[31] Sixteen years later excommunication was threatened against those who declined to pay the twentieth, but on this occasion the consent of a general council had been achieved. In 1228, when a tenth was imposed by Gregory IX for his war against Frederick II, censures were implicit; they

[26] The French and Aragonese Crowns in particular were very dependent on the tenth. See, for example, Henneman, *Royal Taxation . . . 1322–1356*, 313.

[27] Housley, *Italian Crusades*, 131–2, 179–85.

[28] *VMH*, ii, n. 226.

[29] This may have been part of a general trend. See Kantorowicz, 207–32.

[30] See G. Post, *Studies in Medieval Legal Thought: Public Law and the State, 1100–1322* (Princeton, 1964), Part One *passim*.

[31] Lunt, i, 240–1.

were expected by the English clergy at least.[32] Thereafter consent was usually sought when possible. Crusade tenths covering all Christendom were granted in Church councils held at Lyons, and those of purely local application were often debated in regional or provincial synods. But it is clear that consent was not essential. An attempt by Bishop William Durand to establish consent as a condition for the granting of a tenth at the Council of Vienne met with failure.[33] Instead Clement V engaged in informal discussions with national groupings of prelates.[34] The Curia relied on penalties to collect at least a large share of the taxes. The fact that consent was not necessary for a crusade tax, whereas it was for a national tax or subsidy, explains the continuing appeal for the rulers of Spain and eastern Europe of taxes granted by the pope.

The third question about the tenth, and the most difficult to answer with any certainty, is this: to what extent did the tenth, when levied as a crusade tax, represent a moral obligation on the part of the papacy and Church towards a lay ruler engaged in, or about to start, a crusade? The problem is that the Curia and the lay powers held very different views about this issue throughout the fourteenth century. The papal viewpoint is clear enough in outline. The innovations of Innocent III, together with the writings of thirteenth-century canonists, had fixed the legal definition of the crusade as the *negotium ecclesiae*. Innocent and his successors had issued a stream of valuable subsidies not only to crusading kings and magnates, such as Louis IX and Richard of Cornwall, but also to lesser leaders and ordinary knights.[35] The Avignonese Curia accepted the binding nature of these precedents, based on the biblical quotation—cited by the Kings of Castile and Portugal in 1330—that 'he who serves the altar is entitled to live of the altar, and he who is picked for heavy work should not be denied his wage'.[36] A lay prince who went on crusade and spent heavily in the service of the Church was entitled to financial aid. The extent and source of this aid varied. If the campaign was to be of limited scope and duration, a *passagium particulare* or its equivalent, the prince could be granted a tenth from his own lands. Although, as Cardinal Gaucelme de Jean pointed out in 1323, it had been the policy of John XXII's prede-

[32] Ibid., i, 243, 247.   [33] Ibid., i, 395.
[34] *Papsttum und Untergang*, ii, n. 135.
[35] Purcell, 52n and 145–9: a fine analysis of examples from 1244–91.
[36] *AE*, ad annum 1330, n. 44, xxiv, 452. Cf. 1 Cor. 9:13.

cessors (notably Clement V) to deny tenths for such expeditions, by the 1320s realism was dictating a more generous approach.[37] If a prince intended to lead a full-scale general passage, he was entitled to financial help from the lands of other rulers, provided that their consent could be obtained. And if the pope thought that a crusade project merited and needed it, he might grant money from the *camera* itself.

This approach was, however, subject to two important qualifications. One was that the Church could not be expected to shoulder the entire cost of a crusade, both on the grounds that it could not afford it, and because the crusade was the concern of all Christians, lay and clerical. In the case of naval leagues against the Turks, this meant in practice that the other powers involved had to meet their own expenses. John XXII and Clement VI both laid it down that the pope was not the legal *caput*, or head, of the leagues, and that each constituent must pay his own costs without Church aid.[38] The second qualification was that the collection and storage of the tenths levied for the crusade must be handled by the Church itself; this condition was of course rooted in suspicion of the lay powers and what they would do with the money once they were able to direct its movement. Thus the Church was prepared to bear the brunt of major expenditure for the crusade provided the burden was kept within reasonable limits and it retained control of the funds up to the point of expenditure;[39] the latter usually included the expense of preparations.[40]

Lay princes agreed that the crusade was the *negotium ecclesiae* but drew very different conclusions from this definition. For them it meant that the Church, certainly clerics within their own lands and if possible those outside, must pay all or nearly all the costs involved. In addition, it was contrary to royal dignity and detrimental to the planning of the campaign that detailed estimates should be submitted to the Curia and that the king should have to account for every penny spent. A crusade was too expensive, risky, and in some

[37] CC, n. 1695. On the other hand, Cardinal Pierre Tessier considered a *primum passagium* of 26 vessels too small to justify a tenth: ibid., n. 1696.

[38] *AE*, ad annum 1333, n. 15, xxiv, 513; CC, n. 5247; *Acta pont. svecica*, i, n. 337; *VMH*, i, n. 985.

[39] Skilled negotiators like Mile of Noyers were prepared to make token concessions on this point. See 'Les Papiers', 217, and cf. *AE*, ad annum 1332, nn. 5–6, xxiv, 490.

[40] See, for example, *VMH*, ii, n. 272.

cases unremunerative, to initiate without an assurance that the Church would foot the bill and that funds would be made readily available in advance.[41] Theorists like Peter Dubois and William of Nogaret made this approach more attractive by linking it to the reform of the Military Orders, and even Humbert of Romans thought that the Church would benefit from properly administered asset stripping in favour of a crusade.[42]

Moreover, thanks to the Curia's handling of crusade funds in the past, lay princes were almost as suspicious of the financial intentions of the pope as he was of theirs; storage of crusade taxes at the discretion of the Curia was no guarantee of their safety. During the negotiations between Philip VI and John XXII, for example, the King insisted that

from this point onwards, each and every one of the aforesaid donations, legacies, and other collected sums, which, as it has been noted, have been directed towards or spent on other concerns by the [Holy] See, should begin to be directed towards the uses for which they were intended, and spent fully in accordance with the wishes of the legators, donors or other originators.[43]

Philip was by no means alone in voicing such feelings: according to an Aragonese report of 1325, even some cardinals resented the diversion of the Vienne tenth to the wars in Italy.[44]

John XXII's reply to Philip's criticism was an interesting defence of papal policy. The pope's authority to divert money from one pious purpose to another was, he claimed, grounded in both civil and canon law as well as biblical precedents, provided only that the cause was sufficiently pressing.

Why therefore was it illicit, or should it be illicit, for the pope to divert things meant for one purpose to the service of another, when an emergency threatens the common good (*respublica*)? Especially in the case of a matter which relates to the common good no less than that of the original purpose; and what matter could be of greater relevance to the whole Church than one which directly concerns the defence of the Catholic Faith and of Church unity, and the health of the universal Church?[45]

[41] See Housley, 'Franco–Papal Crusade Negotiations', 172–3, 180.
[42] Delaville le Roulx, *La France en orient*, i, 51, 59–60; Atiya, 51, 54; Throop, 198–9.
[43] Mollat, *Lettres communes*, n. 61324, 228–9, and cf. 'Les Papiers', 216–17. Peter Dubois had suggested decentralization as a remedy for this abuse. See *De recuperatione terre sancte*, 91–2.
[44] *AA*, ii, n. 401.   [45] Mollat, *Lettres communes*, n. 61324, 228.

Many secular princes in the recent past had shown that they thought diversion of resources justifiable in certain circumstances: the King of Castile had pocketed the proceeds of the Holy Land tenth, the kings of France the sexennial Vienne tenth, Philip the Fair Holy Land legacies. If a more rigid approach was laid down, John commented, it could make things much more difficult in the future for the King as well as the Pope.

As this last comment shows, differing views about who should pay for crusading activity and how payment should be made were more likely to be reconciled on a pragmatic, *ad hoc* basis than through a genuine consensus. Given the fundamental divergence of approach and great mutual suspicion which existed, this was virtually inevitable. Solutions were reached in each case by careful diplomacy, by demands and offers deliberately pitched too high or too low, by compromises, and ultimately through the studied and sometimes ruthless application of pressure.[46] The result is that when evidence for this diplomatic procedure has survived, it yields unrivalled insights into how relations between the Curia and the chief secular powers functioned in practice. We will now examine the procedure at work on each of the major crusade fronts.

(c) POPES, RULERS, AND TAXES

i. *The Spanish Kings and the Curia, 1327–1334*

In 1325 Alfonso XI of Castile reached his majority. He almost immediately signalled his intention of avenging the deaths of his uncles six years earlier by renewing the war with Granada. In 1326 he founded a confraternity at Seville for the purpose of fighting the Moors,[47] and in 1327 presented his first set of demands for aid from the Church. According to an Aragonese proctor, these included requests for a tenth, for the goods of the Castilian Templars, and the *tercias*, 'which they have already seized, so it is said'. The same report quoted a cardinal's remark that the requests had been made with 'Castilian arrogance' and would not be granted.[48] The Pope's own comment on the demands was that 'some of them were so unusual that we have no record of their being asked for by a prince even for a crusade to the East, let alone granted'.[49]

---

[46] See ibid., *passim*, and for one detailed case-study, Housley, 'Franco–Papal Crusade Negotiations', *passim*.

[47] Goñi Gaztambide, 644–5.   [48] 'Nachträge', n. 32.

[49] '. . . nonnulla satis erant insolita que a nullo principe etiam pro passagio

The demands were, indeed, sent back, because Alfonso's envoys lacked the authority to specify how many troops would be supplied in return for this financial support:

They openly replied to us that they had no mandate on the subject, indeed that they had been expressly forbidden to make a commitment on anything. We were greatly astonished at this, and not without reason. We have not, therefore, made a reply to the said petitions, since it is our responsibility to ensure that any subsidies which we grant to princes from Church property should be spent on the uses for which, and because of which, they were granted, and that God's honour should be preserved and divine worship extended. Without doubt those are the reasons for the said conditions and formulae, as anybody can see who reads them carefully.[50]

John XXII was ready, he wrote, to negotiate about conditions and reduce or remove them as both sides saw fit; but he was not prepared to make an unconditional grant, a refusal which he placed in the context of a remarkably frank statement of papal policy:

We are aware that our predecessors granted subsidies without formulae and conditions to various princes, both for the crusade to the East and for that against the Moors in Spain. But because those subsidies were very frequently diverted to other uses, we want to ensure that from henceforth such subsidies should not be misspent, and that Christian worship should benefit from them. So since our elevation we have laid it down that no such subsidies should be granted except with certain formulae and conditions attached.[51]

---

ultramarino petita audivimus nec fuisse concessa alicui': ASV, Reg. Vat. 114, f. 26ᵛ, n. 747. The Pope was to repeat this comment in 1330: *AE*, ad annum 1330, n. 45, xxiv, 452–3.

[50] '. . . nobis responderunt aperte quod mandatum super hoc nedum aliquod non habebant, imo pocius quod in nullo se obligare presumerent eisdem fuerat expressius interdictum, de quo nec immerito fuimus plurimum admirati. Propter quod a responsione predictarum petitionum duximus abstinendum, cum nostra interesse noscatur ut subsidia que de bonis ecclesiarum interdum principibus facimus in usibus ad que et propter que ea facimus expendantur, quodque honor dei servetur et divinus cultus dilatari debeat providere, ad que proculdubio ordinabantur predicti conditiones et modi, sicut patere poterit cuilibet sedule intuenti': ASV, Reg. Vat. 114, f. 26ᵛ, n. 747.

[51] '. . . licet a nostris predecessoribus diversis principibus tam pro transmarino passagio quam contra parcium Ispanie Agarenos novimusque subsidia sine modis et conditionibus sint concessa, quia tamen subsidia illa frequencius in usus alios sunt conversa, nos propter ea volentes occurrere ne deinceps subsidia talia in usus alios consumantur, ac intendentes quod ex illis cultus divinus debeat ampliari, sic quamdiu in statu isto fuimus duximus observandum quod nequaquam talia fierent subsidia nisi certis modis et conditionibus interiectis': ibid., ff. 27ᵛ–28ʳ, n. 749.

This was an accurate summary of the tougher approach which John was taking. But Alfonso's desire for war with Granada was genuine, and to prove it he took the field and won a notable victory which earned the Pope's praise for the army's commander, the Infante John.[52] Against this background new demands were presented, and Alfonso was granted considerable financial aid, with guarantees attached, in the summer of 1328.[53]

As usual, Aragon was jealous of its neighbour's success. In July 1328 a request was made to the Curia for a tenth of at least six years duration, but this was turned down in September on the grounds of the heavy burdens already faced by the Aragonese church.[54] Alfonso IV was not a man to give up easily. In August 1329 he submitted a fresh petition, which has been described as a request for the greatest possible aid in return for the least possible obligations.[55] Alfonso's envoys were to press for a ten-year tenth to be collected in line with an updated valuation of Church revenues; for intercalary fruits; for a 'voluntary' subsidy from the secular and regular clergy of Aragon; and for a dispensation from residence for clerics who took the cross, with permission for them to employ the income from their benefices for the expenses of the crusade. The ten-year tenth was only an opening gambit, but the envoys were not to settle for less than three years. They were to avoid tying the King down on such matters as numbers, the duration of the crusade or its starting date, and Alfonso was to be left complete freedom of movement in his negotiations with the Moors for an eventual truce or peace.

These were extraordinary demands, but they could not be shrugged aside: we have seen that Alfonso was skilfully orchestrating the considerable extra-peninsular crusade enthusiasm of the 1320s by promoting the war against Granada as far afield as Germany and Bohemia.[56] John XXII would only give a two-year tenth in accordance with the old valuation, and accompanied by conditions which the King described as harsh and novel, the worst being the need for Alfonso's personal participation in the fighting. He voiced the consistent Aragonese claim that the Curia exag-

---

[52] *AE*, ad annum 1327, n. 41, xxiv, 331.
[53] Ibid., ad annum 1328, nn. 76–80, xxiv, 377–80; Mollat, *Lettres communes*, nn. 41541, 41566–8.
[54] Vincke, *SKKA*, 242; Goñi Gaztambide, 297n.
[55] 'Nachträge', 496, n. 42; Goñi Gaztambide, 303–5; Vincke, *SKKA*, 243.
[56] See above, ch. 2, nn. 38–49.

gerated the value of the tenth: 'for the tenth from our kingdoms and lands does not, in truth, amount to 20,000 pounds of Barcelona a year, although it would come to much more if it was paid properly and in full'. This would not be enough to pay the wages of an army of 2,500 knights and 30,000 footsoldiers, together with the expenses of the flotilla of twenty galleys and the various transport ships which would be needed to carry them.[57] At the same time the Kings of Castile and Portugal submitted demands as heavy as those of Alfonso IV, making the same point that the proceeds of the tenth alone were insufficient: 'the amount which can be expected from the said [tenth] may appear to be substantial, but in reality it is small, and would make only a tiny contribution to the said [expenses]'. The tenth had to be granted for ten years, and supplemented by the cession of annates, intercalary fruits, and subsidies.[58]

Clearly John XXII was under great pressure, but he reacted with characteristic stubbornness. To the King of Castile he wrote that the concessions of 1328, themselves very generous, should be enough. The royal demands were without precedent, would ruin the Church if they were granted, and were rejected *in toto*.[59] On the following day, 6 February 1330, Alfonso IV was sent a similar reply: the Church was already overtaxed and the King had been granted all that it could pay.[60] On 29 March Alfonso IV sent proctors to accept the concession of the two-year tenth, and the tax was levied in May 1330.[61] Alfonso IV still wanted his third year, and at the end of May he was granted an extension, but under severe conditions. The King was to fight in person for three months—excluding travelling time— or to appoint a reliable captain with 500 men-at-arms. Only when these three months had expired would he get the tenth. There were other conditions modelled on those laid down in the case of Castile in 1328.[62] The King made one last effort to secure more: he wanted the removal of the clause about personal participation, a new valuation of Church revenues, intercalary fruits for three years, a

---

[57] 'Nachträge', 496, n. 42; Vincke, *SKKA*, 243; Goñi Gaztambide, 305. For the value of the tenth, see also *AA*, iii, n. 90.

[58] *AE*, ad annum 1330, n. 44, xxiv, 452.

[59] Ibid., ad annum 1330, n. 45, xxiv, 452–3.

[60] 'Nachträge', 496–7, n. 42.

[61] Mollat, *Lettres communes*, nn. 49498–9, 50771; *AE*, ad annum 1330, n. 46, xxiv, 453–4.

[62] Ibid., ad annum 1330, n. 46, xxiv, 454. See also Mollat, *Lettres communes*, nn. 49741, 50311.

three year exemption from responsions for the Aragonese Hospitallers, and the grant to the Granada war of money bequeathed to the crusade by Clement V and the French nobility.[63] At the end of 1330 his envoy reported that these demands had been opposed by the cardinals. A new valuation would set a dangerous precedent, and Philip VI would simply not permit the export of the legacies.[64]

So ended the first round of negotiations connected with the Granada crusade. In February 1331 Alfonso of Castile concluded a four year truce with the Moors and all the high hopes for a major expedition evaporated. Alfonso IV of Aragon, it has been remarked, lacked the cool and patient temperament needed for success in diplomacy with the Curia; in this respect he was inferior to his father, James II.[65] Moreover, his plans were vague and aroused great suspicion at Avignon. This point was made by the King's uncle, the Infante Peter, when talks were reopened in 1332 in response to the Muslim offensive. Peter wrote that the Pope and cardinals were not willing to give anything because the King was not acting in a convincingly warlike manner. As soon as he started to behave *baronivolmente* he would begin to get privileges.[66]

Alfonso's reply to this criticism was to reiterate an interesting but probably specious argument previously used by James II.[67] It was not fair for the Pope to impose conditions of timing and numbers on Aragon's contribution to the *Reconquista* because Aragon's war, unlike Castile's, was one of frontier skirmishes and a constant naval blockade. This was expensive, costing 3,000 pounds a day, but it did not call for royal leadership and it precluded the sort of guarantees which the Curia regarded as essential. The man entrusted with this argument, and with a new set of financial demands, was the royal official Bernat Oliver, who was sent to Avignon at the end of 1332. He had a difficult time. John XXII, he wrote in January 1333, was preoccupied with the issue of the beatific vision and with the crusade plans of Philip VI. It was 1309 over again. There had only been one consistory in the past month, at which Bernat had presented his case but no decisions had been taken. Still, the Pope looked favourably on Alfonso's plans and the envoy was optimistic, hoping even that

---

[63] 'Nachträge', 497–9, n. 42. See also Goñi Gaztambide, 306–7.

[64] 'Nachträge', 499–501, n. 42.

[65] See Finke's comments in 'Nachträge', 401. For James II's negotiations with the Curia, see Vincke, *SKKA*, 146–234.

[66] 'Nachträge', 511, n. 50. Cf. Goñi Gaztambide, 310–11.

[67] 'Nachträge', 511, n. 50, and cf. 520, n. 57; Vincke, *SKKA*, 197.

Philip VI might be persuaded to fight in Spain before he set off for the East.[68]

At first Bernat's optimism seemed to be justified. By May 1333 Alfonso IV had been granted a three-year tenth under certain conditions, and he wrote to Bernat to secure the drafting and despatch of the bulls as soon as possible.[69] Then snags arose. On 10 August the King complained that the bulls had not yet been expedited and asked for an explanation.[70] His envoy replied that the Curia was now demanding that the King should lead the army for at least three months of the first year's action, and that he should share the costs of the war with the Church. Part of the problem was the conflicting demands of the French envoys, who insisted, for example, that the crusading energies of the Majorcans be reserved for their *passagium* to the East.[71] Bernat Oliver provided a detailed commentary on these unwelcome developments in a long letter to Gonsalvus Garcia. He could, he wrote, meet the extra demands without exceeding his original brief, but he thought it better that the King himself make fresh offers in letters to the Pope and cardinals. The envoy was concerned about the implications of the six-year tenth granted to Philip VI and was thoroughly exhausted by the negotiations: 'I am so oppressed by sadness and melancholy at the way this business has dragged on, that I can hardly think about anything else'.[72]

In November Bernat Oliver reported that the tenth had now been granted for two years only, and with many unacceptable conditions attached. He added two interesting comments summing up his unhappy experience at Avignon. One was a conventional complaint: 'at this court nothing gets done except for fear or money'. But the other observation was more significant. People at Avignon, Bernat wrote, would be amazed if the King, who had Muslim neighbours (which was not strictly accurate) allowed the extraction from his church of a six-year tenth for a crusade which would not take place.[73] It was probably this consideration which led Alfonso to accept the two-year tenth in March 1334. By doing so he hoped to forestall the levy in his lands of Philip VI's tenth, but the manœuvre failed since the Curia again refused to dispatch the bull.[74]

---

[68] 'Nachträge', 513, n. 52.
[69] Ibid., 514, n. 52.
[70] Ibid.
[71] Ibid., 517–18, n. 56.
[72] Ibid., 519–22, n. 57.
[73] Ibid., 522–4, n. 58, and cf. 519, n. 56.
[74] Ibid., 524, n. 58. In January 1335 the King claimed that only the Pope's death in December had held up the dispatch of the bull. See *Documenta selecta*, n. 509.

During these years Castilian demands for financial aid for the Granada war were usually met. But then Castile was actually fighting the Moors. Aragon's involvement with the *Reconquista* after 1310 was minimal, and it was clearly this factor which frustrated Alfonso IV's attempts to get Church aid. The Curia did not believe that the intermittent land and sea operations which Aragon mounted against the Moors added up to a genuine crusading effort. In addition, Alfonso IV did not forward his own cause by presenting such high demands. In this respect the Aragonese did not learn. In 1340 Peter III demanded, as the price of his participation in the Salado campaign, a six-year tenth, a grant of annates as long as the war lasted, legacies and the sale of indulgences, and the remission of the feudal census due for Sardinia.[75]

What was wrong with the way the Aragonese negotiated for the tenth? Alfonso IV's very high demands, and his obstinate refusal to accept accompanying obligations, were interpreted by both Goñi Gaztambide and Vincke as indicating a lack of real crusading zeal.[76] It is impossible either to prove or to disprove this, but it is also undeniable that Alfonso would have enjoyed winning victories over the Moors which would have earned him a place in the pantheon of his crusading ancestors. If we accept Alfonso's own testimony, the problem centred on an intolerable disparity between the value of the Aragonese tenth and the costs which a major military expedition would entail. The tenth was worth just 20,000 pounds of Barcelona a year if collected under the old valuation, and in 1332 the King asserted that the Granada war would cost 3,000 pounds *a day*. He was probably more accurate when he wrote, in a letter to Philip VI, that a three-year tenth would not meet the expenses of three months' fighting.[77] Hence the Aragonese demands for tenths lasting a decade, for a new valuation, for annates, subsidies, residence dispensations, and the rest. Hence too their insistence on a grant free of conditions relating to royal leadership, for if Alfonso were to abide by an obligation to lead an army in the field for even a year, the result would be financial ruin.

James II's experience of warfare against Granada in 1309–10 tends to support these claims: the tenth, in the Aragonese lands at least, was no longer capable of acting as the corner-stone of crusade

---

[75] 'Aragón y la empresa del Estrecho', 57–9.
[76] Goñi Gaztambide, 305; Vincke, *SKKA*, 243.
[77] Ibid., 247. Cf. Fernández Conde and Oliver, 'La corte pontificia', 379.

finance.[78] But, as Vincke wrote, there were other reasons for Alfonso's failure quite apart from the diminishing capacity of the clerical tenth.[79] First, Aragon had achieved a dramatic overseas expansion which made it impossible for James II and his successors to concentrate on the *Reconquista* as, for instance, James I had done. This was apart from the fact that Alfonso IV enjoyed a splendid court life far too much to make the sort of domestic economies which James I had introduced. Secondly, the success of Aragon had increased the self-esteem of its kings; conditions relating to personal participation which previous rulers would have found quite acceptable, were viewed as intolerable by Alfonso IV. If the king of France would not be dictated to on such matters, neither would his equal, the king of Aragon.[80] Thirdly, the internal position of the king had deteriorated since the days of James I: adventures outside the realm had to be more carefully handled. In such circumstances the problem of finance, allied to the fact that the Granada war was not a profitable one, tipped the balance into inactivity. It was an inactivity which the Castilians, and to some extent the Portuguese, could not afford.

ii. *The French Court and the Tenth, 1323–1363*

If the value of the Aragonese tenth as a proportion of the cost of a crusade against Granada was falling, so too was that of the French tenth as a contribution towards the cost of mounting a crusade of recovery to Palestine. In 1323 the proceeds of a tenth levied on the French church, according to Charles IV, were about the same as in the mid-thirteenth century, 250,000 *livres* of Tours a year. But the annual cost of a *passagium particulare*, again according to the King, was 1,600,000 *livres*. This was more than the entire royal outlay on Louis IX's first crusade, and it would be greatly exceeded by the culminating general passage. Even if we take the rival set of figures put forward by the Curia, of 500,000 *livres* for the tenth and 1,200,000 for the crusade, the disparity is still enormous.[81]

How could this yawning gap be bridged? The French court could of course rely on credit facilities, and Clermont bankers were

[78] The figure of 20,000 pounds of Barcelona can be compared with the sum of 23,000 pounds which the city of Barcelona paid for the arming of ten galleys for just four months' service in 1341. See Robson, 397n.
[79] *SKKA*, 243 ff.
[80] See, for example, *AA*, ii, n. 401.
[81] For the figures see Housley, 'Franco–Papal Crusade Negotiations', 180.

prominent in Philip VI's planning.[82] But for the money itself there were in effect only two sources which could be exploited. One was the French laity, who could be taxed either indirectly, through *gabelles*, or directly, by asking for an aid. Charles IV proposed levying a *gabelle* of 2*d.* in the pound in 1323, but the suggestion aroused scepticism as an unpopular means of raising cash.[83] As for a crusading aid, the abject failure of Philip VI's negotiations with the French towns for a contribution to his crusade, in 1335–6, proved what most people already knew, that the French bourgeoisie had grown too sceptical about the crusade plans of its kings to provide ready cash. While the nobility expressed their doubts by making conditional vows, the townspeople—who had contributed about 274,000 *livres* of Tours to Louis IX's first crusade—showed theirs by either declining to give anything, or by making their grants contingent upon the actual occurrence of the crusade.[84]

The second source of extra finance was the Church outside France. The French court argued that if only the pope would levy a tenth of several years' duration on the entire Catholic Church, enough money would be assembled to launch a crusade.[85] John XXII resisted pressure to this effect in 1322–3, but in 1333 he yielded and levied a six-year tenth throughout Christendom to help finance Philip VI's crusade project.[86] Very heavy French pressure had thus made the Pope contravene a practice which he had generally adhered to, of respecting territorial boundaries when granting crusade taxes: 'We have been accustomed to grant no king a subsidy outside his own kingdom' was how he had expressed it in 1325.[87] As events at the end of the Pope's reign showed, it was an approach rooted in realism, for there was never a chance that most local rulers would permit papal agents to collect the six-year tenth and export it to France.

The most interesting response to the levy of the tenth came from Alfonso IV of Aragon. When he learnt that the clergy of the

---

[82] Cazelles, 107 ff., esp. 110.

[83] CC, nn. 1693, 1695, 1698, 1707.

[84] Jordan, 94–9; J. Viard, 'Un Chapitre d'histoire administrative: les ressources extraordinaires de la royauté sous Philippe de Valois', *Revue des questions historiques*, xliv (1888), 173–5; Henneman, *Royal Taxation . . . 1322–1356*, 104–5; Brown, 243–5 and *passim*. For the earlier failure of Philip V to negotiate a crusading aid, see Tyerman, 30–1.

[85] 'Les Papiers', 216. Cf. Tabacco, 321–2.

[86] Mollat, *Lettres communes*, nn. 61206–7, 61234; *Cal. of Entries*, ii, 369.

[87] *VMH*, i, n. 771.

province of Tarragona were to meet early in 1335 to discuss the tax and arrange its collection, he despatched a royal official, William Boneti, with a brief to persuade the leading prelates to disobey the papal decree. Of the four arguments which the King put forward against the tenth, two concerned only Aragon and the other Spanish *regna*. These related to the threat posed by the proximity and growing strength of the Moors, and to the recently granted two-year tenth—the bulls for which, Alfonso admitted, had not actually been expedited. But the other two points could have been made by any western ruler who wanted to stop the collection of the tenth. First, the crusade was a peculiarly French enterprise in which no other ruler had to date been involved:

The *passagium* proclaimed by the lord Pope cannot properly be described as 'general', since a general passage concerns all the kings and princes of the world, who were not summoned or called by the lord Pope during the negotiations for the said *passagium*. Only the King of France was involved, and it was proclaimed at his request, and his alone; so he should be granted only the tenths of his own kingdoms.

Secondly, and most importantly, the grant of the tax was an intolerable infringement of sovereignty:

It would seem to be very prejudicial to our lord the King, and he would take it ill, that the tenths of his kingdoms should be placed at the disposal of another secular prince or be employed in some such manner, since this would be unprecedented and new, and would seem to be a form of subjection, which would do great harm to the lord King and his realms.[88]

This was surely the crux of the issue. The concept of sovereignty, which ironically received some of its subtlest and most advanced treatment at the French court, made it impossible for Philip VI to finance his crusade with funds collected outside his own kingdom and its satellite territories. And this in turn was a death-blow both to his project, and to all western hopes for the recovery of Palestine by force: in financial terms it was simply impracticable.[89]

This, however, does not exhaust the interest of John XXII's six-year tenth. For while the tax had no future outside France, within the Kingdom it gave rise to a complex and significant sequence of

[88] *Documenta selecta*, n. 509.
[89] The Curia later claimed that its intention was to allocate the collected tenth of each kingdom to its participants in the crusade: Vidal and Mollat, nn. 1620, 1842. This was impracticable, and it would not have solved Philip VI's financial problems.

events. The correspondence about the tenth between Paris and Avignon throws more light than any other contemporary source on the problems which the Curia had to deal with when it tried to prevent the blatant diversion of crusade funds by a hard-pressed and determined lay ruler at the head of the most powerful state of the day.

The death of John XXII at the end of 1334 introduced some confusion into the collection of the tenth, but in January 1335 Benedict XII confirmed the levy of the tax and in June he laid down revised dates for its payment.[90] French pressure had already begun. On the last day of February 1335 Philip VI's envoys, led by Mile of Noyers, presented 'certain petitions concerning the matter of the passage overseas' to the Curia.[91] Two days later the Pope asked for clarification of the requests, which appeared too generalized and obscure. After an initial refusal, the envoys agreed and elucidated the royal requests. There was another consistory and Benedict turned down Philip VI's demands, as he put it, in the name of reason, truth, and fairness.[92] This sequence of events was explained to the King on 12 April, but there was a curious postscript in September. The King was told that there had been a sharp exchange of views during the earlier talks and he asked for details. Benedict replied that the exchange had occurred when he suggested that the royal requests had been forged by an enemy of the King, so detrimental were they to Philip's own interests and honour; this was an ingenious way of saying that they were outrageous without directly insulting the King. Mile of Noyers had replied with 'confused and improper words', and the churchmen in the party of envoys had supported him by their silence. The envoys had, however, gone on to supply the extra details which Benedict wanted and he had drawn up his reply of April. The Pope had forgiven the French prelates and was prepared to forget the insolence of the layman.[93]

Georges Daumet and Francesco Giunta reached the same con-

---

[90] Daumet, nn. 19, 66.

[91] Text in 'Les Papiers', 216. Philip VI had intended to go in person, but was prevented by poor health: Cazelles, 105.

[92] Daumet, n. 44: only a covering letter. Details were given in a secret letter which was not transcribed in the register.

[93] Ibid., n. 103, and cf. Mile of Noyers' own account of what happened, 'Les Papiers', 216–17. The episode was briefly treated by Cont. William of Nangis, ii, 144.

clusion about this episode and they were almost certainly correct.[94] Philip VI had already started to employ the proceeds of the crusading tenth for various other uses and his embassy had the unsavoury task of securing the Pope's open or tacit assent to this diversion of crusading funds, which the King probably promised to restore later. But Philip misjudged the new pope: Benedict XII was a less adroit diplomat than John XXII but was no less determined to defend Church rights and revenues. He demanded that the French envoys lay their cards on the table and then rejected the proposal outright. Not surprisingly, his comment that the King was acting dishonourably, albeit phrased in an indirect manner, drew a stinging rebuke from one of the leading officers of the French Crown: Mile of Noyers even claimed that this was the Pope's intention.[95] Quite possibly Mile's reply took the form of a sharp reminder of the number of times the Curia had diverted crusade funds in the past. Certainly Philip VI must have realized that this would not be an easy pope to deal with. The following years witnessed the clash of powerful wills.

Early in 1336 Philip spent some days at Avignon and discussed the crusade, not as a practical possibility but as the occasion for a series of financial outlays for which the French now wanted compensation from the Church.[96] On 13 March Benedict issued his letter postponing the general passage, which had been planned for the following August. The French King was absolved of his vow to set out in 1336, but was urged to persevere with his preparations for the crusade.[97] By the end of the year, however, the Pope realized that the expedition had no future; collection of the tenth was called off and Benedict decreed the return of the sums which had been collected.[98] A month earlier he had also refused to grant Philip a tenth to help him pay his debts. If this tenth was granted, the Pope wrote, people would conclude that the crusade had been abandoned because the Pope and the King had made inadequate efforts to finance it. Philip had already received various tenths and annates to pay his debts, and the French church could not afford to subsidize him further, at the same time as paying the crusade tenth

---

[94] Daumet, 'Introduction', xlviii–xlix; Giunta, 'Benedetto XII e la crociata', 219–20.
[95] 'Les Papiers', 217.
[96] Ibid., 217–22.
[97] Vidal and Mollat, n. 786.
[98] Daumet, nn. 251–2.

(which was still being collected at this point). But Benedict placed his refusal in the broader context of his policy of retrenchment in state taxation of the Church. If the request of the French King was granted then other rulers would press their case, 'of whom perhaps some need substantial subsidies for the defence of Christians against the enemies of the Faith and the invaders of their kingdoms'. The Church was over taxed: many clerics were already abandoning their benefices and extra taxes would severely hinder the Church's pastoral and charitable work.[99] The Pope's cancellation of John XXII's sexennial tenth in the following month was placed in the same context of papal concern for the well-being of the Church.[100]

Benedict's policy was a courageous and compassionate, but unrealistic attempt to free the secular Church from the heavier demands of lay taxation. Like Boniface VIII's earlier attempt at the same problem, it lacked realism because no contemporary ruler could afford to let it succeed: the loss of the tenth would cripple government finance. French pressure centred on two aims, papal permission for royal seizure of the collected proceeds of the six-year tenth, and the grant of fresh taxes. Early in 1337, Philip VI asked for at least 400,000 *livres* of the crusade tenth as a loan, should Edward III invade France. Benedict rejected this new request in April on familiar grounds. It was directly contrary to the vows of the royal proctors, would scandalize Christendom if it was granted, and would make it impossible to levy future tenths for a crusade to the Holy Land. Of particular interest is the Pope's reference to the common belief—earlier mentioned by John XXII—that previous French kings had incurred God's wrath by seizing crusade funds:

Apart from this, your Royal Highness should prudently reflect on what is popularly believed to have befallen your predecessors as a result of their receiving and spending tenths and other funds levied and collected for the said passage; and on what people would say about you, if anything untoward should happen to you—which the Lord forbid.[101]

But if Benedict remained determined not to give way on John XXII's tenth, his own political needs soon forced him to yield on the

[99] Ibid., n. 240.
[100] Ibid., n. 251.
[101] Ibid., n. 280. Cf. John XXII's similar remark in 1333, quoted above, ch. 4, n. 25, and Daumet, n. 713.

more general issue of taxation. In March 1338 a two-year tenth was granted to Philip to help him to defend France against Louis of Bavaria (or rather his ally Edward III), and in February 1340 he received the grant of another two-year tenth.[102]

It was one thing to issue formal vetoes on Philip VI's use of the proceeds of the crusade tenth, and quite another to stop them finding their way surreptitiously into the royal coffers. The money was held by a number of bourgeois chosen by the King, and the ruling was that nothing should be handed over without the express permission of a four man ecclesiastical commission, of whom two were answerable to the Pope.[103] But this machinery was open to abuse. The papal delegates on the commission were the Archbishops of Rouen and Sens, and Benedict instructed the former in November 1337 to make sure that no money went astray, even as a loan; when the Anglo–French dispute ended the Archbishop was to draw up detailed accounts of the tax.[104] In May 1338 and again in September the two prelates were told to get detailed accounts from the bourgeois and send these to the Curia.[105] Apparently the tenth was still being collected in the province of Lyons, despite the cancellation of 1336, for in June 1338 the Archbishop of Lyons and his suffragans were told to stop collecting the tax.[106]

That the King had been drawing off money from the stored tenth for some time, probably since Mile of Noyers's embassy in 1335, is clear from a frank letter which Philip wrote to the Pope in March 1340.[107] In this he admitted that he had employed part of the tenth, not only for preparations which he had made for the *passagium*, but also for the defence of the realm. He requested absolution for this contravention of his proctors' oath; if necessary he would repay the money, provided repayment could be postponed until after the war had ended. Philip had been assured by his clerical advisers that his use of the tenth 'for the guarding and defence of the realm' was legitimate, and he would have a clean conscience even if no papal absolution was forthcoming. This astonishing self-assurance rested

---

[102] Ibid., n. 420; Vidal, nn. 8095–9.
[103] CC, n. 5211; *Registres du Trésor des chartes. Vol. III: Règne de Philippe de Valois, première partie*, comp. J. Viard (Paris, 1978), n. 2143; Viard, 'Un Chapitre', 211–12.
[104] Daumet, n. 378.
[105] Ibid., nn. 443, 499.   [106] Vidal, n. 6302.
[107] Daumet, n. 708: a rare example of an incoming letter being transcribed in its entirety in the papal register. Cf. above, ch. 2, nn. 96, 98.

on the belief that it was the duty of all Frenchmen, lay or clerical, to contribute to the defence of the Kingdom:

Our war is being fought to resist those who want to deprive both ourselves and our subjects, clerical and lay, of our inheritance. In such a case, as you know full well, everybody is obliged to contribute towards their own defence in the provision of soldiers and expenses, since the matter concerns them as much as it does us.[108]

Benedict replied on 2 April. Not only did he refuse to grant either absolution or a postponement in the repayment of the tenth, but he complained bitterly about the deception which Philip had engaged in and its consequences for the morale of Christendom, already badly damaged by the deferment of the crusade. He was surprised that the King's clerical and lay advisers had treated so lightly the solemn vows of Philip and his son John, undertaken in public and publicized throughout the Christian world. It was already notorious that the French kings had misapplied crusade funds, and this latest example, in which the money would be used to kill Christians, would strengthen the propaganda of France's enemies—which it did, as we have seen. Past experience had shown that postponement was no solution. The Curia was itself under fire because of the tenths of 1338 and 1340 and could not afford to incur extra criticism. Benedict asked the King to reconsider what he had done and its possible repercussions.[109]

This letter must have made it clear to Philip VI that he would get nothing further out of Benedict XII. But in 1342 a more pliable pope was elected, and in 1344 Philip renewed his request for absolution from the sin of seizing and misapplying the crusade funds. On 20 June Clement VI granted the King a pardon, on the sole condition that a new three-year tenth should be levied in France when a general passage or a *passagium particulare* was planned. This money would go to the King or his eldest son if they took part in the expedition, and if they did not it should be stored safely.[110] It had taken Philip VI nine years to achieve the desired objective, but he had finally done so. Nevertheless, the French court found even such liberal terms as these oppressive. In 1351

---

[108] This assurance probably derived from the King's advisers rather than from Philip himself, who was conscience-stricken about his abandoned crusade project. See Henneman, *Royal Taxation . . . 1322–1356*, 103, 304–5.

[109] Daumet, n. 713.

[110] Déprez *et al.*, n. 914. Cf. Viard, 'Les Projets', 316n; Wood, 188–9.

King John asked that the clause about the new tenth should be deleted since he had not benefited from the original tenth and France was exhausted by war. Clement granted what amounted to a *de facto* deletion by conceding that the clause applied only in the case of a general passage.[111] The money remitted came to about 2,800,000 florins.[112]

The key factor throughout these years was the initial levy and collection of the tenth; all the effective power the papacy had was its control over the decision to tax. Once the process of collecting and storing the money had started, the most elaborate precautions and binding obligations were all but useless: the authority of the French king and his financial needs were too great. The anguished phrases of Benedict's letter of 1340 show how powerful an impression this fact made, even on a Curia which was well versed in the techniques of French power. The normal Church sanctions of excommunication and interdict were inapplicable in this instance because of the papacy's reliance on France on other political issues: thus it was the Anglo-imperial alliance which compelled Benedict XII to yield to French demands for a tenth in 1338. All the Pope could do was fulminate, conjuring up the unconvincing threat of a disapproving public opinion and the more disturbing—but nonetheless ineffective—prospect of God's wrath, his punishment of the King in this world or the next. Such criticism could be borne until a new pope was elected. And even in terms of verbal polemic, the papacy was in a weak position because of its own past policy. The argument deployed by Philip VI in 1340 was all too similar to that used by John XXII in 1333.[113] Philip's success in the battle of wills was thus the inevitable outcome of John XXII yielding to pressure in 1333, itself the proof of John's wisdom in not yielding ten years previously. Clement VI, in the actions he took in 1344 and 1351, was not so much displaying his French allegiance as bowing to the inevitable. Benedict XII emerges from the episode with honour—but without achieving his aim of defending the Church.

In 1363 Urban V had to make arrangements for the collection and storage of the tenth and other funds which he granted to King John for the Franco-Cypriot crusade, and his letters enable us to see

---

[111] Déprez *et al.*, n. 4991.
[112] See M. Faucon, 'Prêts faits aux rois de France par Clément VI, Innocent VI et le comte de Beaufort (1345–1360)', *BEC*, xl (1879), 574; Henneman, *Royal Taxation . . . 1322–1356*, 233–4.   [113] Above, nn. 45, 108.

whether the papacy had learnt from the bitter and protracted history of the 1333 tenth. On 31 March Urban issued two different sets of instructions relating to the tenth. In letters to the French King and clergy he duplicated the earlier system. Collectors would hand the proceeds over to 'suitable bourgeois', who would assign them only to a commission of four prelates, two chosen by the Pope and two by the King. Both *burgenses* and clerics were to swear an oath not to permit the diversion of the funds. In addition, no proceeds were to be spent until the Pope was convinced, by the preparations being undertaken, that the project's sponsors were in earnest, 'especially in the preparation of those things necessary for a general passage'.[114] But Urban's second set of instructions, apparently sent only to the clergy of southern France, overrode this procedure. He ordered instead that the collected money should be changed into gold coin, passed on by suffragans to their archbishops at six-monthly intervals, and sent on by the latter to the *camera*. It was to be the Curia which would channel the money into the hands of the King, although royal officials would be kept informed of the amounts involved.[115]

Since the 1363 tenth was never levied, there is no way of predicting which procedure would have been followed, and where. An attempt to implement the second set of instructions would certainly have provoked a conflict between Pope and King; indeed, the fact that the Curia could even contemplate such an approach is a vivid illustration of the collapse of French royal authority, especially in the south, between 1333 and 1363. It also shows that the Curia *had* learnt from earlier events, although its own proposed solution was to reassert its own role as the guardian of crusade funds, impracticable not only because of the reaction of the French Crown, but also because of the way it would heighten Avignon's attractiveness as a goal for the *routier* bands of southern France. The fact was that there was no solution to the problem of crusade funds being diverted and lost, any more than there was to that of finding and channelling adequate revenues for a large-scale *passagium* to the East.

iii. *Crusade Taxation in Sweden and Hungary, 1343–1373*

Taxation disputes between the Curia and the Spanish kings centred on the alarming way in which Spanish demands for financial aid

---

[114] Prou, 91–102.   [115] LM, nn. 346–7.

were becoming greater and more frequent. Clashes with the French court arose from a connected but slightly different problem: that of guaranteeing security for crusade taxes. In the case of eastern Europe the focus of disputes was usually the distribution of the spoils. Sweden under Magnus II and Hungary under Louis the Great are good examples of kingdoms whose clergy the Curia needed to tax for its own ends, and where its policies met with opposition from lay rulers with political aspirations which could be fitted into a crusading framework. Mutually beneficial compromises were reached, but the pope was rarely able to exact his due share of the profits.

In 1343 and 1345 Clement VI included Sweden in the lands covered by his five-year tenth for the crusade against the Turks.[116] In 1349 John Guilbert was sent north to collect the money.[117] He found the Swedish government in acute financial difficulties, partly because of the cost of the expedition which Magnus had directed against schismatic Novgorod in 1348.[118] Under the circumstances, the collector agreed to lend the regent, Blanche of Namur, all the proceeds of the tenth in Sweden and Norway; the loan was to be repaid in 1351.[119] This was followed in 1351 by substantial papal backing for Magnus's war with Novgorod, which the King had successfully presented as a crusading enterprise. In a letter to the clergy of Sweden and Norway Clement VI claimed that he had at first intended to levy a tenth in the northern kingdoms for his own war needs. Then Magnus's envoys had put forward the King's need for financial aid to prevent the Russians attacking the freshly converted communities of Karelians and Ingrians; Swedish resources, they asserted, had been badly depleted by the Black Death. Clement had therefore decided to levy a four-year tenth which would be split equally between Pope and King.[120] By August an extra year had been added to the tenth and Waldemar of Denmark had been brought into the arrangement.[121] Clement also prohibited trade with Novgorod, and asked the Teutonic Knights to help Magnus defend his converts.[122]

The Curia learnt that Magnus collected 10,028 marks in Norway and 22,000 marks in Sweden from the tenth: a total of 19,560

---

[116] Déprez *et al.*, n. 559; *Acta pont. svecica*, i, n. 353.
[117] Riant, 404.
[118] *Chronicle of Novgorod*, 141–2.
[119] Riant, 404–5.
[120] *Acta pont. svecica*, i, n. 398.
[121] Ibid., i, n. 429.
[122] *VMP*, i, nn. 700–1.

florins.[123] Its own share should thus have been nearly 10,000 florins, but the King proved reluctant to honour the agreement. During the last years of Magnus's reign the papacy conducted a long and fruitless campaign to secure its half of the 1351 tax and the repayment of John Guilbert's loan. In February 1356 Innocent VI described his heavy expenses to the King and asked him to restore to the Church, either directly or through its agents in Flanders, the money which he had borrowed.[124] Magnus was threatened with excommunication, but by this point internal conditions in Sweden had made it impossible for the King to hand over any money. In 1358 prelates throughout northern Europe were ordered to declare Magnus excommunicated.[125] In the following year envoys were sent to Avignon to plead the King's contrition and assert that he was prepared to pay 15,000 florins if he was granted a delay. The sentence was suspended in May 1360, but the King was certainly not a reformed character: in August 1361 he levied a forced loan of over 4,000 marks from the papal taxes held by the Archbishop of Uppsala 'because of the evident and obvious need of ourselves and of the realm'.[126] In February 1362 the Pope was willing to lift the excommunication if the King was prepared to pay a half or more of what he owed, but Magnus failed to do so before his death in the following year.[127]

The Curia could take the step of excommunicating Magnus because he was of peripheral importance in papal policies. By contrast, Louis of Hungary had a potentially significant part to play in Italy and the Balkans, and the Curia therefore had to handle his intransigence in financial matters with greater flexibility. Indeed, in its early grants of taxes to the King it made no attempt to reserve a proportion of the proceeds for its own purposes, since these purposes were themselves implicated, directly or indirectly, in Louis's plans. Thus the four-year tenth which Clement VI granted Louis in July 1352—an exceptionally generous concession, as the Pope himself pointed out—took the form of a reward for the King's withdrawal from southern Italy. It was linked explicitly to Louis's release of his high-ranking Neapolitan prisoners, and implicitly to his renunciation of Queen Joanna's war indemnity.[128] Similarly, the three-year tenth which the King was granted in 1356 was intended to

[123] Riant, 405–6.   [124] Gasnault *et al.*, n. 1951, and see too n. 1953.
[125] *Acta pont. svecica*, i, nn. 517, 526, 570.   [126] Ibid., i, nn. 598–9, 622.
[127] Ibid., i, n. 631; Riant, 407.   [128] *VMH*, i, n. 1253.

finance the military aid which ne had undertaken to send Albornoz in Romagna.[129] Louis thus earned seven years' worth of tenths in nine years in the form of reward or incentive.

From 1362, however, papal–Hungarian relations entered a more difficult phase which more closely resembles earlier events in Sweden. The Curia's need to tax the Hungarian church on a more regular basis for its wars in Italy conflicted with Louis's financial needs, a conflict which arose because the King's ambitions were now much less closely aligned with papal policy. Not surprisingly, Louis resorted to the sort of tactics which Magnus had employed, especially the harassment of papal agents and collectors. Thus in May 1363 the King was asked to stop impeding the collection of papal revenue in his lands.[130] The dispute never became as serious as in Sweden, since the Curia continued to hope that Louis might be persuaded to resume his earlier role as 'standard-bearer of the Church', either in Italy or in the Balkans. But in the 1370s the extremely heavy expenses of the Church in Lombardy, allied to continuing royal obstruction and the recalcitrance of Hungarian churchmen, caused Gregory XI to be more severe in his approach than Innocent VI or Urban V had been. Relations perhaps reached their nadir in 1373, when the Pope took the unusual step of stripping the privileges which he granted Louis for his crusade against the Turks of the customary tenths.[131] Gregory subsequently wrote to the Hungarian prelates to tell them that they were to stop preaching Louis's crusade if the King obstructed the collection of the papal tenth.[132] It is doubtful that this hard line approach was more successful than it had been in Sweden.

iv. *The Fate of a Great Crusade Tax: the Vienne Tenth*

The best way to pull together the findings of the preceding three sections about how decisions were reached on the levying and allocation of crusade taxes, is to look at what happened to the proceeds of the only universal tenth imposed and collected during the Avignon period, the six-year tenth levied by Clement V at the Council of Vienne in 1312.

The background and precedents of the tax, which some saw as the

---

[129] Gasnault *et al.*, n. 2320.
[130] *VMH*, ii, n. 98.
[131] Ibid., ii, nn. 270–3; Mollat, *Lettres secrètes*, nn. 1744, 2208, 2318.
[132] Ibid., n. 1769.

Council's chief *raison d'être*,[133] were not promising. Much of the money collected from the two tenths imposed at the general councils held at Lyons in 1245 and 1274 had been diverted from its goal by the papacy and the secular powers.[134] In addition, the crusade plans discussed at Vienne lacked both the background of crisis supplied in 1245 by the fall of Jerusalem and the battle of Gaza, and the vision and driving enthusiasm which Gregory X had brought to bear in 1274. During and after the Council of Vienne too much hinged on the dubious reliability of Philip the Fair and the equally questionable ability of the Curia to get churchmen to pay up, and persuade their rulers to permit the export of the money. Well-informed contemporaries perceived the way the wind was blowing: in 1325 an Aragonese envoy at the Curia, Ferrarius de Apilia, advised James II to resist all papal attempts to export the Aragonese contribution to the tenth on the grounds that the kings of England and France, together with other rulers, no longer permitted such taxation, and 'you are the lord of your Kingdom, just as any other king is the lord of his'.[135]

Consequently, it never appeared likely that the money would be assembled *in toto* to form the great crusade treasure called for by Ramon Lull and others as the financial backbone for a general passage. Clement V admitted as much by making partial grants of the proceeds as soon as the tenth was levied.[136] In this respect the Council and its aftermath form a transitional stage between the great thirteenth-century councils with their aims of crusade, unity, and reform, and the individual, wholly pragmatic sets of negotiations which we have just examined. The overall fate of the Vienne tenth is thus all too predictable, given the history of the preceding half-century; its interest lies in the considerable range of variations in who got the cash, when, and how.

First, there were the countries where all or most of the money ended up in the coffers of the local rulers, with or without papal permission. As always, the history of the tenth in France is instructive; it is also rather complicated. Initially the whole of the tenth was granted by Clement V to Philip IV to help the King prepare his crusade, together with an additional one-year tenth (collected

---

[133] John of St Victor, 19.
[134] See, for example, Housley, *Italian Crusades*, 103–4; Lunt, i, 250 ff., 311 ff.
[135] *AA*, ii, n. 401.
[136] See, for example, *Reg. Clem. V*, n. 7759.

before the Vienne tenth started, in 1312–13), and a four-year tenth intended to follow on from the Vienne tenth. Faced with this extraordinary concession, John XXII decided in September 1316 to treat the first four years of the Vienne tenth (1313–17) as the four-year tenth originally intended to follow it; by so doing, he had some chance of retaining the equivalent four years of the Vienne tenth for crusade purposes, since the tenths of 1313–17 had been swallowed up in royal debts. In the winter of 1317–18, under renewed French pressure, he granted Philip V the penultimate year of the Vienne tenth (1317–18) as a loan, reserving 100,000 florins for the expenses of the Franco-papal naval squadron.[137] He also lent the French Crown the last year of the tenth,[138] and added a new two-year tenth to be paid between 1318 and 1321. The French monarchy thus acquired all six years of the tenth (with the exception of the 100,000 florins), although the first four years in theory constituted a separate tenth: the equivalent four years of the Vienne tenth remained as a 'ghost tax' which John XXII still talked of collecting as late as 1321.[139]

It was of course a combination of royal strength and close ties with the crusade which enabled the French Crown to reap this success, and one or the other of these factors explains similar events in England and some of the Spanish kingdoms. In England only one year's proceeds were collected; these were lent to Edward II soon after John XXII's accession, but the loan was not repaid and it had been written off as a hopeless debt by 1343.[140] The King of Majorca was assigned four years of the tenth in December 1316 for his war against the Moorish pirates,[141] and in 1320 the Portuguese collectors were told to pay their King the proceeds of three years of the tenth so that he could prepare galleys to defend the Kingdom against attacks launched from Granada.[142] In 1317 the Infante Peter of Castile was permitted to use up to 150,000 florins from the proceeds of the tenth and the associated *tercias*, in his war with Granada. If less than 150,000 florins had been collected, he could

---

[137] These 100,000 florins too were later lent to Philip V, but were repaid in the early months of 1319.

[138] This can be deduced from CC, n. 1262.

[139] The whole sequence is explained in Tabacco, 51 ff., 139 ff., correcting earlier accounts of what occurred.

[140] Lunt, i, 395–404.

[141] Mollat, *Lettres communes*, n. 2349.

[142] Ibid., nn. 11495–7.

collect the tenth and *tercias* for up to three years to come, 'using [the money] for the wages of knights, horsemen, and others hired in order to wage this war, and for the arming of such galleys as you find necessary'.[143]

Not all kings were able to retain the proceeds of the tenth for local purposes: some had to agree to a compromise whereby part of the money went to Avignon. The clearest example comes from Sweden. Much of the Vienne tenth was collected in Sweden by 1321, but owing to the civil discord of Magnus's regency the money could not readily be exported. Thus in about 1322 the papal collector and canon of Uppsala, Nils Sighvatsson, noted in a report that members of the nobility were exerting pressure on prelates and chapters holding the tenth in deposit to 'lend' them the proceeds of the tax.[144] In 1326 the envoys of Magnus and his regent petitioned John XXII for help against attacks emanating from pagan Karelia and schismatic Novgorod. The Pope told his nuncios that if they saw a genuine need for the money they were to assign the King a half of the collected tenth: the other half would go to the *camera*.[145] A total of 4,340 pounds sterling was collected, including a contribution from Greenland which was paid in walrus teeth. The Curia received its due share, but only after great obstruction by royal officials, and an attempt by Magnus in 1327 to claim the whole of the money.[146] A similar arrangement was reached with the King of Hungary in 1332, by which the *camera* was to receive two-thirds of the collected tenth. The wording of the letter suggests that it was a response to serious obstacles placed in the way of collectors operating solely on the Pope's behalf.[147] A half of the tenth from the Kingdom of Naples also reached Avignon, though since the money was treated as payment of Angevin census arrears this was rather less of a gain for the Curia than might at first sight appear.[148]

With the kings of Aragon, characteristically, the Curia failed to reach a satisfactory arrangement for the allocation of the tenth; what occurred was a *de facto* rather than a formal division of funds. On several occasions James II and Alfonso IV 'borrowed' the proceeds of the tenth by simply seizing the chests which held it in the

---

[143] '. . . convertenda pro stipendiis militum et equitum et aliorum qui fuerint ad huius negotii prosecutionem assumpti et galearum que adhoc extiterint opportune ipsarumque munitione': ASV, Reg. Vat. 63, ff. 52ᵛ–53ᵛ, n. 155.
[144] *Acta pont. svecica,* i, n. 191.
[145] Ibid., i, n. 207.
[146] Ibid, i, n. 231; Riant, 396–400.
[147] *VMH,* i, n. 867.
[148] Housley, *Italian Crusades,* 104–5.

cathedrals of Gerona, Vich, and Barcelona. A series of royal envoys to the Curia, in 1313, 1316, and annually between 1320 and 1323, were denied the legitimate consignment of the proceeds to the Crown, and to get papal favour on the granting of other tenths James and Alfonso had to permit the transfer of some of the Vienne tenth to Avignon from 1326 onwards.[149] But it is highly unlikely that they repaid their own 'loans' from the tenth. A sequence of events in 1325 forms a very good illustration of how papal resistance could be gradually worn down. In the first instance, James II was granted a loan of 15,000 pounds of Barcelona from the tenth collected in the province of Tarragona, to assist him with the cost of purchasing a castle of strategic importance. Subsequently, the Pope agreed to remit half of the money, specifying that the rest should be repaid from the proceeds of a recently granted two-year tenth. Finally, he yielded to a petition that the whole sum be remitted on the grounds of the heavy expenses incurred in conquering Sardinia and paying its feudal census to the Curia. As so often in such cases, a comment was added to the effect that the Pope would restore an equivalent sum to crusade funds when the time was ripe.[150]

The Curia, then, received some of the proceeds of the tenth from Sweden, Hungary, Naples, and Aragon, at the cost of hard negotiating and compromises with local rulers. Finally, there were some areas of Latin Christendom without strong, unified lay authority, and here the popes were themselves able to collect the lion's share of the tax. Thus the proceeds of the tenth from the dioceses of northern and central Italy, and many of the German dioceses, ended up as pay for the papal armies fighting in Italy in the 1320s. The problem was that without the backing of royal officials, collection in such regions tended to be even slower and more difficult than in the kingdoms; arrears were still being collected decades after the Council of Vienne, a factor which substantially reduced the effective value of the extra revenue.[151] It was ironic that the papacy, which seems to have been singled out for criticism on the grounds of the tenth's diversion from its objective, probably derived less advantage from the tax than most kings did.[152]

[149] Vincke, *SKKA*, 183 ff.

[150] ASV, Reg. Vat. 113, f. 172^{r-v}, n. 1022. Cf. the advice of Ferrarius de Apilia in October 1325: *AA*, ii, n. 401.

[151] Housley, *Italian Crusades*, 104–6.

[152] See, for example, ibid., 107–8. I have found few instances of secular rulers being criticized for their role in the diversion of the tenth.

(d) THE TRANSFER OF PAPAL FUNDS: BANKERS AND HOSPITALLERS

The difficulties which the papacy faced in all these sets of negotiations originated in two developments: on the one hand, the escalating cost of military activity, on the other, the stimulus which this gave to the promotion of such concepts as sovereignty, common responsibility for the defence of the realm, and the duty of the Church to pay for the crusade. As a negotiating power, what hampered the Curia time after time was the disadvantage of being an international institution in a period when compact, national monarchies were in the ascendant. But this also created problems for the papacy as a military power. When they prepared to wage crusades, the kings of Castile, Aragon, France, Sweden, and Hungary collected and disbursed money within their own realms or just outside them. Even Venice, when it sent galleys into the eastern Mediterranean in the naval leagues against the Turks, possessed a colonial bureaucracy well used to forwarding funds over a sustained period.[153] But the Curia drew its revenues from churches stretching from Portugal to Livonia, Greenland to Cyprus, and it had to deploy its money in places where its administrative cadres were either thinly spread—the Latin East—or subject to violent disruption—Italy.

The papacy was enabled to deal with this problem on a regular basis by its privileged access to the services of the Italian banking houses, which were ready and able to do much of its work for it. It is almost impossible to conceive of the popes handling their financial affairs, let alone using their revenues to field armies, without making use of this other international network which so conveniently interlocked with their own.[154] But as Yves Renouard showed in his classic study, it was only in the period up to 1342, when both papal finances and the banking houses were in sound health, that the system worked with maximum efficiency. Under John XXII in particular, the bankers played a prominent role not only in facilitating the finance of the crusades in northern Italy, but also in handling the funding of the two *passagia* of 1319 and 1334, and the transfer of funds sent in aid of Armenia.[155] For a time, the

---

[153] See Thiriet, 181–256.
[154] Renouard, *Les Relations, passim.*
[155] Housley, *Italian Crusades*, 246 ff.; Renouard, *Les Relations*, 166–85.

Curia was no worse placed than the national monarchies in organizing the transfer of its crusade funds.

Then came the crash of the major cameral banking houses, the Peruzzi and Acciaiuoli in 1343, and the Bardi in 1346. These events caused deep and prolonged difficulties for the Curia's crusade finance. Throughout the reigns of Clement VI and Innocent VI the *camera* was compelled to rely on the services of smaller and weaker companies such as the Malabayla. Only after 1362 did the banking houses of Italy experience a gradual recovery, enabling them to resume their former role in papal finance. There emerged at Florence, Lucca, and Pistoia a number of firms which proved strong enough to shoulder the burden of cameral business, the Alberti *antichi* and *nuovi*, the Guardi, the Ricci, the Soderini, the Strozzi, the Guinigi, and the house of Andrea di Tici. Funds could be transferred with relative ease even when the War of the Eight Saints put Florence's banking firms beyond the pale. There could not be a complete return to the smooth-running system of the 1320s, however, because the papacy's own finances were now so unsound; instead of using just the deposit and transfer facilities of the banks, as John XXII had done, Gregory XI had to borrow heavily on the strength of future revenues.[156]

From the point of view of transfer, the most difficult period was thus 1342–62. This affected crusade finance in two ways. First, it made Albornoz's task of reconquering the Papal State harder, since Innocent VI had no regular means of transferring money to his legate. To transfer a total of 531,600 florins to Albornoz, the Pope had to enter into 146 separate contracts with a wide variety of banks. A number of expedients, some of them dangerous, had to be adopted to get money to the papal armies. Forty thousand florins were borrowed from Florence, money was entrusted to clerics and laymen travelling to or through Italy on business, funds were channelled in from neighbouring collectorates, and arrangements were made with people on the spot holding desirable amounts of cash.[157] Secondly, this was also the period when the heaviest call was made on papal revenues for crusading in the eastern Mediterranean, for between 1343 and 1347 Clement VI was maintaining four galleys in the Aegean as his contribution to the naval league against the Turks. These years almost exactly coincided with the collapse of the great Florentine firms. Since this created a mood of

---

[156] Ibid., 197–365.   [157] Ibid., 257–75.

general insecurity, it was impossible to come to an arrangement with smaller firms, which would not have had the necessary agents in the East anyway. Similarly, it was unreasonable to expect to finance the galleys through the sort of *ad hoc* measures which Innocent VI later adopted in Italy. Clement therefore decided to use the services of the Hospitallers, an Order dedicated to the crusade which had high-ranking officials in both East and West. The Pope's well-documented relations with the Order throw much light on the problems which ensued when the normal procedure for the transfer of funds had been thrown into disarray.

Clement was contributing four galleys to the league and at the start his annual payments for these amounted to 38,400 florins, at the rate of 800 florins a month for each galley.[158] He originally planned that the *camera* would pay for the first year's service, after which the proceeds of the tenth levied in December 1343 would be used. On 24 August 1343 he wrote to Hélion of Villeneuve, the Master of the Hospitallers, explaining the arrangements which he was making. The money for the initial four months' service, 12,800 florins, had been paid to Martin Zaccaria, the papal captain, and to the owners (*patroni*) of the vessels. The 25,600 florins for the eight remaining months were being paid to the Marshal of the Hospital and the Priors of Capua and Bari; this money was to be handed over by them or by Hélion to Martin Zaccaria and the owners at the orders of Henry of Asti, the legate, when four months, and then eight, were up.[159] John Amiel, a cameral official well used to crusade business, handed over the money to the Marshal and Priors in Provence.[160] These disbursements were confirmed in the papal treasurers' accounts of October 1343, adding the 1,800 florins paid to Martin Zaccaria as his annual stipend.[161] So far, then, the *camera* had paid out 40,200 florins for the galleys.[162]

In September 1344, Clement wrote to Henry of Asti explaining his revised plans. As the collection of the tenth was taking some time, the *camera* was itself forwarding the money to pay for the next four months' service by the papal galleys (19 December 1344 to 18

[158] This was also the estimated cost of hiring galleys at Venice in 1333 and Genoa in 1340. See *DVL*, i, n. 124; Robson, 400.

[159] Déprez *et al.*, n. 368.

[160] Ibid., nn. 369–70.

[161] Ibid., n. 464.

[162] Setton (*PL*, 186n) reached a total of 53,000 florins for the galleys, but seems to have duplicated the initial four months' payment.

April 1345). Owing to his difficulties in finding merchants to handle the transfer of the money, the Pope would tell Hélion of Villeneuve to lend the legate the funds needed.[163] This money, he assured the Master on the same day, would be swiftly repaid from the despatch of cameral funds.[164] The banking crisis was thus forcing Clement not only to enlist the Hospitallers as his creditors, but also to send money across the Mediterranean, braving pirates and winter storms. This no doubt partly explains his attempt to cut down the Curia's commitment: he told Henry that he was to lay off the crews of the galleys during the winter months, if this could be done without damaging the expedition.[165] From subsequent financial accounts it does not appear that Henry took this line of action. Treasurers' accounts of 1 November 1344 record payments of 12,800 florins for the galleys, 600 for the salary of Martin Zaccaria, and 335 *pro portagio*, to Garin of Châteauneuf, the Prior of Navarre and Procurator-general of the Hospitallers at the Curia.[166] Hélion of Villeneuve did not respond to the letter of September and was again told to carry out the procedure in February 1345.[167] This could indicate the Master's unwillingness to take on this new, and risky, responsibility.

Clement seems to have adopted exactly the same procedure for the next four-month period, starting on 19 April 1345, for the treasurers' accounts of 17 July 1345 record disbursements of another 12,800 florins to Garin of Châteauneuf, and 600 florins for the new captain going East to replace Martin Zaccaria.[168] In May, however, potential confusion was introduced when the Pope wrote to Hélion of Villeneuve and the Marshal of the Order that he had been informed that Martin Zaccaria and the *patroni* had broken the terms of their contracts with the Curia and that captain, owners, and galleys had all been found wanting. The Hospitallers were to investigate the matter, make suitable deductions from the money paid to Martin and the *patroni*, and use the cash saved for the benefit of the league's activities, for the salary of the captain who was to replace Martin, and for the galleys' needs.[169] A quittance issued to Garin of Châteauneuf in January 1346 confirmed that the Hospitallers had paid out all the money they had been entrusted

---

[163] Déprez *et al.*, n. 1114.
[164] Ibid., n. 1115.
[165] Ibid., n. 1114.
[166] Ibid., n. 1209.
[167] Ibid., n. 1463.
[168] Ibid., n. 1834.
[169] Ibid., n. 1713.

with, a total of 51,200 florins given to Martin and Centurione Zaccaria and the *patroni* at Rhodes and Negroponte.[170]

The three years' duration of the league expired in December 1346, but Clement VI assured Humbert of Vienne in June 1346 that he would work for the league's continuation and would keep his own galleys at sea.[171] Recorded payments stop in July 1345, beginning again in the following summer with 58,400 florins sent East with the Hospitallers, and 7,600 paid in the West to the *patroni* of the two new galleys going East to replace the two least seaworthy ones in the Aegean.[172] Payments had fallen into arrears and Humbert of Vienne had stepped in to make provisional payments to the *patroni*.[173] This was the last sum carried by the Hospitallers: the settlement with the *patroni* in 1347 was handled by their proctors at Avignon and by papal agents in Cyprus.[174] In April 1349 Clement specified exactly how much he had spent on the galleys, which represented the most substantial papal contribution to the defence of the Christian East in our period. Cameral officials had paid out 33,546 florins at Avignon, and the Hospitallers had carried 110,800 florins to the East: a total of 144,346 florins.[175] It was not a huge sum when compared with the funds poured into Italy, but even its transfer had proved a strain in the peculiar circumstances of the 1340s.[176]

---

[170] Ibid., n. 2281.
[171] Ibid., n. 2580. N. 2581 is a duplicate.
[172] Ibid., nn. 2752, 2809.
[173] Ibid., n. 2956.
[174] *Die Ausgaben der apostolischen Kammer unter Benedikt XII., Klemens VI. und Innocenz VI. (1335–1362)*, ed. K. H. Schäfer (Paderborn, 1914), 359.
[175] Déprez *et al.*, n. 4130. See also below, Appendix I.
[176] Cf. Renouard, *Les Relations*, 249.

6

Obstacles to Crusading in the Eastern Mediterranean and the Papal Response

THE crusading movement in the eastern Mediterranean during the reigns of the Avignon popes was a failure. This remains a central and unavoidable fact, undisguised by such short-lived or local successes as the capture of Smyrna, the sack of Alexandria, and the fruitful expedition of Amedeo of Savoy. The western powers failed to reconquer the Holy Land or even get close to launching a general passage for its recovery.[1] In addition, the West did not save Cilician Armenia from the Mamluks,[2] it did not send much worthwhile help to Constantinople, and it did nothing to stem the onward surge of Ottoman conquest in the Balkans. This chapter will deal with some of the obstacles which caused the movement in the East to stagnate, a stagnation the more striking when it is compared with successes on other fronts. Some problems are dealt with elsewhere: the rising cost of war and related issues, the problem of control, the difficulties faced by the Knights of St. John. Other obstacles rooted in the West naturally affected all the crusade fronts to some degree. But it is important to focus at some point on the eastern Mediterranean and its problems, because this remained the crusade front *par eminence*. By so doing we are also able to examine the response of papal policy: to see what cognizance the Curia took of these obstacles, and how successful were the measures which it adopted to try to deal with them.

As explained in the last chapter, the financial difficulties involved in promoting a crusade of recovery to Palestine were immense. Even these, however, did not constitute as serious an obstacle, either in

---

[1] They may even have worsened the lot of Christians under Mamluk rule. See Matteo Villani, bk. 7, ch. 3, ii, 7–8, bk. 11, ch. 34, ii, 429.

[2] Cf. Giovanni Villani, bk. 12, ch. 40, iv, 70–1; 'Vita Benedicti XII auctore Heinrico Dapifero de Dissenhoven', in *VPA*, i, 221.

the perception of contemporaries or in objective reality, as the resistance which could be expected from the Muslims once the crusading armies disembarked in the East. The Mamluk armies were formidable opponents and it was acknowledged that a Western force landing in Syria from Cyprus, or advancing from Armenia, had little or no chance of beating them unless it had the assistance of a third power like the Mongols, or other decisive factors in its favour.[3] But serious as the military situation looked, it was not regarded as hopeless; for when Latin Christians considered the rising power of the Mamluk Sultanate in the late thirteenth and fourteenth centuries, they discerned weaknesses which could be exploited in advance of a crusade. Egypt's economic problems were proverbial. The country had very little serviceable iron or timber, and periodically needed to import food in bulk for its large population. In addition, the élite regiments of the Mamluk armies were made up of slaves, many originally Christian, imported from the regions adjoining the Black Sea. Western merchants, mainly from the Italian maritime republics, southern France, and Barcelona, had long built up a thriving commerce with Egypt, supplying it with slaves, food, horses, raw materials, and cloth, and exporting to the West spices and, from Syria, raw cotton.[4]

Crusade theorists used these facts to construct elaborate programmes of economic warfare. Fulk of Villaret, Ramon Lull, Hayton of Armenia, King Henry of Cyprus and others all advocated a partial or total ban on Christian commerce with Egypt in order to weaken the Sultanate before the launching of a crusade to recover the Holy Land.[5] Characteristically, it was Marino Sanudo Torsello who explored the subject in most depth, writing of a threefold blockade. There should be a ban on the export to Egypt of essential war material and, if possible, of foodstuffs too; Christian exports to other Muslim states should be suspended as these might be re-exported to Egypt; and there should be no imports of Egyptian goods, to prevent Christian gold and silver bolstering the Sultan's finances. Two issues now arose: how to stop Christians trading, and

[3] See, for example, 'Le Conseil du roi Charles', ed. G. I. Bratianu, *Revue historique du sud-ouest européen*, xix (1942), 353; Philip of Mézières, 127–8.

[4] See in general E. Ashtor, *Levant Trade in the later Middle Ages* (Princeton, 1983), 3–17. For cotton exports see M. F. Mazzaoui, *The Italian Cotton Industry in the later Middle Ages* (Cambridge, 1981), 23, 38.

[5] W. Heyd and F. Raynaud, *Histoire du commerce du Levant au moyen âge*. 2 vols. (Leipzig, 1885–6), ii, 27–8; Delaville le Roulx, *La France en orient*, i, 16–97.

how to maintain the supply of spices needed by the West. Like others,[6] the Venetian propagandist envisaged Church sanctions backed up by a naval police force provided by those powers with interests in the East. As alternative sources of supply, he suggested either the production of the goods required in Christian states in the central and eastern Mediterranean, or the rerouting of trade from India through Persia and Cilician Armenia.[7] There was thus a rich and fairly well-informed theoretical background to papal policy on trade with Egypt, whose chief aspects we shall now consider.

When Acre fell in 1291 trade with the Muslims in articles which could be used in war had long been banned by the Church, which had also begun the practice of placing temporary vetoes on all commerce with Islamic states while a crusade was in preparation or progress.[8] But the papal decrees of the Avignon period were based on the important bull issued by Nicholas IV in 1291, in which he forbade the export to Egypt and Syria of arms, horses, iron, wood, foodstuffs, 'and any other form of merchandise'; the penalty for contravening the decree was excommunication in the first instance, perpetual infamy in the second.[9] It was this measure which Clement V renewed in 1308 as part of his contribution to the forthcoming general passage. He added that the excommunicated could be absolved only if they gave to the cause of the Holy Land a sum equal to the value of the goods carried,[10] and then only with specific papal authorization.[11] Again, in 1323, it was Nicholas IV's decree that John XXII published.[12]

But what was the extent of the prohibition? So severe in its consequences was the 1291 ban that an interpretation gradually arose which saw it as covering only goods which would aid the Muslims in their conflicts with Christians, a confirmation and strengthening of the longstanding Church ban on such commerce which excluded 'clean' merchandise such as grain and cloth, the

---

[6] See, for example, Servois, 293.

[7] 'Liber secretorum fidelium crucis', 22–33. Hélion of Villeneuve too thought that commerce could be rerouted through Cilician Armenia. See Delaville le Roulx, *La France en orient*, i, 81.

[8] See Purcell, 193–4, 198; Heyd and Raynaud, ii, 23–4; above, Introduction, n. 10.

[9] *AE*, ad annum 1291, nn. 26–7, xxiii, 97.

[10] Not, as Heyd wrote (ii, 27), only profits.

[11] *Reg. Clem. V*, n. 2994. Cf. Atiya, 35.

[12] Mollat, *Lettres communes*, nn. 20313–14.

most important bulk commodities carried.[13] But this interpretation, although aided by the vague wording sometimes used in the
bulls, was unsound. It is clear from the licensing system which we
shall soon examine that throughout the Avignon period the Church
regarded all trade with the Mamluk lands as under a ban. In 1345,
for example, Clement VI wrote of the export of goods worth 3,000
florins to Syria and other regions 'which the faithful are forbidden to
enter'.[14] It is true that the Curia drew a distinction between arms,
horses, iron, timber, and slaves on the one hand, and 'clean'
merchandise on the other. But it was a distinction between two
offences, the one graver than the other. John XXII became so angry
at the common, and convenient, belief that trade in 'clean' merchandise was licit that he denounced it as heretical, instructing
Bertrand Du Poujet in 1326 to commence judicial proceedings
against the Professor of Law at Padua University, who was
championing this argument on behalf of Venice.[15]

In theory, therefore, the policy of the Curia was straightforward.
All commerce with Egypt and Syria was prohibited, and at times the
ban was extended to other enemies of the Church, together with its
companion decree that the persons of those enemies could be
enslaved and their goods confiscated. Trade with Muslim Granada
was periodically banned: for three years from February 1317, for
three years from June 1330, and for five years from January 1334.[16]
The goods and persons of the Venetians were declared subject to
seizure in 1309, a disastrous blow to the city's economy.[17] The
Venetians themselves were asked in 1324 not to prevent Guelfs
seizing the possessions of the people of Fabriano, the Ghibelline
commune in the March of Ancona.[18] And in 1356 and 1363 Venice
was requested to stop all trade with lands controlled by Francesco
Ordelaffi and Bernabò Visconti.[19]

To get its ban on trade with Egypt implemented, the Curia
depended on the support of the civil authorities of those cities which

[13] See, for example, *I libri comm.*, i, 38, n. 166, 183–4, n. 64, 184, n. 65.
[14] Déprez *et al.*, n. 1863.
[15] *AE*, ad annum 1326, n. 24, xxiv, 306–7. See also *I libri comm.*, i, 272, n. 465;
Heyd and Raynaud, ii, 43n.
[16] *Corpus iuris canonici*, ii, cols. 1214–15; Mollat, *Lettres communes*, nn. 50013,
62515.
[17] *Reg. Clem. V*, nn. 5081–5.
[18] Mollat, *Lettres communes*, n. 20387.
[19] *I libri comm.*, ii, 257, n. 207, 258–9, nn. 211, 214, 216; *Codex dipl.*, ed. Theiner,
ii, n. 379. See Purcell, 179n for precedents.

habitually sent ships there. It intended that its prohibition should become part of the common law of Christendom. Thus in 1308 Clement V decreed that his ban be written into civic statutes, and he asked Philip IV to enforce it in the southern French ports.[20] A few states complied, at first. James II of Aragon prohibited all trade with Egypt in 1302, and Genoa was vigorous enough in its execution of the ban to earn the Pope's thanks.[21] But James II did not enforce the embargo very actively. In 1326 he showed himself ready to remit civil penalties imposed on illegal traders in exchange for payments, and it is suspicious that at the end of 1318 he was pressing for absolution from the excommunication which he had possibly incurred by not stopping all Catalan commerce with Egypt.[22] Twenty years later Peter III responded to a plea from the city authorities of Barcelona by cancelling civil law proceedings against Catalans suspected of trading with Egypt.[23] Genoa too let its supervision lapse. It was not enough, Clement V wrote to the city in 1311, to have written statutes: they must also be enforced.[24] The Genoese appear to have done little, for in 1317 John XXII complained that their merchants were still supplying the Sultan with Christian slaves and prohibited goods, even flying flags of convenience which acknowledged Mohammed.[25] Pisa and the French towns made no greater efforts to comply with papal mandates.[26]

Curiously, it was at Venice, which was almost wholly dependent on commercial enterprise and traditionally displayed little tolerance of Church interference in lay matters, that the Curia enjoyed most success. Between 1302, when they concluded a treaty with the Sultan,[27] and 1322, the Venetians traded actively with Egypt and reopened commerce with those Syrian ports which retained their trade facilities; all except war material was carried. Attempts to secure papal permission for this trade by bribery failed, and in 1322 John XXII sent envoys to pronounce excommunication on all Venetians who habitually traded with Alexandria. In the

[20] *Reg. Clem. V*, nn. 2986, 2995. Cf. ibid., n. 3088; *I libri comm.*, i, 37, n. 161.

[21] Heyd and Raynaud, ii, 31, 35.

[22] Mollat, *Lettres communes*, n. 8774; Mas Latrie, iii, 720–2; *Documenta selecta*, n. 335.

[23] Heyd and Raynaud, ii, 32–3. Cf. Mas Latrie, iii, 732–4.

[24] *Reg. Clem. V*, n. 7631.

[25] *AE*, ad annum 1317, n. 36, xxiv, 60. For Genoa and the slave trade, see Balard, i, 289–310.

[26] Heyd and Raynaud, ii, 33–4, 37.

[27] *DVL*, i, nn. 4–6.

204 *Obstacles to Crusading*

following year Venice gave in and banned all direct trade with Egypt. For more than twenty years following this, according to the Sultan, not a single Venetian ship entered his ports.[28] The Republic either traded indirectly, via Cyprus, Crete, and Armenia, or developed alternative markets in Laiazzo, Tana, and Trebizond. Then in 1343 a dispute at Tana, together with political disturbances in Persia, made the northern routes insecure, and Venice approached Clement VI for permission to resume trade with Egypt. In his petition the Doge emphasized his city's contribution to the Pope's naval league against the Turks, a factor which probably helped considerably.[29] In April 1344 this request was granted with the first of the special licences which reopened Venetian trade with Alexandria. Under renewed pressure, Clement extended the grant in August 1345, though not as generously as Venice had requested. But the general veto remained in force, as colonial officials were reminded in 1350 and 1374.[30]

It is hard not to be sceptical about this long break in Venetian commerce with Egypt, given the loopholes which existed and the difficulty of ascertaining whether the Venetian authorities were not secretly sanctioning some trade.[31] Certainly one's dominant impression, necessarily tentative in view of the nature of the evidence, and the length of time and number of cities involved, is that at no point were all the civil powers prepared to back up the papal decrees. At best, like Pisa, they banned trade in war material. Official consulates and *fondaci* of the Catalans, Genoese, Pisans, and merchants of Marseilles were active at Alexandria with few breaks. And even in the case of war material, there were enough unscrupulous traders to keep the Mamluks supplied.[32]

There remained coercion, the arming of a police force of galleys which would capture and retain for sale the goods of Christians who were contravening the ban. Some semi-piratical sea captains took on this function as a means of earning a living, making use of the papal ban as protection against the outraged rulers of the traders

---

[28] Ibid., i, n. 96; *I libri comm.*, i, 246, n. 342, 250, nn. 360–1, 260–1, n. 415; Heyd and Raynaud, ii, 37 ff.; Ashtor, 25 ff.

[29] A similar approach was pursued in 1357: *Régestes*, i, 85.

[30] *DVL*, i, nn. 144, 162; Heyd and Raynaud, ii, 44–8; Zachariadou, 46–7. The 1344 grant cost Venice 4,000–5,000 florins: *DVL*, i, n. 149 and cf. nn. 153–5. That the city took the ban seriously is shown by *I libri comm.*, ii, 237, nn. 116–17.

[31] Ashtor (45) believes that the break was total.

[32] Cf. Heyd and Raynaud, ii, 50: 'jugement d'ensemble'.

whose ships they attacked.[33] Similarly, in the memorandum which he composed for the Council of Vienne, Henry II of Cyprus claimed that he was actively hampering Muslim commerce.[34] But a more systematic approach was called for, and the papacy several times tried to assemble a squadron of galleys to act as an international *custodia maris*.[35] It was one of the roles assigned to the Hospitaller *passagium* of 1309–10, and became a regular duty of the Order at Rhodes.[36] The Franco-papal flotilla organized in 1319 was intended to attack Christian vessels trading with Egypt, and Venice suggested the same task for the naval force which put to sea in 1334.[37] In all these cases the squadrons were hampered by being theoretically attached to a larger French *passagium* which never materialized; they were therefore easily diverted to other enterprises. But even had they set about their work with vigour they would have aroused furious reactions from the home governments of the ships seized. When the Hospitallers captured a Genoese galley trading with Alexandria in 1311, Genoa paid the Turks of Menteshe 50,000 florins to launch hostilities against the Knights.[38] For this reason Henry II of Cyprus argued that the blockade should be undertaken by a powerful state which could not be intimidated, though it is hard to see which Christian power could have fulfilled this function.[39] From 1336 the thrust of crusading naval activity was redirected towards the Aegean and the pressing problem of Turkish piracy, and plans for an international punitive squadron in the south-east Mediterranean were not revived again.

Marino Sanudo's programme had comprised not only coercive measures, but also the positive encouragement of new patterns of trade and cultivation which would enable the West to boycott Egypt and Syria without losing essential commodities like spices, cotton, and sugar. There are no papal letters which address themselves to this approach, nor is it easy to see how the Church could have

---

[33] See, for example, *Reg. Clem. V*, n. 6438; *I libri comm.*, i, 40, n. 176. Cf. *AE*, ad annum 1291, n. 26, xxiii, 97.

[34] Mas Latrie, ii, 121–2.

[35] For late thirteenth-century precedents see Heyd and Raynaud, ii, 28–9.

[36] *Reg. Clem. V*, n. 2988; *Délibérations*, i, 133–4; Luttrell, 'Venice and the Knights Hospitallers', 197 ff.

[37] De la Roncière, 'Une Escadre franco-papale', *passim*; *DVL*, i, n. 110.

[38] *Reg. Clem. V*, nn. 7118–19, 7631–2; Luttrell, 'Hospitallers at Rhodes', 287; J. Delaville le Roulx, *Les Hospitaliers à Rhodes jusqu'à la mort de Philibert de Naillac (1310–1421)* (Paris, 1913), 10–11.

[39] Mas Latrie, ii, 119–20. Cf. James of Molay's comments: *VPA*, iii, 148–9.

helped other than by offering indulgences to traders who co-operated, hardly a practicable notion. To some extent the ban on trade with the Mamluk lands did make people go elsewhere and contribute to the opening up of new routes via the Black Sea ports, Armenia, and Cyprus; the early fourteenth century was Famagusta's heyday.[40] Venice in particular used its colonial stations in Greece and the Aegean to build up its trade in this area, and Genoa relied more than formerly on its colonies at Caffa and Tana. But this was not always possible. In 1326, for example, the Guelf government at Genoa was at odds with its own, Ghibelline-controlled colonies and with the *basileus*, and secured a two year papal grant to use ports in northern Syria as entrepôts for commerce with the Mongol states, Persia, and India.[41] Piracy was rife in the Aegean and the Armenian coastal waters, and no port in this period could compete with Alexandria's excellent facilities, advanced bureaucracy, and well-established links with India.

The Curia was thus unable to enforce its embargo. Under the pressure of petitions and its own financial needs it gradually refined its policy towards trade with Egypt so that it evolved into an important component of the Holy See's fiscal system. The initial policy of outright prohibition was breached in three different ways. First, high-ranking laymen and prelates who were in the East or intended to send ships there for reasons unconnected with commerce, were allowed, by the grant of a special privilege, to use the opportunity to trade with the Muslims in 'clean' merchandise. Hugh IV of Cyprus, a recipient in 1326, was sending envoys and spies to Muslim countries.[42] The kings of Aragon, in 1328, 1354, and 1372, were sending ships carrying envoys who were to negotiate with the Sultan on the translation to Aragon of the relics of St Barbara.[43] The Bishop of Bethlehem, in 1329, was visiting his see.[44] Mary of Bourbon, in the same year, was also visiting Palestine.[45] And Humbert of Vienne, who received the generous allocation of two cogs and twelve galleys in March 1347, was concluding his crusade.[46]

---

[40] See Ashtor, 54 ff.
[41] Mollat, *Lettres communes*, nn. 24872–3.
[42] Ibid., n. 24541.
[43] Ibid., nn. 43003–4; *Documenta selecta*, nn. 547, 643.
[44] Mollat, *Lettres communes*, n. 45717.
[45] Ibid., n. 45766; Hill, ii, 294.
[46] Déprez *et al.*, n. 3181.

Secondly, and of greater importance, absolutions were granted to persons who had been excommunicated for trading with Egypt, but were prepared to surrender some of the profits from this illicit commerce in exchange for forgiveness. This procedure was based on thirteenth-century precedents, and we have seen that provision for paying such a fine as a means of making reparation was written into Clement V's bull of 1308. Throughout the Avignon period there was a steady flow of such absolutions, either issued by the penitentiary or granted by a papal agent in the field, and sometimes linked to the financial needs of the Holy See.[47] I have found examples of absolutions granted to Venetians, Genoese, Catalans, Ragusans, Cypriots, Scandinavians, and others.[48] The country traded with was usually Egypt, but in 1321 a Genoese was absolved for trading with Granada, Malta, and North Africa, and in 1347 other Genoese had traded with Egypt and Sicily (which had been under papal ban).[49] The letters occasionally yield details on the commerce involved. A Venetian in 1331 had sent goods worth 40 pounds of Venice to Alexandria on several voyages and bought pepper there, his profit being 4 pounds.[50] In 1343 another Venetian had traded with Syria in gold thread, copper, tin, and other merchandise to the profit of 2,500 florins.[51] Grants could cover whole communities: in the 1340s there were regular arrangements for Aragon.[52]

How much did such people pay? In 1354 Innocent VI stated that the general rule was that absolution could not be granted 'unless they send in aid of the Holy Land the whole amount which they have gained from this accursed commerce, and as much again of their own property'.[53] This severe ruling, which can be seen to date from the thirteenth century,[54] was not generally adhered to during the

[47] For example, *I libri comm.*, i, 246, n. 342.

[48] The cameral account books in particular are full of examples. See *Die Einnahmen der apostolischen Kammer unter Johann XXII.*, ed. E. Göller (Paderborn, 1910); *Die Einnahmen der apostolischen Kammer unter Benedikt XII.*, ed. E. Göller (Paderborn, 1920); *Die Einnahmen der apostolischen Kammer unter Klemens VI.*, ed. L. Mohler (Paderborn, 1931); *Die Einnahmen der apostolischen Kammer unter Innocenz VI.*, *I*, ed. H. Hoberg (Paderborn, 1955).

[49] Mollat, *Lettres communes*, n. 13102; Déprez and Mollat, n. 1404.

[50] Mollat, *Lettres communes*, n. 52778.

[51] Déprez and Mollat, n. 204.

[52] Ibid., nn. 1734–5; Déprez *et al.*, nn. 578, 1175, 2897–8.

[53] Gasnault *et al.*, n. 1020. Cf. *DVL*, i, n. 10.

[54] See Purcell, 193–4. The Third Lateran Council had made no provision for fines: *COD*, 223.

Avignon period. There were some cases in which absolution was granted free because the recipient had been driven to trade by poverty. This sounds odd, but perhaps, like the Catalan Arnald de Baniheriis in 1316, such men had served as mariners and invested their wages in cargo at Alexandria; Arnald had to surrender all the profits beyond those needed to survive.[55] A similar case from 1376 is interesting because it shows Armenian Christians involved in trade between the Black Sea and the Mamluk lands. Gregory XI ordered that absolution be issued free to three Armenians at Pera who were guilty of illicit commerce 'because the ships on which they had sailed had been wrecked, and they are so poor that they cannot visit the Apostolic See to obtain absolution from the foregoing'.[56]

Normally, however, the Curia expected to receive a fixed percentage of the profits. A good example is an Aragonese case of 1307: mariners who had taken part in the commerce had to pay a quarter of their profits, female investors a fifth.[57] The recipient of the money varied. Two Ragusans fined in 1312 were to pay 200 florins to the Bishop of Sfacia to help him pay his debts, and in 1329 the Patriarch of Jerusalem was given a faculty to absolve forty people—a reflection of the embargo's ineffectiveness—of whose fines he could use twenty to pay the expenses he would incur while in Palestine.[58] But usually the recipient was either a secular ruler with crusade plans, such as James II of Aragon in 1309,[59] or the Curia itself. The pope stored the proceeds for the use of the crusade in the East or used them for other concerns, 'for the defence of the Catholic Faith or for other pious uses, according to the decision of the Apostolic See'.[60]

The third, and most important way in which the Curia breached its own ban was by issuing licences for trade in 'clean' merchandise. Unlike special privileges and absolutions for trade, the licence system was a fairly late development, for until the reign of Clement VI licences were rarely conceded. John XXII made a few grants. The Zaccaria family were permitted to export gum mastic from Chios to Alexandria between 1320 and 1328 in order to pay the heavy expenses of defending the island, which was regarded in the

[55] Mollat, *Lettres communes*, nn. 2235–6. Cf. ibid., n. 44620.
[56] *Acta Gregorii XI*, ed. A. L. Tautu. PCRCICO, xii (Rome, 1966), n. 198.
[57] *Documenta selecta*, n. 119.
[58] *Reg. Clem. V*, n. 8225; Mollat, *Lettres communes*, nn. 45366, 45955.
[59] *Reg. Clem. V*, n. 5090.
[60] *Acta pont. svecica*, i, n. 374.

West as a crusading outpost in the Aegean.[61] More dangerous as a precedent was the grant to Genoa in 1326; this was quite possibly a political move, designed to bolster the city's imperilled Guelf regime.[62] But in general the first three Avignon popes resisted the temptation, which must have been strong, to license some trade and reap the financial benefits. John XXII rejected several insistent advances from Venice. In 1327 the Doge complained that his city was suffering heavily through the ban, petitioned for a licence for thirty galleys and ten cogs, and backed this up with a veiled threat to aid the Pope's Ghibelline enemies if nothing happened: but John does not seem to have responded.[63] This was in keeping with the prevalent hope that a crusade of recovery would soon be launched, so that it was imperative to weaken Egypt as much as possible beforehand. But by 1342 such hopes had vanished,[64] the financial needs of the Curia were rising, piracy was becoming a serious problem in the Aegean, and powers like Venice and Genoa were clamouring for a controlled, limited reopening of the Alexandria route. In 1343 the Curia started issuing licences to trade and for the rest of our period papal licences were numerous.[65]

Through the licence system the Curia was making a profit from a trade which it formally condemned; indeed, it was making money from its own condemnation.[66] In this respect the licences illustrate some of the most striking flaws of the Avignon papacy: its excessive susceptibility to purely financial considerations, its hypocrisy, and its favouritism on political or personal grounds. For the issue of licences was regulated partly by the current needs of the papal *camera*, so that in 1361 Venice received a licence mainly because of the Curia's financial needs.[67] And although many licences were issued directly to individuals or states who wanted to trade or

[61] Delaville le Roulx, *Les Hospitaliers*, 367–8; Mollat, *Lettres communes*, nn. 15644, 21494.

[62] Ibid., nn. 24872–3.

[63] *DVL*, i, n. 105. See also Ashtor, 45–6.

[64] As early as 1326 the realistic Marino Sanudo was advocating a relaxation of the embargo on all but war materials, probably in response to the failure of Charles IV's crusade project. See Laiou, 'Marino Sanudo Torsello', 380 and n.

[65] See, for example, Déprez and Mollat, nn. 756, 2028; Déprez *et al.*, nn. 529, 854, 909, 1176, 1677, 1863, 3316, 4251, 5132.

[66] Strikingly similar was an attempt by Innocent IV to cash in on the Church's formal ban on tournaments. See Purcell, 79.

[67] *DVL*, ii, nn. 41–4; Heyd and Raynaud, ii, 46. On the other hand, in 1365 Venice had paid only a quarter of the sum owed for a licence purchased six years earlier, and originally issued in 1344: *I libri comm.*, iii, 39, n. 202.

organize convoys, there were also grants to people who would clearly sell the licences to third parties in exchange for a cash payment in accordance with the licence's market value.[68] In 1361 the Venetians were desperately attempting to purchase a licence third-hand from some Genoese.[69] Predictably, Clement VI was extremely generous in his grants to his relatives, the Viscount of Turenne and his wife.[70]

In defence of the Curia, it should be added that Innocent VI at least tried to link the granting of his licences to the struggle against the Turks in *Romania*.[71] The Curia also made an attempt to control the trade and ensure that no war material was carried. The licensee's bishop was supposed to exact an oath to this effect and pass on a notarial act to the Curia.[72] This of course placed a heavy burden on the shoulders of the ordinaries, and occasionally they rebelled, as when the Bishop of Castello refused to accept Venetian oaths to the effect that no prohibited goods would be carried.[73] In 1365 Urban V tried to tighten up the system by specifying that the Venetian Republic was not to sell its licences, and that diocesans were to carry out quayside inspections.[74] And in several privileges which Gregory XI granted to John Lascaris Calopheros a few years later even more emphasis was laid on the role of the bishop. The Greek convert, who was one of Gregory's leading agents in crusading matters, was allowed to send one galley to Alexandria as often as he liked in the course of a year. The local bishop was not only to take the oaths of the people who hired and loaded the galley on John's behalf, but also to note its first departure for Egypt and draw up a public instrument, of which a copy should be sent to the *camera*. As if this was not enough, John successfully petitioned for the replacement of the galley by a number of smaller vessels whose loads would add up to that of a galley; the diocesan was now expected to keep track of the voyages made by all the ships concerned.[75] From such grants it is clear that by 1378 the practice of

---

[68] See, for example, ibid., ii, 297–8, n. 109.

[69] *DVL*, ii, n. 46.

[70] Déprez *et al.*, nn. 4613, 5359, 5375. Cf. Guillemain, 169–70.

[71] *Die Einnahmen*, ed. Hoberg, 354, 382.

[72] See, for example, Mollat, *Lettres communes*, nn. 24872–3; Déprez *et al.*, n. 909; *I libri comm.*, ii, 285, n. 45, iii, 76–7, nn. 452–3, 79, n. 479 (a list of prohibited items); *DVL*, i, n. 144, ii, n. 91.

[73] Ibid., ii, nn. 23, 83.

[74] Ibid., ii, nn. 62–3, 67.

[75] *Acta Greg. XI*, nn. 121, 121a, and cf. nn. 189, 199, 236, 236a–c.

issuing licences had become not only a means of raising revenue for the *camera*, but also a cheap, flexible, and convenient way for the Holy See to reward its friends and agents. The system was a headache for diligent diocesans, nor was it so advantageous for men like John Lascaris Calopheros who were not professional merchants.

The papacy made only one serious attempt after 1342 to ban all trade with Egypt;[76] this was when the Franco-Cypriot crusade project of 1363 revived, for a time, the southwards orientation of the movement. In May 1363 the Doge of Venice was asked to help the crusade on the grounds that it would be beneficial to his city,[77] but the Venetians knew that the expedition was more likely to harm their economy, and their support for it was always lukewarm. They kept trading links with Egypt going as long as possible, and in 1370 claimed that Peter I had double-crossed them in 1365 by making an early assault on Alexandria, which led to the robbery and ill-treatment of several of their citizens there.[78] In March 1364 the standard ban on commerce in prohibited goods was renewed,[79] but Urban V continued to issue licences for 'clean' merchandise up to August 1366. Undoubtedly one reason for his generosity was the Curia's need for Venetian ships during the planned return to Rome.[80] Then, on 17 August, the Pope announced the suspension of all licences on hearing of Egyptian war plans against Cyprus and Rhodes.[81] The ban was a failure and in the following May a fresh licence was issued to Venice,[82] though the ban itself, curiously enough, was only revoked in June.[83] But in 1368–9 Venice and Genoa found that diplomatic negotiations with the Sultan were unsuccessful and in July 1369 Urban was able to impose another ban, this time with greater chances of success as the two republics were resigned to using military means.[84] This ban was revoked in

---

[76] Apart from Innocent VI's short ban of 1359–61: *DVL*, ii, nn. 30, 40–4.

[77] Ibid., ii, n. 54.

[78] *Nouvelles preuves de l'histoire de Chypre sous le règne des princes de la maison de Lusignan*, ed. M. L. De Mas Latrie. 2 vols. (Paris, 1873–4), i, 64–5, 71n.

[79] ASV, Reg. Vat. 246, f. 141ᵛ.

[80] *DVL*, ii, nn. 62–3, 67 (June 1366: on condition that nothing is done which would be detrimental to a general passage), 69–70. See too *AE*, ad annum 1366, n. 13, xxvi, 127–8, on Urban's need for Venetian and Genoese ships. Cf. *DVL*, ii, n. 65.

[81] Ibid., ii, nn. 69–70, and cf. LM, n. 2370; *AE*, ad annum 1366, n. 13, xxvi, 127–8.

[82] *DVL*, ii, n. 76, and cf. nn. 75, 79–80.

[83] Ibid., ii, n. 77. In 1368 Venice and Genoa mediated between Cyprus and Egypt: *I libri comm.*, iii, 72, nn. 425–6.

[84] *DVL*, ii, n. 87. See also ibid., ii, nn. 85–6; *I libri comm.*, iii, 84, n. 512; 'Vita Urbani V auctore Wernero', 390.

September 1370 when peace was restored, though only for a two year period to start with.[85] It is possible that the time limit constituted yet another way of squeezing money out of the West's trade with Egypt, and that when it was extended in May 1371 it was in exchange for payment.[86]

From this point onwards licences were again regularly issued.[87] Under Gregory XI, moreover, the Curia seems to have been more generous in the terms of its privileges. In 1374 and 1377, for instance, Venice was permitted to send two galleys from Crete to Syria and Egypt 'as often and whenever you wish' over a three year period, because of the dangers to the city's shipping lanes elsewhere in the East.[88] These were signposts to the open-handed liberality of the Schism; for in 1384 Venice was allowed to send as many vessels as it wished to the Mamluk lands during the course of a year, and in 1390 it was granted the same privilege for a whole decade.[89] Concessions on this scale marked the virtual demise of the licence system, brought about by the political weakness and dire financial problems of Urban VI and Boniface IX. They clearly parallel the trend after 1378 towards a more openly financial administration of the crusade indulgence, and for much the same reasons. In both cases, the popes of the Schism did not radically depart from policies pursued before 1378; they simply accelerated certain trends already present.

The Veneto-Genoese alliance of 1369 shows that western trading cities were only ready to implement the papal ban on trade when it fitted in with their short-term objectives in negotiations with the Mamluks; their long-term aim was peaceful commerce, not the economic crippling or military conquest of Egypt. The terms agreed on by the two cities in 1369 make this quite clear, for their forces were only to open hostilities if the Sultan obstinately refused to release his Venetian and Genoese captives.[90] In normal circumstances it was impossible to prevent all Christian trade with Egypt. Individuals could not be expected to abandon their livelihoods, and states the economic foundations of their prosperity, for the good of

[85] *DVL*, ii, n. 90.
[86] Ibid., ii, n. 94, and cf. n. 102 (1377). For this paragraph, see also Ashtor, 88–102.
[87] See, for example, *DVL*, ii, nn. 96, 99, 102–3.
[88] Ibid., ii, nn. 99, 103.
[89] Ibid., ii, nn. 113, 133, and cf. nn. 118–19, 125.
[90] *I libri comm.*, iii, 84, n. 512.

a crusade which might not even occur.[91] As Anthony Luttrell put it, 'a blockade which could only be enforced by those who stood to lose by it had little chance of success'.[92] By 1378 it had been made amply clear that the western powers could no more hope to bring the Mamluk Sultanate to its knees by means of economic warfare than they could hope to defeat its armies in the field.

To some extent these problems were duplicated in the other main area of crusading endeavour in the East, the defence of *Romania* against the Turks. Here much hinged on the attitude of Venice. Faced by the belligerent and destructive piracy of the Anatolian emirates, Venice was ready to make a substantial commitment to a naval coalition of Latin states, and to encourage others to do the same. We have seen that the Republic even helped to bring about the shift in thinking which enabled the Aegean to be seen as a crusade front in its own right.[93] But it was a key theme of Venetian policy to avoid expensive, long-term commitments. It is possible that the Venetians opened talks with Umur, for example, almost as soon as Smyrna fell in 1344,[94] and they repeatedly failed to pay their subventions for the maintenance of the port's garrison in the 1350s.[95] The main reason for adopting this policy was cost-effectiveness: Venice knew that if it could prevent attacks launched by the emirs, it could rely on its own naval police force to cope with ordinary Turkish piracy.[96] A long-term war, on the other hand, not only disrupted trade and tied down the resources of the metropolis, but also meant imposing extra financial burdens on Crete; on at least three separate occasions in our period these burdens led to serious revolts on the island.[97] The result was that Venice favoured hard-hitting military action with the chief goal of preparing the

[91] Cf. Venice's refusal to cut off trade with lands held by Francesco Ordelaffi: *I libri comm.*, ii, 257–9, nn. 207, 211, 214, 216.

[92] 'The Crusade in the Fourteenth Century', in Hale *et al.* (eds.), *Europe in the late Middle Ages*, 130. Cf. Henry II of Cyprus in his crusade memorandum: Mas Latrie, ii, 19.

[93] See above, ch. 3, nn. 178–96.

[94] 'Historiae romanae fragmenta', col. 371; Zachariadou, 52. Cf. Lemerle, 197n; Setton, *PL*, 207.

[95] See Appendix II, nn. 46–8.

[96] See Thiriet, 165–7, 243–51; A. Tenenti, 'Venezia e la pirateria nel Levante: 1300c.–1460c.', in *Venezia e il Levante fino al secolo XV*. 2 vols. (Florence, 1973), ii, 705–71.

[97] Zachariadou, 26, 44, 68.

ground for talks, in which the Republic would act by and for itself: an approach totally at variance with papal policy and the wishes of other Christian states in the area, which saw the naval leagues as a form of long-term defence strategy.[98] These fundamentally different viewpoints could not be reconciled, any more than could conflicting views in the West about the responsibility for crusade finance.

At the root of the problem was the disparity of Latin objectives and interests in *Romania*. In 1360, for instance, Venice wanted to withdraw its galleys from Smyrna for service in the Black Sea against the Turks of Sinope.[99] The Republic considered that this could legitimately be regarded as league business, whereas it objected strongly when, seven months later, Peter Thomas directed league galleys to Cyprus.[100] Similarly, despite the fair words which it exchanged with Peter of Cyprus, Venice expected little good of his expedition: in July 1365 the Republic made provision for the dispatch of messengers to emirs with whom it had treaties, to assure them that Venice had no part in the King's crusade, should it be directed 'ad partes Turchie'.[101] In fact Venice's interest in the crusades of Peter of Cyprus and Amedeo of Savoy focused neither on Anatolia nor on Egypt, but on Crete. In 1363–4 the Venetians hoped that Peter or Amedeo would go in person to the island to help suppress the revolt there, and even that Urban V might be persuaded to grant Venice's soldiers an indulgence on the grounds that Crete was mainly held by 'Greeks and schismatics', whose rebellion was impeding the *sanctum passagium*.[102]

If the Venetians would not consistently take the lead in sponsoring crusading activity in *Romania*, who else might? Certainly none of the other Latin states and families who ruled in the area. Given the extreme political fragmentation of *Romania*, complicated as it was by the papal outlawry of the Catalans at Athens, absentee rule in Achaea, and the constant ebb and flow of the lesser Latin island dynasties, the only way in which a solid structure of regional defence could have been established was through a firm rapport

---

[98] A good example is Clement VI's rejection of the treaty negotiated with the Turks by Octavian Zaccaria in 1347–8, which secured an early resumption of trade at the cost of demolishing the harbour fortress at Smyrna. See Lemerle, 226 ff.

[99] *Régestes*, i, 95; Zachariadou, 66–7.

[100] *Régestes*, i, 97.

[101] Mas Latrie, iii, 752–3.

[102] Ibid., iii, 744–6; *DVL*, ii, n. 56; *Délibérations*, ii, 273.

between Avignon and Constantinople. For this reason, and also because of the historic role of papal–Byzantine relations in the crusading movement, the influence of the Greek Empire on the Curia's crusade policy during this period calls for detailed attention.

In 1305 the prevailing attitude towards Constantinople in those political circles in the West with crusading aspirations was one of active hostility. An impressive alliance of interests, religious, dynastic, and commercial, was attempting to launch a sea-borne crusade against the Greeks. The Curia was committed to a policy of achieving Church Union through coercion; the French royal family furnished a pretender in Charles of Valois; and Venice, ousted from the markets of the Black Sea by the Genoese in 1261 and since then periodically at war with the Palaeologi, was ready to supply naval aid.[103] But the alliance was much less powerful than it appeared. Neither Charles of Valois nor his successor as titular Latin Emperor, Philip of Taranto, could muster the resources for the task. Venice sealed a twelve year truce with the *basileus* in 1310 and relations between them gradually improved.[104] Without the help of a major seapower the Latin reconquest of Constantinople was out of the question.

In these circumstances papal policy towards the Greeks slowly reverted to earlier plans for a negotiated Union of the estranged churches.[105] Such a Union had been achieved at the Second Council of Lyons, but immediately wrecked by Charles of Anjou's aggression and Michael VIII's inability to persuade the clergy and laity of Constantinople to accept the terms which he had reached. Now Latin hostility had been largely defused, and a new factor had come into play which offered hopes that Greek opposition to Union might be overcome by persistent imperial propaganda. This new factor was the appallingly rapid inroads which the Turkish emirates were making into Greek territory in Asia Minor. By 1300 the Turks had already reduced Byzantine holdings to the coastal towns and river valleys, and in the following years Andronicus II's strenuous attempts to stave off both Catalan and Turkish attacks nearly destroyed his Empire.[106] It was imperative to concentrate military efforts on the East, and if possible to secure western aid against

---

[103] See above, ch. 1, nn. 10–14, ch. 3, nn. 131–2.   [104] *DVL*, i, n. 46.
[105] For the most recent discussion of the issue of Union, see J. Gill, *Byzantium and the Papacy, 1198–1400* (New Brunswick, N.J., 1979), 193 ff.
[106] See Laiou, *Constantinople and the Latins*, *passim*.

the Turks, at the cost of making religious concessions to the papacy.

Negotiations for Union during the Avignon period were therefore closely tied up with Byzantine calculations of exactly how much aid could be expected in return.[107] In practice this meant help in the form of a crusade. The exponents of Union at Constantinople exaggerated not only the political influence of the Curia,[108] but also the military potential of the West. Faced with powerful opposition at home to any rapprochement with the Latins, they welcomed such meagre proof of western prowess as was forthcoming. Thus the success of the 1334 league was celebrated at Constantinople, the capture of Smyrna made a great impression there, and Demetrius Cydones, a leading advocate of Union in the 1360s and 1370s, made much of the sack of Alexandria.[109] Nor were such feelings restricted to the capital. Towards the end of Clement VI's reign the people and clergy of Philadelphia sent envoys to Avignon to say that they were ready to accept the temporal supremacy of the Pope if he would take over their city's defence.[110]

The turning point in Greco-Latin relations was the 1320s, when the acceleration of Turkish naval raids brought Constantinople into the negotiations for a defensive league. It was in the mid-1320s, for example, that Marino Sanudo changed his views on the desirability of attacking the Greek Empire.[111] In 1326 John XXII sent an envoy to the Byzantine court to reopen talks on Union. But although Andronicus III signed an agreement at Rhodes in 1332 for Greek participation in the naval league, no ships were sent two years later. The *basileus* was more concerned at the Ottoman Turks and their advances near Constantinople than the raids of the southern emirates; and he quite rightly feared Italian encroachments on imperial possessions under cover of the league's activities. So although relations between Avignon and Constantinople had greatly improved, active co-operation was a very different matter. As always, there was a basic problem of timing. The Curia insisted on full implementation of Union before organizing a crusade to help

---

[107] See Gill, 193–227. For the political and military background see Nicol, *Last Centuries*, chs. 10–14.

[108] The monk Barlaam, for example, spoke of the Pope '*allowing* the King of France to send help to those parts': *Acta Ben. XII*, n. 43.

[109] See Halecki, *Un Empereur*, 14, 123, 143–4; Loenertz, 184.

[110] Gasnault *et al.*, n. 71; Lemerle, 235–7; Setton, *PL*, 224–5.

[111] Laiou, 'Marino Sanudo Torsello', 381 ff.

the Greeks, whereas the Greek proponents of Union argued that the only way to overcome the deep opposition to their cause at Constantinople was to demonstrate Latin strength and good will through the launching of a major expedition. This was quite apart from the doctrinal issues of papal primacy and the *Filioque* clause.[112]

Surviving documents about the mission of Barlaam, a Calabrian monk sent by Andronicus III to discuss Union with the Pope in 1339, illustrate these problems with great clarity. Barlaam made a number of plausible points about the need for 'aid before Union', concentrating on the urgency of Latin help against the Turks and the role of that help as tangible proof of western sincerity.[113] Perceiving that French manpower would be needed, he conjured up the image of recaptured Anatolian lands, ports, and towns opening up 'a mighty door for the holy passage [to Palestine]', an echo of Venetian arguments for the 1334 league.[114] But from the point of view of winning Benedict XII for his cause, this was probably a mistake, since the Pope certainly did not want the reopening of earlier crusade negotiations with Philip VI. In any case, the papal position was plain: 'If the said Greeks are strengthened, bolstered, encouraged, and comforted by ourselves and others of the faithful before the said Union, they will afterwards turn their backs on us and the Church'.[115]

In 1341 Byzantium was plunged into civil war between the young Emperor John Palaeologus and the pretender John Cantacuzenus. Not surprisingly, the two sides assumed violently pro- and anti-Latin stances, John Cantacuzenus allying himself with the Turks while Anna of Savoy, the mother and regent of John Palaeologus, appealed to the West.[116] Clement VI corresponded with Anna on Greek support for his naval league and allowed Humbert of Vienne to open negotiations about Union,[117] but papal dealings with Constantinople were generally thin, and Clement did not respond to the active overtures made by John Cantacuzenus after the

---

[112] D. M. Nicol, 'Byzantine Requests for an Oecumenical Council in the Fourteenth Century', *Annuarium historiae Conciliorum*, i (1969), 69–95.

[113] *Acta Ben. XII*, n. 43.

[114] *DVL*, i, nn. 110, 124.

[115] *Acta Ben. XII*, n. 42; Gill, 196–9.

[116] Nicol, *Last Centuries*, 191 ff.

[117] For the league as an instrument of Union, see Déprez *et al.*, nn. 466–71; Lemerle, 182–3.

pretender's victory in 1347. In 1348 John guaranteed his personal leadership of 15,000–20,000 troops, if the Pope were to launch a 'sanctum et magnum passagium' against the Turks, or 4,000 if he sent a 'sanctum parvum passagium' as the preliminary to a later general passage. Either of these *passagia*, he claimed, would win the Greeks over to the idea of Union, which could then be rapidly formulated at a synod.[118] Clement's dilatory and lukewarm response to this, the first major Greek initiative for a decade, can be explained by the Pope's uncertainty about John's chances of holding on to power at Constantinople, as well as by the financial plight of the *camera* and the economic troubles of the West.

This sterile period in papal–Byzantine relations ended in 1354 with the restoration of political stability at Constantinople. John V Palaeologus was now unquestioned Emperor, and his long reign produced the richest and most complex contacts between the two courts, in striking contrast to the preceding half-century.[119] The reasons for this were the continuing advance of the Turks, which now began to concern Latin Christendom as well as Byzantium, and the extreme weakness of the Empire, which by now consisted of little more than Constantinople, eastern Thrace, and the southern Morea. The climax of John V's negotiations with the Curia was his own journey to the West in 1369 and his solemn profession of faith in Rome. The years leading up to this momentous event confirmed the impression of the Emperor's pathetic eagerness to convince the Curia of his personal conversion to Catholicism provided that he did not have to start implementing Union before receiving effective Latin aid.

For their part, Innocent VI and Urban V had the problem of actually organizing aid for the Greeks, and as always papal abilities in this respect were exaggerated at Constantinople. In his remarkable chrysobull of December 1355 John V asked the Pope to send an initial force of 500 men-at-arms and 1,000 foot, carried by fifteen transport ships and five galleys. This *passagium* would fight against the Turks and rebel Greeks, under the command of John V, for six months; during this time Union would be implemented. The expeditionary force would then be followed by a major crusade, which would also fight under the Emperor's command as 'principalis capitaneus, et signifer et vexillarius sanctae matris

---

[118] Loenertz, *passim*; Lemerle, 223–6; Gill, 205–6.
[119] See Halecki, *Un Empereur*, *passim*.

Ecclesiae cum mero et mixto imperio'.[120] It is an interesting proposal from several points of view. In the first place, it shows that the Greeks had grasped western thinking about twofold *passagia*, and were using this strategic approach to try to break through the deadlock about aid or Union coming first; for the first *passagium* would show the Greeks that the Latins were worthwhile and reliable allies, while the Greek response would convince the West of their sincerity and thus lead to the major expedition. It may well be that this part of the document was influenced by one of the men who brought it to the Curia, Archbishop Paul of Smyrna.[121] Paul, a friend of John V and a leading exponent of Union, had been prominent during Clement VI's crusade, in which the concept of a twofold *passagium* had first been transferred to *Romania*, albeit in a haphazard and unsatisfactory manner.

Secondly, the chrysobull shows that John V, perhaps again through the advice of Paul of Smyrna, realized the complexity of crusade recruitment at this time, so that the Emperor wrote of 'those paid by the Church or by others following instructions to secure the Church's indulgence, and those who come voluntarily, to save their souls'.[122] Most importantly, the letter reveals the full extent of the Greeks' plight, for the *basileus* was ready to act as a papal lieutenant, albeit an exalted one. There was a precedent in 1347–8, when John Cantacuzenus suggested that he should be appointed captain of the Smyrna crusade and boasted that he could do more in a month than its present leaders had managed in a year.[123] But given the economic state of the West the chrysobull's proposals were out of the question, and the nuncios sent to Constantinople in 1356 had the limited task of converting leading Greeks.[124] Impracticable as the chrysobull was, it remains a key source for Greek perceptions of the crusade in the mid-fourteenth century.

Some Latin aid reached the Greeks, although not on the scale hoped for by John V. When Peter Thomas was sent East as legate in 1359 he was instructed to do all he could to help the Emperor, and he used the naval resources of the revived league to capture Lampsacus in the Dardanelles.[125] Since Peter had been granted

---

[120] *AE*, ad annum 1355, nn. 34–7, xxv, 601–2. See also Gill, 208–10.
[121] Cf. Halecki, *Un Empereur*, 36–8.   [122] See above, ch. 4 *passim*.
[123] Loenertz, 183.   [124] Halecki, *Un Empereur*, 53–7.
[125] Philip of Mézières, 85–6; Boehlke, 166–8; Setton, *PL*, 236–7.

crusade privileges for his legation, this can be considered as the first crusading venture actually intended as military aid for Constantinople since the fall of the Latin Empire in 1261. As news reached the Curia of the gains made by Sultan Murad in the early 1360s, Urban V made some efforts to step up western aid, though he was clearly hindered by the southwards thrust of the Franco-Cypriot project. In an extraordinary letter to John V in October 1364, he wrote as though the general passage, which the death of John of France had already robbed of any practical significance, would proceed to Palestine via the Byzantine Empire, picking up promised Greek aid *en route*.[126] This fantastic suggestion is illustrative of the confusion in the Pope's mind, to which we shall return in the next chapter. For it is obvious that any crusade aimed against Mamluk Egypt could do nothing for Byzantium. Peter of Cyprus's expedition of 1365 was thus irrelevant to the Greeks, but in 1365 and 1366 the Pope wrote to John V outlining his plans for sending help. In the first letter Urban wrote of an expedition by the Knights of St John, the Genoese, and the House of Montferrat; some months later his hopes had switched to another triple alliance, this time Peter of Cyprus, Amedeo of Savoy, and Louis of Hungary.[127] Neither project got very far.[128]

Only one of Urban's many candidates actually went to help the Greeks, Amedeo of Savoy.[129] Not only did the Count's successes act as a much needed boost to the pro-Latin faction at the Greek court, but he also showed that Union and crusade could go together, provided there was good will—or desperation—on both sides. As Halecki remarked, the debate about which should come first had been rendered irrelevant by Turkish advances in the Balkans; the defence of the Latin Christians there, firmly validated as a crusade in 1366, would geographically involve the protection of the Greeks as well.[130] There was thus enough enthusiasm for Union to persuade John V to make his visit to the West in 1369. But the 1370s were a disastrous decade. In 1371 the Serbs suffered a catastrophic defeat at the Maritza river. Constantinople was soon all but cut off from the West by land. John V had to become a vassal of Murad, and in 1377 Gallipoli, Amedeo's chief gain, fell again to

---

[126] LM, n. 1305. Cf. Halecki, *Un Empereur*, 86–8.
[127] LM, n. 1703; *AE*, ad annum 1366, nn. 1–2, xxvi, 122.
[128] Halecki, *Un Empereur*, 98 ff.
[129] See above, ch. 1, nn. 194–9.
[130] *Un Empereur*, 123–4.

the Turks. Although Union had not been implemented at Constantinople, Gregory XI did what he could to help the Greeks.[131] But he could neither persuade Louis of Hungary to honour his commitments to John V, nor assemble a league of the other main Christian powers in the East, Venice, Genoa, and the Hospitallers.[132]

It is striking that of all the crusades envisaged in connection with Constantinople during our period, from Charles of Valois's plans of reconquest to Gregory XI's projects for aid for the Greeks, only one, Amedeo of Savoy's campaign, materialized. The main reason was of course the many problems surrounding Church Union, and the link which the Curia so long insisted on making between Union and crusade. There were difficulties on both sides. Not until the late 1360s, or even the reign of Gregory XI, did the papacy actually define the defence of what remained of the Empire, or the recovery of its lost lands, as a crusading cause. And even if the Curia had agreed to proclaim a crusade, to mount an expedition along the lines requested by Barlaam in 1339, John Cantacuzenus in 1348, and John V in 1355, the response to such a call in the West would probably have been meagre. The powerful pull which Constantinople continued to exert on Latin Christians was one of conquest and plunder, or commercial control and exploitation; not, except in the case of Amedeo of Savoy, that of Christian charity. Despite papal arguments about the strategic importance of Constantinople, few westerners felt personally committed to the defence of Greek lands and towns, and few felt sympathy for a people long regarded as treacherous schismatics. Nor were coinciding interests strong enough to make Latins and Greeks act together against the Turks. We have seen that Venice usually felt that it could best defend its trading routes and markets in *Romania* by negotiating rather than fighting; and when interests overlapped in the Balkans, the western ruler with most to lose, Louis of Hungary, displayed a remarkable insouciance about the Ottoman advance.

Western attitudes might have changed had the Byzantine authorities adopted a consistent and vigorously executed policy of Church Union. Almost throughout our period there was an influential body of counsellors at work which pressed the *basileus* to do just

---

[131] In June 1373 the Pope wrote to John V that he would act with greater urgency if he saw signs that the *basileus* was trying to implement Union. See Mollat, *Lettres secrètes*, n. 1933.

[132] Halecki, *Un Empereur*, 248–324.

that. But it had to contend with a powerful religious opposition with great popular backing, and during the crucial period, 1341–54, when papal attention was focused on *Romania*, the Empire was wracked by civil war. Even after plans for a Latin reconquest had ended, there were well-grounded fears that a crusade might act as cover for further inroads by the Italians, and much less well-grounded hopes that Byzantium could dispense with western aid by forging alliances with the Slav states of the Balkans, or even relying on Russian help.[133] Only *in extremis*, at certain points in the reign of John V, were the Greeks prepared to accept Union at even the official level as the price of Latin aid.

In the south-east Mediterranean a vast and well-run Muslim state at the height of its power blocked all hopes of recovering the Holy Land, slowly destroyed the Christian foothold of Cilician Armenia, and began to threaten Lusignan Cyprus. In the north-east a decaying Christian empire, aided by the splintered and tiny Latin states and colonies which were its neighbours, frustrated by the very complexity of its relations with the Curia all attempts to co-ordinate the defence of the region. The papacy failed in its policies towards them both because they were too ambitious, too out of tune with economic and political reality, and called for greater influence and material resources than the Curia could muster. And this was only part of the problem, for in the West the papacy faced political and economic obstacles which were of an equal severity.

The first of these was warfare between Christian rulers, the *bella intestina* which were both endemic and destructive, and were bound to pose an obstacle to the West's ability to launch any form of crusade to the East. This was readily perceived by the Curia.[134] It focused on the Anglo-French war, which was quite rightly seen as the most damaging dispute of the day. Thus in 1342 Clement VI wrote that the conflict was encouraging not only the Sultan of Egypt but also the Merinid rulers of Morocco to organize invasions of Christian lands.[135] In December 1344 the Pope described peace between England and France as 'pleasing to God, convenient for

---

[133] For the importance of Russia in Byzantine policy in this period see J. Meyendorff, *Byzantium and the Rise of Russia: A Study of Byzantine-Russian Relations in the Fourteenth Century* (Cambridge, 1981).

[134] As well as by others: e.g. *DVL*, i, n. 110; Peter Dubois, *De recuperatione terre sancte*, 3–4, 7 ff., 20–2, and *passim*. See also Throop, 75–82.

[135] Déprez *et al.*, n. 94.

both sides, and very necessary for all Christendom, as well as for the launching in our time of a crusade overseas'.[136] Three months later he made a discreet appeal to self-interest in writing to Edward III that 'the right wars for Catholic kings and princes are those through which their temporal realms are not lost but expanded, and through which they acquire for themselves the crowns of the everlasting kingdom'.[137] The same themes of temporal and spiritual gains within the context of the defence of Christendom were reiterated a generation later by Gregory XI, with even greater urgency as the Curia began to perceive the extent of the Ottoman threat. In 1372 the royal envoys at Bruges were asked to bear in mind 'how harmful to the entire world and damaging to the matter of the Holy Land has been, and still is, the conflict between their Kings'.[138] And in 1375 the Pope wrote to Venice that he was postponing his journey to Rome in order to further the talks at Bruges, because of their supreme importance, 'not just for the kingdoms and lands of the said Kings, but also for the whole of Christendom and for the launching of a general passage'.[139] Like his contemporary Catherine of Siena, Gregory XI continued the very old tradition of regarding peace within Christendom, and the crusade in the East, as two sides of the same coin: 'The crusade is particularly conducive to peace, and peace itself leads to the crusade'.[140]

To the problem of warfare between Christian rulers must be added that of the *routiers*, the mercenary companies which harassed the civilian populations of France and Italy from the 1350s to the end of our period and beyond. The *routiers* were themselves a symptom of almost continual and widespread war, but they complicated the situation greatly, adding to and thriving on civil disorder and insecurity. Even if the major conflicts between sovereign states could be settled by peace or truce, it was necessary, as after Brétigny in 1361, to deal with the activities of these locust-like bands before a crusade could be organized.[141] And there was a third obstacle, more far-reaching and disruptive even than warfare and

---

[136] Ibid., n. 1326.
[137] Ibid., n. 1582, and cf. n. 1590; *AE*, ad annum 1340, n. 55, xxv, 211.
[138] Mirot *et al.*, n. 581, and cf. n. 604.
[139] Ibid., n. 3713.
[140] Ibid., n. 1852. See also Luttrell, 'Gregory XI', 415–17; P. Rousset, 'Sainte Catherine de Sienne et le problème de la Croisade', *Schweizerische Zeitschrift für Geschichte*, xxv (1975), 499–513.
[141] Housley, 'Mercenary Companies', *passim*.

the *routiers*: the economic difficulties which beset the period. Already at the beginning of the fourteenth century there were clear signs that two centuries of expansion both in the West's agrarian economy and in its manufacturing and commercial sectors were coming to an end: the increasing incidence of local famines, social unrest in towns and cities, a credit squeeze, and brutality in the relations between bankers and their princely patrons.[142] Collapse came in the 1340s, with the crash of the Florentine banking houses and the Black Death in 1348. The economic and social dislocation which resulted from the Black Death and the periodic recurrence of plague lasted throughout the remainder of our period.[143]

War brought not only devastation to large areas of the West, but also a heavy fiscal burden to civilian populations wholly unaffected by the fighting itself.[144] The *routiers* forced many towns, seigneurs, and rural communities in France and Italy to think in terms of the immediate defence of their persons and goods, erecting physical and mental barriers against the world outside. And these preoccupations beset people weighed down by appallingly high rates of mortality, less productive, probably poorer than their predecessors in real terms, and more critical of their social fabric. It is no surprise that, from about 1340 onwards, the Curia increasingly dismissed the idea of planning a crusade in such circumstances as hopeless. This was the background to Clement VI's advice to Humbert of Vienne, in November 1346, not to rely on either manpower or money from the West.[145] Twenty years later Urban V wrote to Peter of Cyprus that he could not organize further crusade activity as the West was devastated by war and the companies, and neither Church nor laity could provide aid; the King would have to negotiate a peace, or at least a truce, with the Sultan.[146] And in 1375 Gregory XI described the *populus christianus* as oppressed by wars, plague, famine, and other calamities, 'its faculties exhausted, its numbers reduced', so

---

[142] See, for example, Cont. William of Nangis, i, 427–8, where an account of the crusade enthusiasm of 1316 is followed by a description of the serious famine conditions of that year.

[143] For the consequences of the Black Death and the banking failure, see, for example, Henneman, *Royal Taxation . . . 1322–1356*, 234 ff.; Renouard, *Les Relations*, 197 ff. For economic conditions generally, see the forthcoming revised edition of the *Cambridge Economic History of Europe*, vols. 1–2.

[144] See Hewitt, *passim*; Allmand, *passim*.

[145] Déprez *et al.*, nn. 2956–7.

[146] *AE*, ad annum 1366, n. 13, xxvi, 127–8.

that a general passage either to recover Palestine or to expel the Turks from the Balkans was out of the question.[147]

As Clement and Urban wrote, the Church was especially hard hit by these developments. Newly subject to taxation for national wars, more vulnerable than the laity to the looting and blackmail of the *routiers*, and often burdened with fixed rents and unproductive estates in a period of falling food prices, churchmen complained loudly of their difficulties, which loom large in the papal registers. To take a few examples. Already in 1308 Clement V wrote of falling Church revenues in Scotland, and in 1326 the clergy of Parma were described as weighed down by war.[148] The sufferings of the French church were referred to by Clement VI in 1349 and Urban V in 1363, those of the German church by Innocent VI in 1355.[149] And in April 1374 Gregory XI responded coldly to complaints from the Hungarian church by pointing out the sacrifices of national churches in much worse straits than that of Hungary.[150] As for the Hospitallers, whose help would be important to any crusade in the East, an inquest into their estates carried out at the order of Gregory XI in 1373 is one of our best sources for the period, amply testifying to the poor condition of the rural economy in France, Italy, and Germany.[151]

The papacy realized all too well the gravity and implications of this group of interconnected problems, but what could it do about them? War between Christian rulers was a field in which the Curia had long established a right of intervention, based at least partly on its role in the promotion of crusades.[152] Papal intervention was welcomed as a means of ending disputes peacefully without either side losing face; but as the concept of lay sovereignty sharpened and was advanced more forcefully towards the end of the thirteenth century, it became necessary to create a peacemaking formula which did not smack of papal overlordship. This was found by allowing the pope to intervene as a private individual rather than as Christ's vicar, so that Boniface VIII acted as Benedict Caetani in his

---

[147] *Lettres de Grégoire XI,* iii, n. 3263.

[148] *Reg. Clem. V,* n. 2329; Mollat, *Lettres communes,* n. 24802, and cf. n. 26155.

[149] Déprez *et al.,* n. 4070; LM, n. 221; Gasnault *et al.,* n. 1785.

[150] *VMH,* ii, n. 292.   [151] See below, ch. 8, nn. 110, 119–20.

[152] See Y. Renouard, 'Les Papes et le conflit franco–anglais en Aquitaine de 1259 à 1337', *MEFR,* li (1934), 258–92; J. Gaudemet, 'Le Rôle de la papauté dans le règlement des conflits entre états aux XIIIe et XIVe siècles', in *Recueils de la Société Jean Bodin XV: La Paix* (Brussels, 1961), 79–106.

arbitration between Philip IV and Edward I. In the Avignon period the papal position was weakened even further: the pope now acted not as a judge, but as a mutual friend, a reconciler of the two disputants.[153] In this capacity papal interventions were numerous, particularly in the long-running disputes between England and France, and between Genoa and its various foes, Venice, Aragon, and Cyprus.[154] John XXII and Benedict XII had some successes, but the period was not one in which the Curia excelled as a peacemaker. There was very little it could do to enforce its decision if it proved unacceptable to one side, which usually proved to be the case. More importantly, the pope was often the political ally of one of the powers in the dispute and his attempt at arbitration was partisan, or was seen as such. The problem was typified by Cardinal Talleyrand's unsuccessful arbitration on the eve of the battle of Poitiers.[155] Appealing to the need for a crusade was ineffective since, as we have seen, Christian princes had become adept at incorporating this particular argument into their own propaganda.[156]

Without peace between Christian princes there could be no major crusade; but unless a solution was found to the problem of the *routiers* whom such a peace would release from paid employment, the crusade would be equally distant a prospect. The Curia was therefore just as active in its attempts to deal with the companies as it was in its peacemaking. It adopted a two-edged policy. It regularly issued indulgences to stimulate resistance by local authorities. This approach was not generally successful because, although the Curia made an accurate assessment of the hatred felt by the civilian population towards these bandits, it proved unable to organize proper leadership for its *ad hoc*, anti-*routier* forces. The second approach was to negotiate with the most important leaders of the companies for the departure of their groups on crusades to Spain, the Balkans, and the East. Such a solution appealed in its neat symmetry: it entailed relief for Christendom's interior, help for an embattled Christian frontier, and personal salvation for the *routiers*.[157] A good example is Enguerrand of Coucy's proposal to

---

[153] Ibid., 95 ff. [154] See, for example, Mirot, 13.

[155] See N. P. Zacour, *Talleyrand: the Cardinal of Périgord (1301–1364)* (Philadelphia, 1960), 51–3. See also Wood, *passim*; Faucon, *passim*; Henneman, *Royal Taxation . . . 1322–1356*, 197, 233–4.

[156] See above, ch. 3, nn. 37–45.

[157] See, for example, *Lettres d'Urbain V*, n. 1656.

lead 'a fine strong body of men-at-arms' to Albania to fight against the Turks in 1373. Gregory XI asked Joanna of Naples to permit their transit through the *Regno* since it would 'exalt the Christian Faith and the honour of the Roman church, and be of benefit to your Kingdom of Sicily and its adjacent regions, as well as to the common good'.[158]

Historians have usually dismissed such schemes as chimerical, but there are grounds for believing that the aspirations of the *routiers* included participation in a crusade: it had, however, to be a profitable enterprise and this, with the exception of the sack of Alexandria in 1365, was not easily achieved. For some decades Church and lay authorities nevertheless continued their attempts to 'export' the *routiers*; indeed, their dogged persistence is itself a good reason not to view such projects as hopeless. At the time of the Bruges peace talks Gregory XI conceived a grand design for an Anglo-French peace to be sealed symbolically by the co-operation of the two powers in a crusade, and aided materially by the participation in this expedition of the soldiers in the pay of the two monarchies.[159] It was not to be, although this *mélange* of eminently desirable aims reverberated through the 1380s and 1390s.[160] Moreover, it has been argued that even in dealing with the *routiers* the Curia made decisions which were specifically intended to aid the Valois cause in the Anglo-French war.[161]

In tackling the problems of war and brigandage the international standing and universal role of the papacy were often compromised by its own political aims, especially its close association with the French monarchy. This was strikingly true also of the approach taken by the Curia towards the difficulties created by the economic depression. The reaction of the Curia was to place its own financial needs first. It has been claimed that as early as 1335–6 Benedict XII rejected Hospitaller plans for a limited crusade because this would entail the withdrawal of the Order's funds from the Florentine bankers who acted for the *camera*, thus indirectly endangering papal solvency.[162] This has to be viewed in the context of Benedict's

[158] 'Gregorio XI e Giovanna I di Napoli', *ASPN*, xxiii, 691–2, n. 63.

[159] Mirot *et al.*, nn. 1896–1907.

[160] J. J. N. Palmer, *England, France and Christendom 1377–99* (London, 1972), ch. 11 *passim*.

[161] Id., 'England, France, the Papacy and the Flemish Succession, 1361–9', *JMH*, ii (1976), 339–64.

[162] See A. T. Luttrell, 'Interessi fiorentini nell'economia e nella politica dei

deep-rooted suspicion of crusading projects. At least his letters are pervaded by a concern for the financial health of the Church.[163] Much more serious was the cumulative weight of papal taxation from the 1340s onwards, when the Curia abandoned Benedict's policy of retrenchment in favour of increased taxes against a background of economic decline. From the point of view of paying for a major crusade to the East, and certainly from that of the financial and pastoral health of the western Church, it was essential to lessen the burden of papal taxes as Church revenues dwindled and lay taxation soared. Urban V did halve the assessment of the clerical tenth in northern France, a drastic measure which shows how serious the situation there had become,[164] but the expense of the Italian campaigns of Cardinal Albornoz and his successors led to more taxes, not less. As Gregory XI wrote to the Abbot of Cîteaux in 1372, the *camera* was subject to increasing demands at a time when its revenues were under strain because of the effects of war and plague, 'by which, alas, the Christian people has long been afflicted and to which it is still subject in many parts of the world'. 'The assistance of the devout' was necessary, which in practice meant a heavy burden of tenths, annates, and subsidies.[165] The Curia argued, on traditional lines, that its Italian wars were of importance to the whole Latin Church, but the coincidence of this taxation with the other problems facing the Church inevitably weakened allegiance to the Holy See.

Throughout the period 1305–78 most of the West had domestic cares and preoccupations which prevented it thinking for long of a crusade to the eastern Mediterranean. But apart from people with vested interests, such as the Venetians and Cypriots, were Latin Christians still attracted by the crusade anyway? The view has long been held that a drastic fall off in crusading zeal had occurred in the thirteenth century, possibly as early as Louis IX's first crusade, and that this decline continued in the following decades; the failure of most projects to get off the ground is often adduced in support of

---

Cavalieri Ospedalieri di Rodi nel Trecento', *Annali della Scuola Normale Superiore di Pisa: Lettere, Storia e Filosofia*, 2 serie, xxviii (1959), 317–20; id., 'The Crusade', 134.

[163] See, for example, Daumet, nn. 240, 251.
[164] LM, n. 221; Henneman, *Royal Taxation . . . 1356–1370*, 222.
[165] ASV, Reg. Vat. 268, ff. 171^v–172^r.

this interpretation.[166] But it will now be clear that the stagnation of the crusading movement in the East does not *need* to be explained in terms of declining enthusiasm. It can be accounted for by the many obstacles, political, economic, and financial, examined in this chapter and in the preceding one: this indeed is the advantage of not approaching the question of response at an earlier point of this study. With this in mind, we can now attempt a reassessment of popular feeling about the crusade, still concentrating on the East, though with sidelong glances at other fronts.

Forming even a reasonably accurate impression of what most people thought about the crusade in the fourteenth century is a formidably difficult task. It is complicated by the presence of hired troops in crusade armies, and by the fact that many *crucesignati*, and even more beneficiaries of the indulgence, did not actually fight and left no trace of their zeal.[167] The frequent assertions in the documentary sources that men were less ready to go on crusade than their forefathers were invariably made with a specific purpose—such as the discouragement of a crusade project—and can no more be relied upon than twelfth-century descriptions of crusade preaching emptying towns and villages of their menfolk. The fact is that contemporaries, including the Curia, were not aware of how much enthusiasm remained or would be stirred up if, for instance, a leading western king took the cross. This is evident from a letter which Gregory XI wrote in 1375. Two crusading enthusiasts had informed the Pope that many people in northern France and the Low Countries were eager to fight the Turks; they hoped to be able to raise troops for at least a small expedition, a *passagium particulare*, and asked for papal letters to back up a recruitment drive. Gregory was cautious in his response:

Without anybody preaching, and without calling people together, they are to make diligent enquiries about who is eager for a general passage or a *passagium particulare*, about their rank, resources, and wishes, and about how long they want to fight or serve in person or through others, or contribute from their possessions.

People who wanted to go, send soldiers or donate money were to make a votive obligation (curiously unspecified) before their bishop or vicar, and a sealed document or notarial act was to be drawn up and sent to the Curia, so that it could gauge the response for itself.

[166] See, for example, Throop, 206–13.   [167] Cf. Purcell, 52 ff.

If we can see that it amounts to a large number (*multitudo*) of the *populus christianus*, with enough resources and the other necessary things, then we will launch a *passagium generale* or *particulare*, if and in the way that we believe to be expedient, granting the customary indulgences, graces, and privileges.[168]

In some ways, of course, we are better placed than Gregory XI to work out what his contemporaries thought, and there are several approaches which we can adopt to build up a picture of popular feeling. The first is to evaluate the significance of opposition to the crusades. Views on this subject have recently changed considerably. Mainly through the work of Palmer Throop an orthodoxy was established in the 1940s which saw criticism of the crusades growing in volume and range in the late twelfth and thirteenth centuries after a period of general acceptance between the First and Second Crusades; by this interpretation, repeated failure, the chief cause of criticism, meant that it went on increasing in the fourteenth century.[169] But as scholars have examined the early twelfth century in greater detail, they have demonstrated that deep-seated doubts about the validity of the crusade flourished even in the glowing aftermath of the First Crusade. On the other hand, while criticism of the practice of crusading, particularly the abuses which it gave rise to, grew in the thirteenth century as a response to military failure, there was noticeably less criticism of the idea of Christian holy war. The reasons for this included the prescriptive respectability of crusading, and the achievement of the canonists in giving the crusade a place in the just war framework of analysis. Outside the peculiar circumstances of Prussia and Livonia, the muchvaunted conflict between war and conversion, crusade and mission, hardly existed except in the heads of idealists. More so than in the first third of the twelfth century, the crusade was accepted by Church and laity.[170]

Developments in the Avignon period support this revised picture. Certainly the practice of crusading, or as was increasingly the case, of defaulting on crusade obligations, continued to provoke pungent criticism. Popes attacked kings for failing to keep their

---

[168] *Lettres de Grégoire XI*, iii, n. 3263. See Golubovich, iii, 147–8, for a similar enquiry for purposes of crusade planning, handled by the secular clergy, in 1316.

[169] Throop, *passim*. Accepted by Runciman, Prawer, Purcell, and most others who have considered the subject.

[170] See E. Siberry, *Criticism of Crusading, 1095–1274* (Oxford, 1985).

commitments, while opponents of the Curia and crusade theorists accused the papacy of diverting resources; such criticisms had become well-tried and handy weapons in the armoury of the West's publicists.[171] But the concept of the crusade remained virtually unassailable behind the ramparts of prescription and the just war tradition. Crusades in Spain and along the Baltic had many generations of precedents in their favour.[172] As for the eastern Mediterranean, the treatment of crusades there by Honoré Bonet is typical. He argued that the pope could declare crusades either to recover Jerusalem, 'which was gained by lawful conquest for Christians by the passion of Jesus Christ our Lord', or to liberate Christians who were being oppressed by Muslims outside Syria.[173] We have seen that the Curia adhered very closely to this defensive justification, and there is no evidence in the papal sources of opposition to the crusades in the East on ethical grounds.

Nor did the two approaches of crusade and mission clash any more than they had done in the thirteenth century. In another chapter we shall see that at one point the Curia came close to compelling the Teutonic Knights to abandon their coercive strategy towards the Lithuanians when Gediminas, their Grand Prince, claimed to have been converted; but this was a brief and abortive episode. In the eastern Mediterranean there was never any hope that the rulers of the Mamluks or Turks could be converted, and as an alternative to armed defence, missionary work which could not achieve this goal was useless.[174] It is perverse to dismiss the enthusiastic response to the preaching of the Smyrna crusade as uncharacteristic, as one recent historian has done, on the grounds that 'the Turk had now become an enemy to convert rather than fight against'.[175] This is putting interpretation before evidence.

All this is confirmed by the one critical document I have dis-

---

[171] See, for example, their virtuoso deployment by Guillaume de Plaisians at the Paris assembly of 1303: *Documents relatifs aux états généraux et assemblées réunis sous Philippe le Bel*, ed. G. Picot (Paris, 1901), n. xiv, 43–4, and cf. *Histoire du différend d'entre le pape Boniface VIII et Philippes le Bel roy de France*, ed. Dupuy (Paris, 1655), 342–3.

[172] For an argument from precedent see *Acta pont. svecica*, i, n. 191.

[173] Honoré Bonet, 126–8. See also E. Porter, 'Chaucer's Knight, the Alliterative *Morte Arthure*, and Medieval Laws of War: a Reconsideration', *Nottingham Medieval Studies*, xxvii (1983), 58 ff.

[174] For missions in the Avignon period, see Richard, *La Papauté et les missions*, 131 ff.; id., 'Les Papes d'Avignon et l'évangélisation du monde non-latin à la veille du grand schisme', in *Genèse et débuts*, 305–15.   [175] Papi, 100.

covered which does go into some detail, a letter addressed to Pope Clement VI at the time of the Smyrna crusade and purporting to come from a Turkish emir.[176] In reality it almost certainly originated with the enemies of Venice, probably the Genoese, who saw the crusade as an instrument of that city's colonial ambitions. The emir, *Morbasianus*, wrote that the Pope should not send crusaders (*cruciferi viri*) to fight him. The Turks were innocent of shedding Christ's blood and of occupying the holy places of Palestine; they favoured the Italians, with the exception of the Venetians, who had illicitly seized Crete and other islands belonging by rights to the Turks; and they revered Christ as a prophet so there was no religious motive for attacking them. The gist of the letter was that the crusade was invalid as an exercise of the—unquestioned—papal power to release from sins because the Anatolian Turks were neither occupying the Holy Land nor oppressing Christians without due cause: Honoré Bonet's two justifications. For good measure, *Morbasianus* reminded the Pope that 'your law forbids you to compel someone to embrace your belief'. Clement had been tricked, the emir was made to claim, by Venetian stories of Turkish piracy and raiding. The strained and unconvincing character of this defence of the Turkish position shows how hard it was to establish a case against crusading in legal terms. To do so, the author had to resort to the implausible idea that it was really the Venetians who were the aggressors in the eastern Mediterranean.[177]

That criticism of the crusading idea was muted could of course mean that it no longer aroused much passion for or against, and we need more positive indicators to popular feeling. Despite the problems involved, it is possible to construct a picture of rising and falling enthusiasm, gauged by the numbers who definitely took the cross or showed interest in crusading in other ways. What emerges is a rough division of the period into three phases. The first lasts until about 1340 and is associated above all with the crusade projects of the French Crown and hopes for the recovery of the Holy Land. The crusading enthusiasm of the Western nobility in these decades is striking in its depth and persistence.[178] French nobles in particular were loath to abandon what was, for many families, a rich and

---

[176] Gay, 172–4.

[177] Even the Turks saw the league as a response to their raids. See Lemerle, 181.

[178] Cf. Hillgarth, *Ramon Lull*, 73 and ch. 2 *passim*.

venerated tradition of fighting in the East;[179] and acting through their vociferous representatives in the *Parlement* faction at court they exerted pressure on their kings to act. Thus in February 1332 Peter Roger asserted that Philip VI had been pressed to undertake a crusade by his barons and prelates at an assembly held in Paris.[180] Projects for *passagia* in turn created their own enthusiasm. Chroniclers wrote of the excitement provoked by the glittering Pentecost assembly of 1313.[181] Three years later there were reports of more than 5,000 French nobles taking the cross to accompany Louis of Clermont,[182] and John XXII and others were impressed by the numbers who took the cross for Philip VI's project.[183]

It was in the 1320s and early 1330s that this enthusiasm reached its peak, with a series of major campaigns in Spain, Italy, and Lithuania as well as French plans for a general passage to the East. Spain in particular retained much of its old appeal as a battleground for French and German knights. In 1316 James II was told by an envoy that 500 of the best French and Norman knights had formed a sworn association with the goal of fighting for the King at their own expense.[184] This report is rather suspect, but between 1326 and 1331 Philip of Valois, King John of Bohemia, Philip of Evreux, and William of Jülich, amongst others, actively considered campaigning against the Moors in the peninsula.[185] But the deferment of all their plans was typical of a period in which, time after time, groups of nobles found that they could not fulfil their vows because the campaign in which they were to take part had been abandoned. Disillusionment and anger, caused by military failure in earlier generations of *crucesignati*, was in the fourteenth century the result of the failure of planning and organization, for canon law did not permit individuals to treat their vows lightly. Special consideration had to be given to such oaths as Louis of Clermont's vow not to enter Paris until he went on crusade, and the vow made by the

---

[179] The role of lineage in sustaining enthusiasm for the crusade is a subject which calls for investigation.

[180] *VPA*, ii, 288–9.

[181] See, for example, Cont. William of Nangis, i, 396; *Chron. regum Francorum*, i, 210–11; John of St Victor, 21.

[182] *AA*, i, n. 145. See also Cont. William of Nangis, i, 427–8; 'Chron. parisienne anonyme', 25–6; *Titres de la maison ducale de Bourbon*, i, 259, n. 1509.

[183] CC, n. 5322; 'Chron. parisienne anonyme', 154; Cont. William of Nangis, ii, 134–5.

[184] *AA*, iii, p. L.

[185] See above, ch. 2, nn. 38–49.

Count of Eu—particularly unfortunate in view of the fact that he was Constable of France—not to carry arms until he had gone to fight in Granada.[186]

The repeated postponement or failure of crusade plans in these decades was therefore accompanied by a swelling chorus of popular discontent. There was disappointment at the way the Hospitaller *passagium* of 1309–10 achieved so much less than was hoped for: 'They said the aim was to go overseas [i.e. to the Holy Land], but nothing came of it'.[187] A few years later came the Council of Vienne and the recruitment drive which it launched: 'Money was collected for the *passagium*, and a wealth of arms and other things donated by the faithful . . . But nothing came of the crusade. On this account the *populus christianus* was greatly scandalized'.[188] In 1318 John XXII wrote of the danger of popular discontent should Philip V postpone his crusade, and Louis of Clermont had to contend with great hostility because he proved unable to launch his promised *passagium*.[189] It was not surprising that by the 1330s many had stopped giving credence to the French projects; one chronicler wrote of Philip VI's crusade that 'it did not materialize, and it was generally predicted that very little would be done on the basis of past delusions'.[190] John XXII expected preachers of Philip VI's crusade to encounter hecklers and took measures to deal with them.[191]

This wave of disillusionment did not, however, lead to a final collapse of crusading zeal any more than had similar comments in the thirteenth century: once again Latin Christians displayed a remarkable resilience of faith. The early 1340s thus constitute a second phase, during which enthusiasm, while not as striking as in the preceding decades, could still be aroused in circumstances when military activity proved possible. Once again Spain is important because the presence of non-Spaniards fighting as crusaders both

[186] Mollat, *Lettres communes*, n. 54386; CC, nn. 4870, 5064. See also Philip of Mézières, 124, for Peter of Cyprus's similar vow in 1365.

[187] Mas Latrie, ii, 131n.

[188] 'Vita Clementis V auctore Paulino, Veneto', in *VPA*, i, 82. This passage may relate to the Hospitaller fundraising campaign of 1308–10 rather than the Council of Vienne.

[189] CC, n. 667; Cont. William of Nangis, ii, 65–6, 81; Barber, 'The Pastoureaux', 160–2.

[190] 'Octava vita Benedicti XII', in *VPA*, i, 237. Cf. *Les Grandes Chroniques*, ix, 133–4; *Chron. regum Francorum*, ii, 19.

[191] CC, n. 5220, col. 89.

makes an impact in the sources and cannot be explained in terms of self-interest. At both of the major engagements at this time, the battle of Salado and the siege of Algeciras, there were significant groups of foreigners present; indeed, Philip of Evreux finally achieved his goal of fighting in Spain at Algeciras, where he was a victim of plague during the siege.[192] More striking than Spain, however, is the recruitment for Smyrna in 1344–5. It is especially interesting to find large groups setting out from the Italian inland cities, such as Florence, Siena, and Bologna, which are not usually regarded as promising centres of recruitment for crusades in the East. It has recently been estimated that as many as 100 went from Pistoia and its *contado* alone, out of a total population of about 36,000.[193]

These years mark a watershed. By November 1346 men could not be found to fight at Smyrna, possibly because of the famine conditions of 1346–7 in Italy.[194] If this is correct, it is symptomatic of the onset of warfare, plague, and economic and social dislocation, whose effects on the crusade we have already charted. These difficulties characterize the third phase, which lasted to the end of our period. Even in these decades, however, enthusiasm was only dormant, and could be aroused when a crusade was promoted at a time when domestic peace seemed possible. This is shown both by the response of the French nobility to the Franco-Cypriot project in the 1360s, and by the continuing popularity of the Lithuanian *Reysen*.[195] And when crusading plans revived on a grander scale in the more propitious political, if not economic, conditions of the 1390s, there was enough lay enthusiasm to sustain them.[196]

An analysis based on the collection of alms and legacies for the crusade, although fraught with difficulties,[197] reveals a broadly similar pattern. In the early part of the period the sums collected could still be impressive: Louis of Clermont was allotted 25,000

---

[192] See Goñi Gaztambide, 324–34.

[193] M. S. Mazzi, 'Pistoia e la Terrasanta', in Cardini (ed.), *Toscana e Terrasanta*, 107–9. For the population of Pistoia, see D. Herlihy, *Medieval and Renaissance Pistoia: The Social History of an Italian Town* (New Haven–London, 1967), 76.

[194] Déprez *et al.*, n. 2956. For the famine conditions, see 'Storie pistoresi', 224.

[195] For the Franco–Cypriot project see, for example, *AE*, ad annum 1363, n. 15, xxvi, 82, nn. 20–2, 84–6; Philip of Mézières, 105; LM, n. 1724; Jorga, 165–6.

[196] Atiya, chs. 17–18; Setton, *PL*, ch. 14.

[197] Well illustrated by a recent attempt to analyse testamentary bequests in thirteenth-century Florence: P. Pirillo, 'La Terrasanta nei testamenti fiorentini del Dugento', in Cardini (ed.), *Toscana e Terrasanta*, 57–73.

florins from the proceeds ot French alms and legacies in December 1323.[198] But they later declined considerably. In voluntary contributions to the crusade by Scandinavians, for instance, there was a substantial fall off between the rich pickings of the Hospitallers in 1312 and the thin proceeds of the 1350s.[199] And in England W. E. Lunt detected a decrease in legacies in 1358–63, followed by their virtual disappearance in 1363–78.[200] That this development was caused not only by economic difficulties but also by pessimism about the chances of a crusade actually setting out, is confirmed by the enthusiastic reaction in England to the preaching of the Flanders crusade of 1382–3. Froissart put the total receipt from the sale of indulgences at 25,000 francs: it is clear that people were still prepared to offer money for an expedition which was being actively planned.[201]

It is in the nature of crusade enthusiasm and its sources that our findings concern primarily the nobility, and historians of the later medieval nobility are now tending to reassert the importance of the crusade in its system of values.[202] Recent *Personenforschung* on the fourteenth-century nobility has revealed that quite a high percentage took part in some form of crusade. For England, the crusading careers of Thomas Beauchamp and Henry of Lancaster have already been noted.[203] These were famous names, and it is quite possible that many other Englishmen took the same road but left no record of the fact. For example, one of the reasons why we know that Henry of Beaumont and Henry Despenser fought in the Italian crusades of John XXII and Urban V is their shared baptismal name.[204] And the sole reason we know that Robert Bradeston and John of St Philibert, two men-at-arms, intended to fight against the Turks in 1345 is their imprisonment at Pisa while travelling East, which elicited a letter on their behalf from the Pope.[205] Clement VI's register is also our source for the extraordinary exploits of John

---

[198] CC, n. 1894.

[199] *Acta pont. svecica*, i, nn. 128, 130, 138–9, 197, 311, 409, 412, 421, 425, 486, 488, 541, 547, 563.

[200] Lunt, ii, 525–34.

[201] Ibid., ii, 535–44, esp. 541.

[202] See especially Keen, 'Chaucer's Knight', *passim*; id., *Chivalry*, 155–6, 166–7, 170–4, 194–5, 214–16.

[203] See above, ch. 3, nn. 91–2.

[204] Their lives were therefore included by John Capgrave in his 'Liber de illustribus Henricis', with references to fighting in Italy on 169–70.

[205] Déprez *et al.*, n. 1617.

De River, a knight from the diocese of Worcester who spent some time in the East; in 1348 the Pope wrote that he had fought against the Mamluks as well as the Turks, visited all the holy places of Palestine, and acquired a detailed knowledge of Mamluk military power, techniques, and fortifications.[206] As for France, Philippe Contamine's research on Charles V's war captains in his reconquest of 1369–80 has shown that, out of forty, eight took part in at least one crusade, one or possibly two participated in two, and two fought in three.[207]

What attracted these hardened men-at-arms to the crusade? Assessing the motivation of fourteenth-century *crucesignati* is no easier than in any other period of the crusading movement; wherever they originate, comments on motivation have to be very carefully weighed. In 1363 Urban V described seven German knights who had come to Italy to take part in 'the Lord's war' against Bernabò Visconti as fighting 'because of the zealous devotion which they feel towards the Faith and the Church, so some of them have told us, for reverence towards God and his Church, and for the salvation of their souls'.[208] Foolish as it would be to take such protestations at face value, they cannot be automatically dismissed. In an anti-clerical age, it was equally conventional for lay contemporaries to be sceptical about religious motivation. Typical is Froissart's famous remark that 'men-at-arms cannot live on pardons, nor do they pay much attention to them except at the point of death'.[209] But professional fighters often were at the point of death, and such evidence as exists indicates that men-at-arms were attracted by indulgences, provided they had wages too.[210] Philip of Mézières wrote that most of the fighters who accompanied Peter of Cyprus in 1365 were initially motivated by greed and vanity rather than devotion, but this comment was inserted in order to highlight the great feats of conversion which Peter Thomas, Philip's hero, was described as carrying out in the army.[211]

---

[206] Déprez and Mollat, n. 1605. For John, see also *Cal. of Entries*, iii, 28, 33, 209, 300.

[207] Contamine, *Guerre*, 562–93.

[208] '. . . ex zelo devotionis quem habent ad fidem et ecclesiam prelibatas sicut aliqui eorum nobis exposuerunt, pro reverentia dei et eiusdem ecclesie ipsarumque animarum salute': ASV, Reg. Vat. 245, f. 205ʳ.

[209] Lunt, ii, 541.

[210] See Housley, 'Mercenary Companies', 278–9.

[211] Philip of Mézières, 126.

Whether or not they rivalled religious devotion in leading people to take the cross, the secular attractions of the crusade were undeniably great. The profits of war, wages and plunder, formed an important motivation. Thomas Walsingham described Englishmen returning from the sack of Alexandria with booty in the form of gems and silk hangings of gold, 'in testimony to the great victory achieved there'.[212] There was the status of crusading fronts as places where ambitious men-at-arms could win advancement and renown. According to John Capgrave, Henry Grosmont was a good example of this type of dedicated crusader:

When he was a young man, and the love of hard work came easily to him, he eagerly sought out all the areas where there was war against the pagans, Turks, or Saracens. So he was first in Prussia, then at Rhodes, then in Cyprus and many places in the East, then crossed the regions of Granada and Spain, either putting to flight or killing those who held Christ's cross and Christ himself in contempt.

He acquired such a reputation in this way that French and German youths eager for glory used to follow his standard.[213] Similarly, Froissart wrote of the Lord d'Albret complaining to the Prince of Wales in 1366 that the Prince had persuaded him to hire 800 troops and then had no use for them; this had prevented them from going 'overseas to Prussia, Constantinople or Jerusalem, as every knight or squire does who wants to get on'.[214] Erich Maschke wrote of the *Wanderlust* of young noblemen without heavy responsibilities, and also of some older men (such as John of Bohemia), who made use of the still predominantly international culture of the day to travel from crusade to crusade, just as their ancestors had ridden out in search of heiresses.[215]

Clearly it would be wrong to regard the crusade in the fourteenth century as an unpopular movement. There was a broadly based acceptance of the crusade, characterized by a paucity of opposition

[212] Walsingham, i, 302.

[213] 'Liber de illustribus Henricis', 161. Henry Grosmont's son-in-law and grandson shared his enthusiasm for foreign adventures and holy war: John of Gaunt led a crusade to Castile in 1386 and Henry of Lancaster fought in Prussia in 1390. See ibid., 99; P. E. Russell, *The English Intervention in Spain and Portugal in the time of Edward III and Richard II* (Oxford, 1955), ch. 17.

[214] Froissart, vi, 231–2. Cf. Keen, *Chivalry*, 170.

[215] 'Burgund und der preussische Ordensstaat. Ein Beitrag zur Einheit der ritterlichen Kultur Europas im Spätmittelalter', in *Domus hospitalis Theutonicorum* (Bonn–Bad Godesberg, 1970), 15–34, esp. 26–8.

to the idea of crusading, though criticism of what was happening in practice continued to be vociferous. More importantly, crusading retained a strong appeal amongst fighting men in the West, largely owing to its absorption into the structure of their vocational and cultural aspirations. This appeal was transformed into active enthusiasm, albeit qualified by caution because of past experience of failure,[216] whenever plans were afoot for a crusade to the East in promising political and economic circumstances. From the watershed of the 1340s, as crusading projects gathered dust and the West was crippled by internal problems, the attraction of the crusade was thrust into the background: but it had not yet ceased to exist.

Naturally this has an important bearing on why the crusading movement in the eastern Mediterranean stagnated. Broadly speaking, we need to shift our attention from will to resources, for what was lacking was not enthusiasm but political leadership, domestic security, financial means, and an attainable goal. The papacy identified these problems and made great efforts to come to grips with them, but in almost all cases it failed. There were three main reasons for this. First, the Curia was thwarted by its lack of effective sanctions. It could not compel civil authorities in the West to implement its ban on trade with Egypt, or make powers like Venice and Naples assume their proper role in the defence of *Romania*. Nor could it enforce its decisions as mediator in disputes between Christian states. Secondly, outside Italy the papacy was hampered by its comparative weakness as a military power. It had difficulty in organizing a punitive squadron in the south-east Mediterranean, in sending help to Constantinople against the Turks, and in co-ordinating military action against the *routiers*.

Thirdly, the Curia's own financial and political needs were too often in competition with those of the crusade in the East. In several cases a clash occurred and was resolved to the detriment of the East: with Church taxation, with papal intervention in the Anglo-French war, and to some extent with the granting of absolutions and licences for trade with Egypt. In trying to deal with the problems facing the crusade, the Avignon popes displayed impressive qualities, a keen perception of what was amiss, deep compassion for the plight of Christians in danger or distress, and readiness to alter policies in accordance with changing circumstances. But their

[216] Cf. above, ch. 4, nn. 127–9 (conditional vows).

failure to do much about these problems epitomized some of the outstanding flaws in the Roman church and its role in the crusading movement, flaws which were much aggravated by the constraining political and economic conditions of the period.

7

Crusade Armies in Action:
The Problem of Control

MORE than either the launching or the organization of a crusade, the problem of controlling it in the field taxed the resources of the papacy, revealing the gulf which separated claims from reality. As the vicars of Christ, the popes had the responsibility of ensuring that the *negotium Christi* did not go astray. Extra stress had been laid on this by Innocent III, both because of the added importance which he attributed to military success, to *efficatia*, and because of the dynamic role which he claimed, and to some extent played, in the preparation of the crusades launched during his reign.[1] But Innocent created no new instruments of control or direction; like his predecessors he relied on the vow, on his legates, and on his personal contacts with secular leaders. It was not enough, and Innocent's own reign produced two of the best examples of the Curia losing control, the Fourth Crusade and the Albigensian Crusade.[2] Others followed soon after the Pope's death.[3]

The problem was complicated by three new developments in the ninety years between 1216 and the accession of Clement V. First, the great kings of the West tightened their grip on the leadership and direction of crusading expeditions. The popes acquiesced in this partly because it did not, at this stage, pose a threat to their own authority within the movement, and partly because strong leadership by a resolute secular prince appeared the best way to achieve a campaign's military objective; with the relentless growth of mon-

[1] See Roscher, 58–99, 140–69, 272–3 and *passim*.
[2] Ibid., 99–131, 221–53. Innocent could of course call off the crusade, as in the case of Languedoc in 1213: ibid., 145, 236. But this was hardly satisfactory. Cf. Riley-Smith, *Knights of St John*, 10–11.
[3] See E. T. Kennan, 'Innocent III, Gregory IX and Political Crusades: a Study in the Disintegration of Papal Power', in *Reform and Authority in the Medieval and Reformation Church*, ed. G. F. Lytle (Washington, 1981), 15–35.

archical power in lay society the Curia could not have resisted the trend even had it wanted to.

Secondly, with the creation of several new crusade fronts early in the century, the problem of diversion, which had always been present in the movement, became a major factor. Thus Charles I of Sicily could justify his plan to divert part of his dead brother's army to Constantinople in 1270 on the grounds that the recovery of the city from the Greeks was a recognized crusading objective.[4] Had the example set by the Curia been one of total probity, such diversions might have been harder to carry out, or at least justify. But by 1305 the papacy too had systematically diverted resources from their original goals, and John XXII continued this approach.[5] By his reign, as we have seen, the danger of manpower, shipping, and funds being diverted had come to dominate crusade negotiations: the undignified wrangling of John XXII and Philip VI in 1332–3 on this very issue shows the extent to which control had by this time become the subject of acrimonious debate between parties who all had poor past records. In view of John's diversion of the 1319 flotilla, of Philip's use of ships prepared for his general passage during the opening stage of the Anglo-French conflict, and of Clement VI's partisan support for his King, it was not surprising that early in 1345 English envoys at the Curia feared the 'very likely possibility' that Louis de la Cerda's preparations for a crusade to the Canaries might be a cover for a Franco-papal invasion of England.[6]

Thirdly, and most importantly, the loss of Latin Syria made it even easier to deflect a crusade in the East from its original destination. While the Frankish states in Syria survived, their defence was of paramount concern, whichever strategical approach was taken. But once they had been overrun, the crusade of recovery had to compete with the defence of Cyprus and Armenia, aid for the Latins in Greece, and, towards the end of our period, help for the Greeks at Constantinople. A seaborne expedition launched from a Western port could go virtually anywhere in the East without losing its character as a crusade, especially as papal policy was so malleable. Hence the speculation at Genoa in 1309 about the desti-

[4] *Spicilegium sive collectio veterum aliquot scriptorum qui in Galliae bibliothecis delituerant*, ed. L. d'Achéry *et al.* 3 vols. (Paris, 1723), iii, 667–8.

[5] See Housley, *Italian Crusades*, 97 ff.

[6] Adam Murimuth, 'Continuatio chronicarum', ed. E. M. Thompson. *RS* (London, 1889), 162–3; Wood, 186–7.

nation of the Hospitaller *passagium*: would it try to invade Syria, attack Constantinople, or even spearhead a renewed papal attempt to reconquer Sicily?[7] Amalric of Cyprus, perhaps with memories of the Third Crusade, made military preparations in case the French used the crusade to seize the island.[8] The Venetians feared an assault on their possessions in Greece.[9] And James II of Aragon suggested a sixth possible objective, the consolidation of the Order's conquest of Rhodes.[10] Such speculation was to be repeated whenever a crusade set out for the East, reflecting both the number of possible objectives and the inherent difficulty of controlling a crusade over a distance of several hundred miles. Thus in 1366 Venetian fears for the safety of their colonies and vessels in *Romania* were resuscitated when Amedeo of Savoy sailed with a flotilla of mainly Genoese and Provençal galleys.[11] Coupled with the abiding concern of the Curia about events in the East, this explains the fact that the best examples of how the popes approached the problem of control all relate to the eastern front.

That control was recognized as a grave problem by those with a genuine interest in crusade planning is clear from the writings of Ramon Lull, the Majorcan theorist.[12] Lull was a fierce defender of papal authority in crusading matters, and unlike other theorists who were content to place untrammelled control of a planned expedition in the hands of a lay prince, he addressed himself to the issue of leadership and direction head on. In his *Liber de fine* of 1305 he entrusted the leadership of his proposed crusade to a 'warrior-king' (*bellator rex*). This man would be the master of the united Military Orders and king of the reconquered Jerusalem, and would be obedient to the pope. At this point Lull perhaps had in mind a member of the royal house of Barcelona, James II or his brother Frederick: certainly a man who was already a king. But his views seem to have changed, and in the 'Liber de acquisitione Terrae Sanctae' of 1309 he wanted the crusade to be led by a 'magister generalis miles religiosus', still the master of the combined Military Orders but no longer a king. Instead this individual would be a papal vassal, 'a feudatory of the lord pope and obedient to him'.

---

[7] *AA*, iii, n. 88.
[8] Hill, ii, 239. Cf. *Délibérations*, i, 129.
[9] Ibid., i, 129–31.
[10] *AA*, iii, n. 91, 198–9. See also Luttrell, 'Hospitallers at Rhodes', 285.
[11] *Régestes*, i, 112.
[12] See Hillgarth, *Ramon Lull*, ch. 2 *passim*.

Quite possibly this reflects a growing suspicion of royal leadership, although Lull continued to invest great hopes in Philip IV and Frederick of Sicily.[13]

The *bellator rex* is a fascinating concept, one of the few really innovative ideas coming from the cluster of theorists active at this time. It was a clever attempt to resolve the tension between the need for papal authority to be exercised throughout an expedition, and the clear prohibition in canon law on clerical participation in fighting.[14] But how practicable was it? Ramon Lull turned for his solution to the Military Orders, and the writing of the 'Liber de acquisitione Terrae Sanctae' coincided with the launching of the Hospitaller *passagium*. It is natural to look for links between the two events, and, although there is no evidence that Lull exercised a direct influence on Clement V, Helene Wieruszowski suggested that, in effect, the idea of the *bellator rex* was put into practice in Fulk of Villaret's *passagium*, both Lull's tract and Clement's crusade being attempted solutions to the chronic problem of control.[15] But this is too conceptualized a view of the Pope's aim, for it is clear from his letters about the crusade's command structure that his approach was essentially pragmatic.

The Pope entrusted leadership of the crusade jointly to Fulk of Villaret and a legate, Peter of Pleine Chassagne, the Bishop of Rodez; Fulk himself had suggested that it should be led by a legate, by analogy, so he believed, with the First Crusade, whose exploits he may have boasted that he would repeat.[16] But details of how this joint command would operate in practice were not given either in Peter's appointment as legate in June 1309,[17] or in the papal letter to the Hospitallers ordering them to co-operate with Peter. In the latter the Knights were told simply to honour the legate:

freely receiving him and his entourage, together with their belongings and victuals, in your vessels and galleys either alongside yourselves or

---

[13] Ibid., 66, 105–6.

[14] In the fifteenth century John Capgrave felt called upon to defend Bishop Henry Despenser's vigorous leadership of the Flanders crusade of 1383. See 'Liber de illustribus Henricis', 173–4, and cf. Throop, 31–4, 43.

[15] 'Ramon Lull et l'Idée de la Cité de Dieu: Quelques nouveaux écrits sur la Croisade', *Estudis franciscans*, xlvii (1935), 87–110. Also found in H. Wieruszowski, *Politics and Culture in Medieval Spain and Italy* (Rome, 1971), 147–71.

[16] *AA*, iii, n. 91, 199; *Cartulaire général*, iv, n. 4681, 106–7. See also *Papsttum und Untergang*, ii, n. 126, 243; Thier, 84–5n.

[17] *Reg. Clem. V*, n. 4392.

separately, as best can be arranged, for the benefit of the said enterprise
. . ., offering the legate the right arm of your aid for the defence and
protection of his person and people, as often as, and whenever,
necessary.[18]

It is not surprising that the expedition seems to have been guided
by Fulk alone to the achievement of a specifically Hospitaller
objective.[19] However, it is noticeable that our few references to
Peter of Pleine Chassagne after the *passagium*'s arrival in the East
do not reveal disappointment, or bitterness towards the Hospitallers. On the contrary, he appears to have regarded the enterprise as
a success, and in the summer of 1310, although largely preoccupied
with internal Cypriot affairs, he was awaiting the arrival of the
follow-up crusade which had been planned.[20] And far from showing
any dissatisfaction with his legate, Clement V promoted him to the
Patriarchate of Jerusalem in 1314, a post which kept Peter closely
involved with crusade projects until his death early in 1318.[21] This
forms an apt commentary on the vagueness which surrounds the
expedition's goals; throughout the crusade there is a strange contrast between Clement V's painstaking preparations and the Pope's
few and generalized references to what he expected it to achieve.[22]
This played right into the hands of men like Fulk of Villaret who
knew exactly what they wanted.

It is both logical and instructive to compare the *passagium* of
1309–10 with the one which the Hospitallers led to the East at the
end of our period. In the case of the latter there was a definite clash
about aims. Initially Gregory XI had ambitious hopes of co-
operation between the Order and Louis of Hungary against the
advancing Ottoman Turks. These collapsed when Louis proved
unhelpful, indeed quarrelled with the Pope and Master about a
nomination to the Hungarian Priory, but it is certain that Gregory
still wanted the *passagium* to engage the Turks. Master Robert of
Juilly, on the other hand, planned to use the troops to defend

---

[18] Ibid., n. 3753.
[19] Cf. A. T. Luttrell, 'The Hospitallers of Rhodes: Prospectives, Problems,
Possibilities', in *Die geistlichen Ritterorden Europas*, ed. J. Fleckenstein and M.
Hellmann (Sigmaringen, 1980), 250.
[20] See Hill, ii, 250 ff.; Golubovich, iii, 131–46.
[21] Ibid., iii, 146–53.
[22] See, for example, *Reg. Clem. V*, n. 2988. According to one source, Clement V
had become thoroughly disillusioned with minor *passagia* by 1314: CC, n. 614, and
cf. Housley, 'Pope Clement V', 40–1.

Smyrna and Rhodes, the two eastern outposts now in Hospitaller hands. In the end a number of factors combined to divert the expedition to Albania. First, the political situation in 1377–8 made it very difficult for the Knights to fight the Turks in a fruitful manner. Secondly, there were powerful forces pulling the crusade towards Albania: the Order's own interests at Vonitza and in Achaea, the interests of its Florentine financiers in Albania, and the Greek ambitions of Juan Fernández de Heredia, who succeeded Robert of Juilly as Master at the critical moment, in September 1377. Thirdly, Gregory XI too died in March 1378 without appointing a legate for the campaign, and his successor Urban VI took little interest in it. So it was that Gregory's carefully planned *passagium* against the Turks ended up being ambushed by Christians in an Albanian pass.[23]

The trouble was that neither Fulk of Villaret, Robert of Juilly nor Juan Fernández de Heredia had any intention of acting as Ramon Lull's obedient papal lieutenant. The Order had its own objectives, which certainly overlapped with those of the Curia but were not identical with them; from this point of view there was less difference than one might expect between the Hospitallers and a secular power. Nor was the Curia under any illusions about this. In the case of both *passagia* it saw its co-operation with the Order not as a means of avoiding having to rely on the leadership of secular rulers, but as a *faute de mieux* in the absence of such leadership. This is clear both from Clement V's constant attempts to involve Philip IV in the first *passagium*, and from Gregory XI's tireless work for peace in the 1370s. There is no evidence that the Avignonese Curia tried to effect a shift away from strong, secular leadership in the field. For all the caution which was displayed in the launching of an expedition, *efficatia* demanded that once it was underway the person in charge should take tactical and even strategic decisions.

The clearest proof of this is the freedom of action which the Curia allowed its own legates in Italy. Thus in May 1363 Urban V permitted Cardinal Albornoz to decide the direction of papal policy in northern Italy. Albornoz was to consider whether a peaceful settlement with Bernabò Visconti was feasible. If it was, he had *plena potestas* to establish terms; if it was not, the Pope guaranteed full financial support for continuing the holy war.[24] Two months

---

[23] See the fine analysis of these events in Luttrell, 'Gregory XI', 411–13.
[24] LM, n. 387.

later Urban wrote another letter to his legate covering various aspects of the crusade against Bernabò. Albornoz was given an assurance that his efforts would not be frustrated by the sudden cancellation of the crusade in favour of an expedition to the East, and was informed that a letter was on its way instructing him about the cases in which his preachers had authority to grant absolution. The Pope told Albornoz that he was to arrange crusade preaching in Italy 'as you see fit', and he enclosed a letter to Venice complaining about the Republic's hostility towards a papal ally, Francis of Carrara; this letter the legate was to present to the Doge 'if and in the manner which you consider appropriate'. On two important matters relating to the military conduct of the crusade and its diplomatic background Albornoz was thus given completely free rein.[25]

This remarkable independence of action enabled Albornoz, like his predecessor Bertrand Du Poujet, to become committed to a policy radically different from that desired at Avignon: indeed, such a situation came about very soon after Urban V's letter of July 1363.[26] If such a conflict of interests could occur in the case of papal legates, it was inevitable in that of crusading kings whose aims had from the start been incompatible with those of the Curia. In Spain and eastern Europe the preferred solution to the dual threat of deflection and premature conclusion was the complicated system of conditional grants and guarantees which we examined in a previous chapter: the Curia realized full well that if it did not incorporate its wishes in the early stages of planning, it had no chance of doing so later. It was possible legally to tie a ruler down to fighting for a certain period of time, with a given number of troops, to achieve a specified objective; or alternatively to agree on a plan of campaign like that established by Innocent VI and Louis of Hungary. But Louis's own career as a crusader is a good example of how unsuccessful both approaches were in practice, for attempts to exert control over the King's crusades failed almost totally.[27] Much the same was true in the Spanish kingdoms, where the legates appointed to supervise the expeditions against the Moors were usually native prelates who proved unreliable as the guardians of papal interests.[28]

---

[25] ASV, Reg. Vat. 245, f. 214[r–v].   [26] Filippini, 320 ff.
[27] Housley, 'King Louis the Great', *passim*.
[28] See, for example, *Reg. Clem. V*, n. 4049.

When these interests were themselves unstable or incoherent, the problem was naturally worsened. Confusion in papal policy played into the hands of secular leaders with clear ambitions which they were prepared to pursue with vigour. This was never truer than in 1365, when Peter of Cyprus captured and sacked Alexandria, dramatically reversing a thirty year old trend in the crusading movement—and papal policy—away from the south-east Mediterranean towards the Anatolian emirates. The Alexandria expedition is a classic example of how the general problem of control could be deepened by the temporary collapse of proper strategic thinking at the Curia.

When the crusading project was first put forward in 1363, its aims were twofold. Certainly it was intended to free the Holy Land. John of France, Peter I, and others took the cross 'for the recovery of the Holy Land', which had been enslaved and defiled by the Mamluks. But reference was also made to the plight of the eastern Christians at the hands of the advancing Turks. The deep geographical distinction involved was simply ignored by the Pope, who proclaimed the general passage 'to the said Holy Land and other parts of the East [occupied by] the infidels', wrote of the Mamluks and Turks as though they had common aims and problems, and expected the crusaders to deal with both enemies, a task greater than that given to any previous crusade to the East and wholly unrealistic from the start.[29] Nevertheless, in the ensuing years Urban gave fresh signs that this was his approach. Thus in 1364 he wrote to the Emperor John V that he would instruct the crusade's leaders to do no harm to the Greeks as they passed through his lands *en route* to Palestine. A reference in this letter to the crusaders deviating from their course in order to enter John's lands shows that the Pope at least had some awareness of the region's geography.[30] In January 1366 he hoped to persuade Peter I to send aid to the Greeks, although Cyprus was itself now threatened by the Mamluks,[31] and in October 1366 the Pope again linked *Saraceni* and *Turchi* as though there was no real difference between them.[32]

In one sense then, Peter cannot be said to have diverted the crusade, since papal policy in 1363–6 was so broad as to accom-

[29] *AE*, ad annum 1363, n. 15, xxvi, 82, Cf. LM, n. 1080.
[30] '. . . cum Christi fideles, in prefato profecturi passagio, ad partes tui imperii declinabunt': LM, n. 1305.
[31] *AE*, ad annum 1366, nn. 1–2, xxvi, 122.
[32] LM, n. 2416. Cf. *Acta Urbani V*, n. 166a.

modate any form of attack on the Muslims in the eastern Mediterranean. It is likely, indeed, that Urban V's chief interest in the
project was as a means of ridding France and Italy of the *routiers*; it
was into their recruitment that most of his energy was going, and
what happened in the East was of much less significance to him. His
attitude towards Bertrand Du Guesclin's 'crusade' to Spain followed similar lines.[33] From this point of view, he was quite happy to
relate the crusade to either or both of the policies pursued by his
predecessors at Avignon, the older plans for the recovery of
Palestine or the more recent defence of *Romania*. This, however,
does not answer the question of what the Pope *expected* of Peter's
expedition when it finally set sail in 1365.

There is some evidence that the Pope thought the King would
lead his troops to *Romania* to fight the Turks. In the letter in which
Peter Thomas was appointed as legate in July 1364, Urban described the aim of this preliminary campaign as the relief of the
eastern Christians; it may be significant that Peter's legatine area
excluded the Patriarchate of Alexandria.[34] But this could have been
a ploy to disguise the forthcoming assault on the city from those who
would have opposed it. It is noticeable that papal letters to Peter I at
this time do not specify either his objective or his enemy: even the
brief letter written after the expedition had set out, on 19 July 1365,
is totally uninformative on these points.[35] Similarly, had Urban
really expected the crusade to go to *Romania*, we would surely find
attempts to alert the Greeks of its approach, if not to organize joint
military action. Instead, the forthcoming campaign was not mentioned in the letter which Urban wrote to John V in October 1364.[36]

Other evidence indicates that the Pope had been informed of,
and had sanctioned, the attack on Alexandria. Urban was to
describe the city's capture as accomplished 'with the permission of
the Apostolic See'.[37] More convincingly, the attitude of Peter
Thomas on the crusade supports the view that Urban knew what
was to occur. He not only gave his blessing to the assault, but

[33] Housley, 'Mercenary Companies', 271–7.
[34] LM, n. 1080.
[35] ASV, Reg. Vat. 247, f. 131ᵛ; LM, n. 1724.
[36] Ibid., n. 1305. In April 1365 the Pope wrote to John V that he was trying to
scrape together a western league to come to his aid, again omitting all mention of the
forces assembling at Venice: ibid., n. 1703.
[37] Ibid., n. 2416. The Venetians had been informed that an assault might be made.
See *Nouvelles preuves*, i, 71n.

exhorted the crusaders to remain in the captured city, arguing in terms of the honour of God, of Christendom's benefit, and of 'the possession of the city of Jerusalem through the retention of Alexandria'.[38] In the moving letter which he wrote after the sack, Jerusalem figures prominently.[39] Since the legate had worked so hard in *Romania* in 1359–61, it is difficult to accept that he would have backed the King so strongly had he been a witness to the expedition's diversion from that area and its terrible need for help. Rather, he seems to be expressing the belief of the Curia that a *tempus acceptabile* had come into being and that the old strategy of exchanging Alexandria for Jerusalem could be made to work.[40]

It is highly unlikely that we can ever find out with certainty what Urban wanted of the 1365 crusade, since none of the evidence constitutes a reliable guide to papal aims. This uncertainty is symptomatic of the confusion which characterized Urban's policy in the East. Even if we accept the argument that he was thinking chiefly of Western problems, this was a startling, if temporary, abandonment of the Curia's historic responsibility for organizing the defence of Christians in the eastern Mediterranean. The lame inclusion of the defence of *Romania* in the project shows that the Pope felt guilty about diverting valuable resources from the struggle against the Turks. The Pope created the ideal conditions for Peter of Cyprus to achieve his objective.[41]

The reign of Urban V presents a picture of very loose, spasmodic, and ineffectual papal influence over crusading activity in the eastern Mediterranean; there are, for example, very few letters indeed relating to the expedition of Amedeo of Savoy once it had been launched. But it is important to remember that this was unusual. We shall now examine a period in total contrast, Clement VI's direction of the Smyrna crusade between 1343 and 1351. There are several differences. To begin with, we have the advantage of ample and generally reliable documentation lasting for several years, in the form of the Pope's correspondence. The Curia's aim was relatively specific, to inflict as much damage as possible on the sea power of the Anatolian emirates. Its own commitment was substantial, for there were four papal galleys in the naval league. And it was

---

[38] Philip of Mézières, 127–8, 133–4.

[39] Ibid., 135–40.

[40] Cf. Halecki, *Un Empereur*, 102–3.

[41] For the quite separate issue of what Peter wanted, see Edbury, 'Crusading Policy', *passim*.

presided over by a pope with great political and administrative experience. In such favourable circumstances, and with so much at stake, what degree of control could the Curia achieve?

The immediate precedent for Clement's league was the *unio* of 1334, the contributors to which had already wrestled with the problem of combining military efficiency with the semi-autonomy which they wanted their own galleys to retain. In the agreement of 1332 which eventually gave rise to the league, the Venetians, Greeks, and Hospitallers decided that while each would appoint their own captain,

a single captain will be chosen to command all the said twenty galleys, committing them to an engagement or battle, or declining to do so, as he sees fit. All will be obliged to obey him in such cases, and he is to be chosen from the Venetians, and picked by the Lord Doge and his Commune.[42]

In the expanded league of 1334, Venice handed over the appointment of this officer to Philip VI, but stipulated that the captain-in-chief must be guided by a majority vote. The lesser captains exercised full authority over their own galleys in judicial and disciplinary matters.[43]

Our information on the 1334 league is too meagre to form conclusions about how Philip VI's captain-in-chief, John of Cepoy, handled his severely limited powers, but it is likely that Clement VI realized from the start that Venice's insistence on the semi-autonomy of its contingent precluded tight control of his league's command structure.[44] So too did Clement's own interpretation of the league, his insistence that he was not its *caput* and could not accept overall responsibility for the outlay of money by its members. Nevertheless, in the autumn of 1343 the Pope attempted to bind the various members of his league together by appointing a legate, the Latin Patriarch of Constantinople, Henry of Asti, to accompany the galleys to the East.[45] In a series of letters Clement tried to invest Henry with the powers which he would need to hold the league together and give it direction and thrust. Thus he was authorized to replace Martin Zaccaria, the Genoese captain of the papal galleys, should Martin prove incompetent; and he could compel the captains of all the league's galleys to obey his orders by

[42] *DVL*, i, n. 117.
[43] *AE*, ad annum 1334, nn. 7–9, xxv, 3–4.
[44] See *Délibérations*, i, 202.
[45] *Diplomatari de l'orient català*, n. 181. See also Déprez *et al.*, nn. 388–90.

using Church sanctions against them if they refused.[46] Clement knew, however, that it was the paymasters who mattered, so Venice and King Hugh of Cyprus were asked to support Henry's authority, and the Hospitallers taking part in the campaign were instructed to help settle any quarrels which might occur.[47]

As in 1310 and 1365, papal authority was represented in the field by a legate, but this time by a legate whose terms of commission were fairly well-defined. The league was to take offensive action against the emirates, which in practice meant the most powerful of the emirs, Umur of Aydin.[48] Henry was ordered 'not to allow the flotilla of galleys to be deflected from its proper course or to be held up in any way'.[49] Given the league's ramshackle constitution, this was no easy thing to do. It was difficult even to exercise firm control over the papal galleys. John Amiel was instructed to exact an oath of obedience to the legate from the owners and sailors of the four vessels, but there were still desertions.[50] For authority over the other galleys in the league the Pope relied largely on his influence with the Venetian and Cypriot governments; for example, he supported Peter Zeno, the captain of the Venetian galleys, and recommended that his appointment be extended.[51]

It is no surprise, therefore, that the threat of diversion arose at an early stage in the league's activities. It took two forms. The papal captain, Martin Zaccaria, proposed an assault on the island of Chios, which the Greeks had seized from his family in 1329. Martin had been held in captivity by the Greeks for several years after the island's capture, and it is highly probable that he viewed the league as a means of recovering Chios: presumably he argued the importance of the island as a strategic base for an attack on Smyrna.[52] According to a papal letter to Henry of Asti in September 1344, the captain was already diverting Clement's galleys against Chios, and the Archbishop of Thebes, Henry's lieutenant, was threatening the

[46] Ibid., nn. 405–7.   [47] Ibid., nn. 408, 412.
[48] This was not stated in the papal letters, but was dictated by Umur's predominance in 1342–3. See Lemerle, 182n.
[49] Déprez *et al.*, n. 409.
[50] Ibid., nn. 413, 815–17.
[51] Ibid., n. 882.
[52] Lemerle, 185, 187n; Balard, i, 119ff., 467ff.; W. Miller, 'The Zaccaria of Phocaea and Chios (1275–1329)', *Journal of Hellenic Studies*, xxxi (1911), 42–55, esp. 49–51; Zachariadou, 7–9, 16–17. In October 1343 Clement VI had absolved Martin of an oath which the Greeks had extracted before releasing him, to the effect that he would not take part in an attack on their Empire: *Acta Clem. V*, n. 23.

Cypriots with excommunication if they refused to co-operate. This sequence of events was driving the Greeks to conduct negotiations with the Turks and would wreck hopes of Union; Clement insisted that it should stop.[53]

Just ten days earlier, however, the Pope had himself reacted to pleas from the Armenians by instructing Henry of Asti to send them help if it was at all possible: 'We wish that you do not delay in sending the King of Armenia naval aid and all other forms of help and opportune backing which you can reasonably supply'.[54] With less than thirty galleys, it is hard to see how Henry could have done this without either committing his full resources to Armenia, or so splitting up the league's galleys as to make their military value derisory. The danger of diversion, then, did not only come from self-seeking individuals like Martin Zaccaria; indeed, from the strategic viewpoint, his proposal made better sense than Clement's.

Soon after the capture of Smyrna another of the classic problems of control, the incompetence of delegated leadership, threatened to destroy the league's efforts. Clement VI saw the weak link in the command structure as Martin Zaccaria: in September 1344, and again in February 1345, he told Henry of Asti to sack the captain if he did not start to display better qualities.[55] But it was probably the legate's foolhardiness and obstinacy which committed the Christians to the skirmish of St Anthony's Day, 1345, which resulted in the deaths of Martin Zaccaria, Peter Zeno, and Henry himself.[56] Short of a total débâcle a greater blow could scarcely be imagined, but the Pope set to work to make fresh appointments to the vacant positions, telling the army at Smyrna to obey the orders of the vice-legate, Archbishop Francis of Crete, while awaiting their new leaders.[57] But it was at this point that Humbert of Vienne entered the picture. Towards the end of May 1345 he was designated 'captain of the holy Apostolic See and leader of the whole army of Christians against the Turks', receiving the cross from the hands of the Pope himself.[58] A Bolognese chronicler wrote

---

[53] Déprez *et al.*, n. 1113.   [54] Ibid., nn. 1086–7.

[55] Ibid., nn. 1114, 1464.

[56] John Cantacuzenus blamed Henry of Asti. See Lemerle, 191.

[57] Déprez *et al.*, nn. 1569–72, 1603–9, 1668, 1676. See also *Délibérations*, i, 208–9, 310–11.

[58] 'Capitaneus sanctae sedis apostolicae et dux totius exercitus christianorum contra Turchos': *AE*, ad annum 1345, n. 6, xxv, 358–9. Cf. Déprez *et al.*, nn. 1748–50.

that the Dauphin was given three standards by Clement VI, including one showing the papal arms, symbolic of his lieutenancy.[59]

How did Humbert's appointment alter the distribution of authority within the league? Its main consequence was to complicate still further the issue of control. Humbert's position was one of command, and the vice-legate and other leaders were told to receive him with due reverence.[60] He was in charge of the four papal galleys, and also of the soldiers whom Clement was hoping to recruit in southern Italy in the summer of 1345. In addition, he led a sizeable contingent of his own, at least 100 men-at-arms who were supposed to remain with him in the East for the duration of the naval league, or at least for three years: he was under oath to this effect. In practice however, and despite his high-sounding title, Humbert's authority over the Venetians and Cypriots was no stronger than Henry of Asti's had been; indeed, Venetian influence within the league probably grew with Humbert's arrival, as the Dauphin was accompanied by four Venetian advisers.[61] And as we have seen, he had little control over the flow of voluntary recruits brought to Smyrna by the wave of popular crusading zeal in 1345–6.

The Dauphin's relations with the Pope, too, were ill-defined, reflecting the difficulty which the Curia faced in establishing a theoretical framework for this crusade. Humbert's status in the West prevented Clement treating him as a mere official of the Holy See. More importantly, he received very little financial backing from the Curia for the troops whom he led East.[62] He secured 6,000 florins from the tenth in August 1345,[63] but no specific grants of taxes, [64] and in 1349, replying to a letter of financial complaints, Clement claimed, quite correctly, that before the Dauphin left for the East it was agreed between them that the Church would not be responsible for his expenses.[65] Humbert had rich lands which he was able to tax for his crusade, but he still ended up with heavy debts, partly because of his own extravagance.

---

[59] 'Cronica di Bologna', cols. 396–7. Clement mentioned only one standard in his letter of appointment.

[60] Déprez *et al.*, n. 1837, and cf. n. 2580.

[61] *Régestes,* i, 58.

[62] Cf. *AE*, ad annum 1345, n. 6, xxv, 358–9.

[63] Déprez *et al.*, n. 1906.

[64] Giovanni Villani was probably wrong when he stated that Humbert's troops were paid by the Church, as also in his claim that the transportation costs of crusaders going to Smyrna were borne by the Pope: bk. 12, ch. 39, iv, 68–70.

[65] Déprez *et al.*, n. 4218.

So although Humbert's cautious and indecisive character led him to ask for detailed instructions and advice from the Pope, these could not be orders like those to Patriarch Henry, and one of the reasons why the Dauphin's campaign failed so miserably was his deep uncertainty about his own position. This emerged very clearly when the time came to negotiate a truce with Umur of Aydin: Clement was prepared either to give his captain-general plenipotentiary powers (like those given to Albornoz in 1363), or to examine and ratify the terms himself. It was up to Humbert which he chose, and characteristically he picked the latter.[66] On the other hand, the historian has cause to be grateful for Humbert's weakness because it gave rise to three detailed letters from the Pope to his *dux*, written in the course of 1346 and discussing points raised both about the papal galleys and about the general conduct of the league and crusade. Brief and unsuccessful as it was, this correspondence yields valuable insights into the relations between a pope and a commander in the field: the best-documented ones, in fact, since Charles of Anjou and Clement IV worked together for the conquest of the Kingdom of Sicily eighty years earlier.

The Pope's first detailed letter is dated 15 June 1346, when Humbert was at Negroponte; in it Clement replied to queries raised about several issues. Humbert had brought up the question of Chios, the wealth and strategic position of which attracted him as much as they had Martin Zaccaria.[67] The Pope agreed that the island would be useful as a base if it was held in conjunction with Smyrna; he consented to write to Anna of Savoy requesting that the Greeks place it in Latin hands for three years, the planned duration of Humbert's expedition. Similarly, the Pope allowed the Dauphin to negotiate with Anna on the subject of Church Union, though not with her rival, John Cantacuzenus; Humbert was warned against allowing his forces to be dragged into the Greek civil war. Clement agreed to suspend for three years the sentences of excommunication and interdict imposed on the Catalan Grand Company, in the hope that its members could be persuaded to help the Smyrna garrison. Humbert was permitted to coin money for the use of the league, and Clement assured him that he would not recall the papal

---

[66] Ibid., n. 2957.

[67] Lemerle argued (196n, 200n, 202) that the struggle for Chios lay at the heart of Humbert's actions in the East. This is an attractive explanation of a campaign which otherwise seems lacking in thrust; but it remains conjectural. Cf. Thiriet, 167.

galleys or replace his vice-legate, and that he was working with Venice and Cyprus for the active continuation of the league.[68]

Clearly Humbert was thinking in some depth about the problems facing him. He was quite rightly convinced of the need to get further reinforcements, and since the Anglo-French war was preventing many westerners getting through, he was actively casting about for sources of manpower in the East, notably the Greeks and Catalans; in March 1346 he tried to persuade the government of Crete to send mounted troops, footsoldiers, and archers.[69] His interest in the Catalans is especially significant, showing that he was not caught up in the sterile schemes of vengeance and reconquest which had long constituted the approach of the French and Neapolitan courts towards the Catalan presence in Greece: things looked different from Negroponte and Smyrna. Yet Humbert's fears about papal withdrawal and his request that Clement send him frequent couriers with letters boded ill. There was too much thinking and writing, and not enough action. The Pope did what he could. Letters went out from the Curia to Anna of Savoy, the vice-legate, the members of the league, and others, all trying to give effect to the points agreed on by the Pope and Humbert.[70]

It was up to Humbert to get things done, and he was dilatory and unlucky. For instance, he came off the worse in an entanglement with a Genoese flotilla under Simon Vignoso, who seized Chios before the Dauphin could get there.[71] Disappointed, Humbert proceeded to Smyrna in late June 1346. By this time there were several thousand fighting men in the port, but the Dauphin proved unable to evolve a plan of action beyond a few sorties and a programme of fortification. The Venetians, who had achieved their objective, were half-hearted in their support for further military activity. Ill and dispirited, Humbert sailed on to Rhodes and spent the winter of 1346-7 there.

This was the unpromising background to the two letters which Clement VI wrote to Humbert on 28 November 1346. His main theme was that there was no hope of more men and money from the West. The contingent which was to have been led by Robert of San Severino at the Church's expense could not leave for the East

---

[68] Déprez *et al.*, n. 2580, and cf. n. 2581.
[69] *Délibérations*, i, 209–10, 311.
[70] Déprez *et al.*, nn. 2582–95.
[71] See Giorgio Stella, 147–9, for the Genoese view of events.

because of the Hungarian threat to the *Regno*; crusaders could not go to Smyrna because their services were demanded at home; tenths and subsidies could not be collected and the *camera* could not support the burden single-handed any longer. Possibly under pressure from the Venetians, Humbert had raised the question of a truce. The Pope eagerly took it up, replying that it was not only expedient but essential. It should be negotiated with the other members of the league and should only last ten years; by that time Clement hoped that the Christian advance could be renewed. Humbert's vow to remain in the East for three years was waived, but he was warned not to use the truce as cover for an attack on John Cantacuzenus: even at this late stage the Curia feared a diversion.[72] As in June, these letters to Humbert were backed up by a stream of papal mandates intended to give them effect.[73] Gradually Humbert was released from his obligations. In March 1347 he was permitted to return to the West despite the fact that he had not succeeded in negotiating a truce with Umur; his confessor was to absolve him of his vow to stay in the East for three years.[74] Grief-stricken by his wife's death, his expedition a failure, and his debts mounting, the Dauphin returned to Grenoble via Venice.

Humbert had gone but the league and garrison remained. It was typical of the Dauphin's luck that the league's galleys scored a notable victory over the Turks at Imbros soon after he left for Venice. Clement congratulated the vice-legate and the Master of the Hospitallers on this success: presumably command was again vested in the Archbishop of Crete, with the special backing of Rhodes.[75] But Imbros did not make a truce any less necessary, and it was now papal policy to make the terms of this truce as favourable as possible for a rapid renewal of the crusade once peace in the West made that possible. With this in mind Clement rejected the truce which Octavian Zaccaria negotiated with Umur of Aydin and Hizir of Ephesus in the winter of 1347–8, on the grounds that it entailed the destruction of the harbour fortress.[76] After the death of Umur in an assault on Smyrna, in April or May 1348,[77] the Christians secured better terms which guaranteed an end to Turkish piracy and

[72] Déprez *et al.*, nn. 2956–7.
[73] Ibid., nn. 2958–9, 2962, 2974; Déprez and Mollat, n. 1273.
[74] Déprez *et al.*, nn. 3179–80.
[75] Ibid., nn. 3336–7.
[76] Ibid., n. 3728; Déprez and Mollat, n. 1563.
[77] Lemerle, 228; Zachariadou, 55. Cf. Déprez and Mollat, n. 1697.

good trading conditions.[78] But Clement continued to delay the settlement. In the autumn of 1349 he asked Venice and Cyprus to send envoys to the Curia to decide whether to make peace or renew the struggle. The *camera* could contribute nothing, but if the two powers could raise the money between them, Clement was prepared to release fresh indulgences and to send out exhortatory letters in their support.[79]

Despite his own refusal to grant funds, and growing tension between Venice and Genoa, it seemed for a time in 1350 as if Clement would manage to get the league renewed, mainly because the Venetians were concerned about Turkish infringements of the truce.[80] In August the Pope announced the formation of a modified league, comprising eight galleys supplied by the Venetians, Cypriots, and Hospitallers. As in 1334 and 1343, semi-autonomy triumphed. A papal legate would be in overall command, together with a captain-general appointed by him; they had the power to impose fines of up to 10,000 florins on people who defied them. But they had no right to intervene in the running of individual galleys, and they had to abide by majority decisions on military matters.[81] The ground was thus prepared for a recurrence of the problems faced by the Smyrna crusade, had the new league not been cut short by the outbreak of the Veneto-Genoese war.[82]

Why was papal direction throughout the Smyrna crusade so much more effective than in any other expedition in our period? The answer lies in the nature of the league: a group of Latin powers with broadly compatible aims—initially at any rate—which needed a single leader whom they could trust more than they could each other. Like warring Catholic kings who accepted papal mediation, they tolerated papal control, within strict limits, because it suited them. And Clement VI was prepared to exercise that control, contrary to normal papal practice, because *efficatia* demanded it.

---

[78] *DVL*, i, nn. 168–9.

[79] Ibid., i, n. 172. See also Déprez and Mollat, nn. 2060, 2080, 2193, and cf. nn. 2024, 2078.

[80] See Lemerle, 233–4; Setton, *PL*, 219–20.

[81] *AE*, ad annum 1350, n. 33, xxv, 492; *I libri comm.*, ii, 184, n. 352. Cf. arrangements in 1357 and 1369: ibid., ii, 261, n. 225, iii, 84, n. 512. On the latter occasion mistrust between Genoa and Venice was so deep that they agreed to exercise command on alternate days.

[82] *I libri comm.*, ii, 185, n. 354; *Régestes*, i, 71; *DVL*, ii, n. 1; Déprez *et al.*, nn. 5052, 5056.

This is not to play down the crusade's achievement: triumphing over the ramshackle nature of its constitution, and the incompetence and diversionary tactics of some of its leaders, the league showed by its successes that Latin powers with common goals could still co-operate fruitfully under the cohesive authority of the Holy See.[83] This was significant.

But it was also exceptional: for taking a broader perspective, it is clear that the Avignonese Curia had no more success in regulating the progress of its crusades than earlier popes had enjoyed. It was not to be expected that the Avignon popes would find a solution which had evaded Innocent III. At the beginning of the period the concept was created of the ideal crusade leader, the *bellator rex*, a man obedient to the pope, determined to keep the crusade on course, wise, able, and energetic. But the closest the Curia got to Ramon Lull's ideal was the captaincy of Humbert of Vienne, who was not only obedient but almost totally dependent on papal guidance. If a man could be controlled, he would be a Humbert. *Efficatia* and reliability were incompatible—this was the heart of the problem.

The activities of three leaders of better calibre than Humbert, all active in the 1360s, throw light on the issue in different ways. Amedeo of Savoy managed his expedition with scarcely any reference to the Curia; by displaying firmness and independence, and adapting his aims to the rapidly changing political circumstances which he encountered in *Romania*, he achieved much without falling out of line with papal policy. Louis of Hungary also made some gains, but they were not what the Curia wanted, and often not what the King agreed to do. His career epitomized the problem of control at its worst. Peter of Cyprus used a crusade to bring about a result in the short-term interests of his Kingdom; whether it was what the Pope wanted is open to question. Peter's case is most interesting because its background was deep and grievous confusion within the Curia's crusade policy. That this confusion did not prevent Amedeo, Louis, and Peter from planning and embarking on crusades is a telling illustration of the extent to which initiative now resided with the lay powers in the promotion and execution of crusading projects.

---

[83] Cf. Robson, 395, 402, on the sheer difficulty of maintaining a fleet a long way from its base in the mid-fourteenth century, without the additional problem of international co-operation.

8

The Papacy and the Military Orders: Templars, Teutonic Knights, and Hospitallers

IT is logical to follow an examination of the Curia's very mixed fortunes in controlling crusades in the field by looking at papal relations with the great Military Orders. Here at least, it may be thought, the popes had a good chance of getting their wishes carried out. The Orders owed their very existence to papal ratification, and much of their power and wealth to papal backing during their period of growth; and in the fourteenth century the Curia continued to function as the Orders' court of appeal and as their ultimate protector against secular encroachment on their privileged status.[1] But in practice things were not that simple: the Orders did not see their role as the agents of papal policy and, to the extent that the Holy See was able to influence their actions, it did so by exerting pressure, even force, rather than by simply issuing orders. The fortunes and activities of all three great Orders were certainly shaped by the papacy, but it acted as one factor amongst many.

In 1305 the three Orders were all long-established institutions. The Order of the Hospital of St John of Jerusalem was recognized as an international Order in 1113; the Order of the Knights Templar followed soon after and the Order of St Mary of the Germans, the Teutonic Knights, was founded in 1198. The Orders were very much children of their age. They would not have been possible if contemporaries had not believed that Christians could fulfil a religious vocation by fighting, and that others could benefit from the holy work of the knight-brothers by endowing them with lands and rents; this belief originated in a complicated but decisive break-through in Christian thinking about sacred violence which occurred between about 1050 and the Council of Troyes in 1128. Also

[1] See Riley-Smith, *Knights of St John*, 43 ff., 375–89; Barber, *Trial of the Templars*, 8 ff.

instrumental in the dramatic early growth of the Orders was the accelerating economic revival of the twelfth century, which facilitated the creation of the vast landed estates of the knight-brothers at the same time as those of other new Orders of the Church. And the Military Orders also 'belonged' to the twelfth century in the sense that their charitable aims were part of an important movement in Christian sensibility which placed the expression of brotherly love at the centre of a Latin Christian's aspirations.[2]

As in the case of all religious Orders, enthusiasm was soon followed by criticism.[3] By the early thirteenth century Christians both in the Holy Land and in the West began to portray the failings of the Military Orders in Syria as one of the reasons for the faltering defence of the Frankish states and the setbacks which befell the crusading expeditions. Two criticisms in particular were directed against the Orders. One, wholly conventional but nonetheless damaging, focused on the Knights' supposed shortcomings as regular clergy; it was written that they had lost their initial purity and vigour and had succumbed to such vices as pride, intemperance, greed, deceit, and envy. The second criticism was probably more dangerous. It was that the Knights had started to act contrary to the best interests of those entrusted to their care by their political relations with the Muslims, their hesitation before embarking on military campaigns, and their unwillingness to make fresh conquests. Although there were good reasons for such behaviour, it appeared as a betrayal of holy war to those who had disasters to explain or who arrived in Syria for a short visit with crusade vows to discharge. It seemed that the Knights could not win: by the mid-thirteenth century some commentators were acknowledging that the Orders were committed to holy war, but they saw this as a vested interest which meant that the Orders had no reason to aim at a decisive Christian victory.[4]

The loss of the Holy Land in 1291 appears to have aggravated the criticism levelled against the Military Orders; despite the heroism

---

[2] Riley-Smith, *Knights of St John*, *passim*; id., 'Crusading as an Act of Love', *History*, lxv (1980), 177–92. There is a brief but good account of all the Palestinian Orders in J. Prawer, *The Latin Kingdom of Jerusalem: European Colonialism in the Middle Ages* (London, 1972), 252–79.

[3] Cf. M. Barber, 'The Social Context of the Templars', *Transactions of the Royal Historical Society*, 5th Series, xxxiv (1984), 27–46.

[4] Riley-Smith, *Knights of St John*, 201 ff.; Barber, *Trial of the Templars,* 11 ff.

displayed by individual brethren, the Orders were blamed by some for the fall of Acre. Ideas for improving the efficiency of the Orders and reviving their enthusiasm concentrated on their unification, an approach espoused by many leading theorists but rejected by the Master of the Templars, James of Molay. United or not, the Orders were looked upon as an important weapon in the discussions of the period 1291–1307 about a Christian reconquest of Palestine.[5] But their vulnerability is undeniable. They had enemies of power and influence and their general popularity was low: a scapegoat was badly needed to account for the loss of Palestine.[6] This was the background to the events of the morning of 13 October 1307, when royal officials throughout France arrested all but a handful of the Templars in the Kingdom on the charge of heresy. The arrests formed the first act of a tragedy which culminated in Clement V's suppression of the Order at the Council of Vienne in 1312.

Although it led to the destruction of a great crusading Order, the trial of the Templars is explicable chiefly in terms of internal French developments. Naturally it was facilitated by the Order's unpopularity in the period after the fall of Acre, by the widespread feeling that the Knights lacked a role. But throughout the trial the motive force came from the financial needs and political thinking of the French government, which exploited the Knights' unpopularity and Clement V's weakness, as well as reacting to strong psychological factors at Philip IV's court. The arrests of October 1307 were in themselves a frightening demonstration of how efficiently royal power could operate, and proof of the ease with which the Inquisition could be perverted, for the royal agents functioned technically as the secular arm of the French Inquisitor, William of Paris, who was a creature of the King. It is thus unnecessary to examine the trial in detail.[7] What we do need to look at is the part played by Clement V, since the trial inevitably became an important element in the shaping of later relations between the Curia and the Military Orders.

Clement accurately assessed the arrests of October 1307 as an unprecedented attack on the temporal status of the Catholic Church, fully realizing that if he allowed Philip the Fair to destroy

---

[5] A. J. Forey, 'The Military Orders in the Crusading Proposals of the late Thirteenth and early Fourteenth Centuries', *Traditio*, xxxvi (1980), 317–45.

[6] On this theme, see in particular Barber, *Trial of the Templars*, 243–7.

[7] For a good, recent study see ibid., *passim*. The following three paragraphs are based largely on this account.

the Templars in this way then no churchmen and no Church possessions would be safe. In addition, he saw the King's action as a flagrant insult to the Holy See, the superior and protector of the Order. His initial reaction was thus one of fury, and in a letter of 27 October he criticized Philip bitterly. But he could not simply order the King to release the imprisoned Knights; all he could do was to establish an official Church inquiry in the hope of making it a fair one, in the meantime safeguarding the persons and property of the Templars. This he did with the bull *Pastoralis preeminentiae* (22 November 1307), which asked all Christian rulers to arrest the Templars in their lands. In February 1308 he suspended the activities of the French Inquisition as he became convinced that the confessions which it had received after the October arrests had been extracted by the use of torture.

Philip IV reacted to this surprisingly tough papal approach by summoning a meeting of the French Estates, which convened at Tours in May 1308, heard the royal ministers denounce the Templars, and obediently backed Philip's actions against them. Soon afterwards Philip descended on Poitiers and engaged in a fierce battle of wills with the Pope. Clement behaved courageously in the face of great pressure—it was less than five years since the outrage at Anagni. But he finally yielded by inaugurating his own judicial inquiry in July and August 1308. This was to take two forms. An episcopal inquiry in each French diocese would investigate individual Templars, while papal commissions would be set up in all Christian states to hold general inquiries. The bull *Regnans in coelis* (August 1308) announced that a general council would assemble at Vienne in October 1310 to consider the reports of the commissions and deliberate on the Order's fate.

The Vienne Council finally met in October 1311. To some extent Clement had succeeded in keeping the initiative: the Council was ecumenical, it met outside the Kingdom of France—though only just—and it stood in the great thirteenth-century tradition of Church councils, with similar aims, the reform of the Church and the preparation of a general passage to the Holy Land. But Philip IV's influence was to prove almost as heavy as three years earlier at Poitiers, for a third of the archbishops and bishops, and a half of the abbots, came from France. Nevertheless, the findings of the papal commissions failed to convince the Council of Templar guilt and by the end of 1311 many were calling for another chance for the

Knights to mount a defence. Clement might have given in but for
the arrival of Philip IV in March 1312. In reaction to royal pressure
the Pope finally prohibited debate and on 3 April announced his
decision to suppress the Order, using his plenitude of power.

Clement V's failure to save the Templars has to be viewed in the
context of the French initiative which began the affair and dominated it throughout. Whatever the motives of Philip IV were,[8] his
charges against the Knights were thin and met with scepticism both
from other secular rulers and from Clement himself.[9] But the vigour
of the French attack, coming at a time of papal weakness, put the
Curia on the defensive. Moreover, Clement was protecting not just
the Templars, but also the standing of the Holy See in the perilous
post-Anagni period. When it became clear that the Order could be
saved only at the cost of the unity, perhaps the very fabric, of
Christendom, the Pope was prepared to abandon it in order to
secure other, more limited, objectives. Thus the Order was suppressed rather than condemned; its property, with the exception of
that in Iberia, was to be transferred to the Hospitallers to maintain
the struggle against the infidel; and the French stopped insisting on
judicial proceedings against the memory of Boniface VIII.

How did the fall of the Templars affect the other Orders?[10] The
Order of the Knights Templar had been destroyed on the basis of
unpopularity, hearsay, and evidence extracted under torture: at
first sight, a dangerous precedent. But to approach the issue
properly we have to realize the exact nature of the gravamen
directed against the Orders. Military Orders were not considered to
be contrary to Christian belief, or redundant, any more than was the
crusade itself. Rather, the Orders were increasingly coming into
collision with secular authority on financial and political grounds.
First, those in high secular office were acutely aware of the
resources controlled by the Orders, reserves of land, wealth, and
manpower which they usually exaggerated. Secondly, the privileged status of the brethren was viewed as a serious infringement of
sovereignty, potentially more dangerous than that of other religious
Orders because of the political activity of the Knights. Thirdly,
these concerns, which in essence stretched back to the thirteenth

[8] See review of Barber's book by G. M. Spiegel in *Speculum*, lv (1980), 329–32.
[9] See S. Menache, 'Contemporary Attitudes concerning the Templars' Affair:
Propaganda's Fiasco?', *JMH*, viii (1982), 135–47.
[10] For the Hospitallers and the trial, see Luttrell, 'The Hospitallers of Rhodes',
249–52.

century, acquired greater relevance in the fourteenth because of growing financial pressure on governments and heightened national rivalries. Thus a line of thought was pursued and policies adopted which were precisely analogous to the question of crusade taxes, and the Orders were placed under pressure very similar to that encountered by the Curia in its protracted negotiations about taxes on the Church.[11]

This was clear from Philip the Fair's action against the Templars which, while it certainly sprang from his desire for their money, was justified in terms of sovereignty. But it was at the Aragonese court that the viewpoint of the secular powers was expressed with greatest clarity and self-confidence, thanks in part to the tradition of the *Reconquista* and the tight control exercised over the Church. Typical were the arguments put forward by James II in a letter to the Master of the Hospitallers written in about 1325. The King was angered by Hélion of Villeneuve's refusal to bestow either the Castellany of Amposta or the Priory of Catalonia on royal candidates. According to James, the Master had consistently turned down his requests, showing contempt for the Aragonese branch of the Order and failing to acknowledge the generosity of James's ancestors. The King insisted that the practice of vesting both Castellany and Priory in the Master's lieutenants should end, and that Castellan and Prior should be Aragonese by birth. Apart from the customary responsions, the revenues of the Hospitallers in Aragon should stay there,

so that what has customarily been the case, and ought to be, continues to be so: that is, that if we require the services of the brethren of the said Order of the Hospital for the defence of the Kingdom or for offensive action against the enemies of the orthodox Faith, we can have that service in proper fashion, to the praise of the divine name and the benefit and use of our realm.[12]

A voice in the appointment of high-ranking Hospitaller officials; reluctance to allow coinage to travel outside the kingdom; insistence on the proper performance of military service owed to the crown—such demands were by no means new.[13] But they were expressed with a new sharpness of tone, and the loss of Latin

---

[11] See above, ch. 5 *passim*; Luttrell, 'The Hospitallers of Rhodes', 252.

[12] *Documenta selecta*, n. 419.

[13] Cf. A. T. Luttrell, 'The Aragonese Crown and the Knights Hospitallers of Rhodes: 1291–1350', *EHR*, lxxvi (1961), 1–19.

Syria gave this tone added edge. Thus James II would not permit the export of Aragonese revenue to pay off Hospitaller debts, 'especially since the Holy Land, *peccatis christianorum exigentibus*, is no longer in the hands or power of the Christians, as it used to be'.[14] There was only one solution open to the Hospitallers and the Teutonic Knights: to find a function which would justify their resources and privileges, compel the Curia to give them its full support against aggressive lay rulers like Philip IV and James II, and enlist the sympathy of public opinion. While this approach could not protect the Orders from secular attack, it would rob that attack of a valuable argument, and both Orders rapidly pursued it.

In 1291 the Hospitallers, like the Templars, set up their headquarters in Cyprus. This was unsatisfactory as a long-term base because it involved the Order in Lusignan politics and deprived it of the freedom of action attached to an independent lordship. The initiative for the move to Rhodes appears to have originated with the Master, Fulk of Villaret. Between 1306 and 1310 he conducted the negotiations and warfare which were necessary for the subjugation of the island.[15] The role of the Pope in this sequence of events was minimal. In September 1307 he formally confirmed the Order in its possession of Rhodes, but was probably unaware of the significance of the acquisition. To the Hospitallers, who quickly moved both convent and hospital to the island, the importance of Rhodes was clear. It was well placed for intervention in Anatolia, Syria or Greece and had some commercial value in itself. The defence and colonization of Rhodes were soon being systematically planned.[16]

In 1310, the same year that Fulk of Villaret demonstrated the continuing usefulness of his Order by leading a *passagium* East, the Grand Master of the Teutonic Knights, Siegfried of Feuchtwangen, transferred the administration of his Order from its temporary base at Venice to Marienburg in Prussia. The move had been prepared by the series of crusades spearheaded by the Teutonic Knights in Prussia in the thirteenth century; and more specifically by the acquisition, using underhand methods, of eastern Pomerania and

[14] *Documenta selecta*, n. 419.
[15] Riley-Smith, *Knights of St John*, 198–226; Luttrell, 'Hospitallers at Rhodes', 281–6.
[16] *Reg. Clem. V*, n. 2148; A. T. Luttrell, 'Feudal Tenure and Latin Colonization at Rhodes: 1306–1415', *EHR*, lxxxv (1970), 755–75.

Danzig in 1308–9.[17] The transfer to Prussia was more dramatic than the Hospitaller move to Rhodes, cutting off the Teutonic Knights completely from the defence of the Latin East. Instead the Knights placed their function as a Military Order firmly in the context of defending Prussia and Livonia against the assaults of the pagan Lithuanians and schismatic Russians, in the steady expansion of the Faith by the association of conquest and conversion.

Both Orders had thus carried out skilful moves which gave them the justification for holding onto their possessions and rights. But it was not as simple as that. The Hospitallers were prevented from using their island base to the best effect by their Order's internal problems and by the prevalent confusion of ideas about what should be done in the eastern Mediterranean. By 1343, according to Clement VI, it was the 'virtually unanimous and popular opinion of the clergy and laity' that the Order was doing almost nothing for the defence of the Faith.[18] This we shall examine later. Meanwhile it is important to avoid giving the impression that both Orders found it easy to weather the storms of criticism which hit them in the century's first decades. For while nobody seems to have suggested that the Hospitallers should be suppressed as an Order,[19] the Teutonic Knights faced judicial proceedings which were as serious in their implications as those which destroyed the Templars.

The trouble arose over the Order's activities in Livonia, the Baltic province to the north of Prussia which was conquered and colonized by the Germans in the thirteenth century. The conquest was achieved by an alliance between the archbishops of Riga and the Military Order of the Sword Brothers, which was incorporated into the Teutonic Order in 1237. The government which was established, with the active help of papal legates, was shared between the archbishop, his suffragan bishops of Dorpat, Ösel, and Courland, and the Teutonic Order. Prelates and Knight-brothers made up two powerful and mutually hostile political blocs around which were grouped the vassals and burghers of the colonial class. The arrangement led to friction and eventually to civil war. The Archbishop of Riga, his bishops, and the people of Riga were the weaker force, lacking the Order's cohesion, its single-minded

---

[17] Johnson, 570–7. [18] Déprez *et al.*, n. 341.
[19] Suggestions were made to Clement VI that part of the Order's wealth should be confiscated and used to create a new Order, whose zeal and rivalry would stir the Hospitallers into action: ibid.

pursuit of its aims, and its often brutal use of force. Consequently they appealed for justice to the papal Curia, an action based partly on the fact that both disputants enjoyed clerical status, and partly on papal suzerainty over Livonia itself, which was a province of St Peter's patrimony. Because of a series of these appeals, lodged in 1298, 1300, and 1305, the Curia was dragged into the affairs of a remote Baltic community at almost the same time that it was faced with the French onslaught on the Templars.[20]

The dossier placed in front of Clement V contained many accusations, which boiled down to five general charges against the Teutonic Knights.[21] First, they were accused of numerous offences against the Church in Livonia, ranging from the imprisonment of the Archbishop of Riga and the wholesale flouting of his jurisdictional rights, to the despoliation of the secular Church: of the fourteen Livonian sees the Order was said to have destroyed seven, impoverished the same number, reduced four chapters to its own control, and encouraged three more to show contempt for their superior's authority. Secondly, the Order was accused by the citizens of Riga of impeding their city's trade, murdering its citizens, and blockading it by land and sea, all in an attempt to place the great port in its power. The picture emerging from these two accounts was plain enough: the Knights were trying to make their grip on Livonia as strong as the authority of their Order's Prussian branch further south.

But the other three charges were potentially more damaging because they struck at the Order's *raison d'être*. This, as everybody agreed, was the defence of the Church and Faith in Livonia. Yet the Knights were not fulfilling this function; on the contrary, it was argued that they had abandoned and sold castles built to defend the province against the Lithuanians, and traded with them in essential arms. Not that it was necessary for the pagans to attack the Christians since the Order was itself intent on destroying Livonian Christianity:

As a result of their gross offences, Christianity has to a large extent been wiped out in our province, and, to sum up briefly, both doctrine and practice will soon vanish altogether; unless the Apostolic See in its pious

---

[20] *Das Zeugenverhör des Franciscus de Moliano (1312)*, ed. A. Seraphim (Königsberg, 1912), vii ff.; W. Urban, *The Livonian Crusade* (Washington, 1981), 29–62.

[21] *Das Zeugenverhör*, 146–67.

mercy provides us Christians with a remedy, Christianity will be wholly uprooted in Livonia, just as it was at Acre and Tripoli.[22]

The reference to Acre and Tripoli is particularly interesting because it was made in 1305, the same year that Philip the Fair started hearing detailed complaints against the Templars. The fourth charge was a logical corollary to this. The Knights were said to be preventing missionary work amongst the heathens by the mendicant friars; they persecuted converts and drove whole nations, such as the Semigallians, into apostasy.[23] The last charge was a hotchpotch of details testifying to the internal corruption of the Order: it permitted the mercy killing of badly wounded brothers and the cremation, rather than the burial, of their bodies; it defied the ban on eating meat in Lent; it displayed contempt for papal authority; and it placed excommunicated brothers in the higher Church offices.

The Order's defence against these charges consisted of a formidable collection of denials, counter-accusations, and claims for the achievements of its brethren in Livonia.[24] It denied that it had contravened the authority of the Archbishop of Riga; it had merely upheld its own status as an exempt Order of the Church. When churches had suffered through the Order's activities it had paid damages. The strife between the Order and the people of Riga and Ösel had been started by the latter, who had conspired against the Knights and had called upon the help of the Lithuanians to harm them. As for the charges relating to the Order's betrayal of its function, history proved them to be nonsense. The Order had lost thousands of knights and sergeants in the work of spreading the Faith and defending the newly founded churches. It spent large sums of money on maintaining forts and garrisons on the frontiers, and it had papal privileges permitting it to trade with the pagans. Behind the defensive walls erected and diligently guarded by the Knights, more than 150,000 people had been converted to Christianity, and the Order's authorities had no doubt that many only stayed Christian because of the strength and work of its brethren. And the brethren themselves were not corrupt: they lived pure lives, cared for their badly wounded comrades, and buried their dead.

---

[22] Ibid., 166.   [23] Ibid., 148, 165.   [24] Ibid., 179–207.

Extracting the truth from two such contradictory dossiers was a hopeless task, but the weight of the evidence lay against the Order. For while it was true that the Order's enemies had massacred its commandery at Riga, had called in the Lithuanians on several occasions, and had not answered summonses to field troops, the Knights had committed worse crimes and had usually started the conflict. In June 1310 Clement V commissioned the Archbishop of Bremen and a canon of Ravenna called Albert of Milan to investigate the whole issue.[25] The Order was in trouble, for Archbishop Frederick of Riga had the Pope's ear: in February 1311 he secured a bull telling the commissioners to look into cases of Livonian bishops elected uncanonically, a measure probably directed against the Order's staunch ally, the Bishop of Dorpat.[26] In 1311 Albert of Milan was replaced by Francis of Moliano, who went to Livonia with Archbishop Frederick and gave his backing to the Archbishop's excommunication of the brethren in July. Francis's investigation began early in 1312 and the general flow of recorded evidence was hostile to the Order.[27]

Was there a real danger that the Livonian branch of the Teutonic Order would follow the Templars into infamy and dissolution? Some contemporaries thought so. The King of Denmark's captain at Reval believed that the judicial proceedings might end in the Order's destruction, and the Oliva chronicler saw the period as a very dangerous one, when 'there was great fear of the destruction of the Order'.[28] The editor of the 1312 process thought that the Archbishop of Riga had genuine hopes along these lines, and that in the atmosphere of protest and recrimination which prevailed at the Vienne Council the Pope was sympathetic to the idea: 'It is very possible that at this time the Pope was stirred to accede to the wishes of the Archbishop of Riga'.[29] Yet the proceedings came to nothing, and the excommunication was lifted in May 1313.[30]

The Order was not as devilish as its enemies claimed, but it had committed crimes which far exceeded those of the Templars. Three

[25] *Reg. Clem. V*, n. 5544.
[26] Ibid., n. 6597, and see also n. 6770.
[27] *Das Zeugenverhör*, xiv ff., 1–145.
[28] Ibid., 47; 'Chronicle of Oliva', in *Scriptores rerum prussicarum*, ed. T. Hirsch, M. Töppen, and E. Strehlke. 5 vols. (Leipzig, 1861–74), i, 712–13.
[29] *Das Zeugenverhör*, xii.
[30] *Regesta historico–diplomatica Ordinis S. Mariae Theutonicorum 1198–1525*, ed. E. Joachim and W. Hubatsch. 5 vols. (Göttingen, 1948–73), iv, 53, n. 451.

reasons can be adduced for its survival. First, the Order conducted its defence with an expertise and vigour which the unfortunate Templars lacked. Its proctor Conrad put up a strong case at the Curia on its behalf, and in 1311 the genial and persuasive Charles of Trier was elected as Grand Master.[31] The Order was able to enlist the valuable support of allies such as the Prussian bishops and the Dominicans in Poland, who sent memoranda to the Curia denying the charges against the Knights and begging the cardinals to speak up for 'this great shield of the Church and Faith in our parts'.[32] Secondly, the Livonian enemies of the Order were far less formidable as opponents than the French Crown had been for the Templars. There was very little pressure which the secular Church in Livonia, its vassals and supporters, could apply at the Curia; they relied almost entirely on Clement V's sense of justice and on such alarm as they could instill about the threat to the Church and its missionary activities. That they enjoyed some success is clear from the dispatch of the papal commissioners, but it would take a very much greater exertion of papal will to bring about the dismantling of the Order's solidly entrenched power, let alone its destruction.

Thirdly, there were good reasons for the Pope to withhold that exertion. Even if he accepted that the brethren constituted a greater threat to Christianity on the Baltic than a defence, their removal would dangerously alter the balance of power in the area. The Order might bully other Catholics in Livonia, and might be aiming at the creation of an *Ordensstaat* similar to that in Prussia, but at least it prevented the territorial expansion of the Swedish and Danish monarchies. As the century progressed the importance of the Order in this respect grew very clear. In 1341, for example, the Livonian Knight-brothers were thanked for helping three Cistercian monasteries in the province to resist payment of a tax of 400 silver marks which the King of Denmark's captain had tried to impose.[33] And in 1355 the Pope stepped in to protect the Teutonic Order itself from aggressive moves by King Magnus.[34] The political situation in the north meant that the Knights had to stay.

This was far from being a decisive vote of approval by the Curia for the Order and its activities. Some such approval was vital. The

---

[31] Peter of Dusburg, 'Cronica terre Prussie', in *SRP*, i, 178.
[32] *Das Zeugenverhör*, 175–8.
[33] *VMP*, i, nn. 560–1.
[34] Ibid., i, n. 741.

Order's wars against the Lithuanians, which were its chief military function in the fourteenth century, were justified as defensive on the grounds that *pagani* were by nature hostile to Christians. But one of the charges brought against the Knights was that they were impeding missionary work which would both defuse this hostility more effectively than fighting, and win souls for Christ. Again, the campaigns against the Lithuanians were represented as holy wars, and the papacy had long established a form of authority over such wars, even when they were not technically crusades. To a certain extent the Knights were able to evade both these issues and thus keep papal intervention to a minimum. They could credibly argue that since Lithuania was more advanced, aggressive, and determinedly pagan than any of the other Slav communities in north-eastern Europe, effective conversion was out of the question until the Lithuanian state had been conquered.

The way the conflict was waged also worked to the Knights' advantage. For the wars against the Lithuanians were fought according to an unusual pattern, by raids (*Reysen*) which took place in summer and winter only, were generally on a small scale, and depended on weather conditions and up to the minute reports of enemy activity.[35] For such warfare the traditional organization of a crusade—appeals to the pope, haggling about finance, issuing of bulls, preaching, assembly, and transportation of an army—was far too protracted and cumbersome to be useful. Instead the Knights developed a system which virtually eliminated the need for papal backing. By vigorous publicity they made their wars the focus of German crusading piety, establishing a claim to money which was donated or bequeathed either to the Holy Land or to the Baltic crusades, as well as money raised from the redemption of crusade vows; in 1366 the Order claimed that the Archbishop of Riga had robbed it of 20,000 marks from this latter source over a fifty year period.[36] They also built up an efficient method of recruitment which ensured a regular flow of knights and men-at-arms from Germany and other parts of Europe to participate in the campaigns against the Lithuanians. 'Pilgrims'—the term may have been used in recognition of the fact that these were not, technically, *crucesignati*—were thus reported in Prussia in 1304, 1307, 1316, 1322–4, 1329, 1341, 1344, 1348, 1377, and in general throughout the grand

[35] Good description in Christiansen, 160 ff.
[36] *SRP*, ii, 150. See also *CDP*, ii, n. 55.

magistracy of Winrich of Kniprode (1351–82).[37] For few of these years are there extant crusade bulls for the wars against the Lithuanians, nor do we find a stream of petitions from Marienburg to Avignon asking for the grant of indulgences. Those who went to fight on the Baltic in this period rarely did so at the pope's bidding.

The policy of the Curia towards the Lithuanian wars was thus an inactive one.[38] The Knights asked for, and received, new privileges and the confirmation of those they already held, they sent presents of horses and in exchange were exhorted to persevere with 'the Lord's war'.[39] They were praised, though usually in wholly conventional and rhetorical terms. In 1368 for example, granting a request from the Livonian Knights for a portable altar to be used on campaign, Urban V wrote of

> the constant work and many dangers, which our beloved sons the Master, preceptors, and brethren of the Hospital of St Mary of the Germans at Jerusalem ceaselessly endure for the defence, exaltation, and expansion of the Catholic Faith in the regions of Livonia and Russia, as the athletes and intrepid prize-fighters of Christ.[40]

If there was any deeper thought in this approach it lay in the idea that if the Lithuanians suffered enough at the hands of the Knights, they would accept baptism in order to bring the war to an end. Thus in 1373 Gregory XI responded guardedly to Lithuanian pleas for peacemaking with the assertion that the negotiation of peace went hand in hand with a programme of instruction in the Catholic Faith.[41] The Curia thus showed much the same caution which it displayed towards the Greeks; in both cases military activity was linked to conversion, though in a radically different form.

The Knights' approach to this issue mirrored Benedict XII's response to Barlaam in 1339: they were consistently sceptical about the sincerity of the Lithuanians, and viewed interest in conversion

---

[37] See Peter of Dusburg, 170, 173, 182, 186–7, 189, 215; 'Chronicle of Oliva', 721, 724; Hermann of Wartberg, 'Chronicon Livoniae', in *SRP*, ii, 69, 99–101, 114; Wigand of Marburg, 'Cronica nova prutenica', in *SRP*, ii, 515–88; W. Paravicini, 'Die Preussenreise des europäischen Adels', *Historische Zeitschrift*, ccxxxii (1981), 25–38.

[38] Cf. Muldoon, *Popes, Lawyers and Infidels*, 97–9.

[39] Mollat, *Lettres communes*, nn. 9758–9, 9778–9, 13798; id., *Lettres secrètes*, n. 2734; *CDP*, iii, nn. 48, 81–2; *Tabulae Ordinis Theutonici*, ed. E. Strehlke (Berlin, 1869), nn. 673–85.

[40] *VMP*, i, n. 877.

[41] Ibid., i, n. 934, and cf. nn. 935–6.

on the part of their leaders as a ruse to gain a temporary respite from the Order's attacks and prepare for an onslaught against the Christians. The test case arose in 1323, when the Lithuanian Grand Prince, Gediminas, sent letters to the Franciscans and Dominicans, a series of German towns, and John XXII, claiming that he wanted to become a Christian and to instruct his subjects in the Faith, and that only the ferocious attacks of the Teutonic Order prevented him doing this.[42] The allies of the Order were rapidly pressed into service, and letters were dispatched to the Curia by the Franciscan Custodian of Prussia, two Cistercian abbots, and the Bishop of Ermland, asserting Gediminas's duplicity; this, they wrote, was proved by his cynical blasphemy when envoys were sent to him, and by his unrelenting attacks on Christian lands. But John XXII was impressed by the Grand Prince's letters, coming at a time when he was badly disposed towards the Order anyway. In June 1324 he sent nuncios to negotiate with Gediminas, giving them powers to excommunicate anybody who impeded their mission, and expressly forbidding the Teutonic Knights to attack Gediminas once he had embraced the Catholic Faith.[43] By the end of August 1324 a four year truce had been arranged between Gediminas and the Order. It was extended to both the Livonian and Prussian fronts.[44]

On this occasion the Order and its supporters were proved right. Gediminas did not become a Christian, but continued to direct attacks on Christian lands. In August 1325 the Pope was petitioned to annul the truce so that the Teutonic Knights could resume their role as defenders of the area.[45] But the Order's interpretation of its position was still not accepted without reservation at Avignon. In 1335 and again in 1338 the Order's allies sent letters to Benedict XII testifying to its many good works: it maintained peace, offered hospitality, distributed alms, promoted religious observance, built new churches, and bestowed fiefs and honours on clerics. Above all, it fought the heathen, functioning as 'a wall for the house of Israel', and as 'a light of the Church, and a pillar, shield, and rampart for the *populus christianus* of our parts'. Indeed, if the Order was not present the whole of the Baltic littoral would be overrun by the

---

[42] *Regesta*, iv, 62–3, nn. 520, 524–7; Muldoon, *Popes, Lawyers and Infidels*, 86–8.

[43] *VMP*, i, nn. 290–300.

[44] *AE*, ad annum 1323, n. 20, xxiv, 211–13; *CDP*, ii, n. 110.

[45] Ibid., ii, n. 114. For the Order's view of this sequence of events, see Peter of Dusburg, 190–2.

pagans.[46] It is clear from these encomia that the Order's enemies were still active at the Curia, and that one of their chief criticisms remained the argument that the Knights had no real function to perform.

If the papal Curia was hesitant about intervening in the Order's war with the Lithuanians, it was much less so about acting as mediator in the Knights' tangled disputes with other Christians. It was in this field that relations between the papacy and the Order were most active, and because of the nature of politics in this part of Europe, the interventions of the popes had an important impact on the waging of holy war. Two disputes dominated the period: the continuing struggle for hegemony in Livonia, and the Order's quarrel with Poland.

Clement V failed to take any action on the crimes of the Order in Livonia, but his successor applied himself to the province's problems with his customary energy. At the end of 1317 he prohibited all alliances and pacts between the Knights and the canons of Riga which were detrimental to the rights of the Archbishop or the Holy See.[47] Three months later he issued a bull of considerable authority expressing his feelings about Livonia and its attachment to the papacy.[48] The Roman church, John wrote, had been instrumental in the birth of Christian Livonia. It had sent legates and nuncios to help in the process of conversion, and it had decreed that the Teutonic Order should defend the new province, which belonged to St Peter alone and must never be submitted to the dominion of another. Now things had gone badly wrong. The freedom of the secular Church was imperilled, and the pagans were drawing back from conversion because they saw how wretchedly neophytes were treated. The new pope was determined to finish the investigation begun by Boniface VIII and Clement V. The Master of the Livonian brethren was summoned to appear at the Curia, bringing with him the Order's papal privileges; in the meantime he was to cease harassing the prelates of Livonia, and to restore the lands and rights usurped from the See of Riga. The Bishop of Ösel and the chapters of Riga and Ösel were to send envoys to put their cases.[49]

Powerful and independent as the Order was, it could not ignore such an insistent summons. The result was, at first, not unfavourable to the Knights. In July 1319 John XXII issued privileges on the

---

[46] *CDP*, ii, nn. 151–2, iii, n. 14. [47] *VMP*, i, n. 214.
[48] Ibid., i, n. 218. [49] Ibid., i, nn. 218–19.

Order's behalf, including its exemption from the payment of annates because of its heavy debts, a rare reference to financial problems in the Order. In particular, the Pope confirmed the Order's purchase of the monastery of Dünamunde, which was well placed to exercise strong control over Riga's trade and, according to the town's merchants, had been used by the Knights to stifle their commerce.[50] Five years later, however, these bulls were followed by a weighty and severe *ordinatio* which represented the final papal verdict on the struggle for power in Livonia. It was almost wholly hostile to the Teutonic Knights. They were ordered to stop all policies calculated to reduce the authority and rights of the secular Church; to restore all lands and goods seized; and to allow the Rigans free use of their privileges. They were to co-operate with the vassals of the Archbishop of Riga, and with 'the rest of the Christian populace', in the defence of the province. They should stop hindering the mendicant Orders in their work of conversion and show favour to new converts. And they were to suppress those practices in their own Order which were uncanonical or unbefitting to a religious Order, such as cremation.[51]

After nearly three decades, the opponents and victims of the Order had finally succeeded in getting unequivocal papal support for their cause. But it did them little good. Judging from papal letters of the following years, the Order's tactics changed slightly while it worked towards the same political ends as ever. In 1330 a trio of bishops was told to enforce the provisions of the 1324 bull, compelling the Order to make amends for crimes against the Church of Riga and others; evidently their goods had not been restored.[52] In 1336 one of the trio, the Bishop of Dorpat, was again instructed to effect restitution,[53] and in 1349 came an appeal from Clement VI to the Order and the Archbishop of Riga to make peace.[54] By now fresh causes for complaint had arisen, but the Curia still strove to get John XXII's verdict implemented. In 1353 Innocent VI took the drastic step of sending commissioners to Riga to assume the government of the city in the name of the Holy See.[55] This in itself proved to be a difficult task. There was strife in 1356,[56]

[50] Mollat, *Lettres communes*, nn. 9758, 9764; *VMP*, i, n. 225.
[51] Ibid., i, n. 279.
[52] Mollat, *Lettres communes*, n. 49555.
[53] *VMP*, i, n. 502.
[54] Déprez and Mollat, n. 1939.
[55] *VMP*, i, n. 725. Cf. Gasnault *et al.*, n. 348.   [56] *VMP*, i, nn. 759–62.

and in 1360 a fresh commission was established to enforce the papal verdict that Riga should be subject to its Archbishop, not to the Order.[57] The Bishop of Dorpat secured a papal intervention in 1365, much to the disgust of the Order's chroniclers,[58] and in 1375 the Knights were ordered to stop molesting the Bishop of Ösel.[59] Such letters had little or no impact on local events. Livonia was a defeat for the Avignonese papacy: less spectacular and less important than others, but no less complete.[60]

Further south the Order came into conflict with Poland. The quarrels with the Livonian secular Church and the King of Poland could not be kept separate, since Casimir was a designated 'protector' of the See of Riga, and King and Bishops co-operated at times against their common foe, but the disputes themselves were very different in nature.[61] The conflict with Poland was territorial, centring on the Order's occupation of Danzig and eastern Pomerania (Pomorze), a valuable province, Poland's sea outlet, and an integral part of the historic *regnum Poloniae*. Since Poland, like Livonia, was a dependency of the Holy See, Vladislav Lokietek appealed to John XXII, and in September 1319 the Pope ordered an inquiry.[62] The fact that it was entrusted to three Polish prelates shows that the Pope was not acting impartially: Poland, as we have seen, was an important ally of the Curia and the source of much revenue.[63] But the Order had no defence anyway; its tenure of the disputed land was based solely on an imperial privilege of dubious worth. It was no surprise when the judges ordered the restitution of the province in 1321, and the payment of an indemnity of 30,000 marks.[64]

Once again the difference between a legal verdict and its implementation became glaringly apparent, for the Knights lodged an immediate appeal and refused to move. There was fighting between Poland and the Order in 1327, and in 1329 the Poles helped Gediminas against the Knights and their Western volunteers, led by

[57] Ibid., i, n. 807.
[58] Ibid., i, n. 845; Hermann of Wartberg, 82–4. The Order had its own complaints about the Bishop.
[59] Mollat, *Lettres secrètes*, n. 3364.
[60] Urban, 65–88, 113–30.
[61] For the next three paragraphs, see Tymieniecki, 116–24; Halecki, 'Casimir the Great', 167 ff.; Knoll, *RPM*, 14–120 and *passim*.
[62] *VMP*, i, n. 231.
[63] See above, ch. 2, nn. 103–4.
[64] *VMP*, i, n. 254.

King John of Bohemia. This was a gift to the Order's propagandists.[65] Tied down by imperial and papal affairs, John XXII could do
nothing but send nuncios with the Herculean task of restoring
peace.[66] At the Vissegrad Conference of 1335 the Kings of Hungary
and Bohemia jointly recommended the return of some of the
disputed lands, Kuyavia and Dobrzyn, and the retention of most of
Pomorze by the Knights. King Casimir, Vladislav's successor, was
disposed to accept these terms, but he was opposed by a powerful
lobby of Polish nobles and prelates. These 'hawks' had the influential backing of the papal nuncio Galhard de Carceribus, who
persuaded Benedict XII to take a tougher line towards the Order.
So when Casimir appealed for papal intervention, Benedict's
nuncios found on the King's behalf at the Process of Warsaw
(February to September 1339). They ruled that all Pomorze,
together with Kuyavia and Dobrzyn, should be restored to Poland
and that the Order should pay Casimir an indemnity of 194,500
silver marks.[67]

The Order dug its heels in. It rejected the Warsaw trial as rigged
and exerted all possible pressure on Avignon.[68] By 1341 Benedict
XII must have realized that the 1339 verdict was unenforceable; he
told Casimir that he was unable to confirm the verdict.[69] This
caused the King to seal the Treaty of Kalisz (1343), whereby he
accepted the terms of the Vissegrad Conference and ceded
Pomorze to the Order.[70] But there was no settled peace between
Poland and the Knights. A fascinating three-cornered contest had
developed in this part of Europe between Lithuania, Poland, and
Prussia. Each had reason to be hostile to the other two, but
geography and roughly balanced resources dictated temporary
alliances, of which the rarest was that of the two Christian states
against pagan Lithuania. This vitiation of the purity of holy war was
offensive to the Curia, which tried to stop Christians helping pagans
to attack their fellow-believers and burn their churches: thus the
Lithuanians were aided by the Knights against the Poles in 1356,
and by the Poles against the Knights in 1353, 1357, and 1371.[71]

[65] Peter of Dusburg, 215 ff.; *CDP*, iii, n. 15.
[66] *VMP*, i, n. 447, and cf. nn. 448, 470, 473–6.
[67] *Regesta*, iv, 86, n. 706. See also *VMP*, i, nn. 541–2, 544.
[68] *CDP*, iii, n. 15.
[69] *VMP*, i, n. 568. See also Knoll, *RPM*, 107–8.
[70] *VMP*, i, nn. 581, 590.
[71] Ibid., i, nn. 727, 769, 776; Mollat, *Lettres secrètes*, n. 422.

Events were forged by a complicated interplay of religious and political considerations which the papacy did not fully understand and could only marginally influence.

The Order's position in Prussia was much more straightforward than in Livonia. It held full sovereignty, under the nominal suzerainty of the church of Rome. This was the *Ordensstaat*, one of the most remarkable medieval governments, characterized by outstanding achievements in the spheres of colonization and administration.[72] Because of its efficient management of its demesne lands in Prussia, the Order was relatively unaffected by fluctuations in the rural economy of the West, where its original estates lay. This was of vital importance: it meant that while the Order had its internal problems, it avoided the financial constraints which led to deep papal involvement in Hospitaller affairs. In Prussia the secular Church was dominated by the Order, with the exception of Ermland, which was subject to the same encroachments as the Livonian bishoprics, and like them appealed for papal support. The popes made several interventions on behalf of the Bishop of Ermland, and succeeded in bringing about at least a nominal peace between the See and the Order.[73]

During the reign of John XXII, the Curia's financial needs made up an extra complicating factor in relations between Avignon and the Order. John saw the Order and its lands as a neglected source of revenue. In January 1317 he ordered the Knights to pay the *camera* the arrears due in their feudal census for Prussia.[74] More important was the issue of Peter's Pence, a tax which the Pope devoted much energy to restoring. In February 1317 he demanded arrears of Peter's Pence from the inhabitants of some of the lands occupied by the Knights in Poland, notably those in the dioceses of Culm and Camin.[75] Both laity and Knights objected to the levy of a tax which, they claimed, had not been collected for several generations; furthermore, its payment would amount to an admission that these lands were part of the historic Polish Kingdom, where the tax originated. By 1321 the papal collectors were applying severe sanctions against the clergy of Culm, but in June 1329 the people were still holding out, expressing their resistance in abrasive and

[72] See F. L. Carsten, *The Origins of Prussia* (Oxford, 1954), 5–88.
[73] *VMP*, i, nn. 895–8, 933, 965; *CDP*, iii, nn. 104, 107–8, 111, 114, 116, 118–19.
[74] Ibid., ii, n. 76.
[75] Ibid., ii, nn. 83, 91–3. See also E. Maschke, *Der Peterspfennig in Polen und dem deutschen Osten* (Leipzig, 1933), ch. 2 *passim*.

defiant terms.[76] Then came a sudden volte-face. In February 1330 the Order put pressure on the community to change its mind: evidently the Knights were afraid of reprisals against their privileges.[77] In October 1330 the Pope wrote of an agreement to pay Peter's Pence in future, and this seems to have held.[78]

It is clear that the Knights could yield to pressure, but also that they were not afraid of defying the Curia. Their active, bloody, and costly engagement in holy war on Christendom's frontier was a powerful advantage which they used adroitly. Thus in 1326 they claimed that the levying of Peter's Pence was so severe a burden that neophytes would revert to paganism, and that settlers were so exasperated by the interdict imposed because of Culmerland's refusal to pay that they were threatening to migrate. This would rob the Order of defenders and supplies for its castles and thus expose the entire region to pagan attack.[79] The message was clear: the Pope's selfish fiscal demands were seriously hindering the Order's work of conversion and defence. Similarly, in 1340 some of the tame Prussian bishops excused the Grand Master's failure to answer a summons to Avignon on the grounds of a serious threat from the Tatars and Lithuanians; God's work must come first.[80] Morally bolstered by such arguments, the Order was prepared to withstand even excommunication and interdict, in the confident expectation that papal attitudes would eventually change under a barrage of persuasion, bribery, and pressure.

Since the Teutonic Knights were unable to depend on papal backing to the extent that, for example, the Hospitallers were, they placed great emphasis on the support of secular rulers, especially those of German-speaking lands. John of Bohemia employed his own claim to the Polish throne to cede the Order all it wanted in recognition of its services to Christianity and himself in the struggle against the pagans.[81] The Knights were not afraid of securing the support of the excommunicated and heretical Emperor Louis IV: he granted them lordship and jurisdiction over Riga in 1332, possession of Lithuania and other territories in 1337, and imperial

---

[76] *VMP*, i, n. 257; Mollat, *Lettres communes*, nn. 42083, 44832; *CDP*, ii, nn. 121–2, 124.

[77] Ibid., ii, n. 133.

[78] *VMP*, i, nn. 437, 444, 490. But cf. *CDP*, ii, nn. 134–5; *VMP*, i, n. 531.

[79] *CDP*, ii, n. 120.

[80] Ibid., iii, n. 21. See also Knoll, *RPM*, 108.

[81] *Regesta*, iv, 67–8, nn. 568–70, 81, nn. 668–9.

protection and backing against Casimir and Benedict XII in 1338.[82] Though of little value in the short run, such privileges were carefully stored away in case they would come in useful later. It was thus a combination of the distance between Avignon and Marienburg, the complex politics of this part of Europe, and above all the Order's own formidable personality, resources, and ability, which so often rendered papal interventions of little practical use.

By contrast with its abject failure to protect the Templars, and the barren nature of its relations with the Teutonic Order, the papacy's role in the evolution of the Order of the Hospital of St John of Jerusalem in the fourteenth century was always important and occasionally decisive. When they were not dictated by the Curia's own needs or pressure exerted by a third party, papal relations with the Hospitallers were conducted with two aims in view: to make the Order secure from attack, united, and solvent; and to employ this revivified force in the service of holy war in the eastern Mediterranean. That the Curia was only partially successful in either respect is explained by the serious problems facing the Order, the limited power of the popes and the contradictions in their policy, and the fact that the Knights of St John did not always concur with papal objectives. In the threefold battle of wills between the papacy, the Order, and the secular authorities of the West it was inevitable that much would be lost, but there was enough unity of aim to make some progress.

We will look first at the papacy's actions on behalf of the Order. A continual effort had to be made to uphold the Knights' status and privileges as an exempt Order of the Church.[83] This meant, in particular, resisting attempts by rulers to tax the Order's lands, enlist its brethren into their service, or simply take over its possessions and revenues. The reign of John XXII witnessed a determined drive by the French Crown to diminish the wealth and influence of the Order in France, inspired no doubt by the recent success of Philip IV in the trial of the Templars. Thus in May and July 1317 the Pope asked Philip V to instruct his officials to stop harassing the Hospitallers, and he called for the restitution of property which had been seized.[84] These French initiatives were connected with Philip's attempt to get more of the property of the French Templars

---

[82] Ibid., i, 10, n. 176a, iv, 82–3, nn. 681–3; *CDP*, iii, n. 8.
[83] For the status and privileges, see Riley-Smith, *Knights of St John*, 375–89.
[84] *CC*, nn. 236, 333.

than his father had secured, and in September and December 1317 John XXII had to send strongly worded appeals to stop molesting the Hospitallers, who were vital to the defence of the Christian East.[85] Even when the issue of the Templar spoils was settled, the Hospitallers were occasionally subjected to the fiscal brutality which formed a hallmark of late Capetian and Valois government; in 1338, for example, royal officials seized goods in Hospitaller houses.[86] But the French were not the only offenders. The Kings of Denmark and Norway despoiled the Order, and German princes were guilty of making illegal financial demands on the Knights.[87]

The Order had priories throughout the West, and most faced problems arising from the desire of powerful rulers or nobles to control their revenues, a danger greatly aggravated by the weakness of the Order's constitution and the often undisciplined state of the commanderies. In all their interventions the popes tried to preserve the priories' resources, but tactics varied. Typical was John XXII's forceful intervention in the affairs of the Priory of Hungary in 1318, when a brother called Mesco, the Duke of Beuthen, usurped the priorate in the face of the absentee Italian, Philip of Gragnana.[88] It is possible that John also helped bring about the compromise which ended a serious dispute between Barcelona and Rhodes on the question of the priorate of Catalonia.[89] But in 1344 Clement VI advised Hélion of Villeneuve to grant the Priory of Toulouse to Escout de Rioutier at the request of the Duke of Normandy, despite Hélion's hope of keeping the priorate vacant so that he could use its revenues for the war against the Turks.[90] Characteristically, the Pope thought it more important not to offend the French Crown. Connected with attempts to keep the priories intact and obedient to Rhodes were the successive appointments of 'judge-conservators' for the Order (for example, in 1319 and 1322), and action taken against physical assaults on brethren and houses.[91]

In May 1312 Clement V issued the bull *Ad providam*, granting the bulk of the sequestrated Templar property to the Hospitallers, 'who constantly face danger of death as the Lord's athletes in defence of

---

[85] Ibid., nn. 398, 453–4.
[86] Daumet, n. 548.
[87] Mollat, *Lettres communes*, nn. 12002–3, 16227–8.
[88] Ibid., nn. 6549, 7284.
[89] *Documenta selecta*, nn. 487, 490, 492, 498, 501, 503.
[90] Déprez *et al.*, n. 1099.
[91] Mollat, *Lettres communes*, nn. 8726, 9841, 10461–3, 15411, 16017.

the Faith, undertaking very burdensome and perilous expenses all the time in overseas regions'.[92] Although Clement's feelings towards the Hospitallers were a lot less warm than this would suggest, both he and his successors attempted to get *Ad providam* implemented. Their degree of success varied from country to country, forming an interesting parallel to the division of spoils from the Vienne tenth.[93] In France the goods were handed over, but at the cost of grants to the French Crown of over 300,000 *livres*, an enormous sum. In England and Castile there was opposition from the nobility and other Military Orders, who had occupied Templar lands during the long trial and refused to disgorge what they had swallowed. There was a relatively peaceful hand-over of the estates of the defunct Order in Bohemia, Cyprus, and parts of Italy and Germany, but elsewhere much prevarication and resistance. In Aragon and Portugal new Military Orders took over the lands and possessions, in accordance with *Ad providam*, and the Hospitallers did not benefit. Nevertheless, in general the transfer took place with surprising rapidity, and by 1324 the estates of the Hospitallers had doubled, with attendant administrative difficulties.[94] Without very active papal support the Order would have benefited much less.

Despite the huge increase in its landed possessions thus brought about, the Hospitallers were faced by financial problems on an almost crippling scale in the second and third decades of the century. In dealing with these debts, incurred in conquering and fortifying Rhodes and establishing an administration there, the help of the Curia was important. First, it laid down the principle that the Order should be exempt from clerical taxation, whether imposed for pope or king.[95] Secondly, the popes took active steps to help the convent at Rhodes deal with the debts themselves. The principle was stated both by Clement V and by John XXII that no Hospitaller estates should be lost to the Order, though this was to prove impracticable in the long run.[96] Instead, the debts were to be

---

[92] *Reg. Clem. V*, n. 7885.   [93] See above, ch. 5, nn. 133–52.

[94] See Delaville le Roulx, *Les Hospitaliers*, 28–50; Barber, *Trial of the Templars*, 231–8.

[95] See, for example, Mollat, *Lettres communes*, nn. 5690, 6929, 24364, 40490, 45582, 53881, 55630, 59868, 62086; *VMH*, i, n. 917. But see also Housley, *Italian Crusades*, 215–16.

[96] *Reg. Clem. V*, n. 9835; Mollat, *Lettres communes*, nn. 7316, 7322–3, 7596, 7604–6.

divided amongst the priories, and the priors allowed to run up debts of their own to lessen the burden on the convent.[97] This arrangement was not a success: money was not forthcoming, some priories found the burden too great to bear, and by 1319 the Pope was trying to exploit all possible sources of extra revenue for the Order.[98] In 1320 the debts stood at over half a million florins, and in May 1321 the Pope allowed the Master to mortgage possessions to pay the 320,000 florins owed to the Bardi and Peruzzi.[99] He backed up the measures taken at the chapters of 1320 and 1321 at Arles and Avignon for the repayment of the debts, and in November 1322 took the radical step of permitting Hélion of Villeneuve to sell lands to clear the debts.[100] By selling lands and raising responsions the crisis was overcome by about 1335.[101]

Writing to the King of France in 1329, John XXII claimed that the response of the priories to the convent's debts had not proved satisfactory: many regions had paid nothing to the Master, others very little.[102] It was in getting the priories to forward their annual payments to Rhodes that the Curia made its greatest contribution to improving the Order's finances. The disciplinary powers of the Master, which were weakened by distance and laxity, were usefully stiffened by those of the Curia, with its sanctions, local agents, control of the secular Church, and influence with local lay powers. There are many examples. In August 1318 the Hospitallers in the Kingdom of Naples were told to pay their responsions in kind by sending food supplies to Rhodes.[103] Two years later the Bishops of Limassol and Paphos were instructed to make the brethren in Cyprus pay their responsions to the convent.[104] Urban V threatened a series of priors with excommunication in 1363 if they did not pay the responsions due;[105] and in 1375 Gregory XI ordered the Prior of Ireland to hand over to the preceptor of Rhodes all money collected in the form of responsions.[106] The Curia also exerted pressure on the priories to secure for Rhodes the extra

---

[97] CC, n. 320; Mollat, *Lettres communes*, nn. 4450–72. See also ibid., n. 5691.
[98] Ibid., nn. 8791, 9695, 9839–40.
[99] Ibid., nn. 13407–10.
[100] Ibid., nn. 14454, 16588–97.
[101] Delaville le Roulx, *Les Hospitaliers*, 21–4, 53–6.
[102] CC, n. 4021.
[103] Mollat, *Lettres communes*, nn. 8024–5.
[104] Ibid., n. 11494.
[105] LM, nn. 600–9. Cf. Delaville le Roulx, *Les Hospitaliers*, 142–4.
[106] Mollat, *Lettres secrètes*, n. 3622, and cf. n. 3655.

financial aid which was essential for Hospitaller participation in the war against the Turks. In March 1334 the priors assembling at Le Puy were ordered to pay the convent a subsidy 'in addition to the customary responsions'.[107] Not surprisingly this was unpopular, and when, ten years later, the priors throughout the West were told to pay a quarter of their annual dues immediately for the Order's expenses in the Turkish war, there was fierce opposition.[108]

Many of these orders were ignored or only half complied with; some imperious letters were followed after a few months by others which moderated the original demand or lengthened the time allowed for payment.[109] For although solvency was restored to the convent in the 1330s, the overall financial condition of the Order remained poor. Its revenues in the West came chiefly from rents on agricultural land, and these were badly hit by the falling cereal prices which followed the Black Death. War and brigandage took a heavy toll of houses in Italy, Germany, and France; brethren accepted debts as a fact of life and struggled to keep heads above water.[110] To pay for a *passagium* of limited size it was necessary for Gregory XI in March 1377 to authorize the sale or mortgaging of more than 200,000 florins worth of the Order's lands in Italy, Germany, Spain, Bohemia, and France. This was obviously not a process which could be repeated *ad infinitum*; as Delaville le Roulx commented, it showed both how poor the Order's finances were, and how serious appeared the growing Ottoman threat.[111]

To be an effective fighting force the Order had to be united and disciplined, the convent obedient to the master and the priories ready to supply men as well as money. The internal regulation of the Order was one of the Curia's chief concerns. For the most part this meant backing the master's authority, pressing general schemes of reform, and taking action on individual houses where there was scandalous corruption or abuse of privileges. In May 1313, for example, the prelates of the secular Church were ordered to support the Master against rebellious brethren, and in 1316 the Prior of Navarre was instructed to take action against pluralism in his Priory.[112] There were many such bulls, but in 1317 John XXII

---

[107] CC, n. 5429.
[108] Déprez *et al.*, n. 711.
[109] See, for example, Mollat, *Lettres communes*, n. 8620.
[110] See Glénisson, 'L'Enquête pontificale', *passim*.
[111] *Les Hospitaliers*, 189–91. See also Luttrell, 'Gregory XI', 411.
[112] *Reg. Clem. V*, n. 9398; Mollat, *Lettres communes*, n. 2125, and cf. nn. 4852–6.

was faced by a major constitutional crisis when the authoritarian
and corrupt rule of Fulk of Villaret resulted in a schism, the leading
brethren in the convent following an unsuccessful attempt on Fulk's
life by electing the Draper Maurice of Pagnac as Master. John XXII
sent nuncios to Rhodes and summoned Fulk and Maurice to
Avignon, appointing Gerard of Pins as provisional vicar-general.
Maurice's election was quashed and he was given the Commandery
of Armenia and half the revenues of the Grand-Commandery of
Cyprus as compensation. Fulk was persuaded to resign the
magistracy, receiving instead the Priory of Capua. Then, in June
1319, Hélion of Villeneuve was elected as new Master by a group of
leading priors.[113]

The schism of 1317 had important implications for papal–
Hospitaller relations. The legal basis for the role played by John
XXII was an appeal to the Pope in 1295, but there can be no doubt
that John's own strong views and imperious character helped to
carry through his decisive intervention: Hélion of Villeneuve was
virtually appointed by the Pope like many bishops of the period.
And it was inevitable that, having striven to restore unity to the
Order, the Curia would demand a greater say in its life.[114] Both
Benedict XII and Clement VI were dissatisfied with the conduct of
the brethren. In August 1343 Clement criticized the luxury of their
life in severe if conventional terms and demanded both internal
reform and fuller participation in the defence of the Christian
East.[115] Twelve years later Innocent VI wrote a fiercer letter of
criticism. He expressed his own, and the cardinals', discontent
about the persistent rumours of luxury and inactivity; if the Order
did not carry out its own reform, the Pope would reform it himself,
possibly founding a new Military Order with the Templar possessions. There was an unfavourable and galling comparison between
the Hospitallers and the Teutonic Knights, and Innocent called for a
chapter-general at Nîmes or Montpellier in January 1356.[116] An
assembly was in fact held at Avignon early in 1356, and in May the
Pope ordered that its reforming measures should be inserted
amongst the Order's statutes and enforced.[117]

[113] Ibid., nn. 5579–82, 5592, 5600–1, 5655–6, 9023, 9025–6, 9577, 9608–9, 10264.
[114] See the rich detail on papal intervention in the Order's life in Delaville le
Roulx, *Les Hospitaliers*, 19–27, 57 ff.
[115] Déprez *et al.*, n. 341.
[116] Gasnault *et al.*, n. 1773.
[117] Ibid., n. 2134.

The initiative taken by Innocent VI was pursued by Urban V and Gregory XI. Urban was content to give his backing to the reforming activity of the Master, but the situation called for a more positive intervention, for the chapters-general of 1367 and 1373 revealed the Order to be in dire straits.[118] In February 1373 Gregory XI took the unprecedented step of ordering an inquest by all bishops into the state of the Order's houses and their lands. Thanks to the imminent publication of the inquest's surviving reports it will soon be possible to gauge the internal condition of the Order in the 1370s in great detail.[119] The picture is likely to be a depressing one. Between 1338 and 1373 the number of brethren in south-east France seems to have declined by about a third, and their average age was alarmingly high: more than 80 per cent were over forty. Moreover, the preceptories and commanderies lived in an embattled world; all the energy of the brethren in the West went into keeping their lands together, resisting royal and seigneurial advances, and providing for the military defence of their estates. The poor went unfed, conventual life was slack, and reforming demands and decrees from Rhodes and chapters-general were ignored. In such circumstances neither persuasion nor threats had much chance of succeeding.[120]

Attempts by the Avignonese Curia to gear up the Order and enable it to engage in holy war were thus frustrated in large measure by the economic and political problems of the age and the innate conservatism of a 200-year-old institution. In addition, there were certain debilitating contradictions in papal policy towards the Hospitallers, resembling those examined in a previous chapter.[121] Thus, while the popes criticized secular rulers who employed the Order's resources for their own ends, they themselves could not resist drawing on the expertise of the brethren in the West, causing absenteeism and anomalies in the Order's structure of command: it has been pointed out that in 1340 every province of the Papal State was governed by a Hospitaller.[122] Again, problems arose because the papal *camera* and the Order both used the services of the great Tuscan banking companies. Under John XXII this was advanta-

---

[118] Delaville le Roulx, *Les Hospitaliers*, 161–3, 166–70. But cf. Luttrell, 'Gregory XI', 398n.

[119] The reports are to be published by the Institut de recherche et d'histoire des textes, under the general editorship of J. Glénisson and A. T. Luttrell.

[120] See Glénisson, 'L'Enquête pontificale', esp. 91 ff.

[121] See above, ch. 6, nn. 66–70, 152–6, 164–5.

[122] Luttrell, 'Hospitallers at Rhodes', 300.

geous, in that the Pope gave his full support to the restoration of Hospitaller solvency because the Order's huge debts endangered his own financial operations. But once the convent was solvent it became convenient for the *camera* to keep it that way; this could explain why Benedict XII refused to permit an expensive Hospitaller expedition in aid of Armenia.[123]

Perhaps worst of all, the policy of encouraging and even demanding reform was at odds with the favour which the Curia showed towards individual brethren guilty of misdemeanours. It was ironic that the man who took Innocent VI's complaints to Rhodes in 1354, Juan Fernández de Heredia, was almost the personification of the Order's internal ills: he was systematically accumulating offices, he had defaulted on his responsions, and he had disobeyed summonses from the Master.[124] Some popes, such as Innocent VI, were too ready to believe rumours about the behaviour of the Knights, and the hypocrisy of Clement VI's criticism of their luxurious way of life needs no comment. But despite all this, the aid which the Curia gave to the Order was of vital importance. Quite apart from his help in ending the schism and in working out a solution to the massive debts facing the convent, John XXII issued dozens of bulls defending the Hospitallers from their external foes and internal weaknesses. Of course such vigorous intervention sapped the master's authority, but it is hard to fault Delaville le Roulx's judgement that John saved the Order from collapse, giving it the time it needed to consolidate its position on Rhodes and work out a military function in the East.[125] This may well have been John XXII's greatest contribution to the crusade in the eastern Mediterranean. The support given to the Order by Urban V and Gregory XI was almost as impressive.

The military activity which the Curia expected from the Hospitallers in exchange for this aid varied according to the nature of the Muslim threat in the East and the crusading forces which the popes were able to organize in the West. Naturally the Knights had their own ambitions in the eastern Mediterranean, though distant and hostile observers like James II of Aragon exaggerated when they claimed that territorial expansion dominated the Order's policies. Rhodes was conveniently situated for offensive operations against the Anatolian emirates, and in the difficult years following the

[123] Ibid., 294.
[124] Delaville le Roulx, *Les Hospitaliers*, 125–6.
[125] Ibid., 26.

Templar trial and the 1317 schism the Hospitallers, led by the able Albert of Schwarzburg, inflicted several defeats on the Turks, two of which were carefully reported to the Pope.[126] Rhodes was also well placed to send help to Armenia. In 1320 John XXII tried to make Maurice of Pagnac reside in his preceptory in Armenia, and from this point onwards the Curia regarded the Order as the natural protector of the Armenians, urging it to despatch troops and, in 1332, to garrison castles.[127] The Hospitallers were sceptical about the value of such projects, nor did they respond to Clement V's attempt to direct their military might against the Catalans in Greece, which would have been contrary to one of the Order's *esgarts*.[128]

For some time in the 1320s and early 1330s the Hospitallers were viewed both at Avignon and at Paris as a vital factor in the crusade projects of the French Crown; they were on the spot, knew the terrain and the enemy, and were duty-bound to take part in crusades. Hélion of Villeneuve, who was in the West between 1319 and 1332, had close connections with the French court, and could not avoid backing such schemes, despite his preoccupation with his Order's debts.[129] But again John XXII proved an ally of the Order, refusing to allow the brethren to be committed to a crusade until its details had been fully settled: there was to be no repetition of the 1310 *passagium*, with its appalling financial consequences.[130] This period culminated in the complex negotiations about the organization of a naval squadron in the Aegean and a general passage led by Philip VI. The French King expected the full support of the Hospitallers, and the Pope himself urged the French priories to co-operate with Philip by giving him men and money.[131] Hélion of Villeneuve arrived back in Rhodes in 1332 and the Order agreed to furnish ten galleys for the 1334 league.[132]

Hospitaller inactivity during the reign of Benedict XII showed

---

[126] Mollat, *Lettres communes*, n. 8374; Delaville le Roulx, *Les Hospitaliers*, 365–7; Lemerle, 30–1; Hill, ii, 274–5. News of the successful action of 1320 reached Giovanni Villani: bk. 9, ch. 120, ii, 224.

[127] Mollat, *Lettres communes*, nn. 12388, 14104, 57909; Déprez and Mollat, n. 2503; Luttrell, 'Hospitallers' Interventions', 123–33.

[128] *Reg. Clem. V*, nn. 7890–1; *Cartulaire général*, ii, n. 2213, 543.

[129] He may have written a crusade treatise at this time. See Delaville le Roulx, *La France en orient*, i, 80–1; Luttrell, 'Hospitallers' Interventions', 124n.

[130] CC, n. 1848, col. 403.

[131] Ibid., n. 5292, and see also n. 5429.

[132] Delaville le Roulx, *Les Hospitaliers*, 87 ff.

that, like the papacy itself, the Order relied on the initiatives of others. Then came Clement VI's fierce letter of criticism of August 1343, demanding the provision of six galleys for the new league to fight Umur of Aydin.[133] In addition, as we have seen, the Hospitallers were to act as paymasters for the Pope's own galleys.[134] The Order supplied its ships and played an important part in the capture and defence of Smyrna; in May 1345 the Prior of Lombardy, John of Biandrate, was appointed captain-general of the Christian forces.[135] Hospitallers also participated in Humbert of Vienne's expedition. This help was noted at the Curia and a series of letters showed that Clement VI was gratified by the Order's response.[136] In August 1350 the Hospitallers agreed to take their share of the expense involved in keeping the league in action, providing three galleys and 3,000 florins a year for the defence of Smyrna.[137]

This satisfying burst of activity did not last long. In 1351 both Venice and Cyprus backed out of the new agreement for defending Smyrna and in September Clement VI wrote to the new Master, Dieudonné of Gozon, that the Order too was released from its obligation to provide galleys, though the annual subvention of 3,000 florins for the garrison was still to be sent.[138] The convent at Rhodes feared that the defence of Smyrna, a severe burden, might be imposed solely on the Order, an undertaking which Dieudonné specifically forbade in 1347. But the annual subvention seems to have been regularly sent, despite the economic upheavals of the 1340s and 1350s. The problem now was the lack of initiatives emanating from the West. The Knights showed, both by their help to Smyrna and by a number of small expeditions and raids in Anatolia and the Aegean, that they were willing to act; but they lacked the resources to make a major impact on their own and they needed direction. There were no crusades to reconquer Palestine and the sporadic war against the Turks provided little to boast about. Innocent VI realized that the problem lay partly in the Order's isolation on Rhodes, and considered that the convent should be transferred to the mainland of Anatolia, while in 1356–7 there was even a plan to establish it in Achaea.[139] There was no permanent solution to these difficulties in our period.

[133] Déprez *et al.*, nn. 337, 341.
[134] See above, ch. 5, nn. 158–76.
[135] Déprez *et al.*, n. 1675.
[136] Ibid., nn. 987, 1669; Déprez and Mollat, nn. 671–2.
[137] Déprez *et al.*, n. 4661.
[138] Ibid., nn. 5052–3.
[139] Luttrell, 'Hospitallers at Rhodes', 296–7.

The 1360s, a decade of substantial crusading activity in the East, gave the Hospitallers a chance to prove their mettle. They supplied troops to Peter Thomas and took part in Peter of Cyprus's attacks on Adalia in 1361 and Alexandria in 1365.[140] In July 1365 Urban V had a plan for joint Latin aid to the Greeks, for which the Order was to provide 1,000 men and four ships.[141] This came to nothing, but men and equipment from Rhodes were of great importance to Peter I in his campaigns of 1366 and 1367 in Armenia and Syria. On the death of Peter in 1369 Urban V urged the defence of both Adalia and Smyrna on the Hospitallers, a few months later reiterating his request that they help to protect the Armenians.[142] The Knights failed to help the Armenians in what proved to be the last phase of the Kingdom's existence, but throughout the 1360s they had shown the falseness of the accusation that they were uninterested in fighting the Muslims.

There followed a period of the most intensive papal–Hospitaller co-operation since Clement V's negotiations with Fulk of Villaret. Gregory XI determined to employ the Order's resources to the greatest possible extent both for the defence of Smyrna and for the now popular policy of joining forces with the Greeks against the advance of the Turks. Thus in September 1374, despite the earlier prohibition of Dieudonné of Gozon, the Pope placed the Order in charge of Smyrna for a five year period, a move necessitated by the corrupt captaincy of the Genoese Ottobuono Cattaneo and the disputes between the Latins resident in the port.[143] By June 1373 Gregory had decided to send a Hospitaller *passagium* East to fight the Turks, and was writing to the Venetians and Genoese for guidance.[144] In the course of the next five years much care and attention to detail went into the planning of this *passagium*. But the Pope failed to take into account either the lamentable conditions in the western priories, or the basic dissimilarity of objectives which made co-operation with the Order hazardous. The result was an inadequately financed expedition which met with disaster in the

[140] Philip of Mézières, 125; Delaville le Roulx, *Les Hospitaliers*, 139–42, 151–4.

[141] LM, n. 1703; Halecki, *Un Empereur*, 99.

[142] LM, nn. 2934, 2980; Luttrell, 'Hospitallers' Interventions', 131. The Knights were also ordered to contribute to the Veneto-Genoese league of 1369: *I libri comm.*, iii, 85, n. 514.

[143] *AE*, ad annum 1374, n. 7, xxvi, 236; Luttrell, 'Gregory XI', 396–7.

[144] Mollat, *Lettres secrètes*, n. 1940, and cf. nn. 2116, 2132.

summer of 1378.[145] It was a fitting end to an undistinguished period of Hospitaller history.

The contrast between papal relations with the Teutonic Knights and those with the Hospitallers perfectly reflected the difference between the fronts on which the two Orders now fought. The papacy had a strong responsibility towards the Christian East, based partly on the status of the Holy Land and the origins of the crusading movement, and partly on the inherent political and cultural importance of the eastern Mediterranean. Its frequent interventions in the internal affairs of the Hospitallers sprang from the same deep roots as its long series of attempts to inspire and organize crusades to the East, and its constant preoccupation with the defence and orthodoxy of the eastern Christians. Similarly, the Curia's failure to sustain a coherent policy towards the East was one of the factors responsible for the relative lack of success of the Hospitallers in the fourteenth century.

In its policy towards the Teutonic Order and its neighbours, on the other hand, the papacy found itself hampered time and again by a traditional approach which almost amounted to *laissez-faire*, by reports and complaints which conflicted in every detail, and by the difficulty of choosing between missionary activity and conquest, rebuke and encouragement. What the popes did was of great importance to the Hospitallers: they enabled the Order to survive, solved some problems, and aggravated others. But for the Teutonic Knights the Curia was a long way away; it could be won over, its decisions ignored or delayed, its orders disobeyed—as long as this did not go too far. Meanwhile the struggle against the pagan Lithuanians and the recalcitrant Christians of Livonia and Poland could continue, benefiting from the crusading movement but never wholly dependent on it.

---

[145] Luttrell, 'Gregory XI', 404–13.

Conclusion

IT is no longer necessary for the historian of the crusading movement in the fourteenth century to defend his choice of subject, for
the older view that this period witnessed only an 'epilogue', or at
best an 'Indian Summer' in the crusades, is slowly but surely being
displaced. It is becoming increasingly clear that abortive projects,
expressions of criticism, and signs of indifference or even hostility,
form only part of the picture. They must be balanced by the
impressive list of expeditions which were launched; by a plethora of
treatises and memoranda composed by enthusiasts; and most
importantly by much evidence that the crusade still held a prominent place in the plans and ambitions of rulers, and also in the hopes
of their subjects.

This is not to deny the problematic and complex nature of the
crusade in the fourteenth century.[1] At all points in its long history
the crusading movement reflected the changing society in which it
was rooted, and it is naïve to expect the fourteenth-century crusade
to resemble, in anything but superficialities, the vigorous feudal
expeditions of the twelfth century or the well-planned royal
crusades of the thirteenth. The fourteenth century was an age of
grave economic difficulties, acute political instability, and widespread suspicion and disillusionment about the mechanism and
aims of government in Church and State. These features are very
much present in the period's crusades, dominating in particular
the negotiations which they entailed. Even more so than other
governmental records of the Middle Ages, fourteenth-century
sources are characterized by dissimulation, bias, and propagand-
istic intent.

Nevertheless, enthusiasm for the crusade persisted, and was
remarkably wide-ranging: there was scarcely a major European
power in the fourteenth century which has not appeared as a
protagonist at some stage in this study. It is useful to view this
persistence in terms of the operation of three factors. One was the
acknowledged function of the crusade as a defensive mechanism in

[1] Cf. Luttrell, 'The Crusade', *passim.*

response to a threat posed by Muslim or pagan foes of Christendom. It was wholly natural for the Curia to issue crusade indulgences and privileges for the war against the Turks in *Romania*, or for the defence of Cilician Armenia and Cyprus against the Mamluks. And in 1340, when Merinid Morocco invaded Spain, and Poland was threatened with a Tatar attack, it was expected that Benedict XII would grant crusade bulls to Alfonso XI and Casimir. Such a response by the Curia was more or less automatic, and varied only in accordance with the nature of the threat and the Christian resistance to it. It would serve in itself to keep the crusade alive until well into the sixteenth century.

Secondly, the crusade was sustained by its value to Christian rulers as a source of finance, prestige, and propaganda advantage. The corollary was of course that rulers pressing for the issue of bulls might be insincere in their proposals. Even today it is virtually impossible to be certain of the real intentions of such men as Philip IV of France, Alfonso IV of Aragon, and Louis the Great of Hungary. The current trend amongst historians is to stress that fourteenth-century kings could not take a cynical, opportunist view of the crusade, even though in practice it did, time and again, work to their political and financial advantage; in the case of the French kings this was impossible because of the responsibilities imposed by their own lineage, and the expectations which talk of a crusade would arouse at home, while the rulers of the eastern European and Spanish kingdoms must have been aware of the dangers of crying wolf.[2] This may be true, but it did not make it any easier for the Curia to assess the validity of a project presented to it, or the sincerity of the project's author.

Through the levying of taxes, the crusade had a certain financial value without reference to popular feeling for or against it. But it would have been a waste of time issuing indulgences, or deploying the crusade as a propaganda weapon against one's Christian opponents, had such measures not struck a chord in the hearts of contemporaries. It is this third factor which underpins the other two and furnishes the most convincing explanation for the movement's continuing importance. It has recently been argued that participation in a crusade still retained 'a special, sovereign honour' in the chivalric culture of the day, and one veteran captain at the Tunis crusade of 1390 considered his presence there equivalent to taking

[2] Schein, *passim*; Tyerman, 32–4 and *passim*; Knoll, *RPM*, 174–7.

part in 'three great battles'.[3] None of the crusade projects examined in this study floundered through lack of enthusiasm. On the contrary, it was because great hopes could still be aroused that, once again, the Curia had to be on its guard against deception and poor planning: both postponement and military failure would aggravate anti-clerical feeling which was already alarming in its extent.

Despite their caution, the Avignon popes were themselves the products of a society and age which held the crusade in high esteem, and for most of them their policies reflected a genuine enthusiasm rather than simply a half-hearted response to popular demand. Old views that the Avignonese Curia was singlemindedly dedicated to the crusade[4] need, however, to be refined in view of the considerable difference both in depth of interest and in strategic approach manifested by individual popes. The only one who demonstrated no real interest in the subject was Benedict XII—ironically, since military crisis in Armenia, Spain, and eastern Europe forced him to issue a large number of crusade bulls. But Innocent VI placed the crusade low on his list of priorities, while Urban V's interest was focused on the crusade's potential as a solution to some of the West's problems. The other popes all displayed greater and more consistent enthusiasm, but in very different ways. In terms of the East, for example, Clement V and John XXII can usefully be linked through their close ties with the French court and its projects for the recovery of the Holy Land, while the Roger popes, Clement VI and Gregory XI, adopted a common approach based on the defence of Latin Greece by naval leagues. In terms of Italy, on the other hand, it was John XXII's approach which Gregory XI appears to have revived.

It is clearly impossible to expect to find a single, readily identifiable, and coherent policy running through these seven reigns. But there were certain themes and approaches which recur with impressive regularity and can be said to have constituted policy. They fall into two categories definable as 'priority' and 'responsibility'.

The theme of priority enabled the Curia to deal with the proliferation of crusading zones with which it was confronted. It had three chief facets. One was papal acceptance of the viability and import-

---

[3] Keen, *Chivalry*, 170.
[4] See, for example, Mirot, 5, 11–12; Y. Renouard, *The Avignon Papacy 1305–1403*, tr. D. Bethell (London, 1970), 116.

ance of crusading activity in Spain and eastern Europe, but, except in circumstances of crisis, their treatment as secondary fronts: certainly they were accorded considerably less attention, and Church revenue, than either Italy or the eastern Mediterranean. Secondly, of these other areas, the Church's struggle in Italy was normally given prominence; Gregory XI must have known, when he enunciated the rationale for this approach with great clarity in 1372, that he was voicing a policy which was now nearly two hundred years old.[5] Thirdly, in the eastern Mediterranean there occurred, in the course of the century, a shift away from projects to recover Palestine to the encouragement of the struggle against the Turks. *Romania* never came to enjoy priority over Palestine: it was not at Constantinople or Negroponte that Christ had died. Indeed, it is notable that all the Avignon popes, with the exception of Innocent VI, expressed the hope of rewinning the Holy Land in their lifetime. But feasibility and the growing menace of the Turks together brought about a *de facto* change of approach, nor was it theoretically difficult to encompass: the crusade meant more than the possession of Palestine, and both the Avignon popes and their contemporaries recognized this.

The theme of responsibility constituted the Curia's approach to the period's leading issue in the organization of crusades: who should pay for crusading activity, how, and when. The popes accepted that the financial burden of the crusade should lay chiefly on the Church, but they were concerned to ensure that clerical control over the levying of taxes be maintained, that the money should not be misspent, and that a proper campaign should be mounted, territorial gains duly made and held on to. When John XXII declared that the provision of guarantees had become an integral part of crusade negotiations, when the Curia specified the occasions on which clerical taxes might legitimately be levied for the crusade, and when John XXII and Clement VI outlined their approach to the novel problem of organizing and financing naval leagues within a crusading context, we can discern the broad outlines of what might, in a period of greater equilibrium in relations between the Curia and the secular powers, have evolved into a system of clear-cut responsibilities.

In the fourteenth century, however, this was out of the question. The papacy was on the defensive throughout, and on both priority

---

[5] *VMH*, ii, n. 267.

and responsibility the stances taken by the Curia were reactions rather than initiatives: attempts to counter or neutralize the driving thrust of the national monarchies. Thus, the Curia was excluded from playing a more active role in Spain and eastern Europe; it had to defend its policy on Italy against considerable diplomatic pressure; and it was only able to promote a shift in strategy in the East—which meant reacting positively to Venetian and Cypriot initiatives—when the French obsession with Palestine ceased to dominate its policy in the late 1330s. Similarly, the Curia's attempts to work out a viable system of financial responsibility and security were provoked by the flood of demands presented at Avignon, demands which even today seem astonishingly wide-ranging in scope and aggressive in tone.

At this point one must beware of pitfalls. One such is to assume that there was anything new in initiatives emanating from outside the Curia, in pressure for a crusade being applied by a secular power, and in attempts to impose or sustain papal authority meeting with failure. This assumption can be dispelled by a glance at the origins of the Second Crusade, at the course of the Fourth Crusade, and the history of the thirteenth-century crusades in Prussia. A second pitfall is to regard the papacy as just another European power, whose effectiveness can be measured in terms analogous to those applied to the national monarchies. The direct, rough and tumble nature of fourteenth-century diplomacy makes it easy to overlook the papacy's supra-national dimension, and it was here that its greatest strength still lay. Continuing acceptance of the papacy's role within the crusading movement, and of its headship of the Church, gave the Curia the resilience and inner resources to survive a series of diplomatic defeats.

Nevertheless, it would be quite wrong to deny that a fundamental shift in the balance of relations between the papacy and the secular powers had taken place. Monarchy was more assertive and demanding than in the days of Innocent III and Gregory IX, driven by ever-growing financial needs and encouraged by ideas of sovereignty. Kings no longer hesitated to forbid their subjects to depart on crusade, to ban the export of crusade taxes like the Vienne tenth, to insist that tenths levied for their own crusading uses be transmitted immediately on collection, by their own officials, to their treasury, and to whittle away the privileges of the Military Orders. The germ of such policies—in essence, the belief that national needs enjoyed priority—was as old as the crusade itself, but their acceleration and refinement proved to be a dominant feature of the crusading movement in the fourteenth century: broadly speaking, occasional practice by the more advanced monarchies in the thirteenth century became the norm for governments generally. The appeal of the crusade in this period remained an international one, but in terms of organization and finance it had taken on the form of a national institution.

It was inevitable that as the grip of the monarchies tightened, that of the papacy would weaken. It was competing with these rulers for a limited range of revenues, so that its share of the cake was diminishing, if not vanishing altogether. Moreover, the Curia had its own crusades to fight or contribute to, in Italy and the East, and its expenses were rising at the same time as the revenues which it extracted from the most important national churches were falling. That it was able none the less to fund its armies and galleys, despite the collapse of the banking houses on which it relied, was an administrative achievement of the first order; but it was won at the cost of alienating the clergy and laity and of bringing the Curia's fiscal machinery to the point of collapse in the 1370s. Worse, the control which the Curia could exercise over its own agents was slackening. Legates such as Peter Thomas and Gil Albornoz were capable of acting contrary to papal intentions, perhaps even of altering the terms of the bulls sent them, while crusade preachers regularly exceeded their authority.

Perhaps more disturbing than the stridently aggressive approach taken by the national monarchs and the many indications of papal weakness and loss of control are certain signs that the approval and sanction of the Curia had ceased to occupy a central position in the expression of the West's crusade aspirations. That the Curia was taken by surprise by the popular movements of 1309 and 1320 is less important (there were ample precedents) than the fact that one of the most popular expressions of crusading zeal in this period, the Lithuanian *Reysen*, took place outside any visible framework of papal backing or sponsorship. Much the same can be said of papal relations with those great depositories of crusading tradition and effort, the Military Orders. After the destruction of the Templars, the surviving international Orders adopted policies which were at best out of step with those pursued at Avignon, and at worst all but autonomous. In view of the argument that the popes were better placed to keep in touch with popular feeling at Avignon than they had been in central Italy, it is ironic that they sometimes appear to have been more isolated from it than Innocent III and his immediate successors.

Once again it is important to keep a sense of proportion. The crusading movement had never been a narrowly papal institution. At most, for a short period in the late twelfth and early thirteenth centuries, Latin Christians were so obsessed with the crusade that they gave credence to papal claims to direct and channel, as well as arouse and sanction, their military energies: claims expressed, for instance, in Innocent III's *Quia maior* and *Ad liberandam*. Granted that those extraordinary documents rested upon premises which were contentious even in their own day, it is still surprising how much ground the papacy had lost just a century later. It had been driven back to the central core of its authority, its unchallenged right to proclaim a crusade. In the case of the *Reysen*, even this was effectively bypassed.

We have seen that papal policy was vitiated by internal tensions and contradictions: in the issuing of licences for trade with Egypt, in papal peacemaking, in Church taxation, even in the Curia's interpretation of the Smyrna crusade and its promotion of Hospitaller reforms. While this factor was clearly important in hampering the execution of policy, it fades into insignificance when compared with the external constraints on policy examined above. That it was the latter which mattered most helps to answer the difficult question of whether papal authority over the crusade deteriorated between 1305 and 1378. The answer is yes, but not because of the corrosive effects of Avignon's much-discussed failings. Rather, as secular governments plunged deeper into crisis, they found surviving papal claims and restrictions intolerable, and grew yet more assertive in their demands. The iron fist was increasingly displayed, though the velvet glove had never been much in evidence since Anagni. Gregory XI was thus in a weaker position, on the crusade as on most other issues, than Clement V had been, even though his personality was stronger, his administration more sophisticated, and his aims better defined.

Similarly, the Avignonese Curia was closer in policy and spirit to the rival courts of the Great Schism than to the thirteenth-century Curia. Of course it was heavily influenced by its predecessor on countless important topics: the crusade indulgence, the vow and privileges of the *crucesignatus*, the legal and theological presentation of the crusades, the interpretation of crusading as a *negotium ecclesiae*, and many other aspects of preaching, organization, and finance. The length of the list comes as no surprise in view of the Curia's reverence for precedent. But the really important developments looked forward rather than back. It is becoming clear that the Great Schism had its roots less in the constitutional problems of the Roman church than in the growth of European nationalism and its fixed political alignments.[6] The resulting view is that the Schism represented the Roman church falling into line with this situation, and was not a radical break with the past but a natural development in Church–State relations, the culmination of a trend some decades old. Avignonese crusade policy did indeed resemble what we know of the policies adopted towards the crusade by the two obediences. It accepted the *de facto* existence of national churches when negotiating and levying crusade taxes; it moved, hesitantly but inexorably, towards a financial administration of the crusade indulgence; and it came to embrace a straightforward financial interpretation of the embargo system.

On the other hand, 1378 is not only a convenient point at which to close this study; it also marks a milestone in the history of the papacy's involvement in the crusading movement. For as long as there was only one Curia there was only one crusading policy, however unstable, contradictory, and difficult to implement. The outbreak and persistence of the Schism signalled the breaching of this final line of defence, inevitably bringing about a further, substantial weakening of the papal position. The Avignonese Curia thus deserves to be studied as a separate and highly distinctive period in papal history. The popes of the Schism and Renaissance, like those of the Avignon period, were the conscious heirs to claims over the crusade established by their predecessors from Urban II to Innocent III; but they were to find their legacy even more intractable than had the seven popes who fought with energy and courage, but little success, to defend those claims between 1305 and 1378.

[6] See, for example, Palmer, 'England, France, the Papacy and the Flemish Succession', 362.

The Cost of Clement VI's Contribution to the Smyrna Crusade, 1343–1349

PROFESSOR KENNETH SETTON has written that 'Clement was to keep his galleys at sea for two years, and the *exitus* accounts of his reign in the Vatican Archives show that they eventually cost him almost 200,000 florins'.[1] This comment seems to be based on K. H. Schäfer's remark that 'gegen die Türken liess [Clement VI] im Jahre 1344 4 Galeeren kriegsmässig ausrüsten und unterhielt sie 2 Jahre lang mit einem Aufwende von nahezu 200,000 Goldgulden'.[2] Difficult as it is to investigate the Pope's expenses fully,[3] it is worth making the attempt since Clement's reputation as a crusading pope obviously depends to some extent on his readiness to invest resources in the naval league.

(1) In his letter of 10 April 1349 to the Master of the Hospitallers, Clement detailed his outlays for the papal galleys as follows: 33,546 florins disbursed *per gentes camere*, and 110,800 florins sent East with the Hospitallers.[4] These sums exactly fit the preceding payments:

(a) Sums paid by cameral officials in the West or in Cyprus: 1,800 fl. paid to Martin Zaccaria, October 1343;[5] 12,800 fl. paid direct, October 1343;[6] 7,600 fl. paid direct, September 1346;[7] 11,346 fl. paid as a final settlement, 1347.[8] Total: 33,546 fl.

(b) Sums sent East with the Hospitallers: 25,600 fl., October 1343;[9] 26,800 fl., November 1344–July 1345;[10] 58,400 fl., September 1346.[11] Total: 110,800 fl.

This makes a grand total of 144,346 florins, less if the Hospitallers sent back the 31,500 florins which Clement claimed that they had not spent;[12] in that case the total would be 112,846 florins, far less than the figure given by Schäfer, and for over three years' service, not two (that is, December 1343 to the summer months of 1347).

(2) The figure of 144,346 florins corresponds closely to the outlay reached by arithmetic calculation based on the annual cost of the galleys:

(a) The galleys: 38,400 fl. *per annum* over a period of three years and seven months, making a total of 137,640 fl.

---

[1] *PL*, 187. [2] *Die Ausgaben*, 170; no source is quoted.
[3] Cf. Setton, *PL*, 187n. [4] Déprez *et al.*, n. 4130.
[5] Ibid., n. 464. [6] Ibid., nn. 435, 464.
[7] Ibid., n. 2809. [8] *Die Ausgaben*, 359.
[9] Déprez *et al.*, nn. 368, 464. [10] Ibid., nn. 1209, 1834.
[11] Ibid., n. 2809. [12] Ibid., n. 4130.

(b) The captain's stipend: 1,800 fl. *per annum* over the same period, making a total of 6,450 fl.

This makes a grand total of 144,090 florins, or 144,425 if one includes the 335 florins paid at one point *pro portagio*. As for the unspent 31,500 florins, this could well be the money saved through the economies which Clement called for on two occasions.[13]

(3) What are the implications of the following passage in a letter which Clement VI wrote to Humbert of Vienne in August 1349?

> For you know, unless you feign ignorance, that while it was carefully laid down that a specified number of ships would be maintained for three years in aid of the said Faith and to the advantage of the faithful of those parts, we proceeded to extend their service for a two year period, for your benefit in particular, as a result of which we had to pay more than 100,000 florins.[14]

Since the papal galleys stopped operating in the summer of 1347, the *biennium* referred to (1346–8) was not fully served; even if it had been, two years' service would not have cost more than 100,000 florins. Clement's reference to this sum can only mean his *total* expenditure on the galleys.

In conclusion, I can see no reason for believing that total papal expenditure exceeded 144,346 florins, while it may have been only 112,846.

[13] Ibid., nn. 1114, 1713.

[14] Ibid., n. 4218. This is a tendentious letter and is not wholly accurate in its comments on the league.

Smyrna under Papal Rule, 1344–1374

THE port of Smyrna lies half-way down the western seaboard of Anatolia, at the end of a deep bay situated between the islands of Chios and Lesbos, and about forty miles north of Ephesus. It has a good harbour, and in 1261 was important enough commercially for the Genoese to insist on its cession to their jurisdiction as part of the Treaty of Nymphaeum. By the early fourteenth century, however, its trade had declined. Pegolotti did not mention it and Ibn Battuta, who visited it in 1333, noted that most of it was in ruins.[1] Smyrna's decline was accelerated by Mehmed of Aydin's capture of its upper fortress in about 1317. Some years later, probably in 1329, the Turks took the port area itself and started to use it for piracy.[2] The capture of Smyrna by the forces of the Latin naval league in 1344 was chiefly important because it deprived the powerful Emirate of Aydin of its main sea outlet; by so doing it considerably altered the balance of power in the Aegean.[3] So although the West's problems prevented it from exploiting its tenure of Smyrna by pushing inland, it was important to hold on to the port itself both as a strategic bulwark,[4] and for the achievement and sacrifice which it represented.[5]

Together with Lusignan Cyprus and Hospitaller Rhodes, Smyrna was a Latin outpost in the Levant. But it differed from them in two important ways. First, it consisted of the port alone, with no hinterland or other towns attached: the great prize of Chios was held by the Genoese, and the Latins failed to capture the upper fortress, or acropolis. Smyrna was isolated, vulnerable, and poor. Again, unlike Rhodes or Cyprus, it was governed

---

[1] As Lemerle showed (226–7, and see also 45), the clause relating to trade in the draft treaty worked out in 1347–8 between Octavian Zaccaria, Umur and Hizir, was concerned with Ephesus rather than Smyrna. For Smyrna in the period preceding the Turkish conquest, see H. Ahrweiler, 'L'Histoire et la géographie de la région de Smyrne entre les deux occupations turques (1081–1317), particulièrement au XIIIᵉ siècle', *Travaux et mémoires*, i (1965), 1–204, esp. 34–42.

[2] Lemerle, 50, 57.

[3] Ibid., 212, 221n, 235, 241.

[4] In 1362, for example, Urban V wrote that 'ad ipsorum [sc. the Turks] repressionem, ac defensionem fidelium Regni Cipri et aliarum partium predictarum, multum expedire noscatur quod civitas nostra Smirnen[sis] custodiatur attente per stipendiarios providos et fideles': ASV, Reg. Vat. 245, ff. 31ᵛ–32ʳ. In 1351 Clement VI still had hopes that the Smyrna garrison might be able to help the Armenians: Déprez and Mollat, n. 2503.

[5] See, for example, Gasnault et al., n. 2018.

until 1374 not by a single power but by a coalition made up of the members of the naval league presided over by the pope. The captain of the garrison ruled *nomine unionis*, though the pope took most of the decisions.[6] In fact there are clear signs that the Curia regarded Smyrna as a papal dependency, though for financial reasons it avoided incorporating it into St Peter's patrimony. Urban V and Gregory XI referred to Smyrna as *nostra civitas*.[7]

It was the Curia's intention that Smyrna should be governed by a captain and a vicar. The captaincy was a military appointment, concerned with the command of the small garrison; the post of vicar was at least partly pastoral, though the sources do not support a strict division between the temporal and spiritual (the situation was probably always too fluid for that). In 1348 Barnabà da Parma was captain, but he vanishes from sight and at the election of Innocent VI Archbishop Paul of Smyrna had assumed charge, possibly as captain. In January 1353 he received the thanks of the new pope: Raymond Sacquet, Bishop of Thérouanne and Clement VI's legate at Smyrna, and Dinadanus de Sala, a Bolognese constable there, had with others told Innocent about the diligence, prudence, and good faith which Paul had displayed.[8] Towards the end of the year the Pope was considering replacing Paul with Nicholas Belintioni, a Florentine, and he asked Hugh of Cyprus to permit Nicholas to become captain at Smyrna without forfeiting his Cypriot pension as a *stipendiarius* of the King.[9] Nothing came of this, and in September 1354 the Master of the Hospitallers was told to confirm Paul in the captaincy if he seemed 'sufficiens et idoneus'.[10] By this time there was also a vicar at Smyrna, a Franciscan *conversus* called Peter Patricelli of Fano.[11]

In April 1356 Orso Dolfin, Venetian Archbishop of Crete, was instructed to appoint a suitable captain, 'tam hac vice si non sit in ea aliquis deputatus et residens, quam deinceps quotiens fuerit oportunum'.[12] Apparently the Archbishop himself became captain, combining it with a papal legation. He was replaced in 1359 by a Florentine Hospitaller, Nicholas Benedetti.[13] Four years later a Genoese, Peter Raccanelli, was appointed.[14] He was succeeded in 1371 by another Genoese, Ottobuono Cattaneo, who held the post until September 1374.[15] Pope Gregory XI then placed the custody of Smyrna in the unwilling hands of the Hospitallers for a five year period, which was extended until 1402.

[6] Cf. Halecki, *Un Empereur*, 14n.
[7] Above, n. 4; *Acta Greg. XI*, n. 59; Mollat, *Lettres secrètes*, n. 2700.
[8] Gasnault *et al.*, n. 93.
[9] Ibid., nn. 619 (in which 'Franciscus' should read 'Paulus'), 689.
[10] Ibid., n. 1133.
[11] Ibid., n. 1156.
[12] Ibid., n. 2018.
[13] Setton, *PL*, 234.
[14] LM, nn. 458–61. Text of appointment and oath of office given below, n. 50.
[15] Mirot *et al.*, n. 2140.

The captain commanded the garrison and presumably exercised a form of jurisdiction in the port; thus in 1356 Orso Dolfin was told to ensure that the captain he chose was obeyed by the constables and the other men-at-arms making up the garrison, and by the town's civilian population.[16] In 1363 Urban V told Peter Raccanelli that he would order 'universis stipendiariis ac civibus et habitatoribus dicte civitatis et aliis quorum interest, ut tibi circa premissa officia plene pareant et intendant'.[17] The captain received an annual subvention to pay the garrison and his own stipend. The most interesting appointment was that of Nicholas Benedetti in 1359. He was ordered to build strong walls within a period of seven years, and to maintain a garrison of 150 mercenaries and two galleys. To help pay for the fortifications he was permitted to send one cog and two galleys as often as he wished to trade with Alexandria. If he died, one of his two brothers, Pace and Francis, could take over the captaincy, and the family was granted rights of conquest provided that it held such lands and towns of the Roman church.[18] Such measures form an attempt to make Smyrna a family-based, profit-making enterprise along the lines of Chios under the Zaccarie.

One is struck by the degree of papal suspicion about the captaincy and the amount of fraud associated with it. If possible the pope subordinated the post to the authority of a legate, such as Raymond Sacquet, Orso Dolfin, and Peter Thomas. According to Philip of Mézières, the latter on several occasions accompanied the troops at Smyrna into action against the Turks.[19] Urban V wrote in 1363 that the captain was to be 'sub obedientia et correctione' of any legate whom the Pope might appoint.[20] Otherwise, important on the spot decisions were vested in the Master of the Hospitallers; thus in 1355 he was to decide whether it was a good idea to substitute two galleys' service for the annual subvention of 3,000 florins provided by Cyprus.[21] Nearly all the captains seem to have succumbed to temptation. Peter Patricelli, vicar in 1354, abused a privilege of sending two ships to Turkish ports to purchase supplies by selling the privilege to merchants.[22] In June 1355 Innocent VI instructed the Master of the Hospitallers to appoint 'aliquos viros probos' to supervise the captain both in handling incoming money and in dealing with the port's own meagre revenues: fraud had crept in when wages were paid to the garrison.[23] In April 1356 Orso Dolfin was told to exercise care in spending money on wages and fortifications. Previously some had gone astray: 'Fraudi namque cuilibet

---

[16] Gasnault *et al.*, n. 2018.
[17] See below, n. 50.
[18] Setton, *PL*, 234–5.
[19] Philip of Mézières, 89, and see too 84, 86.
[20] See below, n. 50.
[21] Gasnault *et al.*, nn. 1788, 1791.
[22] Ibid., nn. 735, 1156.
[23] Ibid., n. 1630.

obviandum est, sed ei maxime que in dispendium populi christiani et confusionem posset catholice fidei redundare'.[24]

Nicholas Benedetti was appointed for eight years but was replaced after only four, so he might have been guilty of peculation. Certainly both Peter Raccanelli and Ottobuono Cattaneo were corrupt. In January 1373 the Archbishop of Genoa and a Genoese abbot were told to show Peter letters describing the condition of the Smyrna garrison, which was presumably poor, and to demand an explanation. They were to take measures against the former captain if he did not pay arrears of wages due. Gregory XI claimed that members of the garrison had been deserting the port because they had not been paid.[25] The Pope was also afraid that they might be bribed to hand the town over to the Turks.[26] Ottobuono Cattaneo was guilty of absenteeism, probably because of his lands in Rhodes and Cyprus, and in the period leading up to the Hospitaller takeover the town was riven by quarrels between the Archbishop of Smyrna, the garrison, the Venetians, Genoese, Cretans, and other Latin residents.[27]

This is not surprising since, although Urban V lavished praise on Peter Raccanelli's leadership in his letter of appointment in 1363,[28] the captaincy of Smyrna was unlikely to have been a prize posting for a commander of ambition. The port was the scene of the usual disputes between Italian traders, and the pope wrote that it was subject to regular and heavy Turkish attacks.[29] Victualling was a constant problem. In November 1353 Innocent VI wrote to King Hugh of Cyprus that arrivals at the Curia had informed him that the garrison was in grave danger of being overrun 'ob ipsius neglectam custodiam et defectum rerum'. The Pope supervised the despatch of two ships with supplies, and at the beginning of 1354 permitted the authorities at Smyrna to trade with the Turks to get the necessary provisions.[30] But in June 1355 the Master of the Hospitallers was informed that 'et loci situs . . . et ipsorum Turchorum . . . rapacitas' meant that the garrison lacked essential supplies.[31] The image of a badly supplied, unpaid, and demoralized garrison clinging to the hostile coastline like a limpet is a compelling one: one problem was that, as pointed out above, the port's commercial importance had declined. When Gregory XI wrote in June 1374 'to the constables, paid troops, and people of Smyrna' to assure them that the Holy See would not abandon them in their penury and in the midst of dangers, the situation had obviously reached rock bottom.[32] The Hospitallers probably took over just in time to save the port.

[24] Ibid., n. 2091.
[25] Mollat, *Lettres secrètes*, nn. 1406, 1411, and cf. nn. 2701, 2705.
[26] Luttrell, 'Gregory XI', 397.
[27] Mollat, *Lettres secrètes*, nn. 1540–1, 2700, 2706, 2876.
[28] See below, n. 50.
[29] Gasnault *et al.*, nn. 618, 1488, 1630.
[30] Ibid., nn. 618, 642, 645, 735.
[31] Ibid., n. 1630.   [32] Mollat, *Lettres secrètes*, n. 2700.

The root of the problem, as so often, was financial: funds paid in part, in arrears, or not at all. The expenses of the Smyrna establishment, wages, the cost of fortifications, and presumably a modicum of administration, were supposed to be met by annual subventions of 3,000 florins each from the papacy, Venice, Cyprus, and the Hospitallers. There were, the pope wrote, *conventiones* to this effect, though Venice denied having agreed to them.[33] The papal share was usually forthcoming. Innocent VI renewed payment as soon as he was elected, channelling cameral revenues from Cyprus through his nuncios there.[34] Tenths were levied to pay for the subventions: a three-year tenth at the end of 1353 in the imperial dioceses and Frankish Greece, and tenths in Cyprus in 1362 and 1372.[35] There were the usual difficulties in collecting and transferring the Cypriot tenth, but in general the pope paid his share, organizing also the collection of voluntary donations and legacies.[36] But the Holy See could not support Smyrna by itself. As Innocent VI wrote in November 1353 to Hugh of Cyprus, he was caught in the grip of falling revenues and soaring expenses, and had no intention of burdening himself with Smyrna too.[37]

This cautious approach was common to all the powers involved. Important as Smyrna was as a symbol—'the very symbol of crusading success'[38]— and in theory (though hardly in practice) as a jumping-off point for further Christian advance, it imposed a considerable annual burden in a period of economic difficulties. Cyprus appears to have been quite regular in its payments.[39] There were letters to King Hugh asking for his subvention, but no very severe rebukes, and in 1356 Innocent VI even expressed his pleasure that the King had kept active the galleys armed for the abortive league of 1351.[40] Possibly the Hospitallers were less satisfactory, though papal correspondence with them tended to be more peremptory anyway, and rather more was expected of them as a Military Order committed to holy war. In November 1353 Innocent VI wrote to Dieudonné of Gozon that he should put to one side all excuses and hand over the 3,000 florins which his Order owed for the defence of Smyrna.[41] Yet in April 1356 Innocent admitted that the Hospitallers had in fact paid the Venetian share as well as their own for the past three years.[42] In May 1363 Urban V was counting on the Order's 3,000 florins to pay the wages of the garrison

[33] Gasnault *et al.*, n. 618.
[34] Ibid., n. 80.
[35] Ibid., n. 646; LM, n. 113; Mollat, *Lettres secrètes*, nn. 935, 1369.
[36] ASV, Instr. misc. n. 2493; Gasnault *et al.*, nn. 2019, 2129; Mollat, *Lettres secrètes*, nn. 2697, 2699, 2702; Zachariadou, 41.
[37] Gasnault *et al.*, n. 618.
[38] Setton, *PL*, 328.
[39] See Edbury, 'Crusading Policy', 91.
[40] Gasnault *et al.*, n. 2006.
[41] Ibid., n. 621.
[42] Ibid., n. 2015.

together with his own quota,[43] but in 1365 it is possible that Hospitaller payments were 15,000 florins in arrears.[44] In 1374 Gregory XI relied on the Knights to lend money to the troops at Smyrna until the arrears of their wages had been paid.[45]

The chief defaulter was Venice. The early 1350s were a difficult period for the Republic, faced as it was by a trio of enemies in Genoa, Hungary, and the Carraresi of Padua. Despite the continuing Turkish raids on Venice's merchant ships, it was unable to give the eastern Mediterranean much attention and tried to opt out of even the defence of Smyrna.[46] In May 1355 Innocent VI wrote to Charles IV that Venice had stopped paying its 3,000 florins at the outbreak of the Genoese war, and that others had followed suit. The Emperor was asked to help, a clear sign of desperation.[47] In April 1356 the Doge was asked to renew payments and to pay his arrears, but it is not clear that he did so.[48] Venice's reluctance to pay its subventions fits in with its general policy towards the naval league after its initial successes.[49] Indeed, there are unmistakable similarities between the faltering and ramshackle nature of the Christian presence at Smyrna in these three decades, and the constitution and activity of the league which had brought it into being.

THE APPOINTMENT OF PETER RACCANELLI AS CAPTAIN AT SMYRNA, 12 MAY 1363[50]

Apostolice sedis solicitudo continua, custodie ac saluti fidelium studio materne sedulitatis intenta, viros industrios et probate fidelitatis solerter exquirit, quos ad huiusmodi custodiam, precipue in locis in quibus maius timetur periculum, valeat deputare, in quorum fide ac vigilantia tam sedes ipsa quam iidem fideles quibus est ipsa oportuna custodia, indubia confidencia requiescant. Ad te igitur qui, prout fidedignorum relatione percepimus, in regimine ac custodia civitatis Smirnarum, in faucibus infidelium Turchorum dei et sacre fidei hostium constitute, fuisti laudabiliter comprobatus, digne dirigentes nostre considerationis intuitum, Te Capitaneum et Rectorem ac custodem dicte civitatis usque ad decem annos

---

[43] LM, n. 459. It is not clear at what point the Curia stopped trying to exact Venetian and Cypriot contributions.

[44] Luttrell, 'Gregory XI', 396n.

[45] Mollat, *Lettres secrètes*, nn. 2695, 2703.

[46] *I libri comm.*, ii, 185, nn. 354, 356. But cf. *DVL*, ii, n. 2.

[47] Gasnault *et al.*, n. 1488.

[48] Ibid., nn. 2015, 2088. Cf. *I libri comm.*, ii, 264, n. 241; *Régestes*, i, 93.

[49] See above, ch. 6, nn. 93–8.

[50] ASV, Reg. Vat. 245, ff. 189ʳ–190ʳ. The oath bears a natural resemblance to that sworn by rectors of provinces in the Papal State when taking up office: *Liber censuum*, ed. P. Fabre and L. Duchesne. 3 vols. (Paris, 1889–1952), ii, 72–3. Cf. also the oath sworn by Louis de la Cerda on his enfeoffment as Prince of the Canary Islands in 1344: *AE*, ad annum 1344, nn. 46–7, xxv, 344.

inchoandos in kalendis mensis Septembri proximi futuri auctoritate apostolica presentium tenore constituimus et etiam deputamus, tibi custodiam dicte civitatis ac arcis in ea constitute faciendam tuis sumptibus et expensis, cum salario tamen quod per alias nostras litteras duximus deputandum, plenarie committentes, ac faciendi, gerendi et exercendi omnia et singula que ad huiusmodi Capitaneatus, regiminis et custodie officia pertinent, potestatem plenariam concedentes, ac mandantes universis stipendiariis ac civibus et habitatoribus dicte civitatis et aliis quorum interest, ut tibi circa premissa officia plene pareant et intendant. Volumus tamen quod semper sub nostra ac nostri legati seu illius quem super hoc deputabimus obedientia et correctione existas. Quocirca discretioni tue per apostolica scripta mandamus quatenus, ad partes ipsas te personaliter conferens, officia ipsa ad honorem nostrum et fidei predicte ac ecclesie Romane statumque prosperum fidelium predictorum sic exercere fideliter et studiose procures, quod spei nostre conceptus ex operationibus tuis fructus utiles pariat, ex quibus nobis satisfactio grata, tibi honor et eisdem fidei et ecclesie votiva deo propitio proveniant incrementa. Dat. Avinione, iiii idus maii, anno primo.

Forma iuramenti..

Ego Petrus Racchanelli, Civis Januensis, Capitaneus et Custos Civitatis Smirnarum pro Sancta Romana ecclesia deputatus, ab hac hora inantea fidelis et obediens ero beato Petro Sancteque Romane ecclesie ac domino meo domino Urbano pape Quinto eiusque successoribus canonice intrantibus. Non ero in consilio vel consensu ut vitam perdant aut membrum vel capiantur mala captione. Consilium, quod per se vel nuncium suum seu litteras michi credituri sunt, signo, verbo vel nutu me sciente ad eorum dampnum seu prejudicium nulli pandam. Si dampnum eorum tractari scivero, pro posse meo impediam ne fiat, quod si per me impedire non possem, per nuncium aut per litteras eis significare curabo, vel illi per quem citius ad eorum noticiam deducatur. Papatum Romanum et regalia sancti Petri et omnia iura Romane ecclesie que habet ubique, et specialiter in civitate predicta, manutenebo totis viribus et defendam, dictam Civitatem per me vel alium seu alios fideliter custodiam ad opus sacre fidei et dicte ecclesie. Ipsamque Civitatem cum pertinentiis suis non resignabo nisi legato apostolice sedis si fuerit in partibus illis, aut alteri per dominum papam vel eundem legatum ad hoc deputato. Supradicta omnia et singula promitto et iuro attendere et observare sine omni dolo et fraude ac malicia, sic me deus adiuvet et hec sancta dei evangelia.

Die xii mensis mai, pontificatus domini nostri domini Urbani pape Quinti anno primo, prefatus Petrus in manibus dicti pape in palatio apostolico Avinionensi.

APPENDIX III

A Schedule of Indulgences, 1368

THE following, hitherto unpublished schedule of indulgences was issued in May 1368 for the renewal of the crusade against Bernabò Visconti, in connection with the planned Italian expedition of Charles IV.[1] It is characteristic of Avignonese crusade bulls in following Innocent III's approach to the availability of the indulgence, with a few variations relating to the service of the *crucesignatus*. Two of the latter occur here:

(1) Those who fight for only part of the year prescribed as the period of service are to share in the indulgence.

(2) Those who die while serving their year, or are prevented from completing the full year by the campaign itself drawing to a close, are to receive the indulgence in full.

Omnibus vere penitentibus et confessis qui contra dictum Bernabonem manifestum hostem ecclesie et Imperii predictorum, ac fautores, complices, defensores, valitores et sequaces ipsius ac adherentes seu parentes eidem contra nos et ecclesiam, Imperatorem et Imperium predictos, in personis et sumptibus propriis, necnon et hiis qui in propriis personis, alienis tamen sumptibus, infra duos annos a die qua presentes fierunt publicate, profecti fuerint, et per unum annum continuum vel interpolatum infra dictum Biennium in dicti prosecutione negotii fuerunt commorati, eorumdem Imperatoris et Imperii sequendo vexilla, et eis insuper qui suis duntaxat expensis, iuxta facultatem et qualitatem suam, destinabunt idoneos bellatores per dictum tempus moraturos et laboraturos ibidem, plenam concedimus veniam peccatorum que proficiscentibus in terre sancte subsidium concedi per dictam sedem apostolicam consuevit. Eos autem qui non per annum integrum sed pro ipsius anni parte in huiusmodi servicio dei forsitan laborabunt, iuxta quantitatem laboris et devotionis affectum, participes esse volumus indulgentie supradicte. Quod si forsan ipsorum aliquos post iter arreptum in prosecutione dicti negotii ex hac luce migrare contigerit, vel interim negotium ipsum congrua terminatione compleri, eos assequi volumus indulgentiam memoratam. Huiusmodi etiam remissionis volumus et concedimus esse participes, iuxta quantitatem subsidii et

---

[1] ASV, Reg. Vat. 249, f. 108^{r–v}. For the rest of the bull see *AE*, ad annum 1368, nn. 2–3, xxvi, 150–1.

devotionis affectum, omnes qui ad impugnationem ipsius Bernabonis suorumque fautorum, complicum, defensorum, valitorum eique adherentium et parentium predictorum rebellium ac hostium ecclesie et Imperii predictorum de bonis suis congrue ministrabunt.

Bibliography

I. MANUSCRIPT SOURCES

Archivio segreto Vaticano

Registra Avinionensia, nn. 156–7.

Registra Vaticana, nn. 63, 68, 74, 78, 87, 99, 105, 107, 113–14, 119, 128, 137, 166, 245–7, 249, 264–5, 268.

Instrumenta miscellanea, nn. 490, 2493, 6292.

2. PRINTED SOURCES

Acta aragonensia: Quellen zur deutschen, italienischen, französischen, spanischen, zur Kirchen- und Kulturgeschichte aus der diplomatischen Korrespondenz Jaymes II. (1291–1327), ed. H. Finke. 3 vols. (Leipzig–Berlin, 1908–22).

Acta Benedicti XII, ed. A. L. Tautu. PCRCICO, viii (Rome, 1958).

Acta Clementis VI, ed. A. L. Tautu. PCRCICO, ix (Rome, 1960).

Acta Gregorii XI, ed. A. L. Tautu. PCRCICO, xii (Rome, 1966).

Acta Innocentii VI, ed. A. L. Tautu. PCRCICO, x (Rome, 1961).

Acta Joannis XXII, ed. A. L. Tautu. PCRCICO, vii² (Rome, 1952).

Acta pontificum svecica, I. Acta cameralia, ed. L. M. Bååth. 2 vols. (Holmiae, 1936–57).

Acta Urbani V, ed. A. L. Tautu. PCRCICO, xi (Rome, 1964).

Adam Murimuth, 'Continuatio chronicarum', ed. E. M. Thompson. *RS* (London, 1889).

Analecta Vaticana 1202–1366, ed. J. Ptasnik. Monumenta Poloniae Vaticana iii (Cracow, 1914).

Annales ecclesiastici, ed. C. Baronio *et al.* 37 vols. (Paris–Freiburg–Bar le Duc, 1864–87).

Appendice ai Monumenti ravennati . . . del conte M. Fantuzzi, ed. A. Tarlazzi. 3 vols. (Ravenna, 1869–86).

'Aragón y la empresa del Estrecho en el siglo XIV: Nuevos documentos del Archivio municipal de Zaragoza', ed. A. Canellas, *Estudios de Edad media de la Corona de Aragón: Seccion de Zaragoza*, ii (1946), 7–73.

Die Ausgaben der apostolischen Kammer unter Benedikt XII., Klemens VI. und Innocenz VI. (1335–1362), ed. K. H. Schäfer (Paderborn, 1914).

Bernard Gui, 'De secta illorum qui se dicunt esse de ordine apostolorum', ed. A. Segarizzi, *RISNS* 9⁵, 17–36.

Bulas y cartas secretas de Inocencio VI (1352–1362), ed. J. Z. Aramburu. Monumenta Hispaniae Vaticana: Seccion Registros iii (Rome, 1970).

Calendar of Entries in the Papal Registers relating to Great Britain and Ireland: Papal Letters, comp. W. H. Bliss and J. A. Twemlow. 14 vols. (London, 1893–1960).

Canon of Bridlington, 'Gesta Edwardi III', ed. W. Stubbs. *RS* (London, 1883).

Cartulaire général de l'Ordre des Hospitaliers de S. Jean de Jérusalem (1100–1310), ed. J. Delaville le Roulx. 4 vols. (Paris, 1894–1906).

The Chronicle of Novgorod 1016–1471, tr. R. Michell and N. Forbes. Camden 3rd Series, xxv (London, 1914).

'Chronicle of Oliva', *SRP*, i, 669–726.

'Chronicon astense', *RIS* xi, cols. 139–282.

'Chronicon mutinense', *RIS* xv, cols. 555–638.

'Chronique parisienne anonyme de 1316 à 1339', ed. M. A. Hellot, *Mémoires de la Société de l'histoire de Paris et de l'Ile-de-France*, xi (1884), 1–207.

Chronographia regum Francorum, ed. H. Moranvillé. 3 vols. (Paris, 1891–7).

Codex diplomaticus dominii temporalis Sanctae Sedis, ed. A. Theiner. 2 vols. (Rome, 1861–2).

Codex diplomaticus prussicus, ed. J. Voigt. 6 vols. (Königsberg, 1836–61).

Conciliorum oecumenicorum decreta, ed. J. Alberigo *et al*. 3rd edn. (Bologna, 1973).

'Le Conseil du roi Charles', ed. G. I. Bratianu, *Revue historique du sud-ouest européen*, xix (1942), 353–61.

Continuator of William of Nangis, *Chronique latine . . . de 1300 à 1368*, ed. H. Géraud. 2 vols. (Paris, 1843).

Corpus iuris canonici, ed. E. Friedberg. 2 vols. (Leipzig, 1879).

'Cronaca malatestiana', ed. A. F. Massèra, *RISNS* 15².

'Crónica de Alfonso XI', ed. C. Rosell, *Crónicas de los reyes de Castilla*, i, in Biblioteca de autores Españoles lxvi (Madrid, 1875), 173–392.

'Cronica di Bologna', *RIS* xviii, cols. 241–792.

'Cronica d'Orvieto', *RIS* xv, cols. 643–94.

Délibérations des assemblées vénitiennes concernant la Romanie, ed. F. Thiriet. 2 vols. (Paris, 1966–71).

Diplomatari de l'orient català (1301–1409), ed. A. Rubió i Lluch (Barcelona, 1947).

Diplomatarium veneto–levantinum, sive acta et diplomata res venetas, graecas atque Levantis illustrantia a. 1300–1454, ed. G. M. Thomas. 2 vols. (Venice, 1880–99).

Documenta selecta mutuas civitatis Arago-Cathalaunicae et ecclesiae relationes illustrantia, ed. J. Vincke (Barcelona, 1936).

Documents relatifs aux états généraux et assemblées réunis sous Philippe le Bel, ed. G. Picot (Paris, 1901).

Ecclesiae venetae antiquis monumentis, ed. F. Cornaro. 12 vols. (Venice, 1749).

Die Einnahmen der apostolischen Kammer unter Benedikt XII., ed. E. Göller (Paderborn, 1920).

Die Einnahmen der apostolischen Kammer unter Innocenz VI., I., ed. H. Hoberg (Paderborn, 1955).

Die Einnahmen der apostolischen Kammer unter Johann XXII., ed. E. Göller (Paderborn, 1910).

Die Einnahmen der apostolischen Kammer unter Klemens VI., ed. L. Mohler (Paderborn, 1931).

Froissart, *Chroniques*, ed. S. Luce *et al*. 15 vols. (Paris, 1869–1975).

Giorgio Stella, 'Annales genuenses', ed. G. P. Balbi, *RISNS* 17^2.

Giovanni Villani, *Cronica*, ed. F. Gherardi Dragomanni. 4 vols. (Milan, 1848).

Les Grandes Chroniques de France, ed. J. Viard. 9 vols. (Paris, 1920–37).

'Gregorio XI e Giovanni I di Napoli. Documenti inediti dell' Archivio segreto Vaticano', ed. F. Cerasoli, *ASPN*, xxiii (1898), 471–500, 671–701, xxiv (1899), 3–24, 307–28, 403–27, xxv (1900), 3–26.

Guillaume de Machaut, *La Prise d'Alexandrie*, ed. M. L. De Mas Latrie (Geneva, 1877).

Henry Knighton, 'Chronicon', ed. J. R. Lumby. *RS*. 2 vols. (London, 1889–95).

Hermann of Wartberg, 'Chronicon Livoniae', *SRP*, ii, 21–116.

Histoire du différend d'entre le pape Boniface VIII et Philippes le Bel roy de France, ed. Dupuy (Paris, 1655).

'Historia fratris Dulcini heresiarche', ed. A. Segarizzi, *RISNS* 9^5, 3–14.

'Historiae romanae fragmenta', in *Antiquitates italicae medii aevi*, ed. L. A. Muratori. 25 vols. (Milan, 1723–1896), iii, cols. 251–548.

Honoré Bonet, *The Tree of Battles*, tr. G. W. Coopland (Liverpool, 1949).

Illustrazioni della spedizione in oriente di Amedeo VI, ed. F. Bollati di Saint-Pierre (Turin, 1900).

John Capgrave, 'Liber de illustribus Henricis', ed. F. C. Hingeston. *RS* (London, 1858).

John of St Victor, 'Vita Clementis V', *VPA*, i, 1–23.

Lettres de Benoît XII, ed. A. Fierens. Analecta Vaticano–belgica (Rome, 1910).

Lettres closes, patentes et curiales du pape Benoît XII se rapportant à la France, ed. G. Daumet. BEFAR, 3rd Series. 1 vol. (Paris, 1899–1920).

Lettres closes, patentes et curiales du pape Clément VI intéressant les pays autres que la France, ed. E. Déprez and G. Mollat. BEFAR, 3rd Series. 1 vol. (Paris, 1960–1).

Lettres closes, patentes et curiales du pape Clément VI se rapportant à la France, ed. E. Déprez *et al*. BEFAR, 3rd Series. 3 vols. (Paris, 1901–61).

Lettres closes et patentes du pape Benoît XII intéressant les pays autres que la France, ed. J.-M. Vidal and G. Mollat. BEFAR, 3rd Series. 1 vol. (Paris, 1913–50).

Lettres communes du pape Benoît XII, ed. J.-M. Vidal. BEFAR, 3rd Series. 3 vols. (Paris, 1903–11).

Lettres communes du pape Jean XXII analysées d'après les registres dits d'Avignon et du Vatican, ed. G. Mollat. BEFAR, 3rd Series. 16 vols. (Paris, 1904–47).

Lettres de Grégoire XI, ed. C. Tihon. Analecta Vaticano–belgica. 4 vols. (Brussels–Rome, 1958–75).

Lettres de Jean XXII, ed. A. Fayen. Analecta Vaticano–belgica. 2 vols. (Rome, 1908–12).

Lettres secrètes et curiales du pape Grégoire XI intéressant les pays autres que la France, ed. G. Mollat. BEFAR, 3rd Series. 1 vol. (Paris, 1962–5).

Lettres secrètes et curiales du pape Grégoire XI relatives à la France, ed. L. Mirot *et al.* BEFAR, 3rd Series. 1 vol. (Paris, 1935–57).

Lettres secrètes et curiales du pape Innocent VI, ed. P. Gasnault *et al.* BEFAR, 3rd Series. 4 vols. so far (Paris, 1959–).

Lettres secrètes et curiales du pape Jean XXII relatives à la France, ed. A. Coulon and S. Clémencet. BEFAR, 3rd Series. 4 vols. (Paris, 1906–72).

Lettres secrètes et curiales du pape Urbain V, ed. P. Lecacheux and G. Mollat. BEFAR, 3rd Series. 1 vol. (Paris, 1902–55).

Lettres d'Urbain V, ed. A. Fierens and C. Tihon. Analecta Vaticano-belgica. 2 vols. (Rome, 1928–32).

Liber censuum, ed. P. Fabre and L. Duchesne. 3 vols. (Paris, 1889–1952).

I libri commemoriali della republica di Venezia Regesti, ed. R. Predelli. 8 vols. (Venice, 1876–1914).

Mandements et actes divers de Charles V (1364–1380), ed. L. Delisle (Paris, 1874).

Marino Sanudo Torsello, 'Liber secretorum fidelium crucis', in *Gesta Dei per Francos, sive orientalium expeditionum et regni Francorum Hierosolymitani historia*, ed. J. Bongars. 2 vols. (Hanover, 1611), ii.

Matteo Villani, *Cronica*, ed. F. Gherardi Dragomanni. 2 vols. (Milan, 1848).

'Nachträge und Ergänzungen zu den Acta aragonensia', ed. H. Finke, *Spanische Forschungen der Görresgesellschaft. I Reihe*, iv (1933), 355–536.

Necrologio di S. Maria Novella, 1235–1504, ed. S. Orlandi. 2 vols. (Florence, 1955).

Nicephorus Gregoras, *Rhomäische Geschichte: Historia rhomaike*, ed. and tr. J.-L. Van Dieten. 3 vols. (Stuttgart, 1973–9).

Nouvelles preuves de l'histoire de Chypre sous le règne des princes de la maison de Lusignan, ed. M. L. De Mas Latrie. 2 vols. (Paris, 1873–4).

'Octava vita Benedicti XII', *VPA*, i, 235–40.

'Les Papiers de Mile de Noyers', ed. M. Jassemin, *Bulletin philologique et historique*, (1918), 174–226.

Papsttum und Untergang des Templerordens, ed. H. Finke. 2 vols. (Münster-i.-W., 1907).

Peter Dubois, *De recuperatione terre sancte*, ed. C. V. Langlois (Paris, 1891).

Peter of Dusburg, 'Cronica terre Prussie', *SRP*, i, 21–219.

Philip of Mézières, *The Life of St Peter Thomas*, ed. J. Smet (Rome, 1954).

'Prima vita Benedicti XII', *VPA*, i, 195–209.

Ptolemy of Lucca, 'Vita Clementis V', *VPA*, i, 24–53.

Regesta historico-diplomatica Ordinis S. Mariae Theutonicorum 1198–1525, ed. E. Joachim and W. Hubatsch. 5 vols. (Göttingen, 1948–73).

Régestes des délibérations du Sénat de Venise concernant la Romanie, ed. F. Thiriet. 3 vols. (Paris, 1958–61).

Regestum Clementis papae V, editum cura et studio monachorum Ordinis S. Benedicti. 8 vols. (Rome, 1885–92).

Registres du Trésor des chartes. Vol. I: Règne de Philippe le Bel, comp. R. Fawtier (Paris, 1958).

Registres du Trésor des chartes. Vol. III: Règne de Philippe de Valois, première partie, comp. J. Viard (Paris, 1978).

Scriptores rerum prussicarum, ed. T. Hirsch, M. Töppen, and E. Strehlke. 5 vols. (Leipzig, 1861–74).

Spicilegium sive collectio veterum aliquot scriptorum qui in Galliae bibliothecis delituerant, ed. L. d'Achéry *et al.* 3 vols. (Paris, 1723).

'Storie pistoresi', ed. S. A. Barbi, *RISNS* 11⁵.

Tabulae Ordinis Theutonici, ed. E. Strehlke (Berlin, 1869).

Thesaurus novus anecdotorum, ed. E. Martène and U. Durand. 5 vols. (Paris, 1717).

Thomas Walsingham, 'Historia anglicana', ed. H. T. Riley. *RS*. 2 vols. (London, 1863–4).

Titres de la maison ducale de Bourbon, ed. M. Huillard-Bréholles. 2 vols. (Paris, 1867).

Le Trésor des chartes d'Albret I¹, ed. J.-B. Marquette (Paris, 1973).

Vetera monumenta historica Hungariam sacram illustrantia, ed. A. Theiner. 2 vols. (Rome, 1859–60).

Vetera monumenta Poloniae et Lithuaniae gentiumque finitimarum historiam illustrantia, ed. A. Theiner. 4 vols. (Rome, 1860–4).

'Vita Benedicti XII auctore Heinrico Dapifero de Dissenhoven', *VPA*, i, 216–22.

'Vita Clementis V auctore Paulino, Veneto', *VPA*, i, 81–8.

La vita di Cola di Rienzo, ed. A. M. Ghisalberti (Florence–Rome–Geneva, 1928).

'Vita Joannis XXII auctore Heinrico Dapifero de Dissenhoven', *VPA*, i, 172–7.

'Vita Urbani V auctore Wernero canonico ecclesiae Bunnensis', *VPA*, i, 383–93.

Vitae paparum avenionensium, ed. E. Baluze and G. Mollat. 4 vols. (Paris, 1914–22).

Wigand of Marburg, 'Cronica nova prutenica', *SRP*, ii, 453–662.

Wykeham's Register, ed. T. F. Kirby. 2 vols. (London–Winchester, 1896–9).

Das Zeugenverhör des Franciscus de Moliano (1312), ed. A. Seraphim (Königsberg, 1912).

3. SECONDARY WORKS

Ahrweiler, H., 'L'Histoire et la géographie de la région de Smyrne entre les deux occupations turques (1081–1317), particulièrement au XIIIe siècle', *Travaux et mémoires*, i (1965), 1–204.

Allmand, C. T., *Society at War: The Experience of England and France during the Hundred Years War* (Edinburgh, 1973).

Ashtor, E., *Levant Trade in the later Middle Ages* (Princeton, 1983).

Atiya, A. S., *The Crusade in the Later Middle Ages* (London, 1938).

Balard, M., *La Romanie génoise (XIIe—début du XVe siècle)*. 2 vols. (Rome–Genoa, 1978).

Barber, M., 'The Pastoureaux of 1320', *JEH*, xxxii (1981), 143–66.

—— 'The Social Context of the Templars', *Transactions of the Royal Historical Society*, 5th Series, xxxiv (1984), 27–46.

—— *The Trial of the Templars* (Cambridge, 1978).

Bishko, C. J., 'The Spanish and Portuguese Reconquest, 1095–1492', in Setton (gen. ed.), *History of the Crusades*, iii, 396–456.

Boase, T. S. R. (ed.), *The Cilician Kingdom of Armenia* (Edinburgh and London, 1978).

—— 'The History of the Kingdom', in his *Cilician Kingdom of Armenia*, 1–33.

Boehlke, F. J., *Pierre de Thomas: Scholar, Diplomat and Crusader* (Philadelphia, 1966).

Bourel de la Roncière, C., 'Une Escadre franco-papale (1318–1320)', *MEFR*, xiii (1893), 397–418.

Bridrey, E., *La Condition juridique des croisés et le privilège de croix: étude d'histoire du droit français* (Paris, 1900).

Brown, E. A. R., 'Customary Aids and Royal Fiscal Policy under Philip VI of Valois', *Traditio*, xxx (1974), 191–258.

Brucker, G. A., *Florentine Politics and Society, 1343–1378* (Princeton, 1962).

Brundage, J. A., *Medieval Canon Law and the Crusader* (Madison, 1969).

Burns, R. I., 'The Catalan Company and the European Powers, 1305–1311', *Speculum*, xxix (1954), 751–71.

Cardini, F. (ed.), *Toscana e Terrasanta nel Medioevo* (Florence, 1982).

Carsten, F. L., *The Origins of Prussia* (Oxford, 1954).

Cazelles, R., *La Société politique et la crise de la royauté sous Philippe de Valois* (Paris, 1958).

Cheetham, N., *Medieval Greece* (New Haven and London, 1981).

Chiappelli, A., 'Contributo di Pistoia ad una crociata contro i Turchi', *Bollettino storico pistoiese*, i (1899), 113–15.

Christiansen, E., *The Northern Crusades: The Baltic and the Catholic Frontier 1100–1525* (London, 1980).

Contamine, P., *Guerre, état et société à la fin du Moyen Âge: Études sur les armées des rois de France 1337–1494* (Paris–La Haye, 1972).

Cox, E. L., *The Green Count of Savoy: Amadeus VI and Transalpine Savoy in the Fourteenth Century* (Princeton, 1967).

Daumet, G., 'Introduction' to his edition of *Lettres closes, patentes et curiales du pape Benoît XII se rapportant à la France*, i–lxvi.

—— 'Louis de la Cerda ou d'Espagne', *Bulletin hispanique*, xv (1913), 38–67.

Delaville le Roulx, J., *La France en orient au XIVe siècle*. 2 vols. (Paris, 1886).

—— *Les Hospitaliers à Rhodes jusqu'à la mort de Philibert de Naillac (1310–1421)* (Paris, 1913).

Déprez, E., *Les Préliminaires de la guerre de Cent ans: La papauté, la France et l'Angleterre (1328–1342)* (Paris, 1902).

Dols, M. W., *The Black Death in the Middle East* (Princeton, 1977).

Edbury, P. W., 'The Crusading Policy of King Peter I of Cyprus, 1359–1369', in Holt (ed.), *Eastern Mediterranean Lands*, 90–105.

—— 'Feudal Obligations in the Latin East', *Byzantion*, xlvii (1977), 328–56.

Faucon, M., 'Prêts faits aux rois de France par Clément VI, Innocent VI et le comte de Beaufort (1345–1360)', *BEC*, xl (1879), 570–8.

Fernández Conde, J. (ed.), *Historia de la Iglesia en España II²: La Iglesia en la España de los siglos VIII al XIV* (Madrid, 1982).

Fernández Conde, J., and Oliver, A., 'La corte pontificia de Aviñon y la iglesia española', in Fernández Conde (ed.), *Historia*, 359–415.

Filippini, F., *Il cardinale Egidio Albornoz* (Bologna, 1933).

Forey, A. J., 'The Military Orders in the Crusading Proposals of the late Thirteenth and early Fourteenth Centuries', *Traditio*, xxxvi (1980), 317–45.

Fowler, K., *The King's Lieutenant: Henry of Grosmont, First Duke of Lancaster 1310–61* (London, 1969).

Fraser, C. M., *A History of Antony Bek, Bishop of Durham 1283–1311* (London, 1957).

Garcia de Valdeavellano, L., *Curso de historia de las instituciones españolas de los orígenes al final de la Edad Media* (Madrid, 1968).

Gaudemet, J., 'Le Rôle de la papauté dans le règlement des conflits entre états aux XIIIe et XIVe siècles', in *Recueils de la Société Jean Bodin XV: La Paix* (Brussels, 1961), 79–106.

Gautier Dalché, J., 'A propos d'une mission en France de Gil de Albornoz: opérations navales et difficultés financières lors du siège d'Algéciras (1341–1344)', in *El Cardenal Albornoz y el Colegio de España, i* (Zaragoza, 1971), 249–61.

Gay, J., *Le Pape Clément VI et les affaires d'orient (1342–1352)* (Paris, 1904).

Gill, J., *Byzantium and the Papacy, 1198–1400* (New Brunswick, N.J., 1979).

Giunta, F., 'Benedetto XII e la crociata', *Anuario de estudios medievales*, iii (1966), 215–34.

—— 'Sulla politica orientale di Innocenzo VI', in *Miscellanea in onore di Roberto Cessi, i* (Rome, 1958), 305–20.

Glénisson, J., 'L'Enquête pontificale de 1373 sur les possessions des Hospitaliers de Saint-Jean-de-Jérusalem', *BEC*, cxxix (1971), 83–111.

—— 'Les Origines de la révolte de l'état pontifical en 1375: les subsides extraordinaires dans les provinces italiennes de l'église au temps de Grégoire XI', *Rivista di storia della Chiesa in Italia*, v (1951), 145–68.

Golubovich, G., *Biblioteca bio-bibliografica della Terra Santa e dell' Oriente francescano*. 5 vols. (Quaracchi, 1906–27).

Goñi Gaztambide, J., *Historia de la Bula de la Cruzada en España* (Vitoria, 1958).

Gottlob, A., *Kreuzablass und Almosenablass: Eine Studie über die Frühzeit des Ablasswesens* (Stuttgart, 1906).

Gualdo, G., 'I libri delle spese di guerra del cardinal Albornoz in Italia conservati nell'Archivio Vaticano', in *El Cardenal Albornoz y el Colegio de España, i* (Zaragoza, 1971), 579–607.

Guillemain, B., *La Cour pontificale d'Avignon (1309–1376). Étude d'une société* (Paris, 1962).

Hale, J., *et al.* (eds.), *Europe in the late Middle Ages* (London, 1965).

Halecki, O., 'Casimir the Great, 1333–70', in *The Cambridge History of Poland (to 1696)*, ed. W. F. Reddaway *et al.* (Cambridge, 1950), 167–87.

—— *Un Empereur de Byzance à Rome. Vingt ans de travail pour l'union des églises et pour la défense de l'empire d'orient 1355–1375* (Warsaw, 1930).

Hamilton, B., *The Medieval Inquisition* (London, 1981).

Heers, J., *Parties and Political Life in the Medieval West*, tr. D. Nicholas (Amsterdam, 1977).

Heidelberger, F., *Kreuzzugsversuche um die Wende des 13. Jahrhunderts* (Berlin, 1911).

Henneman, J. B., *Royal Taxation in Fourteenth Century France. The Captivity and Ransom of John II, 1356–1370* (Philadelphia, 1976).

—— *Royal Taxation in Fourteenth Century France. The Development of War Financing 1322–1356* (Princeton, 1971).

Herlihy, D., *Medieval and Renaissance Pistoia: The Social History of an Italian Town* (New Haven–London, 1967).

Hewitt, H. J., *The Organization of War under Edward III 1338–62* (Manchester, 1966).

Heyd, W., and Raynaud, F., *Histoire du commerce du Levant au moyen âge.* 2 vols. (Leipzig, 1885–6).

Hill, G. F., *A History of Cyprus.* 4 vols. (Cambridge, 1940–52).

Hillgarth, J. N., *Ramon Lull and Lullism in Fourteenth-Century France* (London, 1971).

—— *The Spanish Kingdoms 1250–1516. Volume I: 1250–1410. Precarious Balance* (Oxford, 1976).

Holt, P. M. (ed.), *The Eastern Mediterranean Lands in the Period of the Crusades* (Warminster, 1977).

—— 'The Structure of Government in the Mamluk Sultanate', in his *Eastern Mediterranean Lands*, 44–61.

Housley, N., 'Angevin Naples and the Defence of the Latin East: Robert the Wise and the Naval League of 1334', *Byzantion*, li (1981), 548–56.

—— 'The Franco–Papal Crusade Negotiations of 1322–3', *PBSR*, xlviii (1980), 166–85.

—— *The Italian Crusades: The Papal–Angevin Alliance and the Crusades against Christian Lay Powers, 1254–1343* (Oxford, 1982).

—— 'King Louis the Great of Hungary and the Crusades, 1342–1382', *Slavonic and East European Review*, lxii (1984), 192–208.

—— 'The Mercenary Companies, the Papacy and the Crusades, 1356–1378', *Traditio*, xxxviii (1982), 253–80.

—— 'Politics and Heresy in Italy: Anti-Heretical Crusades, Orders and Confraternities, 1200–1500', *JEH*, xxxiii (1982), 193–208.

—— 'Pope Clement V and the Crusades of 1309–10', *JMH*, viii (1982), 29–43.

Huici Miranda, A., *Las Grandes batallas de la Reconquista durante las invasiones africanas* (Madrid, 1956).

Johnson, E. N., 'The German Crusade on the Baltic', in Setton (gen. ed.), *History of the Crusades*, iii, 545–85.

Jones, P. J., *The Malatesta of Rimini and the Papal State* (Cambridge, 1974).

Jones, W. R., 'The English Church and Royal Propaganda during the Hundred Years War', *Journal of British Studies*, xix (1979), 18–30.

Jordan, W. C., *Louis IX and the Challenge of the Crusade: A Study in Rulership* (Princeton, 1979).

Jorga, N., *Philippe de Mézières 1327–1405, et la Croisade au XIVe siècle* (Paris, 1896).

Jusselin, M., 'Comment la France se préparait à la guerre de Cent ans', *BEC*, lxxiii (1912), 209–36.

Kantorowicz, E. H., *The King's Two Bodies: A Study in Medieval Political Theology* (Princeton, 1957).

Kedar, B. Z., *Merchants in Crisis: Genoese and Venetian Men of Affairs and the Fourteenth-Century Depression* (New Haven and London, 1976).

Keen, M., 'Chaucer's Knight, the English Aristocracy and the Crusade', in V. J. Scattergood and J. W. Sherborne (eds.), *English Court Culture in the Later Middle Ages* (London, 1982), 45–61.

—— *Chivalry* (New Haven and London, 1984).

Kennan, E. T., 'Innocent III, Gregory IX and Political Crusades: a Study in the Disintegration of Papal Power', in G. F. Lytle (ed.), *Reform and Authority in the Medieval and Reformation Church* (Washington, 1981), 15–35.

Knoll, P. W., 'Poland as *Antemurale Christianitatis* in the Late Middle Ages', *CHR*, lx (1974), 381–401.

—— *The Rise of the Polish Monarchy: Piast Poland in East Central Europe, 1320–1370* (Chicago–London, 1972).

Laiou, A. E., *Constantinople and the Latins: The Foreign Policy of Andronicus II 1282–1328* (Cambridge, Mass., 1972).

—— 'Marino Sanudo Torsello, Byzantium and the Turks: the Background to the Anti-Turkish League of 1332–1334', *Speculum*, xlv (1970), 374–92.

Lambert, M. D., *Medieval Heresy: Popular Movements from Bogomil to Hus* (London, 1977).

Larner, J., *The Lords of Romagna: Romagnol Society and the Origins of the Signorie* (London, 1965).

Lecler, J., *Vienne*. Histoire des conciles œcuméniques viii (Paris, 1964).

Leclerq, J., 'Un Sermon prononcé pendant la guerre de Flandre sous Philippe le Bel', *Revue du moyen âge latin*, i (1945), 165–72.

Lemerle, P., *L'Emirat d'Aydin, Byzance et l'occident: Recherches sur 'La Geste d'Umur Pacha'* (Paris, 1957).

Loenertz, R.-J., 'Ambassadeurs grecs auprès du pape Clément VI', *OCP*, xix (1953), 178–96.

Lomax, D. W., *The Reconquest of Spain* (London, 1978).

Lot, F., 'Projets de Croisade sous Charles le Bel et sous Philippe de Valois', *BEC*, xx (1859), 503–9.

Lunt, W. E., *Financial Relations of the Papacy with England*. 2 vols. (Cambridge, Mass., 1939–62).

Luttrell, A. T., 'The Aragonese Crown and the Knights Hospitallers of Rhodes: 1291–1350', *EHR*, lxxvi (1961), 1–19.

—— 'The Crusade in the Fourteenth Century', in Hale *et al.* (eds.), *Europe in the late Middle Ages*, 122–54.

—— 'Feudal Tenure and Latin Colonization at Rhodes: 1306–1415', *EHR*, lxxxv (1970), 755–75.

—— 'Gregory XI and the Turks: 1370–1378', *OCP*, xlvi (1980), 391–417.

—— 'The Hospitallers' Interventions in Cilician Armenia: 1291–1375', in Boase (ed.), *Cilician Kingdom of Armenia*, 118–44.

—— 'The Hospitallers at Rhodes, 1306–1421', in Setton (gen. ed.), *History of the Crusades*, iii, 278–313.

—— 'The Hospitallers of Rhodes: Prospectives, Problems, Possibilities', in J. Fleckenstein and M. Hellmann (eds.), *Die geistlichen Ritterorden Europas* (Sigmaringen, 1980), 243–66.

—— 'Interessi fiorentini nell'economia e nella politica dei Cavalieri Ospedalieri di Rodi nel Trecento', *Annali della Scuola Normale Superiore di Pisa: Lettere, Storia e Filosofia*, 2 serie, xxviii (1959), 317–26.

—— 'The Latins of Argos and Nauplia: 1311–1394', *PBSR*, xxxiv (1966), 34–55.

—— 'Popes and Crusades: 1362–1394', in *Genèse et débuts du Grand Schisme d'occident: 1362–1394* (Paris, 1980), 575–85.

—— 'Venice and the Knights Hospitallers of Rhodes in the Fourteenth Century', *PBSR*, xxvi (1958), 195–212.

McHardy, A. K., 'The English Clergy and the Hundred Years War', in *The Church and War*, ed. W. J. Sheils. SCH 20 (Oxford, 1983), 171–8.

Mahn-Lot, M., 'Philippe d'Evreux, roi de Navarre et un projet de croisade contre le royaume de Granade (1329–1331)', *Bulletin hispanique*, xlvi (1944), 227–33.

Maschke, E., 'Burgund und der preussische Ordensstaat. Ein Beitrag zur Einheit der ritterlichen Kultur Europas im Spätmittelalter', in *Domus hospitalis Theutonicorum* (Bonn–Bad Godesberg, 1970), 15–34.

—— *Der Peterspfennig in Polen und dem deutschen Osten* (Leipzig, 1933).

Mas Latrie, M. L. De, *Histoire de l'île de Chypre sous le règne des princes de la maison de Lusignan*. 3 vols. (Paris, 1852–61).

Mazzaoui, M. F., *The Italian Cotton Industry in the later Middle Ages* (Cambridge, 1981).

Mazzi, M. S., 'Pistoia e la Terrasanta', in Cardini (ed.), *Toscana e Terrasanta*, 103–15.

Menache, S., 'Contemporary Attitudes concerning the Templars' Affair: Propaganda's Fiasco?', *JMH*, viii (1982), 135–47.

Meyendorff, J., *Byzantium and the Rise of Russia: A Study of Byzantino-Russian Relations in the Fourteenth Century* (Cambridge, 1981).

Miller, W., 'The Zaccaria of Phocaea and Chios (1275–1329)', *Journal of Hellenic Studies*, xxxi (1911), 42–55.

Miret y Sans, J., 'Negociacions diplomátiques d'Alfons III de Catalunya-Aragó ab el rey de França per la croada contra Granada (1328–1332)', *Anuari del Institut d'estudis catalans*, ii (1908–9), 265–336.

—— 'Ramón de Melany, embajador de Alfonso IV en la corte de Francia', *Boletín de la real Academia de buenas letras de Barcelona*, ii (1903–4), 192–202.

Mirot, L., *La Politique pontificale et le retour du saint-siège à Rome en 1376* (Paris, 1899).

Mollat, G., 'L'Œuvre oratoire de Clément VI', *Archives d'histoire doctrinale et littéraire du moyen âge*, iii (1928), 239–74.

—— *The Popes at Avignon*, tr. J. Love (London, 1963).

Muldoon, J., 'The Avignon Papacy and the Frontiers of Christendom: the Evidence of Vatican Register 62', *Archivum historiae pontificiae*, xvii (1979), 125–95.

—— *Popes, Lawyers, and Infidels: the Church and the Non-Christian World 1250–1550* (Liverpool, 1979).

Müller, E., *Das Konzil von Vienne (1311–1312): Seine Quellen und seine Geschichte* (Münster-i.-W., 1934).

Nicol, D. M., 'Byzantine Requests for an Oecumenical Council in the Fourteenth Century', *Annuarium historiae Conciliorum*, i (1969), 69–95.

—— *The Last Centuries of Byzantium 1261–1453* (London, 1972).

Oliver, A., and Fernández Conde, J., 'La epoca de las grandes conquistas', in Fernández Conde (ed.), *Historia*, 3–60.

Palmer, J. J. N., *England, France and Christendom 1377–99* (London, 1972).

—— 'England, France, the Papacy and the Flemish Succession, 1361–9', *JMH*, ii (1976), 339–64.

Papi, M. D., 'Santa Maria Novella di Firenze e l'*Outremer* domenicano', in Cardini (ed.), *Toscana e Terrasanta*, 87–101.

Paravicini, W., 'Die Preussenreise des europäischen Adels', *Historische Zeitschrift*, ccxxxii (1981), 25–38.

Partner, P., *The Lands of St Peter: The Papal State in the Middle Ages and the Early Renaissance* (London, 1972).

Perroy, E., *L'Angleterre et le Grand Schisme d'occident* (Paris, 1933).

—— *The Hundred Years War*, tr. W. B. Wells (London, 1959).

Piana, C., 'Il Cardinal Albornoz e gli ordini religiosi', in *El Cardenal Albornoz y el Colegio de España*, i (Zaragoza, 1971), 483–519.

Pirillo, P., 'La Terrasanta nei testamenti fiorentini del Dugento', in Cardini (ed.), *Toscana e Terrasanta*, 57–73.

Porter, E., 'Chaucer's Knight, the Alliterative *Morte Arthure*, and

Medieval Laws of War: a Reconsideration', *Nottingham Medieval Studies*, xxvii (1983), 56–78.

Post, G., *Studies in Medieval Legal Thought: Public Law and the State, 1100–1322* (Princeton, 1964).

Prawer, J., *The Latin Kingdom of Jerusalem: European Colonialism in the Middle Ages* (London, 1972).

Prou, M., *Étude sur les relations politiques du pape Urbain V avec les rois de France Jean II et Charles V (1362–1370)* (Paris, 1888).

Purcell, M., *Papal Crusading Policy: The Chief Instruments of Papal Crusading Policy and Crusade to the Holy Land from the Final Loss of Jerusalem to the Fall of Acre, 1244–1291* (Leiden, 1975).

Renouard, Y., *The Avignon Papacy 1305–1403*, tr. D. Bethell (London, 1970).

—— 'Une Expédition de céréales des Pouilles en Arménie par les Bardi pour le compte de Benoît XII', *MEFR*, liii (1936), 287–329.

—— 'Les Papes et le conflit franco–anglais en Aquitaine de 1259 à 1337', *MEFR*, li (1934), 258–92.

—— *Les Relations des papes d'Avignon et des compagnies commerciales et bancaires de 1316 à 1378* (Paris, 1941).

Rhode, G., *Die Ostgrenze Polens. Politische Entwicklung, kulturelle Bedeutung, und geistige Auswirkung. I Band. Im Mittelalter bis zum Jahre 1401* (Cologne–Graz, 1955).

Riant, P., *Expéditions et pèlerinages des Scandinaves en Terre Sainte au temps des Croisades* (Paris, 1865).

Richard, J., *La Papauté et les missions d'orient au moyen âge (XIIIe–XVe siècles)* (Rome, 1977).

—— 'Les Papes d'Avignon et l'évangélisation du monde non-latin à la veille du grand schisme', in *Genèse et débuts du Grand Schisme d'occident: 1362–1394* (Paris, 1980), 305–15.

Riley-Smith, J. S. C., 'Crusading as an Act of Love', *History*, lxv (1980), 177–92.

—— *The Knights of St John in Jerusalem and Cyprus, c. 1050–1310* (London, 1967).

—— *What were the Crusades?* (London, 1977).

Robson, J. A., 'The Catalan Fleet and Moorish Sea-Power (1337–1344)', *EHR*, lxxiv (1959), 386–408.

Roncière, C. De la, *Histoire de la marine française: les origines* (Paris, 1899).

Roscher, H., *Papst Innocenz III. und die Kreuzzüge* (Göttingen, 1969).

Rousset, P., 'Sainte Catherine de Sienne et le problème de la Croisade', *Schweizerische Zeitschrift für Geschichte*, xxv (1975), 499–513.

Russell, F. H., *The Just War in the Middle Ages* (Cambridge, 1975).

Russell, P. E., *The English Intervention in Spain and Portugal in the Time of Edward III and Richard II* (Oxford, 1955).

Schein, S., 'Philip IV and the Crusade: a Reconsideration', in *Crusade and Settlement*, ed. P. W. Edbury (Cardiff, 1985), 121–6.

Schmitz, P., 'Les Sermons et discours de Clément VI', *Revue bénédictine*, xli (1929), 15–34.

Servois, G., 'Emprunts de Saint Louis en Palestine et en Afrique', *BEC*, xix (1858), 113–31, 283–93.

Setton, K. M., *Catalan Domination of Athens 1311–1388*. Revised edn. (London, 1975).

—— 'The Catalans in Greece, 1311–1380', in his *History of the Crusades*, iii, 167–224.

—— (gen. ed.), *A History of the Crusades*. 4 vols. so far. 2nd edn. (Madison, 1969–).

—— *The Papacy and the Levant (1204–1571). Vol. I: The Thirteenth and Fourteenth Centuries* (Philadelphia, 1976).

Smail, R. C., 'The International Status of the Latin Kingdom of Jerusalem, 1150–1192', in Holt (ed.), *Eastern Mediterranean Lands*, 23–43.

Smalley, B., 'Church and State, 1300–77: Theory and Fact', in Hale *et al.* (eds.), *Europe in the late Middle Ages*, 15–43.

Storia di Milano V: la signoria dei Visconti (1310–1392), ed. Fondazione Treccani degli Alfieri (Milan, 1955).

Strayer, J. R., 'The Crusades of Louis IX', in Setton (gen. ed.), *History of the Crusades*, ii, 487–518.

—— 'France: the Holy Land, the Chosen People, and the Most Christian King', in T. K. Rabb and J. E. Seigel (eds.), *Action and Conviction in Early Modern Europe* (Princeton, 1969), 3–16.

—— 'The Political Crusades of the Thirteenth Century', in Setton (gen. ed.), *History of the Crusades*, ii, 343–75.

Tabacco, G., *La casa di Francia nell'azione politica di papa Giovanni XXII* (Rome, 1953).

Tenenti, A., 'Venezia e la pirateria nel Levante: 1300c.–1460c.', in *Venezia e il Levante fino al secolo XV*. 2 vols. (Florence, 1973), ii, 705–71.

Thier, L., *Kreuzzugsbemühungen unter Papst Clemens V. (1305–1314)* (Werl, Westf., 1973).

Thiriet, F., *La Romanie vénitienne au moyen âge: Le développement et l'exploitation du domaine colonial vénitien (XIIᵉ–XVᵉ siècles)* (Paris, 1959).

Throop, P. A., *Criticism of the Crusade: a Study of Public Opinion and Crusade Propaganda* (Amsterdam, 1940).

Tyerman, C. J., 'Philip V of France, the Assemblies of 1319–20 and the Crusade', *BIHR*, lvii (1984), 15–34.

Tymieniecki, K., 'The Reunion of the Kingdom, 1295–1333', in *The*

Cambridge History of Poland (to 1696), ed. W. F. Reddaway *et al.* (Cambridge, 1950), 108–24.

Urban, W., *The Livonian Crusade* (Washington, 1981).

Van Cleve, T. C., 'The Crusade of Frederick II', in Setton (gen. ed.), *History of the Crusades*, ii, 429–62.

Viard, J., 'Un Chapitre d'histoire administrative: les ressources extraordinaires de la royauté sous Philippe de Valois', *Revue des questions historiques*, xliv (1888), 167–218.

—— 'Les Projets de Croisade de Philippe VI de Valois', *BEC*, xcvii (1936), 305–16.

Villey, M., *La Croisade: Essai sur la formation d'une théorie juridique* (Paris, 1942).

Vincke, J., 'Der Jubiläumsablass von 1350 auf Mallorca', *Römische Quartalschrift*, xli (1933), 301–6.

—— *Staat und Kirche in Katalonien und Aragon während des Mittelalters, i* (Münster-i-W., 1931).

—— 'Der verhinderte Kreuzzug Ludwigs von Spanien zu den Kanarischen Inseln', in *Gesammelte Aufsätze zur Kulturgeschichte Spaniens*, xvii = *Spanische Forschungen der Görresgesellschaft, I Reihe*, xvii (1961), 57–71.

Vries, W. De, 'Die Päpste von Avignon und der christliche Osten', *OCP*, xxx (1964), 85–128.

Wadding, L., *Vita et res gestae B. Petri Thomae* (Lyons, 1637).

Wenck, K., 'Aus den Tagen der Zusammenkunft Papst Klemens V. und König Philipps des Schönen zu Lyon, November 1305 bis Januar 1306', *Zeitschrift für Kirchengeschichte*, xxvii (1906), 189–203.

Wieruszowski, H., 'Ramon Lull et l'Idée de la Cité de Dieu: Quelques nouveaux écrits sur la Croisade', *Estudis franciscans*, xlvii (1935), 87–110. Also found in H. Wieruszowski, *Politics and Culture in Medieval Spain and Italy* (Rome, 1971), 147–71.

Wood, D., '*Omnino partialitate cessante:* Clement VI and the Hundred Years War', in *The Church and War*, ed. W. J. Sheils. SCH 20 (Oxford, 1983), 179–89.

Wrigley, J. E., 'Clement VI before his Pontificate: the early Life of Pierre Roger, 1290/91–1342', *CHR*, lvi (1970), 433–73.

Zachariadou, E. A., *Trade and Crusade: Venetian Crete and the Emirates of Menteshe and Aydin (1300–1415)* (Venice, 1983).

Zacour, N. P., *Talleyrand: the Cardinal of Périgord (1301–1364)* (Philadelphia, 1960).

Ziada, M. M., 'The Mamluk Sultans, 1291–1517', in Setton (gen. ed.), *History of the Crusades*, iii, 486–512.

The following relevant works came to my attention too late to be consulted:

Kedar, B. Z., *Crusade and Mission: European Approaches toward the Muslims* (Princeton, 1984).

Tyerman, C. J., 'Philip VI and the Recovery of the Holy Land', *EHR*, c (1985), 25–51.

Index